JOURNAL FOR THE STUDY OF THE OLD TESTAMENT
SUPPLEMENT SERIES

65

Editors
David J A Clines
Philip R Davies

JSOT Press
Sheffield

There is Hope for a Tree

The Tree as Metaphor in Isaiah

Kirsten Nielsen

Journal for the Study of the Old Testament
Supplement Series 65

Dedicated to the memory of my mother
Else Schroll

Translated by Christine and Frederick Crowley

Originally published as *For et træ er der håb*:
Om træet som metafor i Jes 1–39
© G.E.C. Gads Forlag, Copenhagen, 1985

This edition copyright © 1989 Sheffield Academic Press

Published by JSOT Press
JSOT Press is an imprint of
Sheffield Academic Press Ltd
The University of Sheffield
343 Fulwood Road
Sheffield S10 3BP
England

Printed in Great Britain
by Billing & Sons Ltd
Worcester

British Library Cataloguing in Publication Data

Nielsen, Kirsten.
    There is hope for a tree: the tree as
    metaphor in Isaiah. - Journal for the study
    of the Old Testament Supplement series, ISSN
    0309-0787; 65.
    I. Title II. Series
    III. For et trae er der hab
    224'.106

ISBN 1-85075-182-X

CONTENTS

PREFACE

There is Hope for a Tree is a revised and slightly condensed version of my Danish doctoral thesis of 1985: 'For et træ er der håb'. This thesis came into being as a result of a long-held interest in the form and function of biblical language. In *Yahweh as Prosecutor and Judge* (1978), I considered the prophetic lawsuits, and I immediately became fascinated by their imagery. But the use of images raised some problems that a form-critical analysis was unable to answer. I had therefore to consider other approaches to the study of Old Testament imagery.

Since the 1970s, a substantial element of theological discussion in Denmark has been concerned with language. This has inspired my study of imagery; but all too often I felt that in the struggle to establish positions the discussion between advocates of an historical approach to the texts and those advocating a literary approach came to a standstill. I myself wished neither to abandon historio-critical research nor to give up studying the texts as literary works of art. Study of the prophetic texts and the history of their influence rendered it necessary to analyse both the origin of the texts and their reuse, and the vehicle for this was necessarily a redaction-critical analysis of one central and frequently used image.

Since I had earlier taken an interest in the tension between judgment and salvation in the book of Isaiah, it was natural to investigate the way in which imagery was able to interpret the political situation as an expression of Yahweh's intentions for his people to such effect that this tension was retained.

In the autumn of 1979 I spent some months in the USA. During this visit, a significant part of the ideas of the thesis took shape. I owe heart-felt thanks to my uncle and aunt, Thorkild and Katryna Jacobsen, for their informed inspiration and unstinting hospitality. The hours in Thorkild Jacobsen's study surrounded by the books he selected for me from a lifelong study of Assyriology, and with the cats

Enkidu and Gilgamesh as 'heating pads', were a highlight of this period of study. Similarly, the professional contacts arranged by David L. Petersen and our many conversations about the Old Testament and 'literary criticism' were of great importance.

For discussion and criticism I thank my colleagues at Aarhus and my opponents at the public defence of the thesis. I also owe great thanks to the Theological Faculty for the good working conditions it provided, with an appropriate mixture of time for teaching and for research.

The Danish manuscript was translated by Christine and Frederick Crowley, whom I thank not only for their expert translation but also for their high standard of accuracy and willingness to co-operate. The Danish Research Council for the Humanities made available a grant for the translation, making it possible for the book to be published in an international language; for this I am most grateful.

For sympathetic understanding and confidence, for solicitude and peaceful working conditions, I thank my immediate family.

There is Hope for a Tree is dedicated to the memory of my mother, Else Schroll, in humble thanks for what has been most important to me: the wisdom I learnt in 'my father's church and my mother's parsonage'.

Kirsten Nielsen
Summer, 1987

ABBREVIATIONS

AfO	Archiv für Orientforschung
AJSL	*American Journal of Semitic Languages and Literatures*
ASTI	*Annual of the Swedish Theological Institute*
ANET	Ancient Near Eastern Texts Relating to the Old Testament, ed. J.B. Pritchard (3rd edn, 1969)
AOT	H. Gressmann: *Altorientalische Texte zum Alten Testament* (2nd edn 1926)
ATD	Altes Testament Deutsch
Bibl	*Biblica*
BK	Biblischer Kommentar
BZ	*Biblische Zeitschrift*
BZAW	Beihefte zur Zeitschrift für die alttestamentliche Wissenschaft
CBQ	*Catholic Biblical Quarterly*
DTT	*Dansk Teologisk Tidsskrift*
EvTh	*Evangelische Theologie*
ExpT	*Expository Times*
Ges-Buhl	W. Gesenius-F. Buhl: *Hebräisches und aramäisches Handwörterbuch zum AT* (17th edn, 1921)
Interp	*Interpretation*
JBL	*Journal of Biblical Literature*
JNESt	*Journal of Near Eastern Studies*
JQR	*Jewish Quarterly Review*
JR	*Journal of Religion*
JSSt	*Journal of Semitic Studies*
JThSt	*Journal of Theological Studies*
KBL	L. Koehler & W. Baumgartner: *Lexicon in Veteris Testamenti Libros* (1958)
LXX	Septuagint
MT	Masoretic Text
MThZ	*Münchener Theologische Zeitschrift*
NRTh	*Nouvelle Revue Théologique*
NTT	*Norsk Teologisk Tidsskrift*
RSR	*Recherches de Science Religieuse*
RSV	Revised Standard Version

SBU	Svenskt Bibliskt Uppslagsverk
ScrHier	Scripta Hierosolymitana
SEÅ	*Svensk Exegetisk Årsbok*
SJT	*Scottish Journal of Theology*
StTh	*Studia Theologica*
Svensk TKv	*Svensk Teologisk Kvartalskrift*
ThHAT	Theologisches Handwörterbuch zum Alten Testament I-II
ThLZ	*Theologische Literaturzeitung*
ThW	*Theologisches Wörterbuch zum Neuen Testament* (1933-)
ThZ	*Theologische Zeitschrift*
TTKi	*Tidsskrift for Teologi og Kirke*
UF	*Ugarit Forschungen*
VT	*Vetus Testamentum*
VTSuppl	Vetus Testamentum Supplements
VuF	*Verkündigung und Forschung*
ZAW	*Zeitschrift für die alttestamentliche Wissenschaft*
ZThK	*Zeitschrift für Theologie und Kirche*

INTRODUCTION

The title of this investigation of the tree as a metaphor is taken from the book of Job. In his first reply to Zophar, Job throws his own hopeless situation into relief by contrasting it with the tree and its capacity always to survive. If a tree is cut down, it will sprout again; though its stump die in the ground, yet at the scent of water it will bud and put forth branches like a young plant (Job 14.7-9).

The use of the tree by the author of the book of Job to describe the life-force is not an idea that came to him spontaneously but a centuries-old tradition, of which evidence is to be found in several passages of the Old Testament. We shall investigate in the present book the utilization and continuation of this tradition within a limited section of text.

The situation is in a certain sense easy to survey in the history of scholarship. As far as I am aware, the use of the tree as a metaphor in Isaiah 1-39 has not previously been investigated. The literature available on the subject consists of individual treatises of varying length concerned with other images, particularly the prophets' use of imagery.

It is surprising that scholarly literature on the subject is so sparse compared with the great interest shown by New Testament research in Jesus' use of parables. But it is especially surprising that Old Testament scholars have not made serious use of the results achieved by their New Testament colleagues. Only Adolf Jülicher's great work on Jesus' parables has had any real impact on Old Testament imagery research.

In a 1960 article,[1] the Spanish Old Testament scholar Louis Alonso Schökel describes the prophetic use of imagery as a very promising field of research. But at the same time he points out that in biblical scholarship we have not as yet developed a suitable method for such study. Our colleagues in related disciplines—particularly literature—are much more advanced in this respect, and we should therefore make room for some of their methods.[2] What Alonso Schökel is seeking is a method in keeping with the 'modern stilistics' of literary study, which present an opportunity for both scholarly analysis and artistic empathy.[3]

Such close collaboration across the boundaries of discipline and subject is absent in much of European OT research. On the other hand, in the USA it is quite normal for exegetists to make use of methods and attitudes borrowed from other subjects, such as the history of literature, philosophy and psychology. Following Alonso Schökel's call leads of course to the problem that most of us know too little about what is happening within related disciplines. We are—and we remain—amateurs when we venture outside the narrow limits of our own subject. But I am convinced that such attempts must be made if research is not to stagnate.

This book is such an attempt. But if the attempt is to succeed colleagues in related disciplines must be prepared to enter into the dialogue for which this sets the scene, and which Old Testament research needs.

PART A. METHODOLOGICAL CONSIDERATIONS

Chapter 1

PROTO-ISAIAH AS TRADITIONAL LITERATURE AND RELIGIOUS UTILITY LITERATURE

In his analysis of the Ebed Yahweh songs, Johannes Lindblom points out in his introduction the absolute necessity when studying texts of defining the literary genre of the texts.[1] Analysis of the servant songs therefore requires that we should start by defining their genre. Only then can we pass on to the traditional question of who the servant is. But now of course the question must be raised in a different form. Since analysis of the songs shows that they are allegorical images whose interpretation is given in the linking passages, it becomes clear that the usual question is mistaken. It is meaningless to enquire of the allegorical text who the servant is; the question must be: what does the servant-figure signify?[2] Not until the genre is defined is it possible to formulate the questions relevant to the text.

Precisely the same applies when we come to examine the Proto-Isaianic message with special reference to the use of a certain image. Unless we are clear from the outset about the type of text that confronts us, we run the risk of asking meaningless questions.

But it is not sufficient to define imagery as genre; the whole context in which the images stand must be included. The first question must therefore be: What is the literary genre to which the book of Isaiah—and thus Proto-Isaiah—belongs?

Traditional Literature

Like most Old Testament manuscripts, the book of Isaiah is a piece of traditional literature. Rolf Rendtorff[3] emphasizes in his introduction to the OT that Old Testament texts should be analyzed not only as 'unmittelbare Lebensäußerungen der israelitischen Gesellschaft in der Entstehungszeit der jeweiligen Texte', but that as exegetes we must also follow the texts along the way to their final redaction,

'. . . ein Weg, der zu einem großen Teil einhergeht mit der Weiterbildung des Überlieferungsmaterials zur Traditions*literatur*'.

The book of Isaiah as it now exists is the outcome not only of the message of Isaiah ben Amoz propounded in the eighth century BC but also of the interpretation to which Isaiah's prophecy was subjected and the preaching that continued to stem from it over the following centuries. Numerous attempts have been made to reveal this whole process of genesis; but it is useful here to bear in mind what J.H. Eaton has to say; he introduces an article on the origin of the book of Isaiah with the words: 'The more the authorship of the Book of Isaiah has been investigated, the more complicated has the question appeared.'[4] This having been said, Eaton's own point must also be mentioned. The characteristic of the book of Isaiah is not the complexity itself but the unity in the complexity. It is of course true that the book of Isaiah consists of an enormous body of composite material whose individual parts can be dated to a period covering several hundreds of years, but at the same time the collection expresses a conscious attempt to reproduce a certain prophetic tradition whose roots can be traced back to a named person.

Over the last few hundred years of Isaianic research, increasing interest has been concentrated on the first aspect: the complexity. The division of the book of Isaiah into first two, then three, major entities, the further division into smaller constituent parts, the demonstration of original statements (ipsissima verba), etc. were important and demanding tasks. But although the literary-critical approach has gradually been supplemented by a more tradition-related and redaction-related understanding of the process of genesis, the process itself remained the true object of research. The final result, the canonical text in its entirety, more often than not lacked focus, unless one's interest happened to be the canon.

Only in recent years has theology's increasing interest in the texts and the theology-determined redaction of the traditional material led to a return to the complete text as a serious subject for exhaustive study (cf. primarily Brevard S. Childs). But it is important to realize that study of these texts in their final version makes sense only if their history is taken seriously.[5] This renewed interest in the final result should not cause us to neglect the process that led to it.

The book of Isaiah is not the work of one author but the result of continuous redactional adaptation. That it is a piece of traditional literature means that the text we have before us is identicial with neither the prophet's original message nor with the message of a later individual or group. The book of Isaiah is neither an historical document, in the sense of a shorthand report of Isaiah's words, nor a literary fiction, in the sense of an author's free creation of a fictitious prophet and his message; nevertheless, it represents a certain connexion back to Isaiah as well as a certain element of literary fiction, in the sense of an arrangement of the material determined by literary considerations.

This means that the methods to be employed when reading the book of Isaiah must be able to apply both historical and literary approaches to the material,[6] always including aspects of a redactional nature.

Religious Utility Literature

The book of Isaiah is not only traditional literature but also religious utility literature. I emphasized the book's complex genesis by the definition: traditional literature; by this supplementary definition of utility literature, I wish to highlight possible criteria in the selection of material during the process of genesis and special difficulties associated with the historical interpretation of these texts.

The primary function of the texts in the book of Isaiah was to assist the Israelitic-Jewish community to understand and accept what was/is the wish of the God of Israel. Isaiah preached what Yahweh intended in the politically tense situation of the eighth century BC so that the people might learn from it. His disciples passed on his message as they had understood it on the assumption that it was still topical, i.e. usable. What the prophet preached was perceived as the living word of God, and it is not therefore surprising that this word could be used a number of times to interpret different historical situations.[7] The chronicling and collecting of the traditions results, therefore, not from what we see as an historical interest in the past but rather from an interest in the present and the future.

But this raises the question: Which parts of Isaiah's message were considered usable and therefore worth preserving for posterity? This question can of course be answered by referring to the collection available. What has been preserved is indeed assembled there, and what was not included is irrevocably lost and therefore not available for comparison. What does not exist just cannot be used as a control group!

I wish nevertheless to attempt the following approach, which is concerned only with the form of the texts and therefore has nothing to say about the content-related reasons—which of course also existed—for preserving certain parts of Isaiah's message.[8]

We are familiar from the New Testament with many examples of Jesus' tales given in parable form, and when we read the NT we may be left with the impression that this narrative form was one of Jesus' preferences. We are also familiar from the Old Testament prophets with many examples of preaching rich in imagery, and this may well lead us to believe that prophets such as Isaiah and Ezekiel had a predilection for imagery and perhaps special visionary gifts. This may be so, but we should also consider whether the reason may have had something to do with the selection process underlying the genesis of the OT and NT respectively. I thus consider it likely that the *figurative message* was seen as especially suitable for reuse, and therefore ideal for preservation for posterity. And this brings us to the main subject of the treatise: the use of imagery.

Although the actual discussion of the use of imagery is to be found in Chapter II, a number of aspects relative to imagery must also be considered when we discuss the prophetic texts as utility literature.

One characteristic of imagery is its *receptiveness to interpretation/ reinterpretation* and its *context-dependency*. Receptiveness renders it usable in various situations, and context-dependency means that even when reused the image can be perceived as a relevant—i.e. precise—saying in the specific situation. This is one of the factors that has caused some of the changes in the New Testament parables listed by Joachim Jeremias[9] in his detailing of the development of the parables from their use by Jesus to their use by the primitive church. The new historical context meant that the parables were seen as directed towards the community and not towards Jesus' adversaries; indeed, that the community saw them as a whole as spoken into their own situation, marked as it was by the absence of parousia and by the expanding mission. But the literary context, including the generalizing conclusions which have often been added, also leads to a similar change in the understanding of the parables. In the same way, we must suppose that the prophetic oracles expressed in imagery were perceived as particularly suitable for proclaiming the actual Word of God again and again.

When comparing with the evolution of the New Testament parables, it is appropriate to consider in the OT also whether imagery has had a *text-producing* effect. In the specific situation, the very receptiveness of the imagery may have meant that those mediating the image wished to safeguard one specific interpretation of it, and therefore added the application which, in their opinion, was correct. According to Eduard Nielsen, the application of the fable of Jotham, which is normally considered an original part of the fable, in fact expresses a redactional interpretation. And in his opinion this is not unique. 'This is, in fact, the case with most "original" applications of *meshālīm* within the Biblical literature!'[10]

But the redactors may also have sought to safeguard one specific reading of the image in another way, i.e. by placing it into the available context. Cf. e.g. the placing of Isa. 10.33-34 in extension of a number of oracles referring to the king of Assyria. (See my analysis of Isa. 10.33-34, pp. 124ff.)

I therefore find it probable that the reinterpretation which to a great extent occupied Old Testament scholars[11] in the 1970s was carried out largely on a basis of figurative statements, an aspect that—surprisingly enough—has not as yet been included in the debate.

In his book 'When Prophecy Failed' and in a number of articles on the same subject,[12] Robert P. Carroll has advanced the thesis that the lack of fulfilment of the prophecies and the 'dissonance' arising therefrom occasioned the hermeneutic work (reinterpretation) that we can see reflected, for example, in the prophetic books. Carroll himself expresses this as follows: 'The important principle for this study is *dissonance gives rise to hermeneutic*. That is, the experience of dissonance forced individuals or groups to reinterpret their basic material or the contemporary events so as to avoid dissonance'.[13]

Carroll's methodological approach to prophetic literature has been taken from social psychology, in the form of Leon Festinger's 'theory of cognitive dissonance'. Carroll's interest lies in circumstances of a social and psychological nature that may have contributed to the reinterpretation of the old prophetic oracles, and thus to the creation of the book of Isaiah; and in these areas his ideas represent a valuable contribution to prophetic scholarship. But what I miss in his work is discussion of how such reinterpretation was possible, i.e. discussion of the prophetic message's form and suitability for reuse. It is true that Carroll has a section on the language of prophecy, and stresses the importance of concerning oneself with this; but his real interest lies only in the question of whether or not the prophets were heralds

of future events. Carroll believes that this was the case, although he
leaves open the possibility that they were perhaps also something
other than this.

Carroll's work therefore needs supplementation. In my opinion, it
is necessary to examine how the reinterpretation he rightly demon-
strates took place, and in what sense the possibility of reinterpretation
is associated with the form the prophecy took. I believe that an
analysis of the use of imagery is called for here; not because all
reinterpretation is reinterpretation of imagery (let us establish this
once and for all) but because it is true of a substantial part of it.

I have thus indicated two aspects of importance to the study of
imagery in Proto-Isaiah. One is the complexity of the genesis of the
texts; the other is the complexity of the possibilities of interpretation.

From a traditional historio-critical standpoint, ambiguity is seen
as a problem. The aim of the exegesis is to arrive at as precise a
definition as possible of what a specific statement meant at a certain
time in history. The question one asks about the texts is, then: What
was the information the sender of the message wished the recipient
to apprehend? From this aspect, language is a means of passing on
information from A to B in the most certain way possible. Such an
approach is often useful and reasonable; but it can lead one to
overlook the fact that language is not always so unambiguous that
this is its only possible function. Ambiguity forms part of the
language, especially in imagery. Therefore, instead of seeing ambiguity
as a disadvantage[14] it would be more profitable to consider whether
imagery's receptiveness to continuous reinterpretation—one might
call it the *polyvalence* of imagery—is instead something positive;
indeed, something which in reality renders it usable, and has
therefore helped to make it possible to use parts of the prophetic
message over and over again.

The difficulty of such an approach is of course the obvious
absurdity of its caricature: the all-obliterating relativism and
subjectivism that in the final instance renders any form of communication, and thus any form of information, impossible. But this,
as already said, is the caricature. The fact that imagery is characterized
by ambiguity does not mean that everything is possible by way of
interpretation. It is true that I am speaking of polyvalence, but not of
omnivalence; and there is good reason to bear in mind that in the
specific situation not all meanings are active; some are present only
potentially. To be sure, the hearer must interpret the imagery in a

specific situation; but the interpretation should not be seen as a more or less random choice between innumerable possibilities. The difficulties—or one might say the many possibilities—are much more likely to arise if the statement is torn away from its original historical and literary context.

It is thus important to realize that the context (in the broad sense) acts as the interpretation's 'linesman', and thereby safeguards against arbitrariness in the interpretation. It is therefore also necessary for the exegetist, in order to understand the possible meanings which presented themselves most naturally in a specific historical situation, to make himself familiar with this situation, and to permit the ideas of the time, and not his own, to guide the interpretation.

Another form of 'linesman' is the hermeneutic principles that prevailed at the time the text became the subject of reuse. Whereas the hermeneutic principles of the classical exegetist prompt the scholar to try to return to the original author's meaning when the text was written and to refer to this first meaning as the text's meaning, i.e. *the* meaning, the hermeneutical principle of the Bible-user is simply to work out what the text says in his specific situation. The Bible-user (and here I include to some extent the redactors who composed the book of Isaiah,[15] although they had other principles also) is in dialogue with the text as it exists and not with the situation in which the text was created or with the author of the text. Conversely, the author has lost the opportunity of exerting an influence upon the way the text is to be understood in the new situation. The influence the author possesses is to be found only in the text itself.[16]

Exegetic Implications

I have now given a description of the text within which the tree images are to be found, and I have set out very provisionally some of the important characteristics of imagery. In conclusion, I wish to specify the type of question it is relevant to ask about a passage of traditional and utility literature such as Proto-Isaiah. When we are faced with a text that is neither an historical document nor pure literary fiction, and has a genesis extending over several hundreds of years, it is tempting to abandon completely the historical approach, like some followers of 'Literary Critic',[17] and instead to follow a literary approach. In that case, one keeps to the text as it in fact exists, and in doing so one believes one is playing safe. But what is safe also includes the considerations that the book of Isaiah has its basis in an actual person's activities in a known period of Israel's history, and that parts of this message have been rendered in a new situation as an ever-topical message and have even inspired the production of further statements not only within the complex we refer to as Proto-Isaiah but also in the form of Deutero-Isaiah and later Trito-Isaiah.

This means that the completed book of Isaiah has been constructed not in the light of the laws and standards of literature alone, but that it has its roots in a series of historical circumstances which must be taken into account if one wishes to study the available text in its entirety. As regards method, therefore, we must see ourselves as situated in the field of tension between history and literature—a very insecure position, unsatisfactory to both the literarily and the historically informed. But I can see no other possibility if the genesis of the text is to be taken seriously, and study is not to lead to a reduction of the text.

But what will be the practical implications of all this? Let me try to specify what I see as these *implications*:

Because of the nature of the texts as traditional literature, we must in principle abandon the attempt to find our way back to the Isaianic message in the sense of ipsissima verba. We have only Isaiah's message as his disciples understood it and passed it on. This does not mean that we must abandon the possibility of dating specific passages of text, but we must realize that we often find ourselves on insecure ground.

This abandonment in principle of the attempt to find our way back to ipsissima verba also means abandoning the prejudice that consists in attributing the greatest value to the oldest version from the outset, and the least value to the latest, redactional version.[18] It is of course sad that in a number of cases there is very little we can say about the initial significance of an oracle, but this should not overshadow the fact that we have good means available for interpreting it in the existing, redactional context.

The genesis of the texts makes it unavoidable that questions of a *redactional* nature must be asked when we try to reveal the history of individual passages and their redactional treatment. But here the reuse aspect must act as a means of guarding against far too great a certainty as regards our chances of being able to give a precise *dating*. Many of the texts we must date have been preserved for the very reason that they can be used again and again. I am therefore amazed—to put it no stronger—at the certainty with which scholars such as H. Barth and J. Vermeylen date individual passages in the book of Isaiah. For example, in this respect I find R.E. Clements's cautious analysis of the Isaianic oracles' significance during the Exile far more acceptable.[19]

The complexity of the texts, the uncertainty surrounding the dating of individual passages and the many images the passages contain make it necessary to concentrate a substantial part of our study on a survey of the *possible interpretations* implied by the individual statements and of the relationship between the individual statement and the literary context in which it is placed. Especially when the text to be analysed is expressed in imagery, it will often be more reasonable to analyze the text's possible meanings than to try to give a 'final' definition of its meaning.

That the text has a history of use certainly means, in the redactional context (and here I ignore the later use of individual images severed from the literary context[20]), that neither the initial use nor the final use can be referred to as *the* use. Nothing of this is changed because we can select a number of typical situations in which an image will of course have one specific meaning; it merely emphasizes what I consider to be an important point: that the receptiveness of imagery to reinterpretation in no way prevents precise meaning and comprehension in a specific situation.

Determination of the genre of the Ebed Yahweh songs caused Johannes Lindblom to change the traditional question: 'Who is the servant?' to 'What does the servant mean?' Similarly, the definition of the Proto-Isaianic texts as traditional literature and religious utility literature, with frequent use of imagery, must cause us to change the question, 'What does this or that mean?' to 'What possible meanings were in use at that time and within this context?' From questions of the type, 'What is the meaning of the image?', we must become accustomed to asking 'How is the image used in this or that situation, and what meaning is thereby created?'

Chapter 2

THE USE OF IMAGERY IN THE OLD TESTAMENT

Before I try to define what I understand by imagery, it is perhaps proper to establish the *position of research* within this field. While it is possible, in New Testament studies, to refer to specific parable research and to trace a line back to Adolf Jülicher's great work, 'Die Gleichnisreden Jesu',[1] within Old Testament research we can point to no true research into imagery. The existing studies of examples of imagery have not appeared as a link in a continuing debate on the subject, but have generally come into being in the context of Old Testament prophecy. It would therefore be unreasonable to try to write a history of research in the traditional sense, and thereby postulate a correlation for which there is no foundation. I wish instead to outline briefly the main viewpoints that have been advanced regarding the use of imagery in the Old Testament which I have had to consider in the context of my analyses of the tree as a metaphor in Proto-Isaiah.[2] In continuation of this, I wish to outline briefly a number of considerations central to New Testament parable research.[3]

1. *Main Viewpoints in Old Testament Research*

When considering imagery, it is convenient to take as a point of reference a 1949 article by *Joh. Lindblom*: 'Profetisk bildspråk'.[1] This article ushered in and constitutes an important part of the theoretical background to the study of the Ebed Yahweh songs.[2] Lindblom's definitions of the forms of imagery and of its intention in Deutero-Isaiah is representative of what Old Testament scholars have said about imagery in the present century. Like most others, Lindblom develops the views of A. Jülicher, the New Testament scholar.

He shows his dependence on these views at the very beginning of the article, when he quotes Jülicher's definition of metaphor.[3] According to this definition, the characteristic of a metaphor is that it is a word which must be replaced by another word. Briefly: 'When a metaphor is used, one always means something else. Something is said; something else is meant'.[4]

This perception of the metaphor as expressed by Jülicher/ Lindblom means that a metaphor consists of two parts: the matter which is the actual that is meant; and the image, which is the figurative that is merely said. The metaphor is a kind of replacement, and the object of choosing a word other than what is usual is, according to Lindblom, to strengthen the feelings, so that what is said has a convincing effect on the hearer—not so much because of the clarity of the image but because of its force.

In Lindblom's opinion, the metaphor is the basic form of imagery; but there are also metaphorical descriptions, comparisons and parables. In contrast to metaphors, metaphorical descriptions consist of series of figurative words and expressions. They are similar to allegories, but are more loosely linked. The object of metaphorical description is to illustrate a subject or a sequence of events.[5] Comparisons can have different forms which can employ different comparative particles; but they can also be omitted. Finally there are parables, which in contrast to metaphorical descriptions are rounded entities whose individual elements are not to be translated. Only the main point(s) of the parable are to be interpreted.

Despite this distinction between different forms of imagery, Lindblom has in fact only one theory of imagery: the image is used as a replacement for the expression itself to illustrate a subject in such a way that the hearer allows himself to be convinced because of the force of the image.

This perception of the use of imagery is to be found again in such a standard work as Svenskt Bibliskt Uppslagsverk, which includes an article by *Ivan Engnell* on Old Testament imagery.[6] Engnell also takes account of four forms of imagery, but he emphasizes that the boundaries are fluid, and categorization can therefore be dangerous. The aim in using imagery is not aesthetic but practical; what is important is to argue and convince.

Besides Lindblom and Engnell, Old Testament scholars have studied imagery and have generally adopted the same point of reference: the metaphor as replacement.

Whereas, in his book on Old Testament imagery,[7] *Aug. Wünsche* gives great weight to the aesthetic value of the image, for *Johannes Hempel*[8] imagery is primarily a means of passing on the prophetic experience. Imagery must be understood as a reflection of the special experience of God that the prophets received in the form of visions. According to Hempel, an example of this is the many terrible and horrifying features used in describing Yahweh as a fierce animal, for example a lion.

In his book, 'Gott und Mensch im Alten Testament',[9] Hempel again deals with the occurrence of imagery, and emphasizes that these images themselves reflect the basic attitude of the Israelitic religion: the relationship to Yahweh is characterized by a sense of distance and a sense of affinity at the same time. This can be seen in the imagery itself where, for example, Yahweh can be described as the terrifying lion and as a bird who caringly protects its young.

Whereas, therefore, Hempel stresses the experience behind the image, *Harold Fisch*[10] underlines imagery's ability to formulate theological attitudes, i.e. its informative nature. In his article on Old Testament imagery and its structure, he points out that the inclusion of nature in texts such as Deut. 32.1-2 and in Pss. 19, 119, 147 and 93 does not come about from a wish to create a specific poetic effect but rather from the author's insight into metaphysical circumstances. According to Fisch, the choice of special linguistic means such as word-play, paronomasia, ambiguities, images, etc. precisely because of the insight to be communicated has often been overlooked in favour of underlining their poetical and rhetorical effect.

Rudolf Mayer believes that the prophets were primarily concerned not with finding aesthetically acceptable images but rather images that would clarify and illustrate their thought, i.e. images are the servants of the message.[11] In a later article,[12] Mayer shows that imagery can be used to explain to the people the relation between sin and judgment. Images serve to illustrate the subject in order that the hearers may understand it better. But Mayer's articles function very largely as collections of material, in which he carefully lists and groups the images according to the domains from which they are drawn.

As we have already seen, as early as 1960 *Luis Alonso Schökel* was looking for a way of studying the prophetic use of imagery. He has himself given examples of image analyses in a series of short articles and in 'Das Alte Testament als literarisches Kunstwerk',[13] but he is very reticent as regards his own view of what images in fact are. It appears, however, that his point of reference is the definition of imagery as part of poetic language. He rejects the prevalent ideas that images are a specific poetic decoration, and similarly he must also distance himself from a more rationalistic approach that accepts the image as a pedagogic arraying of the idea concerned. According to Alonso Schökel, in the true poet the image arises simultaneously with the experience, and similarly the experience can assert itself at the same time as the image is encountered.

As regards interpretation of the image, Alonso Schökel has to accept that there is really no alternative to adopting some form of paraphrasing if one wishes to render the content—or part of the content—of an image. Such retelling can be useful, but it does not communicate the whole image. Alonso Schökel also refers briefly to the more psychology-orientated approaches to imagery, but here also he is reserved, since he is forced to call attention to the continuing uncertainty of research in this field.

Alonso Schökel's own analyses of the image are primarily stylistic. They lead to many valuable individual observations, including the serviceability of elementary things such as metaphors and the polyvalence of meaning that characterizes water, for example, and makes it so useful an image.[14] But Alonso Schökel's work is primarily a strong reminder of the need for special exploration of the images in the Old Testament.

In her article on imagery in Deutero-Isaiah, *Eva Hessler*[15] emphasizes that the aim of the images is not to create a rhetorical or aesthetic effect, let alone to act as pedagogic aids; if this arises, it is a by-product. The primary function is to express fundamental theological statements.

The same basic view lies behind *Christine Downing*'s interpretation of Exodus as one of the central biblical metaphors.[16] She says that the aim of her article is 'to present the exploration of metaphor as the way of doing theology which grows out of an attentive reading of the O.T. itself'. But it must not be forgotten here that the form of the metaphor itself also plays a part, in that according to Downing the information provided by the metaphors cannot be translated into everyday language without distortion occurring. This is because of the metaphor's capacity for holding to dualities and paradoxes.

G. Johannes Botterweck,[17] who like Hempel has interested himself in the animal images in the Old Testament, attributes an exceptional degree of significance to imagery. He groups imagery into different types; but they have in common that, with the assistance of similarity, they are means of illustrating abstract matters. Imagery is accordingly a necessary part of language.[18] Imagery is a means of giving information that language would otherwise find it difficult to impart.

In an article on parables and imagery in the Old Testament pseudepigrapha, *Erling Hammershaimb*[19] has assembled extensive material not previously included in the study of imagery. Hammershaimb points out that the New Testament scholars' very narrow use of the parable concept is not adapted to the study of the images in the pseudepigrapha. He wishes instead to use the parable in the same way as the Hebraic term for this, māshāl. Hammershaimb then reviews a number of parables, making it clear that the boundary between parable and allegory—so important for Jülicher—is fluid, and that there is much material in the pseudepigrapha which should be taken into consideration when studying the New Testament and Rabbinic parables, for example.

Whereas the scholars referred to above are all clearly dependent upon Jülicher's concept of the metaphor, new trends have arisen in recent years also within Old Testament research.

Anders Jørgen Bjørndalen's 1966 article[20] should be brought to notice here. In this article he considers a number of methodological problems associated with the Old Testament allegories. Bjørndalen defines an allegory as 'a textual entity with two or more metaphors in mutual correlation of meaning'.[21] But to be able to make use of this definition one must of course know what a metaphor is.

Whereas those scholars influenced by Jülicher seemed to be relatively certain that a metaphor was a combination of two things, i.e. an image and a specific fact, Bjørndalen is not in nearly such a hurry to accept this definition. He says, on the contrary, that it is almost impossible to define what a metaphor is. To define it as merely an abbreviated comparison is not a particularly satisfactory definition, and in any case this is to forget the metaphor's aesthetic value. And to say that the metaphor is merely one word used in place of another (the replacement approach) is to overlook an important aspect.

It is correct, says Bjørndalen, that we are concerned with the use of one word instead of another; but this is in fact done in such a way that only parts of the word's meaning are relevant to the subject. The characteristic of the metaphor is precisely that it is only partially consistent with the subject to which it refers. It is indeed this partial aspect that makes it possible to distinguish between the metaphor and the non-metaphor. Finally, Bjørndalen points out that the elements of meaning relevant to the subject are explained in the allegory on the basis of the context.

Bjørndalen's analysis of the allegory and metaphor concept is the result of very wide and profound reading of many works of linguistic theory; he also relies on both Old Testament and New Testament research within this domain.[22]

The article has since been supplemented by a major work on the allegorical language in Amos and Isaiah.[23] The basic view of the allegory[24] is the same as in 1966, when Bjørndalen showed clearly that further study would have to follow the lines established by Anton J.B.N. Reichling's theories. The aim of Bjørndalen's investigations is to describe what an allegory is—and in this connexion what a metaphor is—and to define the manner of interpretation of this specific form of language.[25] The possibility of being able to distinguish between metaphorical and non-metaphorical language is of great significance to his analyses. This acts directly as a self-evident precondition for any study whatsoever of imagery; but Bjørndalen's painstaking review of various theories of metaphor shows how complicated the problem is.[26]

Among possible theories, Bjørndalen chooses a modified edition of Reichling's 'Worttheorie'.[27] It is precisely this which provides the necessary (though not always adequate) criteria for distinguishing in practice between metaphorical language and other forms of language, at the same time giving an indication of how metaphors should be interpreted. The main idea of the theory is that a word's meaning consists of different elements, not all of which need to be actualized in the specific language situation. If they are all in action, i.e. all the elements of meaning of which the user of language has knowledge directly and in the specific connexion are of reference to whatever he/she is speaking about, then we are in the presence of *conjunctive use*. But if only some of these elements of meaning are in action it is *disjunctive use*.[28] And it is then this disjunctive use which manifests itself in metaphorical language.

Bjørndalen emphasizes by his definition of the substance of the metaphor that the same word can be used metaphorically and non-metaphorically. What is involved is not different words but different use. Bjørndalen is also able to utilize Reichling's theory to establish that it is the context which determines whether a statement is or is not metaphorical.

The object of using metaphors is to communicate points of view in a convincing way. The metaphor's function is to be communicative.[29] But the metaphor's different elements of meaning are not in fact all realized in the specific language situation, and this means that the speaker and the hearer do not necessarily activate precisely the same elements. Bjørndalen points out that, in the context of eighth-century prophecy, both the interpretation which took place when the prophet spoke as well as a later interpretation when whatever was recorded was studied and subjected to reinterpretation, with an opportunity for discovering elements of meaning not previously recognized, must be considered. Different hearers activate different elements of meaning. The consequence of this is that Bjørndalen must describe the metaphor as 'nicht-abschliessend-interpretierbar', and therefore non-replaceable.[30]

The second half of the book consists of a number of precise analyses of allegories in Amos and Isaiah. Bjørndalen shows that allegories are to be interpreted in close accordance with the text. This means not only that individual metaphors are to be interpreted in the allegory's context but also that the allegory must be perceived in the light of the situation in which it was created—not in the light of the hearer's/reader's imagination. Isa. 5.1-7 in particular is given thorough treatment here, with meticulous investigation into which elements of the text act metaphorically/allegorically and which are to be perceived as non-figurative.

To summarize, it may be said, as regards Bjørndalen's view of the allegory's metaphorical language, that although, like his predecessors, he distinguishes between image and subject he has not adopted their view of the metaphor as replacement. Moreover, by emphasizing the disjunctive use he has created an opportunity for understanding the metaphor in a way that can seriously consider phenomena such as reuse and reinterpretation, and thereby established a basis for understanding the metaphor's creative potential.

As we have seen, Bjørndalen arrives at this result by involving a special theory of meaning taken from linguistic philosophy. The same receptiveness to the work of neighbouring disciplines lies behind *Leonard L. Thompson*'s book, 'Introducing Biblical Literature: A More Fantastic Country'.[32] Thompson strongly emphasizes that

משל, mashal is able to create insight. It is more than just an illustration of something already perceived. Thompson formulates this as follows:

> Metaphors, and that for our purposes includes all forms of *mashal*, yield 'semantic innovation'. . . . . Words and phrases seem to have an inexhaustible capacity to take on new connotations. Metaphor enriches language by bringing to life new connotations, which open new ways of ordering the world.[33]

According to Thompson, the fact that the metaphor gives an opportunity for new understanding is related to its receptiveness to interpretation, since by definition it offers many potential meanings. The context assists in pointing out that not all potential meanings are equally relevant. This becomes wholly clear when one is faced with the type of משל that Thompson calls 'a narrative *mashal*'. Here the context, i.e. the narrative element, assists in clarifying *and* delimiting the possibilities, while the metaphorical element ensures a certain receptiveness. The parable itself is a good example of such a 'mashal', with the constant tension between the meaning's receptiveness and its enclosed aspect.

L.L. Thompson also considers it important to stress that imagery conveys information; but whereas in reality the majority of the scholars referred to above saw the metaphor's informative possibilities as merely providing a particularly well-suited way of expressing an existing subject, for example God, Thompson points out that, via metaphor, language can impart *new information*, since it not only conveys what non-metaphorical language has difficulty in conveying but can in fact create something new.

Two more works must be included in this survey of contributions to the understanding of imagery in the Old Testament. In his book on comparison and metaphor in the Song of Solomon,[34] *Hans-Peter Müller* has contributed to the hermeneutic of religious language. Müller's basic view is that these images are not merely poetical embellishments but bearers of religious truths, including mythical concepts. In our context, what is of primary significance is Müller's perception of the creative power of images, which in his terminology can be expressed by such words as: 'eine Art atavistischer Sprachmagie', or described as follows: 'eine sprachmagische Handlung: performativ ist sie nämlich in dem Masse, wie sie die Gleichheit von Vergleichs-spender und Vergleichsgegenstand durch den Sprechakt des Vergleichens allererst herstellt und dabei die Welt des sprechenden Menschen, die sprachlich erschlossene Welt verändert'.[35] Hans-Peter Müller includes in his investigations considerations from recent linguistic philosophy, and thereby joins in pointing out the necessity of an interdisciplinary approach to such a complex phenomenon as imagery.

In recent years, *Claus Westermann* has also studied the use of comparisons. In his book, 'Vergleiche und Gleichnisse im Alten und Neuen Testament',[36] he surveys the comparisons to be found in the Old Testament. These are an important means of expressing what occurs between God and man, and are therefore of theological relevance. Westermann points out that they form part of dialogue contexts, on the basis of which they must be interpreted. They must be perceived as apostrophes; they are part of the message, and help to strengthen its effect in their appeal to the hearers for approval. Westermann stresses that Old Testament comparisons and New Testament parables have these functions in common.[37] There follows a summary of recent research into the parable and its results. Westermann points out that the idea that parables function as illustrations must be abandoned, but the strong emphasis on the significance of the context must be retained. A parable should not be interpreted merely in the context in which it was created; its correlation with other parables and groups of parables must also be considered. Scholars engaged in the study of parables must abandon their attempts to find one basic idea in every parable that must be the point of comparison, but should permit the nature of the parable as narrative to stand out clearly. Finally, study involving parables must be specific and historically aware.[38]

Westermann here sets out the limits within which not only further research into New Testament parables but also the study of comparisons and other forms of metaphorical language in the Old Testament must be conducted.

Image Analysis as 'Gattungs-Analyse'
This brings us to the end of the road. But before we leave the OT and turn to New Testament parable research we wish briefly to consider why Old Testament scholars have shown such a limited interest in imagery. It seems to me that the answer is quite simple.

If one wishes to get an idea of the subjects that occupied Old Testament research in a certain period, it is instructive to look at some of the discipline's standard works, for example the introductions to it. And here, as regards the present century, two points attract immediate attention. The first is that scholars' time and effort have been invested largely in questions of dating and, in connexion with this, in classifying sources and traditions as well as genuine and spurious passages and verses.[39]

This concentration on historical questions is not to say, however, that the texts' literary form was completely ignored in the introductions.[40] But the way in which this was done is crucial.

The second point is that when the OT was treated as literature it was from the aspect of the OT's literary forms. Eissfeldt begins his introduction with a long chapter on 'Die kleinsten Redeformen und ihr Sitz im Leben', and similarly Anderson, Weiser and Kaiser have indeed sections on the literary forms (Gattungen). Form criticism has put its stamp on research.

In his instructive chapter on the history, tasks and methods of Old Testament introduction, Aage Bentzen[41] emphasizes that the nineteenth-century's concentration on the problems of dating and on differentiation of sources is about to be succeeded by a broader approach to the subject. The innovation about to take place stems, of course, from Hermann Gunkel's[42] introduction of the form-critical method. But this causes the history of literature to become the history of literary forms, of which Bentzen's own introduction is a good example.

The limited interest in Old Testament imagery is probably also associated with this development. When the study of the OT as literature becomes a study of Gattung, then indeed is there no room for the—in itself banal—demonstration that the OT uses metaphorical language to a marked degree. What there is room for, which has been remarked on now and again, is the particular Gattungen within imagery: fable, parable and allegory.[43]

Apart from mention of these, scattered references are to be found about the prophets' mysterious experiences as a background to their visions and the linguistic impact these have had.[44] But the main approach is form-critical, and it is therefore possible to become aware only of the forms that satisfy Gunkel's classic requirements in regard to a Gattung.[45]

Imagery also plays no part in the most recently published introductions to the OT. B.S. Childs's great introduction[46] is very largely concerned with the reuse of the prophetic texts, but surprisingly it does not discuss whether prophetic language has in any way been especially well-suited to this.[47]

The most recently published introduction, Rolf Rendtorff's Einführung,[48] has a few references to visions and imagery in the context of the book of Ezekiel, but instead of discussing these forms of language he gives primarily a 'translation' of the specific examples. The crucial aspect is plainly the information the images carry.

After this attempt to explain that the lack of feeling for imagery is a general phenomenon, we turn to New Testament parable research which, as can be seen from the description, is also clearly characterized by a form-critical approach.

2. General Principles of New Testament Parable Research

As we know, recent parable research had its beginning in *Adolf Jülicher's* great two-volume work, 'Die Gleichnisreden Jesu', published at the end of the last century.[1] Jülicher, who wished to do away once and for all with the allegorizing interpretation of Jesus' parables characteristic of earlier times, distinguished sharply between *parable* and *allegory*. According to Jülicher, an allegory consists of several metaphors, each of which calls for separate interpretation. The parable, on the other hand, is a comparison consisting of two parts: image part and subject part. In analyzing the parable, one must initially keep the two parts separate one from another and consider the image part as an independent entity, so that one arrives at the point of the image. It is then to this point that the comparison applies; it is the common point between image part and subject part; *tertium comparationis*.

The parable is distinct from the allegory not only in form but also in regard to comprehensibility. Whereas the parable is clear and simple, and is intended to inform, admonish and convince, the allegory expresses the cryptic language that calls for interpretation in order to be understood. According to Jülicher, Jesus' original language was indeed simple and straightforward; but even the evangelists perceived it and transmitted it as if it were allegorical language. (Jülicher's view and the contemporary view of the historical Jesus as 'der Sohn Galiläas' is clearly behind this emphasizing that Jesus spoke in parables and not in allegories.)[2] In consequence of this, Jülicher must also consider the heart-hardening theory in Mk

4.10-12 par. as unhistorical and completely in conflict with Jesus' original prophetic intention.[3]

Both Jülicher's definition of the parable as a comparison consisting of two members and his sharp division between allegory and parable have been of very great significance to parable research. Jülicher's views became very widely accepted and formed the basis for the work that followed, although many had to refute that Jesus' parables were all pure parables, wholly without allegorical features.[4]

C.H. Dodd's work[5] must therefore be seen as an 'approved' corrective to Jülicher. They are in agreement as regards the point of reference; what Dodd finds he must attack is Jülicher's lack of feeling for the significance of the historical context. Despite all his interest in the historical Jesus, Jülicher has nevertheless interpreted the parables as universal religious truths, instead of perceiving them as a link in Jesus' message that the Kingdom of God is at hand.[6]

Joachim Jeremias[7] continues this history-orientated line. According to Jeremias, the parables' original Sitz im Leben is a number of specific situations in which Jesus used them as weapons in the fight against his adversaries. The parables were later used in a new situation as a link in the primitive church's message to the community. Historically, therefore, one must assume two essentially different Sitze im Leben. An important point is that in being transplanted from the first to the second Sitz im Leben the parables have undergone a number of alterations, including the allegorizing pointed out by Jülicher.[8]

Like Jülicher, both Dodd and Jeremias consider the parables to be linguistic means of influencing the hearers. Dodd formulates this as follows in his *definition of the parable*:

> At its simplest the parable is a metaphor or simile drawn from nature or common life, arresting the hearer by its vividness or strangeness, and leaving the mind in sufficient doubt about its precise application to tease it into active thought.[9]

What Dodd means by this is that parables entice the hearers to pronounce a judgment on the matter the parable portrays, subsequently challenging them (directly or indirectly) to transfer this judgment to whatever is the matter to hand, in the way the prophet Nathan applies his parable directly to David.[10]

Joachim Jeremias also stresses the hearers' active role when he concludes his analyses of Jesus' parables with the words '... alle

Gleichnisse Jesu zwingen den Hörer, zu Seiner Person und Seiner Sendung Stellung zu nehmen'.[11]

Whereas scholars such as Dodd and Jeremias are concerned particularly with parables in their historical context, interest has increasingly concentrated in recent years on the parable as a linguistic form and on the hermeneutic aspects of this linguistic form. American scholarship refers to this new current as '*the New Hermeneutic*',[12] and its main concern could be described—rather in the form of a slogan—by the words: the parable as language event.[13]

Regarded in terms of Adolf Jülicher's understanding of the parable, the new attitudes are not merely a portentous corrective but a break. Jülicher's classic distinction between the parable's image part and subject part is debated—and rejected. In his book, 'Language, Hermeneutic, and Word of God',[14] *Robert W. Funk*, who is inspired by E. Fuchs and G. Ebeling among others, defines parables as language events that compel the hearers to choose between the parable's world and the conventional world.[15] The parable is not therefore an illustration of something that exists,[16] an image of a thing, as Jülicher would have formulated it. The parable is a metaphor and, according to Funk, a characteristic of the metaphor is that it creates meaning and gives a possibility of new meaning. That the parable is receptive in this way entails that one cannot in reality refer to the meaning of a metaphor or parable; it is in principle receptive, and is restricted only by the hearer. This also involves that a metaphor cannot be directly translated.

Funk formulates his view of the metaphor as follows: 'The metaphor, like the parable, is incomplete until the hearer is drawn into it as participant; this is the reason the parables are said to be argumentative, calling for a transference of judgment'.[17] That the hearer becomes involved in the parable can also be described by the formulation, so characteristic of 'the New Hermeneutic', 'Language becomes event'.[18]

If one compares Jülicher's and Funk's views of the parable, two essentially different conceptions of what language is are involved—to express it rather simply. For Jülicher, language is a tool, the figurative that illustrates the actual, which is considered as something tangible. For Funk, on the other hand, this distinction between language and the actual is meaningless. As an event, language is both image and subject, but understood in the sense that both are created by the very relating and hearing of the parable. Funk's perception of parables' metaphorical nature makes it possible to see them as meaningful, not only in their original historical context but in every situation. Funk is therefore very interested in parables' use 'today'.

Dan Otto Via's book on parables[19] also amounts to a clash with Jülicher, since Via rejects the method by which Jülicher distinguishes between parable and allegory, i.e. the thesis of the allegory's many images as opposed to the parable's one point of comparison.[20] In his own definition of the relation between parable and allegory, Via emphasizes the linking together of the elements of the narrative and their relation to the outside world. As regards the allegory, the world external to the narrative determines the structure. Therefore, the correlation between the allegory's individual members is often very loose. In contrast to this, the parable is not dependent primarily upon the external world; it is a poetical composition with a close connexion between the individual members.[21]

Dan Otto Via sees the parable as an independent aesthetic dimension that must be understood primarily on the basis of the parable itself. Via expresses this by saying that the parable's meaning is an 'in-meaning' rather than a 'through-meaning'.[22] Its meaning is created on the basis of its own universe rather than on the world to which it draws attention; but both aspects are present. Via hereby distances himself from the radical conception of the work of art as depending solely on itself. 'In this chapter it has been argued that a work of literary art means both in and through itself but that the inner, non-referential meaning is dominant.'[23]

Viewed in relation to earlier parable research, Via's work signifies a movement away from the strictly historical interpretation; but it is obviously important for Via that this should not lead to 'a return to allegorizing'.[24] One might of course be led to suspect Via of 'allegorizing tendencies' by his insistence that parables are aesthetic dimensions and thereby less linked to time. The distance between past and present can more easily be overcome, so that the parables' content, which according to Via is a special way of perceiving existence, can be communicated and the text become an event. 'Jesus' parables were a language event in his day, and the purpose of interpreting them is that that event might occur once more in the exposition.'[25]

That parables were/are language events means that they require a position to be adopted by the hearers, who are compelled to choose between the parable's perception of existence and their own.[26]

Dan Otto Via's views, which as can be seen are very much in line with Robert W. Funk's, may be supplemented by *John Dominic Crossan*'s in his 1973 article 'Parable as Religious and Poetic Experience'.[27] Crossan distinguishes between two forms of communication: the literal, whose purpose is to give information; and the figurative, whose purpose is to create involvement, participation; and he emphasizes that the true metaphor belongs to the latter category. 'A true metaphor is one whose power creates the participation whereby its truth is experienced.'[28] It should however be noted that Crossan does not thereby deny that metaphors can also have other functions, for example as means of information or of embellishment. But he finds it important to stress that the poetic metaphor is something different and something more, and cannot therefore be replaced by the speech forms of general indicative language. Against this background, Crossan defines Jesus' parables as extended metaphors.[29]

In his book 'In Parables' published the same year,[30] Crossan elaborates his views on participation and information. He makes it clear that there are not only metaphors whose most important function is to communicate information, but also metaphors that primarily create participation.[31] But equally as important as this differentiation is Crossan's emphasis that metaphors can give information about something new. 'The thesis is that metaphor can also articulate a referent so new or so alien to consciousness that this referent can only be grasped within the metaphor itself. The metaphor here contains a new possibility of world and of language so that any information one might obtain from it can only be received *after* one has participated through the metaphor in its new and alien referential world.'[32] The sharp opposition of information and participation that the article previously referred to might precipitate, and which Elisabet Engdahl rightly criticizes in her discussion of Crossan, is hereby avoided.[33]

It is noteworthy that Crossan does not use this classification into the two types of communication in his book, but only in his article. In his later book published in 1976,[34] Crossan also modifies his view on the relation between parable and allegory, in that he no longer sees these two as antitheses.[35]

One more parable scholar will be referred to briefly—*Norman Perrin*. Perrin is characterized by his attempt to bridge the gap

between traditional parable research, with its interest in the
historical context, and the hermeneutic trend, with its underlining of
the metaphorical nature of parables. The important problem lies in
the very tension between the specific historical elements in parables
and the form of the parable itself, which is receptive to new
meanings.[36]

In a review of Dan Otto Via's book 'The Parables: Their Literary
and Existential Dimension', Perrin has clearly indicated that the
problem about Jesus' parables is that they were created in a specific
historical situation, but are so worded that they can also be
understood as what Via called 'aesthetic objects'.[37] Against this
background, Perrin criticizes Robert W. Funk and Dan Otto Via for
forgetting the specific historical features in the parables. But at the
same time he stresses that Joachim Jeremias should also welcome the
views that Via presents. Both Via and Jeremias have indeed
meaningful things to say about Jesus' parables.[38]

What Perrin therefore requires of a hermeneutic method employable
in relation to the parables is that it should make room for an historio-
critical analysis, and also take into account what he calls 'the
hermeneutical interaction of author, text, and reader'.[39]

Finally, a brief reference must be made to Perrin's discussion of
the relation between symbol and myth. Perrin points out in a 1975
article[40] that the symbol 'The Kingdom of God' is dependent upon
the myth of God the Creator, who constantly cares for his people.
This dependence is so strong that if the myth dies the symbol loses its
power; for only while the symbol is able to evoke the myth can it
function as a symbol.[41]

In this brief presentation,[42] I have tried to indicate some central
attitudes of significance also beyond the study of the parables in the
New Testament. I have therefore included only those views I have
found it most important to discuss when considering Old Testament
imagery.

Summary and Evaluation
Finally, a brief summary of why I regard the study on New
Testament parable research as so rewarding.

a.   It is useful to investigate the *Jülicher* tradition, since by this
      means we become acquainted with the theoretical prerequisites
      for very many of the views on Old Testament imagery
      advanced in the present century.

2. *The Use of Imagery in the Old Testament*   41

b.   In the *Jeremias* tradition, we encounter a stubborn insistence on the parables' historical basis and their reuse in the new situation, with the consequent changes in meaning (and perhaps presentation). This is a view which must remind Old Testament scholars that the prophetic texts also have several Sitze im Leben.

c.   The *'New Hermeneutic'* of recent years has brought an important corrective to both the Jülicher tradition and the Jeremias tradition, which necessitates a thorough reappraisal of the linguistic form to which not only the parables but also imagery in general belong. The increasing interest in the language-event viewpoint forces us all to give full consideration to a number of vital problems relating to the metaphor's form and function.

d.   In spite of the corrective's fundamental radicality, there is a tendency and a wish not to accept new either-or attitudes, where the parable either does or does not illustrate something tangible, where it is either a matter of information or of participation, and where one works either purely historically or purely literarily. Indeed, there are even trends towards a softening of the traditional opposition between parable and allegory.

I have found especially inspiring the respect for the realities that I encounter in Norman Perrin's emphasis on the fact that Jesus' parables came into being in a specific, historical situation, but have acquired such a form that they must also be treated as 'aesthetic objects'. I find this duality central to the study of Old Testament imagery: the image's genesis in a specific, historical situation and its receptiveness to reuse and reinterpretation in other, equally specific historical situations. (Cf. Chapter 1 on Proto-Isaiah as traditional literature and religious utility literature.)

However, a danger in bringing in New Testament parable research can be, on the one hand, that it is restricted by its form-critical point of reference, with its interest in Gattungen and not in imagery in general, and that, on the other hand, occasionally it is strongly influenced by the fact that the subject is Jesus' parables about the Kingdom of God. Both these factors contribute to a use of superlatives that cannot be transferred out-of-hand to the OT. It is of no use to expect every individual image, traditional or untraditional, to demand of the hearer the great existential choice. On the contrary,

I believe I can establish that the widespread use of imagery in Isaiah 1–39 is closely associated with Isaiah's prophetic intention.

Hans Wildberger, in his discussion of the book of Isaiah's language and language form, describes Isaiah's prophetic intention as follows: '... er will in der Regel nicht Überlegungen weitergeben ... sondern möchte seinen Jerusalemern ans Herz greifen. ... will sein Volk in Bewegung setzen ... Das ist der Grund, warum er seine Sache immer wieder in *Bilder* kleidet, die das Gemeinte weit besser als abstrakte Begriffe zum Ausdruck bringen'.[43] Following this very precise description, Wildberger provides a very traditional listing of the images used, grouped according to subject areas.[44] But we learn nothing from Wildberger about *how* it is that the images can have the stated function.

3. *Description of the Function of Imagery in the Old Testament*

The significance of Adolf Jülicher to parable research can scarcely be exaggerated.[1] Although very many points have been closely investigated, it is his views that have staked out the debate and formulated the questions. Time after time has parable research returned to Jülicher's two central questions: how do imagery's different forms relate to one another? and what is the relationship between image part and subject part?

The first of these questions is of limited significance to Old Testament research. More important than discussion of the demarcation of, for example, parable as compared with allegory is investigation of the metaphorical function itself, and therefore of what separates figurative language in general from literal language. But the other question should also be discussed in our context, where it is important to clarify whether Jülicher's conception of the image as the figurative that illustrates the subject, *the replacement theory* or *language event theory*, as advanced by followers of the 'New Hermeneutic', provides the best basis for understanding the use of imagery in the Old Testament—if, indeed, such an either-or is actually concerned.

If, therefore, imagery is to be described as it operates in the Old Testament, certain questions must be answered by means of this description. We could learn from the history of research that a characteristic of imagery is that it is simultaneously tied to the specific context and receptive to reinterpretation in the new context.

Furthermore, it has become clear that imagery speaks about reality, but not in such a way that one can simply say that the image illustrates reality. And, finally, it has become clear that the use of imagery presupposes that one can distinguish between the use of figurative language and the use of literal language.

This establishes the framework for an analysis of the use of imagery in the Old Testament and formulates the crucial questions. These questions can be made more rigorous by including individual works concerned with the philosophy of language. But neither earlier parable research nor the philosophy of language supplement can be the true object of the investigation. This must be the specific texts. The basis for preparing the description is therefore the textual analyses presented in Chapter 4, where I discuss the use of the tree as a metaphor in Isaiah 1–39. But the awareness of the questions to be asked of the texts has of course been formed and intensified by studying the works of others on imagery, whether exegetic or language-philosophical.

Scholars such as Max Black, J.L. Austin and John R. Searle are therefore included only because I have found in their works usable concepts and useful reflections on the observations I have made as an exegetist. This can of course have the result that the philosophical concepts I am using are the subject not only of reuse but also of different use.

To introduce the discussion of the characteristic feature of the use of imagery in the Old Testament, therefore, it is appropriate to take a specific example from the book of Isaiah. The example is concerned not with trees but with water.

Isa. 8.6-8 as an Example of Old Testament Imagery[2]
I have chosen as an example Isa. 8.6-8, the well-known passage where Isaiah accuses his countrymen of refusing Shiloah's gently flowing waters and threatens that the Lord will in retribution send the mighty river, the king of Assyria, across the land.

That we are in this case in the presence of an example of imagery cannot be determined from the description of Shiloah alone. In one context, v. 6 will function metaphorically; in another, it will be intended and understood literally. The hearer must therefore decide from one situation to another whether a specific statement is to be taken literally. That the hearer will usually choose in accordance with the speaker's intention stems from very many factors, which I shall broadly call the context. The historical situation in which it is spoken, including pre-understanding of a general cultural nature (religious/political) that both parties possess, is part of the context of a prophetic oracle. If the oracle is reused, the context changes. And by fixing it in writing as in, for example, the book of Isaiah the oracle additionally receives the literary context in which the redaction has placed it.

It is, then, the broadly understood context, with all its individual factors, that helps the hearer/reader to decide whether a statement is to be understood literally. If the context makes the literal meaning absurd, and thereby incredible, the hearer must begin to consider what linguistic usage may instead be involved.

It may emerge from the formulation itself that what is said is to be understood figuratively, as can be seen for example from the interpretation of the image in Isa. 8.7. It may also emerge from this that words not normally juxtaposed appear side by side, so that two different lines of thought are activated. Something on these lines occurs in Isa. 8.6, where the use of the verb, מאס, reject, which is frequently used in theological contexts,[3] indicates that in this verse the prophet perhaps also speaks of theological matters, and that the people's rejection applies to Yahweh and not to a water channel.

Who the speaker is and what he usually has in his repertoire also plays a part. One scarcely expects from Isaiah estimates of the supply capacity of the spring of Shiloah, but rather a statement on Yahweh's view of the people's actions. If, on the other hand, the speaker had been one of King Ahaz's officials, the situation could have been entirely different, but the remark the same. If we imagine a specific situation on the lines of that found in Isa. 7.1-9, with the official concerned addressing the king with the words: 'This people refuse Shiloah's gently flowing waters', then the meaning could be literal. For if, for example, the official concerned (and now we enter into pure hypothesis) had been carrying out an investigation of Jerusalem's water supply with a view to deciding whether a siege could be withstood, then he might well, on the basis of 'an enquiry', report back that the people did not believe that the canal would be able to cope with the quantity of water necessary in an acute supply situation. In this context, the statement would have to be taken literally. No-one would understand it as imagery. All one can do is to consider whether there was a special reason for describing Shiloah as 'flowing gently', i.e. in pointing out the slowness of the water's flow.

In the broad sense, the context makes it probable that we are in the presence of imagery. But for hearers to be able to continue to hold to this interpretation it is important that what is said in the image also makes sense in the context. To use the water of Shiloah as an image of Yahweh makes good sense in terms of the perceptions of the time. Shiloah is a canal running from Gihon, the sacred spring, and in a siege situation such as that threatening it was vitally necessary to Jerusalem.

Moreover, by speaking of the waters of Shiloah the prophet could employ a number of concepts associated with the water image. One of the hymns of Zion, Psalm 46, expresses trust in Yahweh (and this is certainly what occupied Isaiah in this situation) precisely with the aid of water images. In Ps. 46.3-4; RSV vv. 2-3, the emergency situation is described as a threat from a tumultuous sea. This is contrasted with the river that makes glad the city of God as the guarantor of Yahweh's redeeming presence. The reference to the holy spring assures the people that Yahweh lives in his city; therefore it will not totter, and 'God will help her right early' (Ps. 46.6).

In the psalm, the tumultuous sea's noise and fury are a parallel to the people's noise. The creation myth and the myth of the battle with the nations operate not only as a framework of understanding but create confidence that Yahweh will even now intervene and, as in the past, save his people from their enemies.[4]

In the same way, the image of Shiloah and the mighty river in Isa. 8.6-8 is able to recall the myth of the struggle against chaos. (Cf. my reference to Norman Perrin, p. 40.) But whereas Psalm 46 begins with the tumultuous sea and ends in trust in Yahweh's victory, Isa. 8.6-8 begins with the reminder that it is he himself who should be the basis of trust, he that the people have rejected. Yahweh must therefore also punish them by sending chaos on them himself—until the water reaches to their necks. This interpretation of Shiloah as an image of Yahweh also fits in well, as can be seen from the following statement that the Lord will send the king of Assyria against his people. Accusation and punishment go together.

That the speaker is speaking metaphorically means that his intention is to cause his hearers to think two thoughts at the same time. One might say that, in the specific case, two statements are to interact in the hearers' minds, as they do in the prophet's. Statement (a) is the statement we can read in the text: 'this people has refused the waters of Shiloah that flow gently'; statement (b) is the statement that must be assumed for the interaction to take place, for example a statement on the lines of Psalm 46's words that God is in the midst of Jerusalem; the city does not totter; God will help her right early.

Because these two statements interact, the image's meaning emerges. We cannot render this exhaustively; but we can come close to it in the following paraphrase of the meaning: 'This people, i.e. ourselves, reject out of fear of the enemy our only possibility of survival, Yahweh, and thereby put ourselves in mortal peril'. This interpretation of the image therefore provides information on the political situation. What the prophet communicates by his image is another way of looking at reality. The hearers believed wrongly that their hope of existence lay in the contact with the king of Assyria (cf. 2 Kgs 16.7); it now becomes clear that it lies in the contact with Yahweh, and that the other contact leads to destruction and ruin.

That the image is able to create something new, another way of seeing, is associated with the fact that the two statements (a) and (b) are not interchangeable; as Bjørndalen expresses it, (a) is used disjunctively. Combined, therefore, they are able to say something other—and more—than (b) could say alone.

But it is not sufficient to point out that the image creates new information by proposing a new way of looking at existence. It must also be stressed that the aim is to influence the hearers' attitude and action. The hearers must go along with the interpretation of the image, and adopt it as their own. They must allow themselves to be threatened by the prophet's imagery, and it is hoped that they will draw some behavioural conclusions from it. A reasonable consequence of the use of imagery would be to resume the life-giving contact in place of the death-bringing contact; in short: turn back to Yahweh. If this occurs, the use of imagery has succeeded.

Finally, we must refer to one more characteristic. If we read the Targum's rendering of this oracle, it can be seen that a reinterpretation has taken place. Shiloah is not expounded about Yahweh but about the House of David. The historical situation has changed, and makes reinterpretation necessary/natural.

Summary

We have now analyzed one example of imagery in Isaiah, and we shall examine whether it is possible in the light of this to arrive at some general remarks about the use of imagery, at the same time, of course, making use of the viewpoints advanced in the sections

2. *The Use of Imagery in the Old Testament* 47

dealing with research, and anticipating the contributions of Chapter 4's analyses.

As we have seen, Old Testament imagery consists of statements that in one context function figuratively but in another context do not need to function figuratively. The metaphorical function does not therefore have anything to do with the statement's wording but with the use of it. As Bjørndalen emphasized, the same word can be used metaphorically and non-metaphorically. It is not a matter of different words but of different use. In other words: it is the context that determines which use is involved.

To be able to speak of metaphorical use, there must be in a specific statement *two statements* (a) and (b) that *interact* with one another. Statement (a) can be identical in its external form with the metaphorical expression, for example as in Isa. 8.6. Statement (b) can be formulated directly, for example as in Isa. 8.7, where the king of Assyria is directly referred to, or be present merely in the mind of the speaker and (if the metaphor succeeds) of the hearers.

An interacting relationship between (a) and (b) is concerned because the two statements are not interchangeable but different. From the metaphorical statement, information can be derived about reality, i.e. about the specific historical situation in which the image is used. This information, the image's meaning, cannot be rendered exhaustively; an image cannot therefore be translated directly. But that there can be no exhaustive representation of the image does not mean that nothing whatsoever can be derived from it. We can say of this information that it functions as a new design for understanding reality, and thereby for relating oneself to reality. In providing this design, the image helps to influence the hearer's attitude and (if it succeeds) his action. Imagery has therefore not only an *informative* but also a *performative function*. The two cannot be separated. Finally, it must be stressed that modified contexts can lead to modified interpretations.

Requirements Necessary for a Usable Definition of Imagery in the Old Testament

Following this attempt to indicate general features of imagery on the basis of an individual example, we shall now proceed to discuss the three requirements necessary for a usable description of Old Testament imagery.

First Requirement: A definition of imagery's bonding to the specific context, and of its receptiveness to reinterpretation in a modified context.

Imagery's usability in a new context is a subject at the centre of recent parable research, which emphasizes that parables are aesthetic objects that, even today, can become language events. There is a clear understanding here of the texts as religious texts with a claim to actuality. We do not find among older parable scholars interested in the original situation in which Jesus' parables were first heard the same direct interest in the use of the texts today, but on the other hand we find clear knowledge of the reuse of which the parables were made the subject in the early church. But the attitude to this reuse is usually negative. Reuse is misuse of Jesus' genuine parables.

But what I miss is a combination of *the historical interest* and the approach that the texts are religious texts with a claim to actuality which by their form are well-suited to be bearers of a *still-topical message*.

As far as my—certainly limited—knowledge of philosophy of language goes, I can find no interest in combining systematic consideration of what, for example, metaphors are with historical investigation of specific metaphors' use and reuse. The metaphor is dealt with as a basic phenomenon of language, and the approach has no historical perspective. An instructive example of this is the frequently quoted philosopher Max Black, whose views deserve closer analysis and evaluation.

Max Black's article on the metaphor[5] presents three types of metaphor theory, of which he himself prefers the last but without rejecting the first two. The three theories are called 'substitution view of metaphor', 'comparison view of metaphor' and 'interaction view of metaphor'. The theory of the metaphor as a form of comparison is in reality a subdivision of the substitution theory, since both have the same main approach: that the metaphor can be replaced by literal language. In contrast to this, the interaction theory maintains that metaphors are irreplaceable. If they are translated meaning is lost, and not only—as traditionally asserted—the specific embellishment value.

Black considers that the interaction theory only is important to philosophy, since it is concerned with those metaphors which are able to create a new meaning. This new meaning arises because two different statements are combined. Black distinguishes between the

metaphorical statement's main subject and its auxiliary subject, and
points out that the metaphor is created by the interaction between
these two subjects. The auxiliary subject acts as a filter by means of
which the main subject can be seen. This causes a reorganization of
the main subject's elements of meaning, and an addition of meaning
normally attributed only to the auxiliary subject. Black is therefore
able to subscribe to the following description of the metaphor, which
originates from I.A. Richards:

> In the simplest formulation, when we use a metaphor we have two
> thoughts of different things active together supported by a single
> word, or phrase, whose meaning is a resultant of their interaction.[6]

Despite Black's preference for this conception of the metaphor, he
has no wish, as we have seen, to reject the other two. The reasoning
in support of this is that not all metaphors are able to satisfy the
demands which must be made on an 'interaction metaphor'. Some
metaphors are so trivial that one can equally well say that the
metaphor is there used as a replacement, or that what is there
concerned is an abbreviated comparison. If we do not do this, the
metaphor material indeed becomes very restricted.

I have chosen to introduce Black's definition of the metaphor at
this stage because his relatively short article may be able to act as a
paradigm of the views we have encountered in OT and NT research.
Black takes seriously both the substitution approach and the
comparison approach, while at the same time emphasizing that the
metaphors of real value to philosophy are 'interaction metaphors'.

If we now 'translate' this to the Old Testament and New
Testament debate, it will mean that Jülicher's (and also the majority
of the other scholars') views are still relevant—as regards certain
images—but that the metaphors of significance to theology are the
'true' metaphors where language becomes event and creates participation. Or, translated into pure 'NT language': what must be of
interest to a modern theologian is Jesus' parables perceived as the
language event that compels the hearers to choose between their own
world and the parable's world.

In committing ourselves to Max Black's views, therefore, we
commit ourselves to the very theories that have characterized Old
Testament and New Testament imagery research and to the very
natural possibility of accepting them all as more or less useful and
usable—but each of them separately.

As we have seen, Black wishes to assert that there are three different types of metaphor; but however tempting this may sound I must reject his views. The reason for my rejection is primarily that metaphors have a history, and cannot therefore be firmly established once and for all as belonging to either one type or another. Black's conception assumes, indeed, that a specific textual example belongs always and per se to the category in which it has once been placed. According to Black's point of view, Jesus' parables are by definition and in themselves examples of language event, whereas the vineyard in Isa. 5.1-7 is merely a metaphorical paraphrase (substitution) for the House of Israel. But experience shows us in fact that images can begin by acting as images, but after a long period of time and use end up as clichés; and likewise a cliché in a new situation can regain a figurative function. Experience also shows that what one hearer perceives as an image, and therefore as an offer of a new understanding, another may perceive as empty and trivial embellishment. One must not forget here what Perrin called 'the hermeneutical interaction of author, text, and reader'.[7]

A characteristic of Black's view of the metaphor is that he *works synchronously* with language, i.e. he sees language as it operates at one specific point in time in history. If one takes a cross-section through a certain language today (and preferably within a defined and homogeneous group of language users), then it is indeed possible to find metaphors that by far the majority consider they can translate without loss of meaning, as well as metaphors they consider they cannot translate without loss of meaning. But this is not because these 'translatable metaphors' are of another type which is essentially different from the 'true metaphors' but because they have become sealed by convention, so that they evoke only a specific, greatly restricted number of meanings, often perhaps only one.[8]

To students of Old Testament imagery, a very important aspect is that images can for a time lose their figurative function, Old Testament texts being traditional texts which have been used again and again. Many of the images used have therefore become extremely well-known, and demand only very limited interpretation by the hearers. The interpretation is obvious when Yahweh is referred to as a rock in the Psalms (cf. e.g. Pss. 18.3, 32 [RSV vv. 2, 31]; 19, 15 [RSV v. 14]; 28.1; 62.3, 7, 8 [RSV vv. 2, 6, 7]; 78.35). But this is not to say that 'rock' *is* in this case a substitution metaphor. 'Rock' can still act as an interaction metaphor. But if this image is to be revived and force the hearers to see reality in a new way, the expression must be used in a new context. And this is precisely what occurs in the book of Isaiah, where a number of traditional images from the Psalms are used in a new way, and the rock becomes a rock over which one stumbles (Isa. 8.14). Here the prophet can utilize his knowledge of how his contemporaries will interpret the image, just as in his song of the vineyard he can utilize the fact that the traditional interpretation of the vineyard as a woman goes without saying.

We meet the same technique in Ezek. 15.2ff., where the vine is used as an image of Jerusalem's inhabitants. By the rhetorical question—what is the advantage of the vine compared with the other trees of the forest?—the prophet appeals to the hearers' pre-understanding of the vine as the noble and valuable tree. But immediately afterwards it is stated what the yardstick in this comparison is to be: the value of the timber—and not, as is normal with vines, the value of the fruit tree. The context is new compared with the traditional context, and it therefore becomes possible to activate elements of meaning other than those customary. A traditional image set in an unexpected context causes the hearers to look with new eyes, not only at their own situation but also at the vine. They receive new information in both domains that converge in the image.

Conversely, an image used in a well-known context can lose its metaphorical function. But it must be stressed that in such an event a dead metaphor is concerned,[9] i.e. a metaphor that does not at present function as a metaphor. This does not concern a special group of metaphors characterized by being translatable. What is involved therefore is not essential differences but the question of whether a metaphor is successful, i.e. a functional question. As referred to above, we shall ask of the metaphor not the essential question, 'What *is* a metaphor?', but the functional question, 'How does a metaphor *function?*'

The definition of the functioning metaphor is associated with the fact that it represents a tension between two thoughts that come together. If the tension is absent, for example when in everyday usage we speak of a table's four legs, the 'legs' do not function as a metaphor. And it can be disputed whether the expression was once a metaphor but is now a dead metaphor, or whether the intention of the word 'leg' is such that supporting a table-top is just as much part of being a leg as supporting a body.[10]

One of the aspects most strongly emphasized in recent definitions of the metaphor is its receptiveness to reinterpretation. This receptiveness is associated with the fact that the metaphor is not only based on the similarity principle but also presupposes dissimilarity. The cliché brings us face to face with the phenomenon that the relation between similarity and dissimilarity has become established by convention. The tension is relieved, and no-one any longer expends energy in adopting a position on this point; or, more correctly, no-one who is aware of the convention! The child, the linguistically less well-informed (the foreigner or others who marginally fall within this group) and those who in any other way have ears to hear can experience the tension between similarity and dissimilarity and feel themselves challenged to adopt a position. In this way, a metaphor sealed by convention can be opened again, the dead metaphor can come to life.[11]

Metaphors have a receptiveness to interpretation because they apply only partially to that to which they refer.[12] This is the aspect of the comparison that is sometimes overlooked when the comparison concept is reserved to those metaphors which are directly understood conventionally, and denied to those metaphors which appear to create rather than to single out similarity. But if one is to distinguish between singling out and creating similarity one must always introduce the question: For whom, where and when?

Moreover, it must be said of Max Black's definition that since all metaphors are based on both similarity and dissimilarity, and therefore on comparison, it is less desirable to employ a special group called 'comparison metaphors'. 'Interaction metaphors' also make use of comparison; but this must be understood neither as relating to comparison in the sense of identification, i.e. that only the similarity is important, nor as relating to a comparison between tangible things.

The *conclusion* from this last aspect is, then, that I must uphold it as a characteristic of the metaphor that, by bringing together different statements, tension is created between similarity and dissimilarity, or as Paul Ricoeur formulates it in his definition of similarity: 'To see *the like* is to see the same in spite of, and through, the different. This tension between sameness and difference characterizes the logical structure of likeness'.[13]

If the tension is absent and the metaphor does not call for interpretation, but can automatically be translated as a cliché, this does not mean that we are in the presence of a special type of metaphor, but that the metaphor concerned has been sealed by convention at the time concerned. The reason for the absence of tension must be sought outside the metaphor, not in the metaphor. But such 'dead metaphors' are able to come to life again in a new context.

What I have drawn attention to here is of course the reuse potential which is so characteristic of imagery. The image of, for example, the vineyard/vine turns out to be usable in different situations, and with the altered situation new meaning is created (cf. the analysis of Isa. 5.1-7 and 27.2-6). Conversely, the reuse of Isa. 11.1's image of the 'root' in Isa. 11.10 and the reuse of the branch image (although with a terminology different from that in Isa. 11.1) in Jer. 23.5; 33.15 shows that, when reused, an image can lose its image function and become a dead metaphor that in no way evokes two different statements which can interact (cf. p. 142).

Second Requirement: A more explicit statement of the relation between image and reality.

If we return to our point of departure in Black's definition of 'interaction metaphor', it becomes clear that, in regard to this theory, two linguistic dimensions are concerned which are active at the same time. It is 'two thoughts of different things active together' that creates the metaphor. We do not have on the one hand 'reality', 'the hard facts', and on the other hand a linguistic statement. It is not reality and language which are interacting.

The Jülicher tradition's distinction between image part and subject part can certainly be interpreted to mean that its concern is to keep together language and reality; but it is precisely there that criticism comes into action. Jan Lindhardt's formulation (and to refer just once, in spite of all, to the indestructible example of Achilles and the lion) from his criticism of Jülicher reads:

> It is correct that there is a common point between Achilles and the lion, for example courage. But it is wrong to call the one the image part and the other the subject part, since it cannot be said that Achilles is reality, whereas the lion is an image. Both parts are of course equally real . . . 'Achilles is a lion' is an image or a linguistic expression that claims to represent/say something about reality. In other words, the comparison takes place in the image itself or the linguistic expression, which—if it is correct—also expresses a

comparison that applies in reality. Both the metaphor and the simile therefore make comparisons in the language with the aid of the language, and there is no reason therefore to distinguish sharply between them.[14]

As we have said, it is in the language that the interaction takes place; but this must be seen as an interaction not merely between two individual words but between two contexts. The metaphor functions always on the sentence level as a metaphorical statement. Ian G. Barbour stresses that in the metaphor there is created 'a novel configuration ... by the juxtaposition of *two frames of reference* of which the reader must be simultaneously aware'.[15]

It is important that there are two domains which meet in the formation of a metaphor. A metaphor is not merely one word used instead of another, for example 'the river' instead of 'the king of Assyria' in Isa. 8.7; an interaction takes place between on the one hand 'the river' and the entire context in which this word is normally used, and on the other hand 'the king of Assyria' and the context to which he normally belongs. Not everything associated with the river context[16] is similar to the king of Assyria; what is concerned is figurativeness and not identity. The two statements are different.

Nevertheless, it is worth noting that this interaction also implies that 'the river' takes over significance from 'the king of Assyria'. The river 'takes on the colour' of the great king. This interaction can perhaps be seen more clearly in the use of the tree image in Isa. 2.13, where the meaning 'pride' is taken over. The eyes of the hearer are thereby opened to aspects of the tree he has not seen before. What was previously perceived as independence and strength now bears the stamp of pride. This means that the hearer can receive new information about both of the two domains that collide in the metaphor. As an example along these lines, Earl R. MacCormac refers to the statement 'man is a wolf'. In this example, it is not only the man who takes on the stamp of a wolf; our understanding of what a wolf is becomes affected by what we understand by a man.[17]

The interaction therefore takes place within the language; but the meaning created is concerned with reality. We know something different and something more about 'the world' when we have perceived it through the metaphor. But how are we to define this fact more precisely?

What we are faced with is the classic problem of the relation between language and reality/the world.[18] And the answers group

themselves over the entire spectrum, beginning at one extreme with
the world as something tangible, and towards which the language/
image points, to the other extreme where the language's/image's
creative and recreative force is urged. In our context, I consider it
important to maintain that there is a connexion between language
and reality/the world. This connexion is not unambiguous,[19] and we
must therefore warn against too simple a solution in which one sees
language either as a tool and nothing more or exclusively as the
creator and the innovator.

I consider it important to point out that *imagery*, when functioning
according to its intention, offers a new way of seeing reality, and
thereby creates something new. But this may appear to be something
very 'expensive' if one has at the back of one's mind Robert W.
Funk's description of the position in which the hearer of the parable
is placed in the choice between the world of the parable and of the
conventional. One then perceives that, if the imagery is successful,
the choice is between eternal damnation and eternal salvation. But
this of course is because most of imagery research is based on Jesus'
parables.

To choose between the image's world and the conventional world
may also mean having to choose between seeing the king of Assyria
either as a common enemy or as a chaotic force, to have to choose
between seeing the king either as a scion of David or as a proud and
swaggering tree; indeed, to have to choose between seeing an actual
girl either as a quite ordinary girl or as the rose of Sharon. The new
does not have to be radically new; it may merely be a matter of
nuance compared with what one expected.

If imagery works to the effect that one chooses the image's world
rather than the conventional, then what is described as a language
event takes place, or to express it less dramatically one looks with
new eyes upon the reality around one, one's world is being recreated
because one experiences the world in a different way.

When I say in this connexion that the image creates, it means quite
simply that I act differently in relation to specific phenomena in my
surroundings after I have seen them through the image. I say here
nothing about the extent to which reality as 'fact', or what one would
call the world of phenomenon, is changed, let alone whether there is
such a world which is unaffected by my behaviour towards it. What I
am trying to establish is two things: (1) that imagery, if it succeeds,
changes *my reaction to the surrounding world*; (2) that there is *a*

surrounding world that the imagery interprets, and to which I relate
through language.

I have emphasized that there is such a connexion between imagery
and the world because imagery's intention is to change the hearer's
attitude towards the world. The experience of the image does not
take place within an enclosed space of a purely linguistic nature, as it
may sometimes seem. Neither, of course, is space so enclosed that
concrete external events cannot initiate usage. Isaiah speaks of
Shiloah and the great river because he and his contemporaries are
experiencing a political crisis, with all that this involves by way of
discussion of coalitions and political initiatives. But he does not give
a description of the political circumstances; in his imagery, he
provides an opportunity for interpreting events through the images
referred to. And he does not do this in order to describe how the
majority views the situation but to influence his contemporaries to
look at the situation in a different way.

The relation between image and reality can also be looked at from
a somewhat different angle, taking as our point of reference the
discussion of the relation between information and participation.

Information—Participation

While, on the basis of the traditional substitution theory, a
distinction is made between image and subject, this distinction is
impossible on the basis of the language-event theory, since the
'subject' has not been created before the linguistic formulation but eo
ipso comes into being with it. Whereas one would be able, on the
basis of the substitution theory, to pose questions about whether the
information the image conveys is true or false, whether image and
subject correspond to one another, this is not possible on the basis of
the language-event theory. The relevant question here is whether the
imagery acts according to its intention, so that it succeeds. The
criterion for this is whether the hearer allows himself to become
involved in the image, i.e. whether it creates participation.

It is in the light of this that it has been possible to press the
question of imagery's function as an either/or question: either
imagery is a tool to pass on information, and then it can be judged as
true/false, and in that case there must be a direct connexion between
language and the world; or it is its performative function to create
participation, and then one must ask whether it has succeeded or
failed, and in that case imagery is not connected with the world in the

same direct way, and we therefore cannot raise the question of truth.

In my opinion, this contrast is both unreasonable and unacceptable. Imagery has both an informative and a performative function. This view is not mine alone. Even *J.L. Austin*—who introduces his renowned 1955 series of lectures, 'How to Do Things with Words', with a clear distinction between what he calls constatives that can be true or false and performatives that cannot be true/false, but like acts can succeed or fail—shows in the course of his teaching that it is necessary to abandon such a sharp differentiation. One simply gets nowhere if one operates with these aspects of language as antitheses excluding one another.[20] In the act of speech itself, which must be the point of reference for the analysis of language, both dimensions of language are indeed normally present. This must mean that both questions are relevant.

Austin's ideas, which apply to language in general and are therefore also relevant to imagery, have since been corrected and developed by *John R. Searle*. Searle emphasizes even more strongly than Austin that every utterance is a speech act. 'As Austin saw but as many philosophers still fail to see, the parallel is exact. Making a statement is as much performing an illocutionary act as making a promise, a bet, a warning or what have you. Any utterance will consist in performing one or more illocutionary acts.'[21]

Imagery research has long felt that images contain more than information in the traditional sense; and it has been attempted in various ways to define this other aspect. OT research has emphasized that imagery has a special power which acts convincingly upon the hearer; one thus has here a perception of imagery as both informative and something different and supplementary. Recent NT research has concentrated on what this difference and supplementation represents to such an extent that the *informative* side has slipped completely into the background in favour of insistence on the *performative* (referred to as the parable's ability to create participation), as encountered in the 'New Hermeneutic'.

I include the term 'performative' as a counterpart to 'information' in order to have a collective description of that aspect of imagery whose purpose is to involve the hearer in the image's world, so that the hearer participates in it. The speaker thereby utilizes the image's performative power in such a way that the result, if it succeeds, becomes participation. The speaker performs a speech act which—if it succeeds—becomes a language event for the hearer.[22]

As we have said, the performative aspect is part of language, and thus also of imagery. But it must be stressed that the performative function does not exclude the informative. I am therefore in complete agreement with Elisabet Engdahl when, in her criticism of John Dominic Crossan, she points out the absurdity: that Jesus' parables are meant only to create participation; whoever hears the parable also receives, of course, certain information about what he or she is invited to participate in, for example the Kingdom of God.[23] On the other hand, of course, the primary purpose of Jesus' parables is not to give 'Landeskunde' about Heaven.

A characteristic of imagery is, then, *the dialectic relation between the informative and the performative functions*, in the sense that imagery is the bearer of information that can be derived from the image without thereby exhausting it. This happens when the hearer enters into an interpretation of the imagery. The salient point, then, is how is one to understand this 'entering into an interpretation'. Is it what one describes by the expression 'to participate'?

On the basis of Western thought processes, it is reasonable to distinguish between (a) an interpretation of imagery in which one merely 'decodes' it, and thereby extracts information that can be verified/falsified, and (b) the acceptance of what is interpreted which occurs if one allows oneself to be convinced. One of the objects of imagery is, then, to lead the hearer from interpretation to conviction. This occurs when the hearer in his interpretation of the imagery takes over responsibility for what is said and adopts it as his own. The hearer becomes a collaborator in the imagery, which is unfinished until the hearer has completed it and thereby vouches for it. Imagery entices the hearer not only 'into active thought', as Dodd expresses it, but requires what Funk describes as 'a transference of judgment'.[24]

The hearer can extract information (about the relationship between Yahweh and Israel and about Yahweh's plans for Israel) from the imagery to be found in a text such as Isa. 5.1-7. And one can adopt a view on whether this is true or false, depending upon whether or not the plans materialize; the imagery does not therefore in principle avoid the possibility of verification. But this information is given in a form whose effect is that it is at least as relevant to ask of the text whether the message was successful; did the people really allow themselves to be judged? If the people did so, the imagery's performative side has worked, and then the hearer has not only decoded the message but has himself completed it by applying the judgment to himself.

The relation between the two sides of imagery is often very difficult to determine. This has to do with imagery's structure. Since imagery relies on the tension between similarity and dissimilarity, the external historical situation, inter alia, will be determinative not only of the hearer's/reader's interpretation of the information but also of the weight attributed to the informative and performative functions respectively. To illustrate this, we can refer to the prophetic oracles' use and reuse.

In his book on prophecy's failure to come to pass, *R.P. Carroll*[25] has pointed out that the hearers of the prophetic oracles of course experienced frustration when the information on the future which it was thought could be derived from the prophetic statement did not become reality; but that on the other hand they did not thereby consider the oracles as conclusively falsified and therefore worthless (cf. p. 19, where I quote Carroll's thesis). Even though the descriptions of the glorious future to be found in the book of Isaiah could not for the moment be verified, they were not discarded. But why not, I wonder? Apart from having to do with the difficulty of conclusively falsifying a prophetic statement, it would be reasonable to consider whether this might also be related to their dual function, since the prophetic oracles' function was seen not only as purely informative; they did not stand or fall on their value as true/false but were also seen as performative, i.e. their value lay also in their function to console, encourage, etc.

In his book, Carroll himself entertains this possibility; but his treatment of the language's performative function appears to be somewhat pro forma. The position is simply that in the interest of his thesis he has to make the informative function the all-important point of prophecy. Unless the prophets really spoke of the future as something that was to come and could be controlled, i.e. if their prophecies avoided in principle the demand for verification, then there was no reason to become frustrated, and therefore no reason for hermeneutic effort in order to make expectations and reality correspond. Carroll is himself fully aware that his thesis is based upon this assumption, and therefore he also considers the possibility that prophetic language is of a nature other than purely informative, which is a danger that must be investigated; but the arguments in favour of not really taking these possibilities into consideration are very weak.[26]

What I have said here is closely associated with what we touched upon in connexion with the definition of the prophetic texts' genre. These texts are not only *traditional literature* but also *religious utility literature*. They have been suitable as utility literature because of, inter alia, the widespread use of imagery and its receptiveness to interpretation.[27] Not only can imagery's informative possibilities be considered not to be exhausted by the first announcement itself, but even where the informative side lost its actuality the performative side did not necessarily have to fail; whereas the kingdom of David did not become realized in reality, the Isaianic oracles concerning its re-establishment could still succeed as Yahweh's words of comfort and encouragement for the oppressed.

We must therefore emphasize that *imagery has both an informative and a performative function*, whose mutual relationship depends upon the actual text and the situation in which it is used. Imagery provides an opportunity to conduct oneself towards the world in a manner other than the conventional. It is able to communicate something other—and more—than a pure reflection of reality; it not only extends meaning but innovates.[28] I relate myself to the world through imagery, so that it becomes my environment, structured in the special way made possible by language. The relation between imagery and reality is therefore an *interpreting and understanding relationship*.

And this brings us to the *Third Requirement*: A more precise definition of what distinguishes imagery from literal language

Imagery and Imagery's 'Gattungen'

I pointed out earlier that Old Testament research has been inspired by form criticism to such a degree that by and large imagery has been understood to refer only to the special 'Gattungen' of imagery: fable, parable, allegory. For this reason, imagery as a general feature of, for example, the prophetic message has received almost no consideration. The form-critical grouping into Gattungen is fully justified, but if we are to reach an understanding of how images function we must investigate whatever is common to all imagery.

As I have shown, my own understanding of how imagery works is inspired by recent definitions of metaphor, especially Black's view of the metaphor as 'interaction metaphor'. But since I have previously referred to imagery only generally, it is appropriate to set out how I wish to define the metaphor. This I can do quite briefly:

The metaphor consists of two statements that interact with one another by reason of their mutual dissimilarity.

Apart from metaphors, we encounter in Old Testament literature figurative expressions normally described as *comparisons*. The difference between the metaphor and the comparison is usually defined in that in the comparison the two members are presented side by side, whereas in the metaphor the image replaces the second member.[29] But this difference is purely syntactical. The comparison's 'the same as' has the function of emphasizing that what follows is to be understood as an image; in the case of the metaphor, however, this marker is not present. This also means, therefore, that in every comparison, as in every metaphor, both similarity and difference are concerned. I therefore see no fundamental difference between the metaphor and the comparison.

Apart from metaphor and comparison, we encounter examples of imagery in which a combination of metaphor and narrative occurs, i.e. *parables* and *allegories*. As we have seen, very much of New Testament research has been concerned with establishing a clear definition of, and thereby a reliable distinction between, these two forms. But it is precisely within this recent research that critical questions on this matter have been raised, not only in regard to the historical question of which genre Jesus made use of but also in regard to the principle involved in this differentiation.[30] Dan Otto Via rejects Jülicher's method of defining the two language forms. Jülicher's conception of the parable in fact leads to one element in the parable becoming separated from the context as tertium comparationis, thereby breaking the unity of the narrative.

The emphasis on *the parable* as a narrative, i.e. as a chain of events, is in my opinion important. As we had to emphasize in connexion with the metaphor—that it operates on the sentence level and not on the word level—the metaphorical aspect in the parable operates on the narrative level (composition level). The parable as a whole, heard or read as a narrative (chain of events), must be understood metaphorically.

But this must also apply to *the allegory*, which is also a sequence of events that must be understood metaphorically. In the case of the allegory, it has been traditionally emphasized that each individual member must be translated, whereas in the case of the parable this applied only to the one member; but this means, both for the parable and for the allegory, that one fails to appreciate that a chain of events is concerned in which the individual members are bound up with one another.

In addition, it must be pointed out that although it is correct to say that we encounter, in the context of allegories, many individual members which must be interpreted—or rather which, because convention seals them into a certain culture or group, we simply translate as accepted—this in fact means merely that we have in the allegory a greater number of metaphors (dead or moribund) sealed in convention than in the parable. Both are metaphorical narratives, and both include individual metaphors. The difference is not therefore a fundamental difference but a difference of use. I therefore prefer to speak of different use (depending on how many individual metaphors are 'translated') rather than different form. This is discussed in detail in the context of the analysis of Isa. 5.1-7, pp. 87ff.

Both parable and allegory must be understood as metaphorical narratives. What is said about the metaphor is also relevant to parable and allegory. A description of what imagery is can therefore include the two forms of image narrative. It should thus be possible to prepare a general description of imagery; but we still have to define what it is that characterizes imagery compared with literal language.

Literal Language

Although a distinction between imagery and literal language should be fundamentally and naturally demanded of whoever concerns himself with imagery, there appear to be surprisingly few suggestions regarding how one should actually define literal language.

The philosopher *John R. Searle*[31] points out that it is quite normal in analyses of metaphors to assume automatically that everyone knows what literal language is. But if one does not bother to try to define literal language one runs the risk of defining metaphorical language in such a way that one has difficulty in distinguishing it from literal language. But Searle must also concede that 'to give an accurate account of literal predication is an extremely difficult and subtle problem'.[32] In fact, Searle finds it easier to say what literal language is not. It is not, for example, as is sometimes said, a statement's context-less meaning, its 'zero-meaning', for there is no such thing as a context-less meaning. According to Searle, it would be better to say that we are in the presence of literal language if what the speaker says and what the sentence predicates coincide. But to me this definition also seems to be insufficient. There are many cases other than that of figurative language where one cannot say as a matter of course that there is coincidence between what the speaker says and what the sentence predicates. An obvious example of this is irony. The sentence, 'You really are a lot of help in an emergency', can be meant literally as well as ironically, and only the situation can explain how the sentence is to be understood. In the first instance, there is coincidence; in the other, there is not; but under no circumstances is it imagery. A 'no' which in the situation means 'yes' is not entirely unusual; but it does not for this reason become imagery.

In his philosophy of language, *K.E. Løgstrup* has attempted a very restrictive definition of what a metaphor is, inter alia in a polemic against the philosopher I.A. Richards. Richards uses the word metaphor very broadly indeed, and considers the metaphorical to be language's normal way of working—but in reality, in doing this, he makes the word unemployable in the context of those statements which are traditionally described as metaphorical.

Løgstrup's own attempt to demarcate the metaphor from non-metaphorical language is not without its problems. Løgstrup indeed supports simultaneously that 'no word is tied to a specific domain' and that this nevertheless applies to the metaphor when 'the metaphorically-used word is employed within a domain to which it is alien. But for this to be possible the word must already have a domain to which it belongs and is at home. . . '[33] Løgstrup's solution to this conflict is that one uses names in particular metaphorically, for example the names of animals (which does not however apply to the OT), or one uses locutions instead of an individual word, 'and if they are figurative they of course belong to a certain domain different from that depicted'.[34] The argument ends, as can be seen, by going round in a circle.

If we instead look at the features we have pointed out en route as characteristic of imagery, it will be seen that in most cases these features are also to be found in non-figurative usage. This applies for example to the *context dependence*. Non-figurative words and statements are also context-dependent (cf. Searle's refutal that literal meaning is non-contextual meaning). Non-figurative usage also has both an *informative* and a *performative* function (cf. Austin and Searle). The *possibility of reuse* which is so characteristic of imagery does not apply to images alone. Non-figurative language can also be—and is being—reused. It is only necessary to call to mind the use of established rituals.

If on these points we speak of differences between imagery and literal language these are *differences of degree*, not fundamental differences. The features referred to must therefore be included in any description of imagery; but they can scarcely be used as criteria for demarcation.

I find it, on the contrary, more useful to return to the definition of metaphorical language that we encountered in *Anders Jørgen Bjørndalen*. As we saw, he distinguishes between conjunctive and disjunctive use of language, and shows that a characteristic of figurative language is that not all the image's elements of meaning are active, as they are in literal language. If we now combine this with what Black et al. have to say about the interaction between the two different statements, it becomes clear that *the decisive factor* in imagery is its ability to provide new insight, to say something more than and something different from what literal language is able to say. Because this is a matter of two different statements, each of which holds to its own context, *the image is able to activate elements of meaning that in literal language are not cognate with the subject concerned.* And because not all the elements of meaning are activated the statement avoids becoming meaningless.

This does not mean that we now have an infallible means of deciding at any time whether or not a statement is used metaphorically. Whether a statement should be or will be understood figuratively depends upon the specific context. And since the context is so crucial, we must also take into account the consensus that at a given point in time surrounds a word's meaning. I have repeatedly said that a metaphor can die, and so enter into language in such a way that it no longer functions as an image. Those elements of meaning which are active are precisely the elements of meaning which are considered as the word's total number of elements of meaning. For example, 'legs' means neither more nor less in the context of 'table' than it does in the context of the word 'man'.

Whether we are in the presence of literal language or imagery is, therefore, in a number of cases, a matter of opinion. We might also say that this is sometimes more of a psychological question than a literary question. We judge in the light of the linguistic conventions with which we have grown up, i.e. the tradition in which we find ourselves, and it may be that we judge mistakenly. We perhaps do not discover that a certain expression in a certain context interacts with an unexpressed statement. We perhaps do not discover that there is here not one but two statements expressed by one word or expression—and then all that remains is to confirm that the image is unsuccessful. That the speaker meant what he said figuratively does not ensure that it will always be understood figuratively. Isa. 7.23-25 is an obvious example where in the present literary context one naturally perceives the description of the vineyard literally—even though it perhaps originally represented the use of a traditional image (cf. p. 105).

Analogously, the speaker, and especially the writer, whose works are preserved for a—perhaps distant—future risks that what in his mouth/by his pen was literal language is later (perhaps so that the statement can be made meaningful in a new situation) interpreted as imagery. An obvious example of this is so-called allegorizing.

In continuation of my discussion of imagery's suitability for reuse, therefore, it is essential to add that not only images can be reused; non-figurative statements have also in fact been preserved in the OT. But in the case of specific reuse (just think of the homilies) it often occurs that literal language is interpreted as if it were imagery.

My reference to this is primarily in order to stress that, as concerns literal language and imagery, we are in the presence of functional possibilities. Reuse can mean different use. It is therefore much more profitable to attempt to describe these different forms of use than to commence a futile search for inherent characteristics in particular forms of language.

Against this background, we are then in a position to present the following *description of imagery's function* in the Old Testament:

a. Imagery acts in a specific context by an interaction between two different statements.

b. Information can be derived from imagery in the form of new proposals for understanding reality.

c. The object of imagery is to involve the hearers in such a way that by entering into the interpretation they take it over as their own perception of reality (performative function).

d. Imagery can be reused in another context, with possibilities

of new interpretation and new evaluation of the informative
function and the performative function respectively.

Exegetic Consequences
Following these fundamental considerations and the concluding
proposed description, it is appropriate to raise the—wholly banal—
question: What is its use? Has it any significance at all to the way in
which we analyze specific Old Testament texts, to whether we
consider one theory of metaphor more correct than the other?

The question must be asked, and I wish to point out some of the
exegetic consequences that I believe can be drawn from these
theoretical considerations.

1. The demonstration of imagery's strong context-dependence
    must imply the analysis of every figurative expression,
    stating clearly the context on the basis of which it is to be
    understood.
2. Images have a history, and analysis of a certain image must
    therefore include an element of the image's history, giving as
    far as is possible an account of the use made of the image
    before and after its placing in the existing literary context.
    For important images, of course, this task is unending, if we
    include use outside the OT. I shall therefore generally
    confine myself to use within Isaiah 1–39.
3. Since the context is not only the specific historical situation
    and the specific literary placing but also the culture in which
    the image acts, analysis of an image must assume that one
    obtains a reasonable knowledge of the notions that are
    associated in the given culture with the image analyzed. If
    this is neglected, one risks interpreting the image in the light
    of one's own preconceptions.
4. Since imagery must be understood not as a way of reflecting
    reality but as a proposal for a new way of looking at reality,
    analyses must adopt a position towards both the informative
    and the performative functions.
5. Since imagery can be reused in another context, with the
    possibility of new interpretations, one specific meaning
    cannot be demarcated as *the* meaning. It is legitimate to be
    interested in how a specific image was used and understood

the first time, in the way that exegetes have traditionally tried to find a path back to the original situation. But it is important to be clear that our knowledge of this is more often than not extremely limited, and that the result we arrive at is therefore usually no more than a rough outline.

6. The constant reuse of images also makes it questionable to attribute such great authority to first use, as scholars of historical criticism normally do. Redactors of, for example, the book of Isaiah have manifestly assessed the value of Isaiah's message in the light of its utility in their own days, and not in the light of its historical value as a source. In analyzing an image, therefore, the problems of historical redaction and definition of the use of imagery in the redactional context must receive great attention.

7. And, finally, it should be stressed that, since it is very largely a matter of opinion whether a specific expression is perceived as imagery or literal language, it is important to investigate how the expression relates to any literal language in the associated literary context. An image must never be analysed in isolation.

PART B. TEXTUAL ANALYSES

Chapter 3

THE TREE AS A CENTRAL METAPHOR IN PROTO-ISAIAH

1. *The Choice of the Tree Image*

Isaiah 1–39 contains not only a relatively large number of examples of metaphorical use of the tree; if one examines these examples it will be seen that the tree is singularly suitable for communicating *important theological views*. By using the image of the tree, Isaiah not only gives the hearers new proposals for understanding the *political situation* in which they find themselves; he also tries to involve them in the world of the image so that they *take over the image's interpretation* of reality and orientate themselves in accordance with it.

The main problem of the time was the threat from the Assyrians. Would Judah be able to survive, and what could Judah itself do to ensure its future? These were the main questions. Isaiah's answer (and the answer of Isaiah's circle) was ambiguous; but the tree image made it possible to handle the paradox which is the characteristic of the Isaianic message: Yahweh has planned both judgment and salvation for his people. And the image has made it possible to vary the view of the situation. The tree must certainly be destroyed, but it can sprout again.

The use of the tree image may vary; but the significant point is always maintained: there is organic correlation in life; nothing happens accidentally. This point is very precisely formulated in another image, i.e. the image of the sensible farmer, Isa. 28.23-29, which is central to an understanding of Isaiah's message. As the farmer ploughs, harrows and sows his field in a sensible sequence and prepares his corn with the proper tools, so is it with the work of Yahweh; he also leaves nothing to chance, neither does he thresh his corn for an unreasonable time so that it becomes crushed. 'This also comes from the Lord of hosts; he is wonderful in counsel, and excellent in wisdom' (Isa. 28.29). For, using the tree image, he who ensures this sequence is the Yahweh who can both fell a tree and cause it to sprout again.

It is apparent not only from the use of the tree image that it was important to Isaiah's circle to hold to the judgment—salvation paradox. Other striking images are the purification of the metal, Isa. 1.25; the washing of the daughters of Zion, Isa. 4.4; the decimated army, a remnant of which returns from the battlefield, Isa. 7.3; the olive harvest, where only a few berries remain on the top of the highest boughs, Isa. 17.6; 24.13;[1] and the judgment where Yahweh appears in the dual role of prosecutor and judge, Isa. 1.2-3, 18-20; 3.13-15; 5.1-7,[2] to mention only the most important examples. But in this connexion we most frequently encounter the image of the tree.

It is not only, however, the frequent and central use of this image that makes the tree suitable for analysis of Isaianic imagery. In undertaking an analysis of imagery, it is important to understand the image in the light of its context. And this includes the culture within which the image was used. As regards the tree, we have the advantage of a reasonably good knowledge of the ideas associated with it in the Near East (including the Palestinian area), and it is with these ideas that we, who come from a different culture, must familiarize ourselves. The way we look at trees depends of course upon the circumstances under which we live. The pioneer in a forest clearing who must fight to keep the soil clear for cultivation is unlikely to have the same view of trees as the gardener who lives on the fruit his trees bear.

The material circumstances under which people live affect their conceptual world. If we who have not grown up with sycamores and cedars are to understand the Old Testament's use of these trees as images we must learn the taxonomy on whose basis they are assessed. And if the tree image is used, as it is here, in a culture in which the tree also has a religious significance we must look into this. In this section, therefore, we shall investigate the 'material status' of the tree as well as its 'ideological status'.

This does not of course mean that we are not in a position to form associations with the Old Testament's use of the tree as an image unless we familiarize ourselves with the cultural history of the time. A characteristic of the major images is that they are of an elementary nature: water, fire, air, earth. We all have a spontaneous, although not the same, attitude towards them. This is also true of the use of the tree. We all have an elementary understanding of the tree as a living organism that grows and becomes old, that can renew itself by producing shoots even if the wood-cutter or drought arrests growth for a time. Gilbert Durand points out that the tree is one of the archetypal symbols. It connotes progression, and therefore communicates what he refers to, in a characteristic phrase, as 'le complexe de Jessé'.[3]

It is indeed this spontaneous perception of what a tree is that makes it a good image, well-suited for reuse. Without the basic experience 'For there is hope for a tree, if it be cut down, that it will sprout again, and that its shoots will not cease' (Job 14.7), the ideology associated with the tree as a symbol of life in the Near East would not only be incomprehensible; it would not have arisen.

If, therefore, we are to follow the history of the tree image within Isaiah 1–39 we cannot avoid investigating the ideas generally associated with the tree at this period. Only then will it be possible to attempt a detailed determination of the elements of meaning actualized in the specific examples at specific times.

In approaching image analysis, we are in need of the general ideas that were known to Isaiah and his hearers/target group. In our context, it is of limited interest to undertake a major study of the previous history of the tree image. Neither shall we try to become experts in forestry or horticulture. Isaiah did not speak as an expert, and no-one expected expertise from his mouth.

As regards the religion-related assumptions of the tree image, we shall restrict ourselves to what Isaiah appears to take as general knowledge. Whether these ideas had their origin—and a special meaning—in various Near-Eastern cults means no more in our context than it means to the ordinary language-user that the words he uses and hears have an etymology. This is not without interest; but he will scarcely speak any differently and his language will not be understood differently by his surroundings because he has etymological knowledge. Our interest therefore is the connotations that the Proto-Isaianic use of the tree image may/must reasonably be thought to have evoked among the audience Isaiah addresses, and among the redactors who have created Isaiah 1–39.

Only the following will be said about the procedure in the textual analyses: Not all examples of the tree image will be considered in equal depth. I have selected what are in my opinion the major texts, and I wish to begin with an analysis of the best-known, a text in which the image is very carefully developed, i.e. the song of the vineyard (Isa. 5.1-7). The sequence of the texts is not chronologic but pedagogic, in that I am trying to illustrate the less clear by the more clear.

2. *The Cultural Background to the Use of the Tree Image*

a. *Timber Tree and Fruit Tree*

Trees performed an important role as *building material*[1] in Palestine. The most valued species was *the cedar*, which formed an important component of Solomon's temple. According to 1 Kgs 5.20ff.; RSV 5.6ff., Solomon obtained the necessary cedars from Lebanon by sending word to Hiram king of Tyre, who promised to do all that Solomon desired in the matter of cedars and cypress timber.[2] In addition to these types of tree, wild olive is also used. The cedar's great importance is also clear from the description of the palace, one wing of which is referred to as the 'House of the Forest of Lebanon' (1 Kgs 7.2 et al.). David's house was also built of cedars supplied by King Hiram (2 Sam. 5.11), and the house of god rejected by Yahweh is referred to as a house of cedar (2 Sam. 7.7). It thus appears to be taken for granted that the dwellings of the king and the god are built of cedar.

It is clear that the cedars of Lebanon were much-coveted not only from the Old Testament but also from other Near-Eastern texts. Thus, Nebuchadnezzar tells that he fetched cedars from Lebanon for Merodach's temple.[3] Lebanon is described as Merodach's fertile forest, and the cedars are praised as suitable for embellishing a palace for the ruler of heaven and earth because they are tall, beautiful and of the finest quality.[4]

Lebanon is also referred to as a place from which timber is obtained in texts from Ugarit. II AB VI, 18ff. is concerned with the building of Baal's palace, for which trees from Lebanon and cedars from[Siri]on are employed.[5]

Finally, it should be noted that Egypt also sent for the trees of Lebanon for, among other things, ship building.[6]

The texts referred to thus indicate a constant interest in the exploitation of the trees of Lebanon. This has prompted some scholars to assert that, even earlier, such exploitation was so ruthless that a large part of the forests disappeared during the Bronze Age.

This view is however rejected by M.B. Rowton,[7] who believes that the expansion of settlements led to the removal of forests only in valleys and plains, and did not prevent continued forest growth in the mountainous areas. An important argument in support of this is that access to the great mountain forests called for quite sophisticated tools. This was costly, and it cannot be assumed that it could be undertaken by anybody. The Great Kings' boastful accounts of how they penetrated as far as this and felled the great forests indicates that it was no simple task.

It can therefore be established that the cedar especially was known as very valuable building material. The importance of the cedar manifests itself indirectly in Old Testament imagery, only a few examples of which will be mentioned. Where Isa. 9.9 (RSV 9.10) reads: 'The bricks have fallen, but we will build with dressed stones; the sycamores have been cut down, but we will put cedars in their place', use is being made of the hearers' foreknowledge that the cedar tree is by far the more precious of the two types of tree. Analogously, it is the cedar's great value which is played on in 2 Kgs 14.9, where a thistle on Lebanon is contrasted with a cedar on Lebanon; in Judg. 9.15, the fable of Jotham, where the destruction of the cedars forms part of a serious threat; and finally in Ps. 80.11 (RSV 80.10), where the extent of the spread of the vine is described by reference to its branches covering God's cedars.[8]

In this connexion, we have not considered the use of trees such as the oak, the terebinth, the pine, etc. as building material because these trees play no part in Isaianic imagery qua building material, although they do so in the context of other ideas. For the same reason, we do not consider the use of trees in the context of, for example, sickness (cf. Lev. 14.4ff.).

Another aspect of the tree is *the tree as fruit-bearer*. That fruit trees are included among the vital necessities is apparent from, for example, Deut. 20.19-20, where destruction of fruit trees in the event of war is meticulously legislated against. Only trees that do not bear edible fruit may be felled and used for siegeworks, since fruit trees give man his food.

The trees that may have been referred to are apparent from, for example, Deut. 8.8, where Palestine is described as a land of wheat, barley, wine, figs, pomegranates, olive oil and honey. These crops amount together to all that the heart can desire, and in the traditions of the wanderings in the wilderness are contrasted with the wilderness, so that even Egypt becomes attractive (Num. 20.5).

The most important of the trees named is the *olive*.[9] This is reflected in the fable of Jotham (Judg. 9.8ff.), where the olive is the tree the other first request to be their king. The olive tree has good conditions for growth in the Palestinian region, since its long roots can penetrate down to the water-retaining rock crevices. The olive tree's frugality also means that olives can be cultivated outside the normal agricultural areas, leaving these areas for the cultivation of grain, for example.

Harvested olives are widely used in everyday housekeeping in the form of olive oil. Oil was the fat of the time, and was therefore important for cooking, lighting, wound treatment, cosmetics—and as an offering.[10] The olive is harvested just before the fruit is ripe. The fruit high on the tree is knocked down with sticks (Isa. 17.6; 24.13; Deut. 24.20), while the rest is picked by hand. This method of harvesting, which means that individual fruits remain at the top of the tree, has meant that harvesting of olives can be used as an image of judgment, as Isaiah sees this (Isa. 17.6; 24.13).

The reasoning may here appear to be circular, since an image is exploited to extract the realities later used for interpretation of imagery itself. One must be aware of this danger when studying imagery, but at the same time insist that a large part of imagery's power is that it keeps as close to reality as is at all possible. The more authentic the effect of the image, the greater is its power of conviction.

The olive tree is recognized as a particularly luxuriant and vigorous tree. It not only bears a considerable quantity of fruit, but also produces strong shoots from the roots. The image in Ps. 128.3 of the sons as olive shoots can thus reflect the young olive trees that have shot up around the trunk.[11] Moreover, the fact that the olive tree is an evergreen has made it a suitable image for representing vitality. Cf. Ps. 52.10; Jer. 11.16; Hos. 14.7.

Although the olive tree must be judged as the most important of Palestine's fruit trees, and olive oil as a highly significant ingredient in daily housekeeping, the olive tree is mentioned in the Old Testament not nearly as frequently as *the vine* and its fruit. Similarly, the vine and the vineyard play a far greater part in Old Testament imagery.

Like that of the olive tree, the vine's great importance is apparent from the fable of Jotham, where it reads that its wine cheers gods and men (Judg. 9.13). Cf. also Deut. 8.8; 2 Kgs 18.31f.; 1 Kgs 5.5 (RSV 4.25); Mic. 4.4; and Zech. 3.10. While the olive is a relatively hardy tree, the vine requires much attention. It must be protected not only from external dangers (wild animals, thieves, enemies, etc.) (cf. Isa. 5.2; 27.3), but the soil around it must be ploughed and cleared of stones; it must be supported by low walls (terraced cultivation), and the plants must be pruned, supported and staked if they are free-standing and not decumbent vines.[12]

The fact that a vineyard involves much work and that man is in close contact with his vineyard also means that there is simply more to say about a vineyard than about an olive tree for example. And the more there is to say the more elements can be employed figuratively. Cf. Isa. 5.1ff.

Gustaf Dalman points out that the olive tree does not need nearly as much attention as the fig tree and the vine, and that therefore olive trees are not normally planted in the same place as the fig and the vine. 'Der Ölbaum gleicht darin einer Beduïnin (*bedawïje*), die sich selbst zu helfen weiß, während der Feigenbaum als Bauerin (*fellāḥa*) und vollends der Weinstock als Dame (*sitt*) ganz andere Beachtung verlangen'.[13]

That the vine resembles a lady demanding attention and consideration is not without significance to understanding the frequent use of the vine or vineyard as an image of Israel (cf. Isa. 1.8; 3.14; 5.1-7; 27.2-6; (37.30) and, for example, Ps. 80.9ff.). It is scarcely fortuitous that the authors of the Old Testament prefer to use the vine as an image of Israel rather than the hardy and self-reliant olive tree. Used in relation to Israel, the vine is able to connote the election and the greatness as well as the judgment and the insecure position.[14] A completely different connotation is represented by today's favourite metaphor for the indigenous Israeli: Sabra, which is of course the name of a cactus!

Whereas the olive is evergreen, the vine loses its leaves in the autumn. This difference is also of significance to the use of images. Whereas the evergreen olive is suitable as an image of the vigorous and lasting, the wilting vine (and fig tree) can be used to describe disintegration and destruction (Isa. 34.4; Jer. 8.13). Conversely, the lively vine producing new shoots can be used as an image of future happiness (Hos. 14.8; RSV v. 7).

But it is neither the vine's foliage nor its trunk that makes it valuable; it is the fruit and the wine that can be made from it.

Gathering the grapes is among the most crucial events of the year, a time characterized by joy and festivity. Only a remnant of less-good grapes is left as an 'aftercrop'. According to Deut. 24.21, they are to fall to the sojourner, the fatherless and the widow. After gathering, the grapes can be used directly in housekeeping. They can also be dried into raisins, as is necessary if they are to be stored for later use; for example for raisin cakes, which appear to have been a favourite food (cf. e.g. 1 Sam. 25.18; 2 Sam. 6.19).

Finally, we know that they can be pressed for their juice (the grapes are trampled in the press) and converted into wine.[15] The intoxicating power of wine has generated an ambiguous attitude towards it. On the one hand, it cheers gods and men (Judg. 9.13), as the gift of God which it is (Ps. 104.15); but on the other hand, according to Lev. 10.9, Aaron and his sons, i.e. the priests, are not permitted to drink wine and strong drink when they are discharging their office.[16] Wine forms part of the daily meal, and is naturally present at the feast; but intoxication can have unfortunate consequences (Prov. 21.17; 23.29ff.), and therefore woe to those who are heroes at drinking wine and valiant in mixing strong drink (Isa. 5.22).

This negative attitude towards wine is presumably associated not only with the 'hangovers' of a more or less general nature that wine can cause but also with the role wine-drinking played in the Canaanite fertility cult. It is probably such a fertility festival which is described in Judg. 21.19ff. and which forms the background to the Benjaminites' abduction of the young dancing girls. In his sharply polemic message in, for example, Hos. 4.11ff.,[17] the prophet Hosea leaves no doubt about how such a combination of sexual display (= sexual cult) and wine-drinking should be judged.

In our context, therefore, it is worth noting that although Isaiah's attitude towards wine can clearly be negative, for example Isa. 5.22, his use of *the vineyard* as an image always presupposes that the vineyard is something positive, even when he accuses it of behaving unnaturally (Isa. 5.1-7).

The fig-tree,[18] the third of the important fruit trees, is often referred to together with the vine (1 Kgs 5.5 [RSV 4.25]; 2 Kgs 18.31; Mic. 4.4; Deut. 8.8), which has to do with the fact that the fig and the vine were often planted side by side. The fig-tree could then act as a 'climbing frame' for the vine. Figs were a favourite food, both when picked directly from the tree (Isa. 28.4) and when used for fig cakes (cf. 1 Sam. 25.18; 30.12). Moreover, the Old Testament tells us about the use of fig plasters in the event of sickness (2 Kgs 20.7).

Since the fig-tree is one of the most valued fruit-trees, the destruction of fig-trees, like the destruction of vines, is often used to express a disastrous situation (cf. Isa. 34.4; Jer. 8.13). But true figurative use of the fig-tree appears in the book of Isaiah only in Isa. 34.4.

Fruit-trees play an absolutely fundamental part in the Palestinian region. If the trees bear fruit, the country is under Yahweh's blessing; if the fruit harvest fails, it represents a curse. The time of disaster can therefore be described as a period during which thorns and thistles overwhelm the vineyard (Isa. 5.6; 7.23; 27.4; 32.13); whereas the happy times are when the wilderness becomes an orchard and the orchard is deemed a forest; i.e. it reaches as wide and as high as the great forests. Cf. e.g. Isa. 32.15 and Isa. 29.17, where there is clearly a play on the double meaning of כרמל, the Carmel locality and the word for orchard. The hoped-for future is a paradisial existence such as that described in Ezek. 47.12, where the fruit-trees along the temple river (the holy spring) will bear fresh fruit every month, and where the leaves on the trees will never wither, but have even healing power. This brings us to the religious conceptions associated with the tree.

b. *Conceptions of the Tree as Holy*
Conceptions of the tree as holy are a universal feature of almost all 'primitive' religions. If we consider the climatic conditions in the Palestinian region, it can come as no surprise that here also the tree was considered a *symbol of life*. Where trees can grow there is water, and where there is water there is the possibility of life. Thus, here also are the fundamental day-to-day experiences that underlie the idea of the tree.

The tree signals *the holy*, as Karl Jaroš[19] formulates it. This is the background to the association of trees with oracle activity, for example Gen. 12.6; Hos. 4.12; that it is preferable to bury one's dead under trees, for example Gen. 35.8; 1 Sam. 31.13; that one associates trees with various deities, for example Gen. 13.18; Judg. 6.11; and that one can consider the tree stump as well as the manufactured wooden pole as a symbol of life, for example Judg. 6.25; Deut. 16.21.

It is clear that the holy trees also played a part in the Yahweh cult from the fierce prophetic polemic against this in the second half of

the eighth century.[20] In the Canaanite religion, the holy grove with
its life-giving spring and the fertility-giving trees formed a framework
to a number of sexual rites which the prophet Hosea condemns to the
utmost. Hosea can only interpret what the Israelites are about in the
holy grove as fornication, a concept which, interestingly enough,
assumes that Hosea also sees the relationship between Yahweh and
Israel as a sexual relationship, i.e. a marriage.

This cult in the groves must have been very widespread and
popular, if one is to believe the repeated accusations of the prophets.
The people appear to fornicate under every green tree.[21] (Friedrich
Lundgreen, incidentally, is careful to point out that although any
green tree could be used in a cultic context, oak and terebinth had a
special position.)[22] According to 2 Kgs 16.4, King Ahaz, Isaiah's
contemporary, sacrificed under all green trees, and according to
2 Kgs 18.4 the cult reform of King Hezekiah, Ahaz's son, included
his cutting down the Asherah pillar.

However, side by side with the polemic attitude towards the holy
trees and what they represented there is also a positive, or at least
neutral, attitude towards the phenomenon. Evidence of this is to be
found in, for example, the imagery in the book of Hosea, which
surprisingly enough Karl Jaroš has not fastened upon. Reading the
book of Hosea shows indeed that the prophet can perfectly well use
tree images about Israel (Hos. 9.10; 10.1; 14.6ff.), and in such a way
that he must presuppose that the tree is positively connotated. In
fact, his is the only instance in the Old Testament where the image of
a tree is used about *Yahweh himself*, when he permits Yahweh to refer
to himself as an *evergreen cypress* from which Israel's fruit comes (!)
(Hos. 14.9). In spite of all the polemic, the tree has clearly retained its
positive connotations, as is apparent from, for example, the use of the
dry tree in Isa. 56.3 as an image of a dry human being, a eunuch.

That trees, indeed vegetation as a whole, bore this positive
connotation in Israel is also to be seen from the embellishment of
Solomon's temple. The two pillars at the entrance, Jachin and Boaz
(1 Kgs 7.15-22), which must be seen as stylized trees,[23] and the many
carvings using motifs from the vegetable world (trees, fruits, flowers,
leaves)[24] both indicate the widespread idea of a connexion between
vegetation and whatever is holy.

As we know, it was in this temple that Isaiah had his vision (Isa. 6).
There is no doubt that Isaiah's message is strongly influenced by
what the prophet heard and experienced within the temple cult. One

has merely to refer to Hans Wildberger's study of the high degree to which Isaiah, as a Jerusalem prophet, is embedded in Jerusalem traditions. But, analogously, it is possible that what he saw in the temple building also influenced his message. After all, the domains from which one draws one's images are not fortuitous.[25]

Similar examples of this positive connotation are the conceptions of the *Garden of Eden*. They also clearly reflect the Canaanite holy grove[26] with the holy trees at the life-giving spring, the place where man participates in the divine life. These conceptions are best known from Genesis 2-3, but in my opinion also lie behind the figurative description of the bride in Song 4.12-15. She is a locked garden, filled with trees bearing choicest fruits and with a well whose water comes from Lebanon. It is into this not easily accessible garden that the bridegroom is invited to enjoy its fruit. Like the guarding of the holy grove, the bride/garden is locked so that not everyone can gain entry; like the holy grove, the garden has life-giving trees and water.

If we compare this version of the paradise myth with Genesis 2-3, it becomes clear that Genesis 3's account of the Fall is a variation of the myth of Eden as the life-giving place (= the holy place) and that the Song of Solomon comes closest to this tradition, where entry into the garden and eating from the trees is the height of happiness and not a Fall, and where the bride is not the temptress but paradise itself for her bridegroom.

Behind these conceptions of the holy grove lie clearly the Middle-Eastern ideas of the tree of life.[27] According to *Ivan Engnell*,[28] the Israelites had completely taken over the Canaanite ideas of the tree of life and the cult associated with it. This occurs not only at the less holy places but also in the context of the temple cult in Jerusalem. The prophetic protest attacked above all the cultic practice, which gradually became restricted; but *the ideology behind the tree cult* could not be eradicated; at most, it could be changed in form.

An important feature of this ideology is the close association between *the tree of life* and *the king*.[29] For example, it is the ideas of the tree of life that form the background to the description of the coming king, the Messiah, in Isa. 11.1 and Isa. 53.2. However, not only the king but also the people can be 'identified' with the tree of life (Ps. 80.9ff.; Jer. 5.10; 11.16f.), and similarly an individual can be described by using tree metaphors, as occurs positively in Ps. 1.3 and negatively in Ps. 37.35.

In 'Studies in Divine Kingship in the Ancient Near East',[30]

Engnell discusses *the felling of the tree of life* as part of the Tammuz cult, and emphasizes in this context that the Western Semites also identified the god of growth with the trunk of a tree. Engnell in fact intended to supplement his investigations with a discussion of the Old Testament material, including a detailed analysis of the relationship between the king and the tree of life; but the book on this subject never appeared. It was instead *Geo Widengren* who wrote the 'classical' exposition of Scandinavian scholarship's view of the relationship between the king and the tree of life,[31] in which the Old Testament texts are also discussed. Widengren's results are clearly an extension of Engnell's, and he is indeed able to establish, with a reference to Engnell, that '. . . this Tree of Life is nothing but a mythic-ritual symbol of both god and king'.[32]

Neither Engnell's nor Widengren's views were allowed to remain unchallenged. For example, *Sigmund Mowinckel* sharply rejected Engnell's reference to an identity between the tree of life and the king, pointing out that it was not a matter of identity but of a figurative use of concepts from the Tammuz cult, for example.[33] Engnell has subsequently denied that this 'identity' was to be seen as an absolute identity on the physical-metaphysical level, a frequent misunderstanding.[34]

This whole discussion is not, however, of great significance to the textual analyses we are about to undertake, in that what we find in Isaiah is clearly a figurative use of trees. Neither is it crucial whether Isaiah's hearers themselves practised a tree cult now and again, for example when felling a tree (cf. the rite known from Egypt of felling the djed pole) or cultivating quick-growing plants in the so-called Tammuz gardens (cf. Isa. 17.10f.). The crucial point is to establish that they knew and were influenced by these ideas of the tree as holy and closely linked to the fertility-creating forces of life, and in this connexion were familiar with the felling motif and the sprouting motif.

The question therefore is whether, in addition to these general concepts of the tree as the tree of life, we are in a position to suggest a more coherent complex of ideas that *may* have lain behind the way in which the tree is employed in Proto-Isaiah. To answer this, we turn to *Fritz Stolz*'s article, 'Die Bäume des Gottesgartens auf dem Libanon'.[35] Stolz here submits the thesis that a myth existed telling of a garden of God in Lebanon. (Cf. the excursus on Lebanon pp. 126ff.) In the garden stand some special trees, perhaps a world tree, which someone fells. This is the myth that the Old Testament authors use in different versions. According to one version, Yahweh is the owner of the garden, and the tree-feller is a destroyer coming from without; according to the other version, it is Yahweh himself who fells the trees of Lebanon. In support of his thesis, Stolz draws on the following Old Testament texts: Ezek. 31; Isa. 14.8; 2 Kgs 19.23ff.; Ps. 80.11; Ps. 104.16; Isa. 60.13; 51.3; 2.12f; 10.33f.; Jer. 22; Zech. 11.1f.; Gen. 2.4ff.; Ezek. 28; and Ps. 29.5f.

But it is not in the Old Testament alone that Stolz finds traces of such a myth. Behind the Old Testament version(s) lie Mesopotamian traditions. We thus hear in the Epic of Gilgamesh how Gilgamesh and Enkidu wish to fell the great cedar forest guarded by Ḫumbaba. By drawing on this epic and the Sumerian Gilgamesh poetry underlying it, Stolz reaches back to a basic narrative according to which there was someone (the person concerned is quite quickly identified with Gilgamesh) who attempted to capture the garden in Lebanon from Lebanon's god. He thereby tried to arrogate to himself the highest divine power, and as punishment he was banished to the nether world.

In an early Canaanite version, the god in Lebanon was El (cf. Ps. 80.11). According to Stolz, we hear about the theophany of this god in Psalm 29,[36] which describes the violent appearance of the atmospheric god. This causes even the cedars of Lebanon to shatter. This is El as he was known in the Jerusalem traditions, and it is here that the transference to Yahweh has naturally taken place.

The entire motif is utilized in different ways in the Old Testament,[37] in that the destroyer of the garden can be considered on the one hand as a criminal coming from without and on the other hand as Yahweh himself. In those cases where the tree-feller plays a positive role, the felling of the trees is perceived as punishment for the trees' pride. The material has thus undergone a clearly theological treatment.

In his analysis of the myth of the garden of god in Lebanon, Stolz suggests a complex of ideas that may help to explain the formation and use of some of the tree images in Proto-Isaiah. But it is noteworthy in this connexion that the only reasonably coherent version of the myth is to be found in Ezekiel 31. On the one hand, therefore, what is concerned is a relatively late text, and on the other hand a very strong theological treatment of the mythical material, to

which Stolz himself meticulously draws attention. Cf. pp. 165ff., where
Ezekiel is discussed in detail.

The other examples in the Old Testament are similar reinterpretations of Stolz's basic narrative and shorter statements that *may* be
associated with the Lebanon myth but are not necessarily linked to
it.

I find Stolz's thesis both acceptable and useful in spite of these
reservations, because it can to a certain extent explain how some of
the tree images have been employed. We encounter in Isaiah 1–39
both the concept of the destruction of the great trees of Lebanon as
sacrilege (Isa. 14.4b–20; 37.22b–32) and the concept of the destruction
as justified punishment for pride (Isa. 10.33–11.9, 10; 2.12–17). There
is no doubt that the latter is the result of theological reflection, and
that it represents a conscious attempt to play on the preconceptions
of the time. Neither can there be any doubt that these preconceptions
centred on the holy tree, the tree of life. Stolz's thesis has therefore
contributed *a possible narrative correlation* that helps to explain the
Isaianic texts' very terse style and the frequency of tree images.

The extent of the role the Lebanon myth may be considered to
have played in Isaiah's representation of the tree images and the
hearers' understanding of them is, however, best seen from the
specific text analyses. I shall merely premise the following here:

In the myth of the felling of Lebanon's trees, the positive
perception of the holy trees has been contrasted with a negative
possibility. Life can be destroyed, the tree can be felled, but in the
Isaianic texts the positive background can break through despite this
and create a *new variant*, where the felling of the tree not only
signifies (justly or unjustly) destruction of life but also creates a
precondition for new life. Although the tree is felled, its roots and its
stump can produce new shoots. The tree image thus becomes able to
create a prophecy that contains in a new way both a negative aspect
and a positive aspect, both judgment and salvation.[38]

We have considered so far only one kind of threat against the tree,
felling, but to conclude we wish to suggest another danger, i.e. *fire*.
This also appears several times in Isaianic imagery.[39]

During the summer, vegetation in Palestine is constantly threatened
by desiccation. When the scorching east wind, the khamsin, strikes
the country it can cause not only famine, because plants become
desiccated, but also pasture fires and forest fires.[40] This is the east
wind that dries up everything, referred to in Hos. 13.15 as the wind

of the Lord, רוח יהוה. In Joel 1.19-20, the dessication of the country is described as a fire, where grass and trees are burned and the water brooks dried up. In Ezek. 19.10-14, the forest fire is used as an image of the political situation in Judah.[41] It is King Zedekiah's mother who, as a fertile vine, was plucked up in fury and cast down to the ground, was dried up by the east wind and consumed by fire. There is scarcely any doubt that the east wind and fire are here conceived as entirely parallel. It is the east wind that ignites the desiccated growth.

The image of the consuming fire destroying the trees of the land has therefore a natural background in the climatic and vegetational conditions under which the Israelite lives.

Conclusion
We have now discussed the connotations associated with the tree. It is true that it is meaningful in a certain sense to distinguish between what I have referred to in quotes as the tree's 'material status' and its 'ideological status', but in both cases *concepts* are concerned, and in both cases it became apparent that the background to the concepts was to be sought in the *material circumstances*. The grouping should therefore be seen primarily as a practical way of achieving a certain comprehensive view of the material.

After this revealing of the concepts[42] associated with the tree, we continue with an analysis of the use of the concepts in specific images.

Chapter 4

ANALYSIS OF TREE IMAGES IN ISAIAH 1-39

1. *Analysis of Isa. 5.1-7 and Isa. 27.2-6*

Introduction

Whereas in Chapter 1 we attempted a general definition of Proto-Isaiah as traditional literature and religious utility literature, in Chapter 2 we were concerned especially with imagery. It became clear here that imagery is well-suited for reuse in new situations because of its ability to draw the listeners into the interpretation and because of its receptiveness to reinterpretation. We investigated in Chapter 3 the connotations associated with the tree in the Old Testament. This should have outlined the framework of meaning within which listeners of the time saw the tree image and which restricted the risk of insertions into the text by the interpreter.

The textual analyses will be introduced by an analysis of Isa. 5.1-7, the so-called parable of the vineyard. I have chosen to begin with this not only because it is one of the best-known examples of Isaianic imagery but mostly because this text is well-suited for substantiating and testing an essential part of the argument presented in Chapters 1 and 2.

Isa. 5.1-7 is a long and clearly demarcated textual entity that concludes with an interpretation of the vineyard. No-one can therefore be in any doubt *that* this is imagery. It should also be pointed out that the continuous debate about the form of the text renders it necessary to consider once again whether Isa. 5.1-7 is a parable, an allegory or something entirely different. I have emphasized in my definition of what characterizes imagery that images have an informative as well as a performative function. But here also Isa. 5.1-7 calls for more detailed investigation, in that v. 7 seems to render superfluous any participatory activity, the information being presented in the form of an interpretation of the image. Does this mean that this image has no performative function, but is intended only to inform?

Finally, Isa. 5.1-7 exemplifies that an image can be reused, as well as giving rise to a production of new text. The text is therefore well-suited for investigation of what is to be understood by these important concepts.

The Dating of Isa. 5.1-7

In the history of research, Isa. 5.1-7 is one of the most frequently discussed passages of Proto-Isaiah.[1] Almost everyone except J. Vermeylen, whose approach we shall return to below, considers the text to be genuine. There is also wide agreement that it originates from the early period of Isaiah's activities, the period preceding the Syrio-Ephraimite war.[2] The arguments in support of this rely in part upon examination of the content and in part upon analysis of the style.

As regards content, the judgment on the faithless people is well in line with what we otherwise know of Isaiah's early message. According to Isa. 5.7, Yahweh's judgment must overtake the people because they do not satisfy Yahweh's expectations as concerns right and justice, and instead answer him with injustice and a cry. In a number of lamentations dating from the same period[3] (Isa. 5.8-24 + 10.1-4), those who call evil good and those who reject the word of the Holy One of Israel and oppress the needy are similarly condemned. Since Yahweh's anger is not turned away, his hand is still stretched out.

The *style* of the text is also thought to favour authenticity, since the text is one of the most well-formed in the book of Isaiah. Isaiah here displays all his masterly command of language in a sophisticated use of imagery. He makes use of alliteration, the antithetical use of the same word (cf. the repetition of the root עשׂה, in v. 2 and v. 4 respectively) and an antithetical juxtaposition of words based on phonetic similarity. This latter is to be found in v. 7, where Isaiah uses the phonetic similarity between משׁפט (justice) and משׂפח (injustice) and between צדקה (righteousness) and צעקה (a cry) to create what Luis Alonso Schökel defines precisely as 'eine konzise antithetische, durch eine Paronomasie verstärkte rhetorische Schluß-sentenz'.[4]

As regards dating and authenticity, therefore, we should be on relatively safe ground.

The Form of Isa. 5.1-7

Isa. 5.1-7 forms a clearly demarcated entity.[5] In relation to the preceding chapter, with its expectations of Zion's future, as well as in relation to the subsequent lamentation, we are faced with an independent entity. The text is compactly structured; but this does not mean that the form of the text can be determined directly. There is an old tradition of referring to the text as *the parable of the vineyard*; but although this description suggests something major, and for the sake of convenience will be employed occasionally in this treatise, there is much more to be said about the form. And much has already been said.

A good idea of the results of research to date may be had by reading John T. Willis's excellent summarizing article, 'The Genre of Isaiah 5:1-7',[6] in which Willis lists 12 different suggestions: 'An Uncle's Song', 'A Satirical Polemic against Palestinian Fertility Cults', 'The Prophet's Song concerning His Own Vineyard', 'The Prophet's Song Expressing Sympathy for His Friend Yahweh', 'A Drinking Song', 'A Bride's Love Song', 'A Groom's Love Song', 'A Song of the Friend of the Bridegroom', 'A Lawsuit or Accusation', 'A Fable', 'An Allegory', 'A Parable'. After critically reviewing each suggestion, Willis himself decides to call it 'a parabolic song of a disappointed husbandman'.[7]

It will be seen from this listing that the stress is on its being, alternately, a song, a lawsuit and figurative language. None of the definitions therefore, including Willis's own definition, makes clear the crucial point of the text: that it is built up like a Chinese system of boxes, involving all three genres.[8]

Isa. 5.1-7 is presented by Isaiah as a *song* about a man and his vineyard. The listeners see the vineyard as an *image* of a woman. They soon discover that the song takes the form of a *lawsuit*, and it is finally confirmed that it is demonstrably a *metaphorical narrative*— although Isaiah's interpretation shows that the vineyard is not a woman but the people themselves. And it is precisely this surprising point that made it necessary to present an explicit interpretation. If Isaiah had left it to his hearers alone to interpret the vineyard image, they would have followed convention and seen it as referring to an unfaithful wife. Therefore, v. 7 forms part of the Isaianic vineyard parable.

Isa. 5.1-7 is a very sophisticated composition with a complicated use of forms. This has not only a reason but also implications.

One of the important aims in analyzing Isa. 5.1-7 is therefore to show, on the one hand, the intended message behind the specific wording and, on the other hand, how later times have made use of the text.

A. *Isa. 5.1-7 as an Authentic Isaianic Statement*

The frame of reference for detailed analysis of Isa. 5.1-7 must be the form of the text.

A Love-Song, vv. 1-2
If in the first instance we hold to what the text itself says, it will be seen from 5.1a that it is a song; indeed, a love-song.

Isaiah begins with the verb שיר (to sing), pointing out that it is his ידיד with whom the song is concerned, i.e. a person close to him, and he elaborates this further by using the description שירת דודי, the direct meaning of which has an erotic implication.[9] What the prophet wishes to convey to his hearers is disclosed very slowly, and for the time being they must assume that it is to be a love-song.

Another possibility that has played a certain part in research should, however, be mentioned briefly here. This relates to the thesis that דוד was the name of a *god of vegetation* worshipped in Jerusalem. Hans Wildberger refers to this thesis in his comment on the passage and, with a prudent reference to G.W. Ahlström's treatment of the question, leaves open the possibility that certain of Isaiah's hearers, 'sofern sie hellhörig genug waren, vermuten konnten, daß der 'Freund' oder 'Geliebte' Jesajas Jahwe sein müsse'.[10] This is rejected by A.J. Bjørndalen[11] who, following meticulous examination of the material, is forced to conclude that the god's name can be demonstrated neither in Ugarit nor in Syria-Palestine in Old Testament times. It would therefore be unreasonable to assume that the hearers of Isa. 5.1 would see דוד as such a naming of a god.

Bjørndalen's argument appears to be convincing, and can be supplemented by a further consideration, not based on the hearers' or the author's 'religion-related assumptions' but on the text's own strategy. Wildberger works from the possibility of a special type of responsive audience which would have already sensed from v. 1 that the song related to Yahweh as the prophet's friend. If Wildberger is correct in this, it would mean that Isaiah, by choosing the word דוד, risked that from the outset the audience anticipated the interpretation which he is so carefully keeping until v. 7. And thereby the entire strategy of surprise which characterizes the text would lose its impact. Since in his analysis of Isa. 5.1-7 Wildberger relies upon Aage Bentzen's interpretation, in which it is wholly crucial that up to and including v. 6 the audience believes that the song concerns a man and his unfaithful wife, his acknowledgments of Ahlström etc. appear to lack careful reasoning.

What Wildberger's approach reflects, however, is a phenomenon worth considering for reasons of principle. For *which audience* is the exegete in fact working when he or she analyses a text such as Isa. 5.1-7? What assumptions can be attributed to the transmitter of the text and expected among the recipients? Many subtle interpretations are perhaps not incorrect in the sense that they go beyond the potential meanings of the text, but they are questionable if the intention is to assert that this is how the text was understood by the originator and his audience. It is often very difficult for us to decide whether it was possible for the hearers of the time to grasp precisely the nuance and the association that the exegete himself finds obvious. That the possessor of special knowledge, the philologist or the scholar trained in the history of religion, can see more—and different—connotations in a text than an untrained person is not surprising. But care should be exercised in postulating that these connotations were intended and were understood in the original situation. Wildberger's attentive audience is perhaps more likely to be the exegete who has read his Engnell and his Ahlström than Isaiah's contemporaries.

And here we return to the text itself. Apart from anticipating that it is a *love-song*, the hearers must anticipate that the song concerns neither the prophet nor the hearers themselves, but the prophet's friend, *Isaiah's* ידיד. According to H. Junker,[12] because of the central role the groom's friend plays in the wedding, it is reasonable to assume that it is not the principal male character himself who sings the song but someone with whom he is on friendly terms (cf. Jn 3.29).

The question now is whether the subsequent definition of the song as לכרמו supports this view. While the modern reader would probably be surprised at the juxtaposition of love-song and vineyard, Isaiah's contempories would scarcely have found it surprising. To them, the vineyard was a well-known metaphor for the bride (Song 1.6; 2.15; 8.12[13]). And so there is good reason to assume that the audience,

92 *There is Hope for a Tree*

when it heard the word כרם in association with the word דוד, had its first impression still further reinforced. It is also possible that the beginning of the song reflects a familiar profane song of erotic content, which is now exploited by the prophet for the purposes of the message. If this is so, the listeners' preconception would be further strengthened and the prophet even more assured of an approving audience.

We do not know whether, in addition to this, Isaiah in his choice of time and place (some scholars have suggested that the song was recited in connexion with a wine-harvest festivity,[14] where the fertility motifs were especially dominant) or in his manner of presenting the song (we have no possibility of knowing anything about gestures or inflections) from the very outset helped the audience in a certain way to understand what he was saying. But, for our context, it is important to point out that it would be possible with very modest means to guide the hearers towards one specific understanding of the song, i.e. as a narrative about a man and his wife, but with the special refinement that the narrative is formed in imagery.[15]

After the introductory presentation follows the song itself, with its description of how the owner of the vineyard lays out and looks after his vineyard in conformity with all the rules of the time, but to his great disappointment he discovers that the noble vines yield wild grapes (Isa. 5.1b-2).

In his analysis, A.J. Bjørndalen[16] argues against the view that the song is a love-song, and says that whereas lyrical love poetry would concentrate on the vineyard's/woman's charms this song speaks of the owner's work-effort, which should make an erotic interpretation impossible.

Bjørndalen is right in saying that the subject deviates from what one might expect from a love-song. But there are reasons for this deviation which the hearers are also able to understand. From v. 3 onwards, Isaiah changes over to a different genre: the description of a lawsuit.

A Lawsuit, vv. 3-6

The listeners are called not only as witnesses in the case; they are directly asked to be judges in the matter between the owner of the vineyard, who now himself speaks, and his vineyard. The song is thus not an ordinary love-song; in reality, the prophet wishes to involve his listeners in a litigation in which a judgment must be reached here and now. A new image has thereby been activated: *the trial image.*

Viewed in this light, the meticulous description of the owner's care becomes fully comprehensible. One of the stages known from the lawsuit, the *rîb* pattern, is the introductory description of the plaintiff's kindnesses towards the accused.[17] The purpose of this account of the plaintiff's solicitude and fidelity is of course to emphasize the seriousness of the accusation. In Isa. 5.2, it is not the plaintiff himself but the friend who describes his kindness, so testifying that the plaintiff has met his obligations. The importance of this motif is also shown by its resumption in v. 4, where the plaintiff himself asserts by his rhetorical question that he has done all that could be expected of him, and can therefore with every justification pronounce the sentence that the vineyard must be destroyed.

But in regard to the problem earlier raised about the significance of the vineyard image, what will be the implications of the fact that the song now appears to take the form of a lawsuit? Will the hearers still be able to hold to their first-hand impression that the song is a figurative description of an erotic relationship? Yes; there is no doubt that they will. The narrative about the ungrateful vineyard which, quite contrary to nature, yielded wild grapes can most certainly be seen as a narrative about an unfaithful wife who bore her husband illegitimate children. We know this motif from another prophetic description of a lawsuit of this period, Hos. 2.4-17,[18] where proceedings are in progress by reason of an unfaithful wife's adultery. The trial is a *divorce case.* Viewed in the light of the erotic code, therefore, the vineyard image and the trial image are well-matched. It is not unreasonable for the 'owner' to permit his mortification to have juridical consequences.

But in the Hosea text the unfaithful wife is an image of Israel, and it is therefore worth considering whether the hearers might not have come to the conclusion in the circumstances that Isaiah also uses the unfaithful wife as an image, i.e. for the people themselves. To this it may be answered that the hearers would be unlikely to consider whether two layers of imagery are involved, of which the first interpretation is fully understandable and acceptable in the light of the actual situation. That Isaiah sings a love-song in order, in fact, to denounce a woman living in adultery must be seen as wholly probable. The hearers would have been taken aback if the prophet had suddenly begun to sing a love-song with no form of 'deeper meaning'; but they are unlikely to have been surprised if he made one of his usual attacks on the wickedness of the time. His condemnation of the haughty upper-class women who toss their heads and trip along in full war-paint, and who will certainly get their just deserts (Isa. 3.16ff.), shows that the subject was not unkown (unwelcome?) to him.

The Vineyard Image as the Story of a Man and his Unfaithful Wife
We shall now examine whether it is possible to hear/read the whole of Isa. 5.1-6 as a narrative about a man and his unfaithful wife; i.e. we shall examine the thesis presented by *Aage Bentzen* in 1927, which has since won many supporters.[19]

The vineyard is described in v. 1 by its location. Precisely what is meant by בקרן בן־שמן (a fertile hill) cannot be determined, according to Hans Wildberger,[20] but he sees שמן (oil) as describing the rich soil giving good growth potential. קרן indeed refers to the horn = promontory on which the vineyard is located. Such an interpretation is acceptable, but the unusual term makes one ask whether it is more probably chosen because of the erotic code than because of the vineyard image. If we translate the term literally, it must mean 'a horn of oil', but this is not a normal term for a horn of oil; according to 1 Sam. 16.13 and 1 Kgs 1.39, this is called קרן השמן. But it is so close to the normal term that the hearer must pause and relate to a 'horn of oil'. What is meant by a woman in a horn of oil other than that her surroundings are being described as the finest possible? She is really in clover we would say, using a metaphor. If the hearers have in fact, as earlier indicated, been steered into the erotic code, the idea of oil does not surprise. In the Song of Solomon, fragrant oils are included in the description of the bridegroom and bride; they are both anointed, Song 1.3; 4.10.

But this does not mean that the 'horn of oil' effects a break in the vineyard image. In Isa. 28.1, 4, for example, the hillsides of Samaria are described by using the concept, שמן. This is done in such a way that the context evokes associations with both the geographical circumstances (Samaria lies on a hill in a fertile valley) and the flower-decorated but intoxicated inhabitants whose crown of flowers lies faded על־ראש גיא־שמנים (on the fertile hillside). There is no doubt here that we should keep in mind both the head from which the ointment flows and the 'fertile' slopes.

Whereas Isa. 5.1 refers to קרן בן־שמן (horn of oil), which *can* be understood figuratively as hillsides, Isa. 28.1, 4 speaks of גיא־שמנים (fertile slopes), which *can* be understood figuratively as a person's anointed temples. So there is reason to consider the term קרן בן־שמן as a deliberate and well-chosen expression that permits the hearers to hold in their minds simultaneously both the vineyard image and the erotic code.

In *v. 2*, the characterization of the owner of the vineyard is amplified by a description of his various activities in the vineyard; but here also it is possible to follow the erotic code. Cultivating a field is an image of sexual intimacy frequently employed, and it does not call for much imagination to read in this way the passage about planting cuttings, building a tower in the centre of the garden and cutting out a vat, expecting proper grapes but finding wild grapes.[21]

What is crucial here is not how many of these associations the individual hearer picks up but that Isaiah expresses himself in such a way that the hearers at no time pause and say: This cannot be the story of the unfaithful wife after all; Isaiah must want to tell us something else.

In *v. 3*, the author interrupts the song and reveals that what began as a love-song has developed into a trial. The third person singular is changed to the first person singular, and the distance previously present between the prophet and the owner of the vineyard disappears. It is the betrayed himself who now begins to speak, asking his neighbours for their verdict and asserting his own innocence in the form of *v. 4*'s rhetorical questions.

These two verses still operate within the vineyard image but make equally good sense on the basis of the erotic code, where the subject should be seen as a case against an unfaithful wife who bore her husband illegitimate children (cf. the trial in Hos. 2.4-17). It must also be emphasized that when the hearers are directly asked to be judges in the case they are not given a new and surprising role but are merely asked explicitly to go on being what they have been all along. From the very moment that they thought they understood the drift, they have sat and listened as judges of the unfaithful wife.

Instead of waiting for the hearers' verdict, the owner of the vineyard passes judgment himself in *vv. 5-6*, but its content is no surprise since he speaks on behalf of a unanimous audience. The case is indeed open-and-shut; all that needs to be agreed is the grounds for the judgment. This is what can happen if one takes a wife; but she for her part will not be allowed to get away with it; she must suffer her well-deserved punishment.[22]

We must again consider, however, whether Isaiah succeeds in maintaining the erotic code. The punishment consists in his intention to remove the vineyard's hedge, break down its wall and leave the vineyard to be laid waste by wild animals. This is fully comprehensible in the light of the vineyard image itself. From the erotic code, the hearers will see the punishment as removal of the protection the owner/husband has so far given to his wife. In the lawsuit against the unfaithful wife in Hos. 2.8 (RSV 2.6), the husband threatens that he will prevent her from seeking lovers by hedging up her way with thorns and by building a wall against her. We can also find a parallel to wild animals devouring the vineyard in the Hosea text, i.e. in 2.14 (RSV 2.12) where it is said that the husband intends to lay waste her vines and fig trees and make them a forest so that they can be devoured by the beasts of the field.

Despite a difference in the choice of words and presentation the same images are employed in the two places, making it probable that the hearers of Isa. 5.1-7 can still feel convinced that the matter relates to an unfaithful wife. That the wild animals which devastate the vineyard can be an image of the young woman's lovers we also know from Song 2.15, in one of the passages where the vineyard is used as an image of the bride and the foxes as an image of those that destroy the idyll.[23]

The description of the punishment continues in v. 6. The vineyard is to be permitted to fall into decay, the cultivated land is to become like an uncultivated wilderness again.[24] The vines are not pruned, the soil is not hoed, briers and thorns are to grow over it and the clouds shall no longer rain upon it. The description of the vineyard's entire destruction is completed by a few vivid expressions. The cultivated land returns to its natural condition, which is not idyllic and free growth but wilderness.

If this description is read in terms of the erotic code, it must similarly be seen as a description of the woman's total destruction. Here also comparison with Hos. 2.4ff. is informative. In this trial scene, the husband threatens to strip her naked and make her a wilderness, כמדבר, a drought-stricken land, כארץ ציה, so that she dies of thirst. The images in the two texts are similar, but display such a different choice of words that there can be no direct dependence but rather the different use of a general image: the wife as a field.

The reference to the husband's forbidding the clouds to give rain has caused a number of scholars to question whether Isaiah here abandons the image and passes on to the interpretation; i.e., he reveals that the matter is not concerned with a vineyard and its owner, let alone a man and his wife. Indeed, only Yahweh himself can issue such orders.[25] To this argument, Aage Bentzen[26] says it is unreasonable to imagine that Isaiah would give the hearers an opportunity to realize at the penultimate moment that it is they themselves who are concerned. But he does not do this. It is only we moderns who are taken aback when a human being expresses such a curse. The lamentation over Saul and Jonathan (2 Sam. 1.21) includes an analogous demand, that no dew or rain is to fall upon the mountains of Gilboa. Apart from Bentzen's comments on this, it is perhaps reasonable to bear in mind that if the hearers listen on the basis of the expectations created by the erotic code the husband is demanding something from himself here—and he surely can decide for himself whether he can satisfy that demand?

We have now attempted to read vv. 1-6 in the light of the erotic code. We have seen that the text is easy to understand in these terms, and it has been established as probable that Isaiah's hearers, with their preconceptions, also interpreted the song as the story of an unfaithful wife.

In v. 7, however, Isaiah reveals that the vineyard is the people themselves. Just as in the Hosea text the unfaithful wife was an image of faithless Israel, so in Isaiah is Israel's case brought before the court. The erotic code which the hearers believed to be the key to understanding the song of the vineyard was one of several possible keys, but not the correct one.

Having established this, the question again arises of the form and function of imagery. Why does Isaiah choose to describe Yahweh's case against Israel in imagery, and how are we to decide the form of imagery Isaiah employs? Let us begin by considering the form of the imagery.

Parable or Allegory?
As indicated on p. 89, I perceive a text of this type as a metaphorical narrative. But why choose this designation and not one of the two traditional ones: parable or allegory?

Discussion of—and the clear distinction between—these two concepts has played a vital part in New Testament research, but in my opinion this does not assist us to understand Old Testament imagery. I shall now try to identify the reasons for this on the basis of Isa. 5.1-7.

We all agree that Isa. 5.1-7 uses imagery. This means that the language functions in a special way. The key to understanding this special function in the present case must be sought in the interpretation (v. 7). Here, כרם (vineyard) is interpreted as בית ישראל (the house of Israel) and נטע שעשועיו (pleasant planting) by איש יהודה (men of Judah), and in addition an interpretation is given indirectly of דוד/ידיד (the friend), in that the vineyard is defined as the Lord of Hosts's vineyard. But does this mean that the hearers have now been given the key-word, and are thereafter to 'translate' the remainder of the text's meaning-bearing words in order fully to understand the text, as is believed in principle by those who see the text as an allegory? Or is it sufficient to take the interpretation in v. 7 as the one point of comparison in the light of which the meaning of the text is to be understood, as is presumably believed by those who see the text as a parable?[27]

The key-words given in v. 7 cannot of course contain the total meaning of the text, since the text describes a sequence of events and v. 7 merely translates a few individual nouns. The hearers must enter into the interpretation and extract the information now made available. How much or how little of the text is understood metaphorically, in the sense that it is translated, depends, indeed, on the culture within which the hearers exist. Some metaphors are so general that more or less all hearers will translate them, and will do so in the same way. These metaphors, sealed in convention, can be bearers of new meaning only in a changed situation. What this means in reality is apparent if we remind ourselves of the difference between the original situation, where the hearers first listened to the prophet's word-of-mouth song, interpreted it—*mainly individual key-words*— as it proceeded, and on this basis saw that the accused was about to receive a just sentence, and the situation underlying the Targum's paraphrase of the existing text, for example, where the building of the watchtower is translated to mean that Yahweh gave them his altar for atonement of their sins. In the first case, we would say that in the light of traditional terminology the hearers heard and interpreted as if the prophet were introducing a parable; as regards the second, we would have to say that they interpreted it as if it were an allegory. But what about the text itself, we would ask. *Is* it a parable, or *is* it an allegory?

As far as I can see, the question is lopsided. If we can question at all what the text *is*, then the answer must be the open-ended definition: a metaphorical narrative. If, in addition, we are to define the form of the text, this we must do by stating the *use* made of it at *various* times within its history of use and reuse. All metaphorical narratives are not the same, in the sense that there is an equal number of elements in them which can be directly translated by those that accept them. If we look at the meaning of a text in its original Sitz im Leben, the author had of course an intention in formulating his message in the manner he has chosen. He knows what he can reasonably expect the hearers to understand from the images chosen, and the better known the images the more certain he can be that they will interpret them as expected. The more metaphors sealed by convention an author employs in a story and the longer the narrative links he creates, the greater will be the probability that the hearers will interpret allegorically; i.e. try to translate as many as possible of the individual terms and, on this basis, understand the entire sequence of the narrative.

In the case of Isa. 5.1-7, it is reasonable to assume that Isaiah's intention was to make use of familiar metaphors to argue that the unfaithful should receive their just punishment, so causing the hearers to pass judgment on themselves. The metaphors are well-known, which may have given the hearers a better opportunity to 'translate' details than if lesser-known images had been used. But in this case the point of the message does not depend upon how many of the individual metaphors are 'translated'. The individual metaphors form part of the narrative context, and therefore contribute to arrival at the crucial point.

But even if this was the understanding of the text that the author had in mind in the original situation, neither he nor other people can prevent a more allegorizing interpretation, such as we find in the Targum. What we as exegetes must do is to investigate the text's history of use and reuse and consider for each individual phase which interpretation (including which method of interpretation) must be considered as most probable in precisely this context— context being understood in a broad sense.

The main difference between my understanding of imagery and

the traditional understanding is therefore that whereas the focus is traditionally on *the form* I speak of *the function* as the crucial aspect. Whereas scholars like Adolf Jülicher are interested in whether a specific text is to be defined as a parable or an allegory, as if two different modes of existence were concerned, I am interested in the ways the specific text *can function*, the hearers carrying out a translation of the main content of the text, or at least managing to translate a large number of the individual metaphors. The advantage of this approach to imagery is of course that it becomes possible to distinguish between the hearers'/readers' *different use* of the image at *different times* in the history of the text. And in my opinion this is the crucial aspect when dealing with texts which not only have a long tradition behind them before they were written down but which have also been exposed to continuous reuse in new situations. But interest in reuse should not lead us to neglect to ask the question: What was the original intention of Isa. 5.1-7?

Isa. 5.1-7 as a Description of a Lawsuit: Performative Function

As we have said, Isa. 5.1-7 is a metaphorical narrative, but it is also a *trial*. We have two images in this text, the vineyard image and the lawsuit image; and almost imperceptibly the two images gradually merge into one another. Moreover, this description of a lawsuit is presented as a song, which more than suggests that the situation in which the lawsuit takes place is not what is usually referred to as the function-typical Sitz im Leben.[28] The situation can in fact be wherever a prophet may have an opportunity to speak to a group of people.

But the lawsuit uses the language in a special way that requires the hearers to enter into an interpretation of what is said, in as much as they see the entire trial of the vineyard as imagery. In this specific case, the imagery has a further consequence for the form of the text that has nothing to do with the form of the lawsuit, namely v. 7, the prophet's own interpretation of the imagery. What in other contexts is left to the hearers is here undertaken by the prophet himself.

The imagery does not therefore preclude the texts' being structured in specific Gattungen, although this can mean certain alterations, and will always mean that the question must be asked: how are imagery and Gattung related to one another? Are competing phenomena involved, or is there a certain amount of collaboration?

The answer is that, for Isaiah, the *intention* of Isa. 5.1-7 is to *pronounce judgment* on the hearers. This judgment is created by collaboration between the lawsuit form and imagery. The lawsuit form ensures that the hearers are formally appointed judges, and that the case ends in a decision. The imagery's receptiveness and demand for interpretation draws the hearers into the case; they participate in it, they become part of it—if it is successful of course.

By choosing the vineyard image, the prophet can argue that judgment *must* come and that it is righteous—since the vineyard has behaved entirely contrary to nature—and, thanks to the hearers' direct interpretation of the vineyard as an image of a woman, he can be sure that they actually pronounce a judgment which only at the end proves to be self-condemnation. Now, as we have seen, the vineyard image is a traditional image. It is relatively easy therefore for the hearers to decide that the song concerns an erotic relationship. But this does not mean that they thereupon lose interest. What occupies them on the way is not merely the choice of code but interpretation of the narrative's whole development, from its poetic beginning, via the owner's disappointment and the decision to bring a case against the vineyard (with the hearers themselves as active participants), to delivery of the judgment. Imagery and the lawsuit form co-operate here to include the hearers in the narrative so that they make it their own and see reality through it.

Isa. 5.1-7 has therefore a clearly *performative function*: to deliver a convincing judgment. The function of the text corresponds entirely to what we encounter in 2 Sam. 12.7, where David pronounces judgment on the rich man who took the poor man's only lamb and was only then confronted with Nathan's 'You are the man'. As in Isa. 5.7, this interpretation, held to non-figurative language, creates the certainty that the hearer does not escape. There is now no longer a possibility of his thinking: It's the other people.

Gale A. Yee[29] criticizes John T. Willis for not showing how the parable makes the hearers pronounce judgment on themselves. This is a justified criticism, and similarly I am completely in agreement with Yee that what she refers to as the parable effect is based on the presumption that the hearers believe the judgment to be aimed at 'the other people'. But it is true that Yee rejects the erotic interpretation, arguing that the hearers believed it was the Northern Kingdom Isaiah was speaking against, an interpretation to which we shall return on pp. 108ff.

The crucial aspect of this use of common imagery is that it leads the hearers to a certain interpretation predictable by the author. The hearers do not concentrate on the choice of code, since this appears to be obvious and gives them confidence that the reference is not to them but to someone else. What they go along with and allow themselves to be caught up in is the interpretation of the text's individual points and the sequence of the narrative as a whole. The fact that the hearers follow the erotic code creates a distance that permits them to accept as a matter of course that the case will end in judgment; indeed, to accept themselves as co-judges.

The image used—the vineyard behaving contrary to nature—is a convincing argument that the judgment is just. And it is equally inevitable that an unfaithful wife must be punished; therefore they do not bother to ask whether the accusation against her is correct, or whether she should be allowed to speak in her defence. Why should it not be just? And how could she defend herself against such an open-and-shut case? But now that the correct interpretation is emerging it is too late to reject the legitimacy of the accusation or ask for an opportunity to put forward a defence. Sentence *has* been pronounced on the basis of the premises advanced, and these cannot now be attacked merely because it turned out that the sentence was to apply to the hearers themselves.[30]

Informative Function
We have now seen the supreme skill with which Isaiah, by his use of imagery, exploits the hearers' preconceptions in order to argue, on the one hand, in support of the justice of the negative judgment and, on the other hand, to camouflage the fact that the hearers are judging themselves.

As is clear from v. 7, the true meaning of the image is that Yahweh must punish his people. Read on the basis of this code, the vineyard text becomes a trial scene in which Yahweh is prosecutor and judge, but makes the accused co-judges. The accusation and the judgment are turned against the people, and must therefore be seen in the light of the historical situation within which Isaiah speaks. By using the vineyard image, the hearers must have an opportunity to interpret their own situation. That they themselves *have* pronounced judgment does not mean the end of any reappraisal of what the image means. The *performative function* does not exclude the *informative function*.

There is nothing surprising about the fact that the people's situation can be interpreted through the image of a vineyard. In another description of a lawsuit from the same period (Isa. 3.13-15), Isaiah uses the devouring of the vineyard as an image of the exploitation of the poor by elders and princes, and in a somewhat later text (Isa. 1.8) the siege of Jerusalem in 701 is described by the words: 'And the daughter of Zion is left like a booth in a vineyard, like a lodge in a cucumber field, like a besieged city'. But at the same time these examples show that the use of images is not deadlocked. The vineyard may be the inhabitants in general; it may be the disadvantaged; or it may be an image of the country. For this very reason, it was important for Isaiah to begin his presentation of the vineyard song by defining it as a song with an erotic content. It was this definition, together with the culture-inspired possibility of interpreting the vineyard as an image of the bride, which ensured that the hearers permitted themselves to be convinced that in this case the man-woman/groom-bride code was the correct code.

That care of the vineyard is to be seen as Yahweh's care of Israel is unlikely to cause difficulty. We cannot determine how many of the individual terms were translated by the hearers on the basis of the Yahweh Israel code. The revelation in Isa. 5.7 gives an interpretation of the grapes. The fruits Yahweh expects from his people are justice and righteousness; but he received injustice and a cry. According to Isaiah, the people's offences are thus of a social nature, which on the one hand answers well to the social accusations in the preceding chapters and on the other hand to the subsequent lamentations.

The *Targum*'s rendering of Isa. 5.1-7 shows how details were translated at a late date so that the audience could understand not only the kind of benefits Yahweh had given them in his care for them—the sanctuary and the altar of atonement—but also what his punishment would be—he will remove his Shekinah, שכינתי, so that they will be destroyed; he will demolish their sanctuaries, so that they will be trampled down; he will drive them out of the country and refrain from giving them any kind of support; indeed, Yahweh will even forbid the prophets to speak to them.

Whereas later reappraisal may be very interested in considering the reasons for the calamity and the justice of it, for the hearer who apprehends the message as an *actual judgment*, and has even, as co-judge, to accept and fall into line with the judgment, it must be more essential to come to understand how the judgment will in fact be realized. Verses 5-6 are therefore those in which the hearers will seek this *information*. The first part of v. 5 refers to removing hedges and walls. Isa. 3.1ff., which must also be included among Isaiah's early prophecies, describes how Yahweh is about to remove Jerusalem's and Judah's stay and staff: the mighty man and the soldier, the judge and the prophet, the diviner and the elder, the captain of fifty and the man of rank, the counsellor, the skilful magician and the expert in charms. When they are gone, the people will be led by boys and louts, and civil war will break out.

Against this background, it would be natural to imagine that the hearers of the vineyard parable would have understood the removal of hedges and walls as removal of their lawful leaders. When they are gone, others will come, but they will devour, i.e. despoil the poor and crush the people as described in Isa. 3.14-15. These new rulers over the decaying vineyard are also described as thorn and thistle, שמיר ושית, a typical Isaianic expression exclusively used as an image. Figuratively, it can be used of internal or external usurpers in contrast to lawful leaders, or it can be used more generally of groups considered inferior in social standing.

A brief survey of the passages in which שמיר ושית is to be found will support this:

Excursus
Apart from Isa. 5.6, שמיר ושית is to be found only in Isa. 7.23, 24, 25; 9.17 (RSV 9.18); 10.17; 27.4. In addition, שמיר is to be found in Isa. 32.13. The term שמיר ושית consists of two words, which are similar not only in content but also in their sound. This suggests that the words were more likely to have been chosen because of their sound-effect than to ensure botanical accuracy, which in turn suggests that the term is used figuratively. As a good example of this, we shall begin with Isa. 9.17, where godlessness is compared with a fire consuming thorns and briers and the large forests, סבכי היער. A parallel to the juxtaposition שמיר ושית—סבכי היער is to be found in the fable of Jotham (Judg. 9.8-15), where fire out of the bramble, האטד, shall devour the cedars of Lebanon, and in 2 Kgs 14.9, where a thistle on Lebanon, החוח, is contrasted with the cedar on Lebanon. It will be seen that the same words are not used, but both passages contain figurative narratives which refer to the political circumstances. In the fable of Jotham the subject is the election of Abimelech as king, and in 2 Kgs 14.9 the subject is the challenge of the king of Judah, Amaziah, to king Joash to try their strength in war. The cedars of Lebanon are thus an image of what is valuable, the bramble and thistle of what is of no value. Similarly, it is natural to see Isa. 9.17 as a description of a society in which wickedness and godlessness have spread from top to bottom

so that the whole of society is saturated with it, leaders as well as the most wretched prophet who teaches lies (Isa. 9.14; RSV 9.15).

Isa. 10.17 (here the expression has been reversed: שיתו ושמירו) is clearly dependent upon Isa. 9.17. In the present context, the oracle is directed against the king of the Assyrians, and it is said that fire, i.e. Yahweh, will devour his thorns and briers and sweep away the glory of his forest and his fruitful land. Here also thorn and brier are contrasted with the forest to signify the top and bottom of the social hierarchy.

In Isa. 27.4, as in Isa. 5.6, we encounter שמיר [ו] שית[31] in association with the vineyard image. There is little doubt that Isa. 27.2-6 is founded on Isa. 5.1-7, but at both the beginning and the end the interpretation has broken through the image. Yahweh is the keeper of the vineyard, and should thorn and brier enter his vineyard he will battle against them and burn them up unless they call for his protection. Thus, שמיר ושית is an image of a group of people who may be persuaded to revert to Yahweh. The background is presumably the internal unrest during the post-Exile period,[32] and therefore again concerns a group which, through the image, is branded as unco-operative, although there is still hope for them.

In Isa. 7.23, 24, 25, the term שמיר ושית occurs three times, just once supplemented by the preposition ל. The passage 7.23-25 is an oracle about what will happen on that day. The prospects are not bright. The vines are to be replaced by thorns and briers (cf. Isa. 5.6); all the land is to become thorns and briers; cattle and sheep will take it over as a grazing area (cf. 5.5). Isa. 7.18-25 consists of a number of loosely connected oracles, all referring to future events. It can be seen from the imagery in vv. 18-19, 20 that Yahweh will summon the enemies and let them raze the land. The train of thought is then broken by a positive statement (Isa. 7.21-22) which speaks, without use of imagery, of living conditions on that day. This is rounded off by 7.23-25, which must be interpreted as negative.[33] If 7.23-25 is read in direct continuation of the down-to-earth description in 7.21, these verses will of course be seen as an equally down-to-earth description of how cultivated land becomes a wilderness. Nevertheless, the link back to Isa. 5.1-7 is so distinct and the use of imagery in Isa. 7.18-19, 20 so clear that one is left with a feeling that it is an original image which in its *present context* has lost its figurative function. What the image originally concerned would then correspond to the image in 7.20 on the one hand and to the image in 9.17 on the other: all the elders and honoured men will be removed; only thorns and briers will remain.

Finally, Isa. 32.13 must be briefly mentioned, where שמיר is not combined with שית but is a link in a description of the time of chaos when everything dies away, and it is probable that the text does not use the established metaphor שמיר ושית but קוץ שמיר from a desire to ensure that a disaster such as the destruction of nature is understood literally.[34]

The analysis of שמיר ושית is thereby completed. *To summarize*, it can be said that in most places the term has a figurative meaning. In Isa. 32.13, where the established term is not in fact used, שמיר is used in the direct sense, and likewise Isa. 7.23-25 in the *present* context must be accepted without figurative meaning.[35] The meaning of the term is not always precisely the same; but it has negative connotations on every occasion. A common feature of the figurative use of שמיר ושית is that a political code lies behind the use in all cases.

If we now return to Isa. 5.6's use of the term שמיר ושית, it should be clear that contemporary hearers would naturally interpret this image as referring to *internal or external usurpers* who take over power in the land after the fall of the lawful leaders. Whether the hearers expected the destruction from within or from without depends, therefore, on the precise historical situation and their political evaluation of it.

The terms used in v. 5 to describe the wreckers' behaviour may, however, have led their thoughts in one specific direction. The removal of the hedge takes place לבער and the breaking down of the wall takes place so that the vineyard can become למרמס. The first expression, לבער, is used here in the same sense as in Isa. 3.14 and 6.13, i.e. about the devouring of the vineyard.[36] This is to be seen from, for example, the parallel placing in relation to למרמס, which can be used about cattle trampling down the soil (cf. Isa. 7.25 and Ezek. 34.18f.). But what is significant about these two expressions is that whereas בער can also mean 'burn down',[37] מרמס can be used as an image of the advance of an enemy army; i.e. the two expressions contain potential meanings which make them well-fitted for implying that punishment will come in the form of an enemy attack. In Isa. 10.5 where Assyria is cursed, the ravaging and plunder of the king of the Assyrians is described by, for example, such figurative use of מרמס.

We do not know how Isa. 5.1-7 was seen later in the eighth century. We do know that this song about the vineyard was preserved, and we must consider it probable that a *'re-reading'*, occurring while either the Syro-Ephraimite or the Assyrian troops were marching towards Jerusalem, must have made it natural to see in these formulations a prediction of Judah's destruction at the hands of an enemy. It is well-known that this was no more than a threat in the eighth century, but with the destruction of Jerusalem in 587 BC the Exile generation must have seen it as a fulfilment of Isaiah's judgment statement.

It may indeed appear speculative to consider how any possible re-reading or reinterpretation of the vineyard parable can have occurred over time. Nevertheless, I find that certain features in the composition of the book of Isaiah show that the redactors' work on the surviving words of the prophet reflect just such a procedure.[38]

One of the problems raised by the construction of Isaiah 1–12 is the placing of the lamentations and curses. The redactors have placed the majority of them (Isa. 5.8-24, and the description of the approach of the Assyrians, Isa. 5.25-29) in direct extension of the vineyard parable and its terse exposition. In my view, it is reasonable to see this placing as expressing a conscious desire to clarify, in the light of historical realities, what it means to yield wild grapes and what it means to be trampled down by cattle when all protection is removed. By placing this description of the onward-marching Assyrians as an extension of the vineyard parable and the lamentations and curses (both sections should be read as primarily literal language), the redactors succeed in interpreting the threat of war as Yahweh's righteous punishment for the sins of the people. It is also clear from Isa. 10.5ff. that the Assyrians are Yahweh's instrument of punishment. This may perhaps help to explain the very striking separation of Isa. 9.7-20 and Isa. 5.25-29, as well as of Isa. 5.8-24 and Isa. 10.1-4, although this does not represent a complete explanation of the phenomenon.

We have now carried out two interpretations of the vineyard parable: one on the basis of the *erotic code*, husband–unfaithful wife, the other on the basis of the *political code*, Yahweh–Israel. The analysis showed that the first was consciously a false trail on Isaiah's part, but it was precisely this use of traditional imagery and his presentation of the vineyard parable as a love-song that enabled him to keep his hearers on this trail right up to the disclosure in v. 7. The other interpretation—Isaiah's own—is scarcely an innovation in imagery, but the use of the vineyard/vine to refer to Israel proves to be relatively flexible in the various texts. The images can be employed about the country, about the entire people, or about a group of the people. This means that the range of meaning of individual metaphors is not clearly demarcated in advance, but depends largely on the context (literary as well as historical) in which they occur. It is, for example, difficult for us to establish on the basis of the vineyard image alone whether the hearers, in the light of the political code, were able to associate something with the forbidding of rain.

The Targum translates the forbidding of rain from heaven as a ban on prophetic preaching; but we do not know whether the Targum is founded on an established tradition in imagery on whose basis and within which Isaiah also speaks. We have examples of heaven raining things other than rain, but such texts are relatively late. These texts are Isa. 45.8, where the skies are asked to rain down righteousness; Isa. 55.10-11, where the rain and the snow watering and fertilizing the earth are used as an image of God's word doing God's will; and Deut. 32.2, where the dropping rain is an image of Moses' teaching. In relation to this latter text, however, it must be added that the dating is unusually difficult.[39]

If we are to try to find some connexion within Isaiah 1–12 itself, which the Targum may have employed for its interpretation of the cessation of rain as the absence of the prophet's words, it is tempting to refer to Isa. 8.16, since Isaiah's 'Denkschrift' ends with the sealing of the message. Yahweh has spoken to his people through Isaiah, but from now on he will keep silence. But such attempts to find interpretation possibilities can easily approach guesswork—entertaining for whoever searches and thinks to have found, but almost impossible to support if the individual interpretations do not together reflect a coherent pattern.

To summarize, we must therefore be content to say that the vineyard parable is very much open to *reinterpretation* as regards its details in new situations.

B. *Reinterpretation of Isa. 5.1-7 in the Eighth Century*

We have arrived now at the question of the possible later use of the text, a question already briefly referred to in the analysis. In my opinion, we encounter an example of a possible reinterpretation in *Gale A. Yee*'s reading of the text. In her analysis of Isa. 5.1-7, Yee[40] has emphasized mainly the text's legal aspects. The two forms on whose basis the text has been composed, song and trial parable, are exploited by Isaiah in such a way that the inhabitants of Judah pronounce sentence on themselves.[41] The vehicle for the denunciation itself—and here I fully agree with Yee—is the use of an imagery that makes the hearers believe the judgment to be aimed at 'the other people'.

But who are these others? According to Yee, they are *the inhabitants of the Northern Kingdom*. Yee argues in support of this interpretation (a) by drawing attention to the house of Israel,

בית ישראל, in v. 7, which appears in no other place as a parallel to Judah or Jerusalem but in fact in Hosea, Amos and Micah (and later in Jeremiah) always refers to the Northern Kingdom; and (b) by indicating that wine and vineyard are often used in reference to the Northern Kingdom, i.e. in Hos. 10.1; 9.10; 14.8 and Ps. 80. Yee concludes from this that if it was usual in Isaiah's time to use the vineyard motif in reference to the Northern Kingdom it is very possible that the hearers also believed, in the context of Isa. 5.1-7, that it was their rivals and not themselves on whom the judgment was to fall. And all the more so since at the time Isaiah was writing the text the Northern Kingdom had already witnessed Tiglath-Pileser's conquests in this region. Isaiah's point was in fact that Judah should not rejoice too soon, since it was to suffer the same fate as Israel—unless it reformed.

But Yee's interpretation does not hold water as an interpretation of Isaiah's original intention. As already indicated, Yee bases her reading on the interpretation of the vineyard as בית ישראל, equivalent to the Northern Kingdom, but here she introduces a distinction between the vineyard and the vines planted in the vineyard, since the latter are of course clearly an image of the Southern Kingdom, Judah. This distinction not only breaks the unity of the image but at the same time makes the point imprecise. Yee says on the one hand that the hearers are lured into believing that the judgment applies to the Northern Kingdom, but discover in the end that it applies to themselves, and on the other hand that the vineyard is in fact the Northern Kingdom. The Northern Kingdom interpretation thus becomes both correct and incorrect: correct in the sense that the Northern Kingdom did in fact witness a destruction that could be described in the vineyard imagery; incorrect if the judgment became applicable to the Northern Kingdom alone, since the true accused is Judah.

I call this point imprecise; but it would be equally justifiable to call it over-precise. It acts like an interpretation *ex eventu*, in which one attempts to extract from the available text as much *information* as possible about what has already occurred so as to be able to argue from the text that Yahweh had already predicted the course of history. To me, such a reading is a typical reinterpretation in the light of a new historical situation. In spite of Yee's insistence on this very aspect, the emphasis is no longer on the text's event-nature. The *performative*, the sentencing, has been pushed into the background to the advantage of the *informative*, and the purpose of the text is no longer to cause the hearers to judge themselves but to produce theodicy, i.e. to function as legitimation of Yahweh's action.

I therefore wish to maintain that my interpretation of the text's original meaning is more probable than Yee's, although I cannot do this without having at the same time to oppose her argument that the hearers would *as a matter of course* have understood the vineyard image as an image of the Northern Kingdom. Again, her understanding of בית ישראל indeed calls for closer investigation. I here take her two arguments in reverse order—and this I do deliberately. The point is simply that if we wish to say anything about Isaiah's intentions and how the original hearers associated with Isa. 5.1-7 we must accept that they listened to the text from the beginning—and not backwards as Yee in fact presumes. We therefore have to consider whether on hearing the word כרם (vineyard) they would rather associate this with the Northern Kingdom than with a woman. Yee rejects the erotic interpretation without argument; but this means that she does not commit herself as regards the concepts דידי and דוד. She speaks of the text only as a song, and jumps straight to Deuteronomy 32 and the rîb Pattern. But that will not do; the song is defined in detail on the basis of these two concepts; it is only secondarily that the rîb Pattern can be considered.

It is quite correct that Hosea uses images taken from the vineyard. In Hos. 10.1, the prophet uses the image of the luxuriant vine, גפן בוקק, to polemize against the idol-worship in the Northern Kingdom; in Hos. 9.10 Israel is described as grapes in the wilderness, כענבים במדבר; and finally in Hos. 14.8 (RSV 14.7) the image of the vine whose wine is like that of Lebanon, כגפן זכרו כיין לבנון, is used about Israel. It will be seen that there is no great coincidence between the terminology in Isa. 5.1-7 and these texts; only the word for grapes, ענבים, is repeated. For example, כרם is not used[42] in the Hosea texts, which twice refer to vines by using the word גפן. On the other hand, גפן is not used Isa. 5.1-7, where the individual vines are described by the words שרק (v. 2) and נטע (v. 7). However, גפן is frequently used in Psalm 80, which Yee includes as an example of a North Israelitic hymn in which the vineyard is an image of Israel = the Northern Kingdom (Ps. 80.9, 15). But it is not as certain as Yee implies that this hymn is in fact North Israelite.[43]

So there is not much to indicate that in Isaiah's time there was an even fairly well established tradition of using the vineyard image as a reference to the Northern Kingdom, as Yee assumes despite her reservations. It is much nearer the truth to say that in a culture such as the Israelite one the vineyard is a natural image which can be used in many different contexts. Cf., for example, Isa. 3.13-15, where the image is in fact used to refer not to the Northern Kingdom but to the Southern Kingdom. It will therefore be the specific formulations of the vineyard, for example by means of the words ידיד and דוד, that determine the use of the image the hearers will expect.

Yee's other argument concerns the use of the term בית ישראל (the house of Israel). But if Yee is correct in saying that this refers to the Northern Kingdom it must be made clear that this interpretation would have surprised the hearers just as much as the interpretation that followed: It is Judah! After having believed that it was all about an unfaithful wife, they now learn that the vineyard is the Northern Kingdom, to be corrected once again immediately afterwards: No, it is in fact you yourselves! The malice is then transferred from the female sex to the political rivals. This is possible, but is it likely?

I have pointed out earlier that one reading of v. 7, which takes the house of Israel and the men of Judah as indicating two different population groups, causes a break in the image; but this argument is not of course compelling. Isaiah may have been a poor user of imagery. The vital consideration must therefore be to investigate what Isaiah and his hearers directly associated with the statement that the Lord of Hosts' vineyard is the house of Israel. Isaiah here uses the name for God particularly associated with the cult in Jerusalem. It is thereby revealed to the hearers that the owner of the vineyard is the God they themselves worship. This is not to say that it must also be the hearers themselves who are the vineyard; but nevertheless it follows naturally.

As Yee points out, בית ישראל is also used by Isaiah's contemporaries, Hosea, Amos and Micah. According to Yee, all three use the term to refer to the Northern Kingdom. That Amos and Hosea use it in this sense is not surprising, but it must be meaningful that Isaiah's colleague in the Southern Kingdom, Micah, uses it significantly to refer to the Northern Kingdom (Mic. 1.5; 3.1, 9). Mic. 1.5 refers to both Israel and Judah, but the verse is so constructed that whereas the name of Jacob clearly indicates the Northern Kingdom (Jacob's transgression was caused by Samaria) the house of Israel in v. 5b stands in the same place as Judah in v. 5d, i.e. the natural understanding of the verse is that the designations Judah and Israel

are both used to refer to the Southern Kingdom, whose capital is
Jerusalem. In my opinion, therefore, the house of Israel is not used to
refer to the Northern Kingdom but to the Southern Kingdom. It
should also be noted that some scholars believe the verse to be a later
addition,[44] which would mean that this passage can scarcely be used
as an argument in support of a specific meaning at the time of Micah
and Isaiah.

In Mic. 3.1, 9, בית ישראל is parallel with יעקב (Jacob), and here also
indicates Judah. This is clear from 3.10, which details the crimes of
which the judges of the house of Jacob are accused, i.e. that Zion is
built with blood and Jerusalem with wrong. Mic. 3.12 then
pronounces the punishment for this, which rationally consists of the
destruction of Zion and Jerusalem.[45]

The book of Micah therefore provides little support for the
argument that Isaiah uses the term, the house of Israel, to refer to the
Northern Kingdom. Quite the reverse; it shows that Micah and
perhaps the redactors of the book of Micah use it to refer to the
Southern Kingdom.

Yee has evidently not investigated how Isaiah uses בית ישראל
generally, or the name Israel at all, which would however be natural.
In Isa. 1–39, the term בית ישראל appears only in Isa. 5.7; 8.14; and
14.2. Isa. 8,14 speaks of Israel's two houses, i.e. Israel is used to
describe neither the Northern Kingdom nor the Southern Kingdom
but as a name for the great kingdom. Isa. 14.2 is a later addition
which combines the two prophecies about the destruction of Babel in
Isaiah 13 and 14. Neither, for good reason, is the house of Israel here
a description of the Northern Kingdom; but this later usage cannot of
course be employed as an example of Isaiah's use of the term at the
time when both kingdoms existed.

If we then investigate the use of the name Israel generally—and
here it is sufficient to look at Isaiah 1–12, the section where most of
Isaiah's original utterances are to be found—it appears that Isaiah
used Israel almost exclusively as a description of the people as
Yahweh's people, without giving a precise geographical demarcation.[46]

An example of such use is to be found in Isa. 1.3 (Israel has broken
the covenant with Yahweh); Isa. 8.18 (Isaiah and his children/
disciples are signs and portents in Israel); Isa. 10.20, 22 (the remnant
of Israel);[47] and very many passages where the name of God is
combined with Israel: Isa. 1.24 (the Mighty One of Israel); Isa. 10.17
(the light of Israel); and especially Isa. 1.4; 5.19, 24; 10.20; 12.6 (the

Holy One of Israel). Only in one passage is the name Israel used unambiguously for the Northern Kingdom, namely in Isa. 7.1, where Pekah is described in an historical context as מלך ישראל (the king of Israel), in contrast to Ahaz who is מלך יהודה (the king of Judah). Finally, the historical paraenesis in Isa. 9.7ff. should be noted, where the name Israel occurs three times. It can be seen from the historical context in which the name occurs that geographically it must refer to the Northern Kingdom. In Isa. 9.7 Israel is analogous with Jacob, and v. 8 makes it additionally clear that it refers to Ephraim. Similarly, in 9.11, where the attack of the Syrians and the Philistines is described, it must, from a geographical aspect, be the Northern Kingdom that was intended, as is also true of 9.13.

Study of Isaiah's use of the name Israel shows therefore that Israel is used primarily to describe Yahweh's people seen in relation to Yahweh. In only a few passages is geographical differentiation involved. In Isa. 7.1, there is clear opposition between Israel and Judah, whereas the use of Israel in the historical paraenesis derives more probably from a wish to stress that it is Yahweh's people who will not permit themselves to be admonished rather than the Northern Kingdom. This latter aspect is evident, in that the geographical specification follows later. It is apparently not enough to use Israel to indicate that the reference is in fact to the Northern Kingdom.

If we compare this result, and in particular the use of the name Israel in Isa. 9.7 (RSV 9.8) with the use in Isa. 5.7, the *conclusion* must be that in 5.7 Israel is also used to describe Yahweh's people. Whereas in Isa. 9.7 Israel as a religious concept is defined geographically by the parallel statement in 9.8 אפרים ויושב שמרון (Ephraim and the inhabitants of Samaria), Israel is defined in Isa. 5.7 by the term איש יהודה (the men of Judah), a term that in its short form refers back to v. 3's יושב ירושלם ואיש יהודה (inhabitants of Jerusalem and men of Judah), which in turn is strikingly similar to the formulation in Isa. 9.8.

I must therefore reject Yee's interpretation as the most natural in the environment in which Isaiah speaks. On the other hand, I consider it probable that, in the context of the Northern Kingdom's destruction and ruin, this text has been reinterpreted in the light of the actual historical events, and that the name Israel was then taken as a description of the Northern Kingdom and—with 722—seen as a partial fulfilment of Isa. 5.7. Yahweh's punishment had now really fallen on *Israel*, as he had said, and *Judah* had now to understand that they were sharing the same fate.

C. *The Exile Period's Reinterpretation of Isa. 5.1-7*

The authenticity of Isa. 5.1-7 was until recently considered as beyond dispute; but *J. Vermeylen*'s great work on Isaiah[48] forces scholars to reconsider the matter. According to Vermeylen, the vineyard parable was a Deuteronomistic insertion. The subject is a legal action between the vineyard owner and the vines. This action is described in parable form, but it is at the same time an indictment, *rîb*. That the parable has this *rîb* structure is Vermeylen's most important argument in support of a later dating of Isa. 5,1-7, since in his opinion this structure is characteristic of the Deuteronomists.

In addition, Vermeylen says that Isa. 5.1-7 is so similar to 2 Sam. 12.1-12 and 1 Kgs 20.35-43, which also contain a judgment communicated in imagery, that contemporaneity must be present— which incidentally is not a binding conclusion; other forms of dependence might equally well be involved. And since these two texts are probably inserted by the Deuteronomists, this must also be true of Isa. 5.1-7, according to Vermeylen. Jeremiah's use of the vine image should point in the same direction—but here also perhaps one should consider whether other forms of dependence are involved. Finally, in spite of the uncertainty of such investigations, to which Vermeylen sensibly draws attention, the choice of words itself can be cited in support of the thesis that Isaiah is not the author of the text.

The similarities indicated by Vermeylen are correct; but whether they necessarily lead to the conclusion is questionable. Closer analysis of *rîb*[49] shows that the *rîb* speeches have their Sitz im Leben in the specific emergency situation in which the prophet announces Yahweh's accusations arising from the people's breach of the covenant, i.e. he interprets the actual historical situation in the light of the covenant's concepts. Such emergency situations can scarcely be confined to 'the Deuteronomists' period'. But what we can say is that Jerusalem's destruction has without doubt caused a genre such as *rîb* to become especially topical. *rîb* has been able to explain the events of 587 as Yahweh's just punishment of the disobedient people. And we know that this was necessary from Deutero-Isaiah's particular use of the lawsuit form.[50] But if one comprehends *rîb* on this basis alone one grasps only the theodicy element, and so overlooks the genre's nature of topical proclamation, including the aspect that I have elsewhere called '*rib*'s event character'.[51]

The descriptions of a lawsuit are not created as rationalizations after the event. Their original purpose was not to explain a course of events; they are, like the prophetic word in general, actual words used in a crisis situation; they are not descriptions of something tangible, but new suggestions for understanding reality. But this does not prevent the ability of the genre itself and a number of older *rib* texts to enter into the theological considerations and explanatory models that we encounter in the Deuteronomists.

When Vermeylen defines Isa. 5.1-7 as belonging to the Deuteronomists' environment in the Exile period, and stresses that it is precisely there that v. 4's clearly apologetic function and the images of the destruction in vv. 5-6 have been given meaning, he is correct in that those who experienced Nebuchadnezzar's destruction of Jerusalem and were familiar with Isa. 5.1-7 must have interpreted this text as a striking expression of their own experiences. But this is not to say that the text was written with the intention of interpreting the Exile.

In his conclusion, Vermeylen himself points out that the language is not particularly Deuteronomist, but he is content that this must be partly because a special technical viticultural language is concerned and partly because the Deuteronomists were using old material. Vermeylen is correct in saying that it is old material; but he has not shown in his analyses that this would have undergone any form of Deuteronomistic processing. Moreover, he owes us a detailed explanation of how this text about the Exile came to be placed together with a passage from Isaiah's earlier message, where the enemies were Ephraim, the Syrians and, especially, the Assyrians.

I see no reason therefore to abandon, because of Vermeylen, the traditional assumption that Isa. 5.1-7 is an authentic statement by Isaiah. What Vermeylen has to say about the text's significance in relation to the destruction of Jerusalem is striking. This is indeed how the parable must have been understood. The Exile period was able to reuse the text without amendment to interpret the historical situation. It was possible to reuse Isa. 5.1-7 at this date not only because *rib* convincingly explained the Exile's misfortune as Yahweh's punishment of the disobedient people; the text's imagery has also made it suitable, since the vineyard's destruction is so described that it can be interpreted as the enemies' attack on and ravaging of the land.

Just as in the eighth century's possible reuse of Isa. 5.1-7, the Exile period's possible reuse is an expression that the *performative* function is pushed into the background to the advantage of the *informative*. The object of the text is no longer to cause the hearers to pronounce judgment on themselves but to explain that the catastrophe which had already occurred was Yahweh's just punishment of the people's sins.

In this section, we have considered how it was possible to re-read Isa. 5.1-7 in new *historical situations*. But it must be emphasized that the potential for certainty about this is very limited if there is no *literary context* to reflect how the redactors understood the text at the time in question. Since I am considering Isa. 5.1-7's literary context—the lamentations and descriptions of the advancing Assyrian army, Isa. 5.8ff.—as an example of redactional interpretation of parts of the vineyard image, I have included this to throw light on the eighth century's response. We lack direct redactional clues in the immediate context in regard to the Exile period's interpretation. We can only submit that the similarity between 701 and 587 (notwithstanding the different outcomes) made it automatic for redactors to re-read the statements about the king of Assyria as utterances about the king of Babylon. Cf. my discussion (p. 160) of Isa. 14.4a, for example. It is possible perhaps that the interpretation of the vineyard image could have been similarly taken over. But from our knowledge of Deutero-Isaiah's use of the *rîb* pattern we must stress the significance of the theodicy aspect at this time.

D. *Isa. 27.2-6 as a New Production of Text Based on Isa. 5.1-7*

'Il est assez évident que le deuxième chant de la vigne entend être une réplique à celui du chapitre 5.' With these words, Edmond Jacob introduces his analysis of Isa. 27.2-5.[52] According to Jacob, the two vineyard songs stand in an *antithetical relationship* to one another, in that Isa. 5.1-7 describes a failure and Isa. 27.2-5 a success. Whereas the former originates from Isaiah himself, the other came into existence in post-Exilic times, where against the background of the strife between the Jews and the Samaritans the writer describes the latter as destructive elements, thorns and briers, and offers them a choice between annihilation and refuge with Yahweh.

I agree with Jacob in this interpretation. It is fairly evident that the two songs stand in an antithetical relationship to one another. Yahweh is here represented in ch. 27 as the protector of the vineyard he gave up to destruction in ch. 5 by eliminating hedge and wall, so that it now has an opportunity of growing and bearing fruit. But what calls for closer investigation is the purpose of the choice of motifs and of the changes carried out by the author of Isa. 27.2-5, as well as the purpose of the addition of v. 6.

Jacob does not concern himself with this addition. The reason is evidently that in terms of rhythm (but not in terms of theme) v. 6 differs from vv. 2-5. But Jacob is not quite clear on this point, since in his translation of the song he includes v. 6, although in parenthesis. We find a similar uncertainty as regards the demarcation of the song in Hans Wilderberger, who clearly bases himself on Jacob but gets into difficulties when he comes to define v. 6's function in the passage on 27.6-11. 'V. 6 ist *wohl so etwas wie* eine Überschrift über das ganze Stück' (my emphasis).[53]

To this I must say that what evidently disturbs the commentators is that, on the one hand, it is an extension of the original vineyard song and, on the other hand, that it represents a change of rhythm. In my opinion, this is because v. 6 must be seen as subsidiary to vv. 2-5, a conscious supplement reflecting the author's particular intention. The verse is therefore also held within the plant image, but as we shall see later the author here also exploits the available material, which may explain the change in rhythm.[54]

Similarities and Differences

Let us begin the analysis with a brief review of the similarities and differences between the two texts. Both passages are about a song of a vineyard (but different verbs are used for 'to sing') and about the figurative use of the vineyard. But whereas in Isa. 5.1-7 the hearers are given Isaiah's interpretation only in the last verse of the song, in Isa. 27.2-6 the interpretation comes through in the imagery right from the beginning. It is Yahweh who is the vineyard's guardian. It is clear from the different techniques that the purpose of the two texts is different. It was crucial in Isa. 5.1-7 that the hearers did not know the correct interpretation, and therefore unwittingly pronounced judgment on themselves. But this cannot be the point in Isa. 27.2-6.

Whereas Isa. 5.1 says that Isaiah will sing of his beloved and his vineyard, in Isa. 27.2 it is the hearers who will one day sing of a pleasant vineyard, כרם חמד. In Isa. 5.1, it is the beloved who is positively connotated; in Isa. 27.2 it is the vineyard.

Isa. 5.2 describes the vineyard owner's careful preparation of the ground, whose quality has already been described in v. 1, his construction of the vineyard, his positive expectations and his unexpected disappointment; 27.3 mentions only the guarding of the vineyard by its owner, Yahweh, and his constant watering of it. It is clear from 27.3f. that Yahweh guards it against outsiders, against thorns and briers.

The *similarities* are clear enough, but it is equally important that the *differences* are not fortuitous; the contrasts are deliberate. According to 27.2-6, the negative aspect is not to be found within the vineyard, for that is obviously כרם חמד; it is something external that threatens. In Isa. 5.1-7, on the contrary, it was the vineyard itself, the vines, that acted negatively.

Isa. 5.3-5 seems to be completely 'missing' in the later version, unless 27.4's reference to Yahweh's lack of wrath is to correspond to the wrath that presumably lies behind the vineyard owner's description of what he will do to his vineyard (Isa. 5.5).[55] This means that the trial motif has been omitted.

On the other hand, Isa. 5.6, with its description of the invasion of the vineyard by thorns and briers, is retained; but whereas in 5.6 these formed part of the vineyard owner's punishment of the vineyard, in 27.4 the vineyard owner wishes to combat them with all his might to protect his vineyard. Similarly, the motif of failing to water the vineyard as a punishment has been turned around, so that careful watering is introduced as an expression of the vineyard owner's continuing solicitude (Isa. 27.3).

That the watering itself is used to exemplify this is perhaps related to the interpretation we have briefly discussed on the basis of the Targum (cf. p. 108). If there is a connexion between the rain image and the prophetic message, it is understandable that the author, who must see himself as representative of 'the rain', emphasizes this very feature.

The use of שמיר ושית (thorns and briers) as an image of the negative forces is common to both versions; but whereas in 5.6 these are a link in the owner's punishment, in 27.4 they are a threat against which the owner wishes to fight. The wrath has turned against the vineyard's enemies, who are to be battled against, במלחמה אפשעה בה,

and burnt up, אציתנה יחד. These formulations are not chosen fortuitously, if we remember that the description of the punishment in 5.5 employed the words בער and מרמס, which can be seen as referring to burning up (but also cropping) and the enemy's devastation (but also trampling down) respectively. Common themes are therefore involved, although the same words are not employed.

Whereas the punishment in 5.5-6 is unrestricted, 27.5 leaves open an opportunity for the enemies to make peace with Yahweh if they lean on him—the expression should perhaps be understood as 'seek asylum with'.[56] Whereas 27.5 concludes with the possibility of שלום (peace) between the enemies and Yahweh, 5,1-7 mentions no such possibilty of a restoration of relations. The שלום that had been the natural state between Yahweh and his people, characterized by משפט (right) and צדקה (justice), does not become reality; in its place came the opposite to משפח:שלום (injustice) and צעקה (a cry).

But the clearest contrast between 5.1-7 and 27.2-6 appears in 27.6, where the people's happy future is described by using a plant image. Jacob/Israel shall in the days to come take root, put forth shoots, blossom and fill the world with fruit. Which plants are referred to is not said; but in the light of the context it is only logical to imagine a vine that grows, spreads and bears fruit. This is what the owner in 5.1-7 hoped for, but did not witness; according to 27.2-6, it will happen 'in that day'.

If we now *summarize* the observations we have arrived at from a comparison of the two texts, it becomes clear that there are in fact two *contrasting texts*. The older is characterized by Yahweh's wrath and judgment, while the later describes the end of the wrath—or rather its shifting on to those who threaten the people—and the positive future to follow.

The Intention of the Message
That the author of Isa. 27.2-6 chooses to formulate his text in such contrast to the original song about the vineyard is bound up with the intention of his message. He chooses a well-known and earlier-used image as an image of Israel, so that his message assumes some of the authority borne by the old Isaianic text. On the other hand, he renounces the surprise effect which the interpretation of the image had in Isa. 5.1-7. But the author has no need of this effect. From the very beginning, therefore, he can indentify the owner of the vineyard with Yahweh.

The author does not use imagery to conceal who the vineyard is because, as we touched upon earlier, the new song is not a lawsuit. Everything that in the old version showed it to be a disputation speech is consciously omitted. The intention of Isa. 27.2-6 is not to pronounce judgment on the vineyard, and not therefore to make the hearers pronounce judgment on themselves. The intention is primarily to *comfort and encourage* the hearers, who are Yahweh's vineyard. Only secondarily is it the purpose of the text to *exhort* the harmful elements to seek refuge with Yahweh.

We can see that this is the purpose of the text from the following: In Isa. 27.2, the author addresses himself directly to his hearers, with the imperative ענו־לה (sing of it!); he describes them positively as כרם חמד (a pleasant vineyard), and goes on to say that every threat against them is warded off by their God. The vineyard is cared for and guarded by the owner, and logically the pleasant vineyard will take root—ישרש יעקב probably means not only 'take root' but 'throw out suckers'[57]—put forth shoots, blossom and fill the whole world with fruit. Just as it was unnatural for the vineyard in Isa. 5.1-7 to bear wild grapes, so is the vineyard's reaction in 27.6 natural and convincing.

To understand fully the author's prophetic intention, however, one must investigate *the historical situation* in which the text came into existence and was spoken. There is wide agreement that this text from the Isaianic apocalypse belongs in time to the post-Exile period. In his discussion of the text, J. Vermeylen[58] emphasizes that, in its moderate attitude towards the enemies, it reflects a time when internal strife had created disruption within the community, but when there still existed an opportunity for atonement. Hans Wildberger[59] similarly considers the post-Exilic period's internal strife between *Jews and Samaritans* as a probable background to Isa. 27.2-6, but he points out that precise dating is not possible.

Viewed in the light of this situation, Isa. 27.2-6 contains not only a promise to the faithful in the community but also a warning to 'the others', to those who behave like thorns and briers, to face up to the fact that in reality they thereby become the enemies of Yahweh himself. They should therefore see the error of their ways and make peace with him, so that all Israel can bear fruit. Whereas the *performative* function of Isa. 5.1-7 consisted in the original situation of condemnation, it is here concerned with comforting and warning respectively the two groups in the community.

In analysing Isa. 5.1-7, I strongly emphasized the erotic connotations associated with the vineyard image. From the very beginning of the new version, we know that the song is to be about Yahweh and his vineyard, and this of course has the effect of moderating the erotic aspect; but it does not disappear.

The vineyard in 27.2 is described as חמד, a word that can be used about desire (cf. Exod. 20.17; Prov. 6.25; Song 2.3); Yahweh waters it, אשקנה, a formulation which is possibly a play on the root נשק, to kiss (cf. Song 8.1); יפקד עליה can indicate both protection against attack from the enemy and against visits from outside; חמה אין לי can be part of the suitor's courting, and other possibilities of this type might be mentioned.[60] Although I do not wish to go as far as Luis Alonso Schökel and say that Isa. 27.2-6 is a disguised love-song, like him I find it reasonable to submit that erotic imagery may be used elsewhere in the Old Testament about the relationship between Yahweh and Israel, for example in the book of Hosea and in Ezekiel.[61]

What is important in our context is, then, that whereas the essential function of the marriage code (the erotic element) in Isa. 5.1-7 is to conceal what is the correct code, in Isa. 27.2-6 it assists in giving the Yahweh-Israel code a special intonation. It is the beloved whom Yahweh will protect, just as, according to Isa. 5.7, it is Yahweh's favourite plant that is involved.

Apart from the vines, other plants appear in both texts, i.e. thorns and briers. Of whom the thorns and briers are images is not said directly; but it appears (cf. v. 5) that the reference is to people who might be conceived as converting to Yahweh and making peace with him. In the analysis of Isa. 5.6, we interpreted שמיר ושית as an image of the negative forces (lower social groups or external enemies) that wished to seize power if Yahweh's protection in the form of lawful leaders were absent. The intention in Isa. 27.4 must be the same, and depending upon the historical situation in which the text is employed the image can be understood as relating to internal or external enemies.[62] But it is most probable that Isa. 27.2-6 was originally directed against groups which were interpreted as enemies, but for whom there was still a possibility of repentance. As pointed out earlier, the *Samaritans* would correspond well to such a group that threatens to destroy the pleasant vineyard but cannot summarily be given over to extermination.

The situation is known from, e.g., Hag. 2.10ff., and we can

supplement the attitude Isa. 27.2-6 expresses by Isa. 4.2ff., where we encounter the concept of a necessary purification. Only when this has taken place can it sprout again. In post-Exilic times, the Samaritans were looked upon as impediments to the rebuilding of the Temple, and so to the coming time of joy.[63]

Before we leave the analysis of Isa. 5.1-7 and 27.2-6, one question must be asked. As we have said, Isa. 5.1-7 operates as the material for 27.2-6; but comparison of the two texts shows that Isa. 27.6 has no formal source in 5.1-7. In the original version of the vineyard image, the natural development in which the vineyard bears good fruit is a prerequisite expressed only in the owner's disappointed outburst in v. 4. Here, in Isa. 27.6, the thought has been given form. But does this form of language result from the author's own creative ability, or is it here also a reuse of existing material? This can only be answered after close analysis of the other tree images. Cf. pp. 136 and 226.

Conclusion

Apart from providing a number of results in regard to details, the analyses of Isa. 5.1-7 and 27.2-6 have outlined parts of what we may call the history of the utility of the vineyard image.[64] We have considered three phases which in my opinion reflect an important aspect of the prophetic message in use and reuse.

In the *first phase*, the original utility situation, Isaiah's intention is to involve his hearers in the message in such a way that they themselves pronounce the necessary judgment. The function of the image is primarily performative.

In the *second phase*, reuse in the eighth and sixth centuries, the image is utilized especially to give the information necessary for understanding the connexion between bearing wild grapes and being destroyed; most clearly of course in the context of the Exilic period's theodicy considerations.

The *third phase* is the contrasting version presented by Isa. 27.2-6. The original text could no longer be merely reinterpreted; a new presentation of the text was necessary in order to mould the message to the generation that experienced the home-coming from the Exile. But this new text is in fact a development of the old image. The object is not to condemn but to console and admonish. The text has a clear performative function, but at the same time it gives information about the necessity of purification before the positive time to come.

Both Isa. 5.1-7 and 27.2-6 can be used by the hearers/readers to adduce *information* about Yahweh's wishes for his people and his reasons for acting as he does. In other words, the image has been used to give *theological interpretations of the political situation*, just as Isaiah wished to give his interpretation of the political events of his time. The connexion between the people's actions and Yahweh's actions can be upheld by means of the vineyard image, and Yahweh's fairness established. Particularly in the original situation, the image has been instrumental in making the people pronounce judgment on themselves and thereby take over Isaiah's way of interpreting reality. But, as we have seen, the image has a *performative function* in reuse also.

A characteristic of the vineyard image is that it has been receptive to reinterpretation, and that it has occasioned a *production of new text*. Further analyses of tree images will show that we are in the presence of a phenomenon with something important to say about the prophetic message, as we know it from the book of Isaiah. The central apophthegm, often worded in imagery, can be reused in new situations, exposed to reinterpretation of various kinds, and in individual cases give grounds for a production of new text.

2. Analysis of Isa. 10.33-11.9, 10

Whereas in the case of Isa. 5.1-7 demarcation of the vineyard image presented no problem, it is very open to discussion whether the forest- felling image in Isa. 10.33-34 is an independent oracle, located only secondarily before the oracle about the new shoot of Jesse's stump, or whether Isa. 10.33-34 and 11.1-9 are so closely connected that they must originally have been one entity.

It has been stressed repeatedly that the context in which the image is placed is crucial to its understanding. But the context can change—and has quite certainly changed in the case of this image. The analysis must therefore fall into three sections: A, a section in which 10.33-34 + 11.1-9 are interpreted in the light of the existing, redactional context; B, a section in which we attempt to reveal the image's history of utility and to discuss the connexion between 10.33-34 and 11.1-9; and C, a section in which the reuse of 11.1 in the form of 11.10 is analysed with a view to closer analysis of v. 10's function in the chapter as a whole.

A. *Isa. 10.33-34 + 11.1-9 Read in the Redactional Context*

The oracle of Yahweh's destruction of the high trees of Lebanon (Isa. 10.33-34) is a direct extension of Isa. 10.5-32's description of the arrogant king of Assyria. Two parallel sequences disclose ch. 10's main theme, i.e. that *Assyria's pride* is about to fall, but this will be to the advantage of Israel.

In the first sequence, the king of Assyria is presented in a number of quotations (10.8-11 + 13-14) which disclose his overrating of himself and his failure to understand that in reality he is only a tool in the hands of Yahweh (10.5-7, 15). It is made clear by means of the quotations that this pride is not just something of which he is accused by others; in fact, his own words betray him. This provides the necessary proof of the justice of the subsequent judgment oracle (Isa. 10.16-19).

The second sequence is also introduced with proof of the king of Assyria's pride, i.e. in the description of his successful advance against Jerusalem (Isa. 10.28-32). The names of the towns the Assyrian army passes in its forced march are reeled off in short, sharp sentences. The descriptive technique is the same as in Isa. 10.8-11, where the captured towns are listed from Carchemish to Samaria, and in both texts the North-South movement acts as a strong threat against Jerusalem. Like the quotations in Isa. 10.8-11 + 13-14, the situation report in Isa. 10.28-32 also acts to provide authenticity: so has the king of Assyria notoriously spoken, we heard it ourselves; this is what he did, we saw it ourselves. In the light of this, Yahweh must in justice pronounce judgment upon him (Isa. 10.33-34).

Both *chains of reasoning* conclude in judgment oracles, and the use of tree images is common to both oracles. The king of Assyria's punishment is described by the image of a forest fire (Isa. 10.16-19) and of forest-felling (Isa. 10.33-34).

The redactional composition is therefore clear and symmetrical, as is further underlined by glancing at the oracles that follow the two judgment oracles. Both Isa. 10.20-27 and 11.1-9 contain promises of a positive future for Israel. Assyria's fall signifies Israel's rehabilitation.

Against whom the judgment oracle is directed is a question that has been exhaustively discussed in the context of both Isa. 10.16-19 and Isa. 10.33-34. But the majority believe[1] that 10.33-34 must be read in the light of its literary context—i.e. the polemic against the king of Assyria in 10.5-15—as a judgment upon the king of Assyria by reason of his hubris.

J. Vermeylen and H. Barth

An example of such an interpretation is to be found in J. Vermeylen.[2] *Vermeylen* defines Isa. 10.33-34 as an addition to 10.27b-32. Whereas, in Vermeylen's opinion, 10.27b-32 is probably a description of Sargon II's march against Ashdod in 712,[3] written anonymously, 10.33-34 is a redactional addition, meant—together with 10.27b-32— as a commentary on Isa. 10.5-14*, which at this time was placed directly before 10.27bff. The prophecy is specified in 10.27b-32: the king of Assyria wished to attack the holy city, Jerusalem. '... le rédacteur, qui tient Sion pour la cité inviolable de Yahvé, l'accuse du crime de lèse-majesté.'[4] Assyria's punishment is then described in vv. 33-34. What is therefore involved is reinterpretation, or, as Vermeylen calls it, 'relecture'. This re-reading has taken place in the context of reappraising the events at the end of the eighth century: Samaria's destruction and Jerusalem's miraculous salvation.

Moreover, Vermeylen sees Isa. 11.1-5 as a consciously constructed antithesis to Isa. 10.33-34. The little shoot of Jesse's stump is contrasted with the great trees. Now that Assyria has fallen, Judah can sprout. Analysis of the vocabulary and ideology leads to the result that Isa. 11.1-5 belongs to the time of Josiah's assumption of power in 639. Josiah was only eight years old, a little sprout, when he came to the throne after the murder of his father, King Amon. As we know, this assumption of power coincided with the Assyrian nation's decline; the great trees are felled.[5]

If we follow Vermeylen's interpretation, we are faced with the phenomenon that a redactor undertakes a re-reading, and so an interpretation, of an older text, *in casu Isa. 10.5-14**. But not all scholars will be in agreement with this. In his book on the productive new interpretation (Barth's description of reinterpretation) of the Isaianic tradition in Josiah's time, *Hermann Barth*[6] has undertaken a fundamental analysis of Isa. 10.27bff. Barth emphasizes the distinct link with Isa. 2.9-17, in that he sees Isa. 10.27b-32 + 10.33b-34 as a substantiation of the judgment (*Isa. 2.9-17*) proclaimed upon all the high and the proud. Isa. 10.27b-32 + 10.33b-34 make it clear that the destruction coming from the north, which in 2.12ff. is described as a theophany, will become a reality if the Assyrians march against

Jerusalem and the city receives its punishment. Barth therefore interprets Lebanon as Jerusalem, not as the king of Assyria!

Vermeylen and Barth agree that Isa. 10.27b-34 is the result of reinterpretation, i.e. a more detailed commentary on an older Isaiah text. But they do not agree about which older Isaiah text it is. According to Vermeylen it is Isa. 10.5-14*, which describes the *king of Assyria's* pride. What this pride consists in is explained in 10.27b-32, which shows that the king of Assyria commits 'lèse-majesté' by marching against Yahweh's own city. Verses 33-34 describe the punishment for pride. According to Barth, it is Isa. 2.9-14 that is commented on. What is described in 2.9-14 as man's pride, which is to be punished, is now referred to more precisely as *Jerusalem's* pride.

In my opinion, the disagreement between Barth and Vermeylen is bound up with the fact that they are concerned with Isa. 10.33-34's significance at different times in the oracle's *history of utility*. Analysis of the tree image in this text therefore renders necessary a clarification of the text's history.

B. *Isa. 10.33-34 + 11.1-9's History of Utility*

By way of introduction, we shall analyse the judgment oracle in 10.33-34 as an independent entity, disregarding the redactional context. In both form and content, it is a well-balanced oracle about a coming calamity. The calamity is described as a felling, in which Yahweh fells the trees of Lebanon. Read in continuation of the oracles about the king of Assyria, it was most natural to understand this as *imagery*. But to perceive the trees figuratively in the existing context does not automatically mean that they were always used and understood figuratively, irrespective of context. In order to determine whether Isa. 10.33-34 is to be understood figuratively even without the existing context, it is appropriate to investigate whether Lebanon may perhaps be a traditional image.

Excursus
Lebanon[7] is referred to about seventy times in the Old Testament, but of these references only just over a third are a purely geographical designation (cf. Deut. 1.7; Josh. 1.4; 11.17) or used in the context of exploiting the trees of Lebanon as building material (cf. 1 Kgs 5.23ff. (RSV 5.9ff.); Ezra 3.7). The remaining two-thirds all show a direct figurative use of Lebanon (cf. Judg.

9.15; Ezek. 17.3; 27.5; Ps. 92.13) or a use clearly exploiting the connotations associated with Lebanon as the exemplary place (cf. Isa. 33.9; Ps. 29.5f.; Song 4.8).

If we compare the many texts that refer to Lebanon, a picture emerges of a fertile and beautiful place. The glory of the new time can indeed be described in terms of Lebanon's glory (Isa. 35.2; 60.13), and similarly the extent of the disaster becomes evident when the prophet describes how Lebanon withers and mourns (Isa. 33.9; Nah. 1.4).

Lebanon is in fact not just a place with positive connotations; it is also a threatened place.[8] Its trees are in danger of felling and other forms of destruction (Isa. 2.13; 10.34; 14.8; 37.24; Ezek. 31.10ff.; Zech. 11.1; Ps. 29.5). As we have seen, Stolz has pointed out that behind many texts about the felling of Lebanon's trees lies an old myth, according to which a garden of God with special trees is to be found at the top of Lebanon. There is little reason to doubt that ideas about such a garden existed, and that these ideas were known in the Palestinian region; cf. merely the descriptions of the Garden of Eden in Genesis 2–3 and the reference to Eden, the garden of God, Ezek. 28.11ff. But in the Old Testament there are different traditions about the location of the garden.

In an article about the four rivers of paradise, Sigmund Mowinckel[9] has advanced the thesis that the garden of paradise was thought to be located in the Armenian mountains in the farthest north, i.e. in almost inaccessible regions. Mowinckel himself points out that this is only one of the traditions about the location of the garden of God. What is important in our context is that we probably have a similar tradition in the case of Lebanon.

In support of this, we can turn, as we have seen, to Ezek. 31.16, where the trees of Eden are referred to as the trees of Lebanon. But Walther Zimmerli[10] believes that there is no compelling reason to associate with Lebanon the ideas about Eden on which Ezekiel 28 is based, and he therefore sees no connexion between these ideas in ch. 31. But it must be said here that, although the ideas about Lebanon and Eden have *different origins* in the history of tradition, the repeated use of the names Eden and Lebanon in Ezekiel 31 itself means that these ideas are associated in the hearers' minds, and that Lebanon thereby assumes connotations from Eden. It is clear therefore that a text such as Ezek. 31 is helping either to create or (and I believe this to be the case) to strengthen an already-existing connexion between the ideas about Eden and the ideas about Lebanon.

Fritz Stolz also goes to much trouble to emphasize that the traditions about Lebanon's garden of God and those about the Garden of Eden are two different traditions. The cedars of Lebanon are not trees of life, but must be seen as expressing the world-tree concept. But, in constrast to Zimmerli, Stolz believes that Ezekiel in fact combines the two themes as an innovation.[11] In this connection, one might also point to the ideas in Dan.

4.10ff., where there is an analogous combination. It is true that this is a late text, but many of its ideas are old.

Whereas the book of Daniel does not associate the tree with Lebanon, in the Song of Solomon's imagery we encounter a combination of Lebanon and the garden of paradise, which in my opinion also deserves consideration. Song 4.12ff. describes the bride as a locked garden filled with trees, with a fountain whose water comes from Lebanon. For my part, there is no doubt that we are here confronted with an exploitation of the paradise motif, but with the change, compared with Genesis 2, that the garden is not placed far away in the Armenian highlands but in the familiar and highly esteemed Lebanon.[12]

In imagery, therefore, nothing prevents a combination of these motifs. The similarity between the ideas of Eden and Lebanon is fully able to overcome any differences (particularly if these differences are primarily of an *historical* nature). That such a combination is possible and has occurred is not of course evidence that this also took place in all other texts which use Lebanon as an image. Whether this is so must be decided in the light of analysis of the text concerned and its context. What we have indicated here are just some of the *potential meanings* Lebanon implies.

But to return to Stolz's thesis: a characteristic element in the ideas about the garden of God is that it is subject to destruction. It is either a stranger who perpetrates an injustice against it or it is Yahweh himself who destroys the trees. In Isa. 14.8; 37.24 (2 Kgs 19.23), the felling is seen as an act of violence that merits punishment; in Isa. 2.13; 10.34, on the other hand, it is an act of punishment executed by Yahweh. The fact that it is Yahweh who destroys the trees of the garden of God calls for an explanation. This explanation is found in Ezekiel 31: the trees have been guilty of pride. Whereas in Isa. 14.8 and 37.24 (2 Kgs 19.23) pride is a characteristic of the destroyer who fells the trees, in Isa. 2.13 and Ezekiel 31, for example, it is a characteristic of the trees which are destroyed. We can see here how the motif is turned, and thereby used to give a theological interpretation of the destruction.

We have now come to the end of the discussion on the use of Lebanon as an image. *To summarize*, it can be said that Lebanon has frequently been used as an image, and connotes an especially fertile place. According to certain traditions, there was at the top of Lebanon a garden of God; this is sometimes identified with the Garden of Eden. Lebanon is at the same time exposed to threats of destruction, either by external powers or by Yahweh himself. But this does not preclude that the fundamental connotations are positive. Lebanon is the epitome of fertility, beauty, greatness and power. We shall now investigate whether these concepts underlie Isa. 10.33-34.

Isa. 10.33-34

The judgment oracle is introduced by a description of Yahweh as a tree-feller. Verse 33a emphasizes Yahweh and his activity. It is pointed out that it is the Lord, the Yahweh of Hosts, who lops the boughs with terrifying power. It then focuses on the fallen trunks, characterized by their height (v. 33b); but only in v. 34 does it become clear that it is Lebanon which is struck by the Almighty.

There are strong indications that the oracle is a genuine Isaianic oracle. The designation האדון יהוה צבאות (the Lord, the Yahweh of Hosts) is to be found, apart from here, in Isa. 1.24; 10.16; 19.4 (cf. אדני יהוה צבאות in Isa. 3.15; 10.23, 24; 22.5, 12, 14, 15; 28.22). Among the quite rare words the oracle includes, there is reason to note the expression used for the terrifying force במערצה (hapax legomenon). This has presumably been chosen for the sake of the wordplay on מעצדה, axe, the word one would expect in connexion with felling. Whereas מעצדה does not arouse associations other than the tool the word indicates, מערצה causes the hearer to think of both the implement itself and the terror the use of it provokes.

Apart from this, it must be said as regards the *choice of words* that the words רום, גבה, שפל and לבנון are repeated in Isa. 2.9-17. For example, רום/רם is used in Isa. 2.11, 12, 13, 14, 17; גבה is used in 2.11, 15, 17; שפל is used in 2.9, 11, 12, 17, and finally לבנון is mentioned in 2.13. A remarkably large degree of congruence is therefore present in regard to the choice of words in these two texts.

If one investigates the semantic domain of the words referred to above, it appears that the root רום, apart from being a spatial statement, can also signify 'to be proud' (cf. Deut. 8.14; 17.20; Ezek. 31.10; Hos. 13.6; Dan. 11.12; Ps. 131.1; and Prov. 30.13, etc.) or mean, as a substantive, 'pride' (cf. Isa. 2.11, 17; 10.12). It is indeed this meaning that comes through Isa. 2,9-17's polemic against all that is high, including the high trees and the high mountains. Similarly, one might imagine that the description of places of worship as high-lying in, e.g., Ezek. 6.13 and 20.28 indicates not only this spatial location.[13]

The root גבה, as well as having the meaning 'to be high', also means 'to be arrogant'; cf. as to this latter meaning, e.g. Isa. 3.16; 5.15; Jer. 13.15; Ezek. 16.50; 28.2, 5, 17.[14]

The root שפל similarly belongs to the domain surrounding the concept of pride, in that שפל, apart from indicating purely spatially a low location, very frequently describes the humiliation of the proud.

Cf. e.g., apart from the passages in Isaiah 2, Isa. 13.11; 25.11.

The similarity between Isa. 10.33 and Isa. 2.12-17 causes Hermann Barth to draw the conclusion that Isa. 10.27b-32 + 10.33b-34 is a reinterpretation of 2.9-17. But, according to Barth, that a reinterpretation is involved does not mean that Isaiah is not himself the author of Isa. 10.27b–11.5, although it is most probable that a traditionist whose theology is closely related to that of Isaiah was concerned. But Barth does not seem happy with this solution, which if one follows his argument is indeed constructed on a somewhat speculative foundation.[15] It is therefore much simpler to see Isa. 2.12-17 and 10.33-34 as related oracles, both of which go back to Isaiah. But this need not imply that Isaiah reinterpreted 2.9-17 in the later oracle in order to make it clear that the Assyrians are Yahweh's tool.

Whereas it is clear from the beginning of v. 33a who the subject of the action is, only at the end does it become apparent what the object is, i.e. the majestic trees of *Lebanon*. But the clarification is only apparent; the hearer must himself carry out a further clarification: what does the trees-of-Lebanon image represent?

That the image attempts to exploit the connotations of the name Lebanon, implying greatness, is apparent from the description of the trees, which are characterized only by their height.

Isaiah employs a traditional image, and evokes a great number of associations of a positive nature among his hearers. But his own description of these trees and his definition of who the tree-feller is represents a twist in the well-known motif. The trees are not the holy, protected trees, the tree-feller is not the usurper who tries to seize power; it is the proud trees that fall under the Almighty's hand. Confronting these trees, whose greatness and strength is interpreted as pride, stands Yahweh, whose power and might is so integrated and so naturally part of his nature that the greatness can be discerned from his names.

In the redactional context, the trees of Lebanon are an image of the haughty king of Assyria; but read outside this context, as an original Isaianic text, this image need not refer to the king of Assyria. The proud trees can equally well be used figuratively to refer to, for example, the king of Judah. What the tree image originally represented depends on the specific context in which Isaiah uttered the words.

Isa. 10.33-34's Original Context

The question is, then, whether we are able to say anything at all about the original context, or whether any attempt at this remains pure guesswork? We are not in a position to determine what preceded v. 33's הנה. On the other hand, it is worth considering whether the existing passage, Isa. 11.1-9, would have been the tree-felling image's original context, i.e. whether the existing literary context reflects the original situation in which Isaiah uttered the oracle.

The conjecture that *Isa. 10.33-34* also originally continued in *11.1-9* is supported by the fact that 11.1 is formulated in imagery, and even employs a tree image. Whereas vv. 33-34 describe the felling of the trees, v. 1 describes a shoot growing out of the stump, and in vv. 1-9 it becomes clear that this shoot is an image of the righteous king, the scion of David.

The observation that Isa. 10.33-34 and 11.1ff. are closely associated is not new. Herder[16] already interpreted 10.33-34 as referring to David's line, from whose roots grow the new shoot (Isa. 11.1). If these three verses are read in context, we get a picture in which the negative and the positive are held together organically, and in which the hearers' 'glance' performs a natural movement from the high trees' branches, which are lopped, onwards to the trunks, which fall to the ground, and finally to the stump, from which sprouts the new shoot.

Read together, then, the image expresses the same basic idea, which we are familiar with from Job 14.7-9: even if the tree is felled, it can sprout again. That the Job passage is somewhat later than the Isaiah text is of no significance in this context, where the point is that the image expresses an every-day experience which has found linguistic form also in a text such as the book of Job.

But there are certain problems about this interpretation. Whereas 11.1 speaks of the stump and root of Jesse, 10.33-34 describes the felling of a forest; it is not a single tree that is felled, subsequently to sprout again. Whereas 10.33-34 clearly keeps within the plant image, the trees of Lebanon, 11.1 speaks of the stump of Jesse, i.e. Jesse's line. These differences may arise because it is not an original cohesive image that is concerned but, in fact, an original redactional marrying together, whether one supposes Isaiah himself or another to be the redactor.

Isa. 11.1

We shall therefore look a little closer at the *choice of words and construction* of 11,1. To describe the new king, the words חטר (branch) and נצר (shoot) are employed. Apart from here, חטר is used only in Prov. 14.3 where it is normally read as an instrument of punishment, a rod (cf. Prov. 10.13, which in general terms says the same but uses the word שבט). In Isa. 11.1, חטר, describes something that grows from the root, i.e. a shoot. But the distance between shoot and instrument of punishment is not as great as may immediately appear. Gesenius–Buhl point out that חטר is related to the Assyrian ḫuṭaru and ḫuṭartu, which means sceptre, while Baumgartner refers to the Accadian ḫaṭṭu, which also means sceptre. This connexion between sceptre and shoot corresponds entirely to the connexion, demonstrated by Geo Widengren in particular, between the concept of the king's sceptre and the concept of the tree of life.[17]

The word חטר is used in parallel with נצר. In addition to Isa. 11.1, נצר is used in Isa. 60.21, where it similarly refers to the vigorous shoot as an image of each individual of the people who, when the time comes, will enjoy a 'royal' existence in the new Jerusalem. In addition, the word is used in Dan. 11.7 (in a description of the king who will replace the other) to describe the new king who grows from the roots of his predecessor (the queen of the south), i.e. entirely parallel with Isa. 11.1. But it should be remembered that the book of Daniel is a late text.

Finally, נצר is employed in Isa. 14.19 in the satirical song directed against the king of Babel, a text to which we shall return. After his fall, the king lies 'like a shoot that is loathed'. נצר is thus employed in association with concepts of royal ideology. There is scarcely any doubt that the image in Isa. 11.1 is also based on Near-Eastern royal ideology.[18]

The shoot comes forth from the stump of Jesse, מגזע ישי, the branch grows from his roots, משרשיו. The word גזע is employed only three times in the Old Testament. As in Job 14.8, it is used here about the stump that can put out new branches, while the meaning in Isa. 40.24 corresponds precisely to the meaning of שרש. שרש is the normal word for root. It is frequently used figuratively, e.g. Hos. 9.16, when Ephraim's root is said to be dried up; Hos. 14.6, where Israel is promised to strike root like Lebanon; Ezek. 17.6, 7, 9, where the vine is an image of Israel; Ezek. 31.7, where Pharaoh is described as a great cedar; Dan. 11.7, where the new king is described as a branch,

נצר, of the roots of the queen of the south. Hans Wildberger[19] refers to שרש as typical Isaianic usage; it should be added that Isaiah's contemporaries Hosea and Amos (cf. Amos 2.9) also use שרש in the context of tree images. Ezekiel's frequent use, on the other hand, may very well reflect a later reuse of precisely Isaiah's tree images.

It is clear from the combination with the name of David's father, Jesse, that root is used figuratively. The proper name Jesse is of course used quite literally, so that it comes to function as the interpretative key to the image. The point of mentioning the name Jesse is to designate the future king not as a fortuitous member of the line of David but in fact as a new *David*, a point scarcely surprising in an Isaianic context.

The family tree must of course be an individual tree from whose stump the new branch grows—and not from an entire forest. What we learn about in Isa. 10.33-34, on the other hand, is the felling of an entire forest. *Hermann Barth* suggests, as a solution to this problem, that the original image consisted only of 10.33a + 11.1. 11.1 relates to an individual tree, i.e. the king, whereas 10.33b-34 concerns more generally the 'high' and the 'lofty'. Whereas 10.33a describes the lopping of one tree, where the naked trunk remains, according to vv. 33b-34 the trees are hewn down. Whereas the destruction in v. 33a presumably occurs during a violent storm (Barth's interpretation of what lies in the expression במערצה), vv. 33b-34 speak of iron tools. Barth must therefore conclude: 'Die alte, jesajanische Einheit am Übergang von c. 10 zu 11 umfasst 10,33a + 11,1-5; 10,33b-34 ist späterer Zusatz'.[20]

Barth's solution is initially tempting. The problem quite simply disappears—but the method of removing the problem is alarming. Barth's claim to logic and cogency does not seem reasonable, and in reality strikes at his own attempt at a solution. For if only v. 33a describes the destruction of the tree as a prerequisite for the new sprouting it is necessary to identify the remaining trunk with 11.1's גזע and שרשים (stump and roots), which is scarcely possible.[21] 10.33a + 11.1 do not therefore provide the clear, logical and coherent image of one tree's 'felling' that Barth seeks. Moreover, one must perhaps ask Barth why the redactor supplements this short and clear image with his extra sentences about the felling of a forest, and why he does this so awkwardly?

I must therefore prefer the reading already proposed of *Isa. 10.33-34 + 11.1* as a *coherent image*. But this is not to say that I close my eyes to Barth's observation of the complexity of the image, for he is of course right that it relates to both one tree and an entire forest. That I nevertheless find it acceptable to retain the image as an entity is not only because of the precariousness of Barth's method but because this tree image is not alone in this complexity, not alone in operating with both an individual tree and an entire forest.

The use of the tree image in the book of Ezekiel also reflects gradual transitions between the concepts of a large forest and of a particularly high tree, perhaps a tree of life or world-tree. For example, Ezekiel 31 deals primarily perhaps with the misfortune of the great cedar tree, but the cedar is apparently one of Eden's many different trees, and in the final instance they suffer the same fate when all trees crash down into the nether world.

As will be clear from the analyses of Isa. 14.4b-20 and Isa. 37.22b-32, here also both the forests' trees in general and one particular tree are concerned, and in Zech. 11.2 there is to be lamentation over the fallen cedar and the fallen forest.[22]

Unless we are to assume secondary additions in all the passages referred to, the very moment that our train of thought moves from the one tree to the many trees it would probably be wise to accept that we are in the presence of a complex of ideas involving both aspects. Whether this results from a combination of originally different traditions or from a conscious desire to refer, via a complex image, to both a king and a dynasty (cf. Zech. 11.2) I am unable to decide. But I believe there is reason to stress that what, in our opinion, the complex image loses in lucidity and logic is perhaps gained in the form of greater usability, i.e. because of its increased potential meanings.

Isa. 10.33-11.9

Before we leave discussion of the authenticity and scope of the tree image in Isa. 10.33ff., there is just one further observation I wish to make. The analysis of Isa. 5,1-7 showed the sense for effect that Isaiah was able to formulate in his message. From a literary aspect, Isa. 10.33-11.9 is not perhaps on a level with the vineyard song and its surprising interpretation; but nevertheless a little of the technique and a little of the author's awareness of what it means to speak to the audience so that they permit themselves to become involved in what is being said is recognizable.

That the tree-feller is Yahweh is said right from the beginning of v. 33, but only at the end of v. 34 is it explained that the forest is in Lebanon, and only then does 11.1 give the information that it is the stump of Jesse that puts out a new shoot, after which 11.2-9 elaborates on the implications of this.

The image clearly shows that the great trees resist Yahweh with their pride, and the frequent use of the image of a large tree or trees to refer to the king/dynasty makes it probable that the hearers' associations were moving in the direction of the royal house. Moreover, Isaiah appears to have made no secret of his views on, for example, king Ahaz (cf. ch. 7), when he haughtily relies on his own military forces (perhaps in league with various coalition partners [Isa. 31.1ff.]),[23] and not on Yahweh.

The specifying of Lebanon seems merely further to strengthen the connexion with the royal house. It is the great trees of Lebanon, i.e. the cedars, that are felled. They are not random trees but the kind of tree used especially as the royal symbol. And the use of the name Jesse not only makes it clear that the people's own king was earlier concerned but also—and this is in contrast to the original basic narrative—that this felling will not after all be the catastrophe it is for Pharaoh, for example, in Ezekiel 31; for after the felling follows new budding.

After the image of the new king as a shoot from the old stump, there follows an informative description of this king's weapons. In our connexion, it is important to point out that, in the context, the description of the new king operates to interpret the image of the shoot/branch. This interpretation is given primarily in non-figurative language, so that the earlier image's meaning is defined and protected against arbitrary interpretation. In the same way that Isa. 5.7 settled all discussion about to whom the image of the vineyard referred, Isa. 11.2-9 establishes, although without using the word 'king', that the new shoot is a king. According to 11.2-5, he is equipped with the spirit of Yahweh, the spirit that gives wisdom, counsel, might, knowledge of Yahweh and fear of Yahweh. The king can therefore pronounce righteous judgment and help the weak against the wicked and godless. In consequence of this just rule, his kingdom becomes a kingdom of peace to which paradisiacal conditions have returned (Isa. 11.6-9).

We have now read Isa. 10.33–11.9 in context, and in the course of this we have been able to show a close connexion between 10.33-34 and 11.1-9. Both passages employ the tree image, and both passages use this as an image of a king and a dynasty, a use corresponding entirely to the image's king-ideological background. The analysis has also shown that there is nothing against, but much to support, the tree image as an authentic Isaianic oracle—and we cannot expect to get any closer than this in regard to the question of authenticity.

Read as suggested, Isa. 10.33–11.9 forms a consciously created entity that interprets the *fall of the proud king of Judah* as resulting from Yahweh's righteous *punishment*, but then proclaims that the dynasty will nevertheless endure; a new king, a *new David* will appear, and he will be a regent favoured by God over the kingdom of peace. The connexion between tree-felling and new sprouting is as organic as it is possible to imagine: from the lineage of the old king is born the new king of Judah. It is otherwise in the redactional context, where the punishment of the king of Assyria, the felling of the great tree, is the negative background to the promise of the shoot from the root of Jesse.

But the analysis has also shown something further which is worthy of note. If we compare the Isa. 10.33ff. version with the tree-felling myth Stolz has demonstrated, then the Isaiah text is not merely a manifestation of a theological treatment, whereby the tree-felling becomes a righteous punishment of Yahweh's own king, but has been supplemented by a new motif: the promise of the new king's birth, indicated by the image of the new shoot budding forth. Here, Isaiah has not only reinterpreted the old myth but has also created, in extension of it, a new and crucial link. We are therefore confronted with an example of *production of new text*, a phenomenon we also identified in the analysis of Isa. 5.1-7's history of utility.

This reconstruction, therefore, returns us to the question we were forced to leave open at the end of the analysis of Isa. 5.1-7 + 27.2-6. We considered there whether the positive conclusion of Isa. 27.2-6 was the result of the author's own creative power or whether it was a matter of reusing available material. The analysis of Isa. 11.1 has made it very probable that we are confronted with such reuse. Further argument in support of this is to be found in the analyses of Isa. 37.31 and Isa. 4.2.

Isa. 10.33–11.9 in the Wider Literary Context

We have now analysed Isa. 10.33–11.9 as an independent entity that prophesies collectively Yahweh's judgment upon the king of Judah and Yahweh's wish to restore the fallen dynasty by providing it with an heir apparent. But, as we know, this oracle is not isolated in the book of Isaiah; it is placed in continuation of a number of oracles directed against the king of Assyria. We shall therefore return below to the tree image's meaning in the wider literary context.

Since the Assyrians gradually assume an increasingly active role on the political scene, their role must also be seen as a link in Yahweh's plan for his people, and it is this attempt at interpretation which is reflected in some of the redactional work relative to ch. 10.

It is evident from, for example, the additions to Isa. 7.17: את מלך אשור and in 7.20: במלך אשור that it is important for redactors to define the function Yahweh intended for the Assyrians. The king of Assyria is seen here as Yahweh's instrument of punishment following the people's disobedience.

The interpretation of the king of Assyria as an instrument of punishment is to be found, however, not only in the redactional additions but also in Isaiah's own prophecy. One example of this is the oracle in Isa. 10.27b-32, which may very well reflect one part of the Assyrian king Sargon II's punitive expedition against Judah in 712. According to Isaiah, this march, which did not lead to an attack on Jerusalem, was Yahweh's clear warning to the leaders in Jerusalem not to continue in their current policy.

There is no reason to doubt that Isaiah saw *the Assyrians as Yahweh's tool*, and the king of Assyria as the cudgel with which Yahweh would strike Judah in his wrath (cf. Isa. 10.5). But as the situation evolves towards 701 the Assyrians' role in Yahweh's plan must become increasingly uncertain. Although the leaders in Jerusalem do not heed Isaiah's warnings to keep quiet and to abstain from political transactions in the form of alliances against the Assyrians, and although Isaiah still has something to say to his countrymen about this, *the events of 701* must have caused a *change* in attitude towards Assyria. The king of Assyria's siege is and remains an insult against Yahweh himself, and this cannot go unpunished. Isaiah must therefore curse the king of Assyria, who did not understand that he was only an axe in Yahweh's hand, and believed that he himself was the hand (Isa. 10.5ff.).

This change in attitude towards the Assyrians' role, which must of course have increased throughout the following century as the destruction of the kingdom of Assyria approached, has, then, formed a basis for reinterpretation of parts of Isaiah's message. The crisis forms a foundation for hermeneutic activity, as R.P. Carroll expresses it. We do not know whether Isaiah himself, shortly after 701, contributed to this; on the other hand, the redaction of Isaiah 10 shows that such reinterpretation took place in the circles which passed on the Isaiah tradition. In the light of 701, some of the words of judgment that in the earlier period were directed against Judah can now be interpreted as referring to the Assyrians. Yahweh's wrath is soon gone; Zion will no longer be afraid of the king of Assyria, for now Yahweh directs his wrath against him and removes the yoke that Judah has borne (cf. Isa. 10,24-27a). Now it is the king of Assyria's richness and magnificence—not Judah's—that Yahweh attacks (cf. the analysis of Isa. 10.16-19); now it is the king of Assyria who is to have his boughs lopped and to fall like the trees of Lebanon (Isa. 10.33-34); and now it is this destruction that forms the background to the promises about Judah's future, of which Isaiah has been the prophet (Isa. 11.1ff.)

It is, then, this sequence of developments to which Isa. 10.5ff. bears indirect witness by the redactional placing of the individual oracles. At the redactional point in time, the relationship to the Assyrians played such an important role that it is the punishment of Assyria which becomes the *leitmotif* of the chapter. We do not know when ch. 10 received its final form. Hermann Barth, who sees Josiah's time as a very productive period of continual reinterpretation, considers surprisingly enough, in the light of the role the Assyrian kingdom played,[24] that the juxtaposition of Isa. 10.27b-11.5 is not the result of reinterpretation of that period but of an older reinterpretation, perhaps even the result of Isaiah's own redactional work. This is bound up with the fact that Barth has an eye only for the connexion between Isa. 10.27b-34 and 11.1-5, and does not concern himself with the new interpretation of which the precedent of Isa. 10.5ff. is an expression.

J. Vermeylen believes that the combination of Isa. 10.27b-32, 33-34 and 11.1-5 belongs to 639, when Josiah came to the throne. On that occasion, 11,1-5 was composed as a tribute to the new young king and as a deliberate contrast to 10.33-34's description of the fall of the king of Assyria.[25]

Dating

If in the light of the analysis undertaken we now try to date the juxtaposition of the oracles in Isa. 10.5-11.9, I see it as important to start from the fact that Isa. 10.33-34 is formulated in an imagery that permits the oracle to change its meaning according to the situation and the context.

This is what occurs when the cursing of the king of Assyria in Isa. 10.5ff and the description of the march in Isa. 10.27b-32 precedes Isa. 10.33-11.9.[26] This juxtaposition must have come into being after the events of 701, and must have taken place before the fall of the Assyrian empire, when it still had a function beyond the purely retrospective and explanatory. An important aspect of the prophetic use of cursing is, in fact, that the person cursed appears to enjoy the best of health! But we have little chance of determining how close we are to 701 or how close we are to 612, the fall of Nineveh. I do not believe that, like J. Vermeylen, we can identify a precise year, for example 639. Vermeylen's belief that he can be certain that Isa. 11.1-5 was written on the occasion of Josiah's assumption of power must be because he overlooks not only that these verses contain images which can be used on many different occasions but also that the entire linguistic usage is so characteristic of liturgical language as to make precise dating almost impossible. For example, there is nothing in these verses to suggest that they are not Isaiah's.

On the other hand, what we can say with some degree of certainty is that the juxtaposition of Isa. 10.33-11.9 with the polemic against the king of Assyria in 10.5ff. expresses a view of the political situation which corresponds very closely to the view that must have prevailed in the period leading up to Josiah's assumption of power. In this situation, Isa. 10.33-34 could of course have been seen as Yahweh's righteous punishment of the arrogant king of Assyria, and as an appropriate background to the new period soon to come—perhaps even imminent—with Josiah's kingdom.

The relation the imagery postulates between tree-felling and new sprouting, originally a relation between the fall of the haughty king of Judah and the dynasty's continuation, is now singled out in another place, i.e. as a relation between the destruction of the kingdom of Assyria and the flowering of the kingdom of Judah. The political events are here once again made to act as a coherent link in the divine plan, in which the punishment of the kingdom of Judah may be seen as a stage over and done with. The plan now brought to accomplishment has two vital elements: punishment for Assyria—salvation for Judah.

Summary
What we have been able to show, then, in this analysis is how a specific image has been able to function as an interpretative key to the political situation. It has become possible, via the image, to look at relationships which the people had until then been unable to see. The image has suggested a new way of perceiving reality.

The image is taken from the flora. Its strength lies in its evident accuracy; everyone knows from his own experience that this is the way things are with trees.[27] The tree as a metaphor is among the elementary metaphors whose suitability and capacity to survive are evidenced by their continual reuse. But in regard to the Old Testament's tree images there is the additional fact that they came into being in a culture in which the tree's holiness was a natural assumption, and in which the fundamental myth of the fertility cult, which affected everyone, had the same elementary message as the image of the tree that is felled but sprouts again: despite all, death is overcome by life.

In Isaiah's version, the image is employed to argue indirectly that *imperatives*, as recognized by nature's world and the world of the myth, are also present in—and will prevail in—the political world. Whatever holds good within the code to which the tree belongs is also postulated, via the imagery, as holding good within the political code. Isaiah's original prophetic intention, then, was to warn his contemporaries against the coming calamity, and to comfort them by saying that even though the present king is about to fall Yahweh has not abandoned David's dynasty; it will sprout again!

C. *Isa. 11.10's Meaning and Function*

One of the characteristic features of imagery is, as frequently emphasized, its context-dependency. This means that a figurative statement can often act as a connecting link between two passages. Such use of the tree image is to be found in Isa. 11.10, where part of the image in 11.1 is re-employed as an intermediary between the chapter's two main passages, 11.1-9 and 11.11-16.

J. Vermeylen dates this verse to the post-Exile period. In his opinion, it was added to 11.1-9 before the addition of vv. 11-16, and its function is to explain vv. 1-9, especially v. 1. This is not a literal resumption of v. 1, since it speaks of the root and not of the branch that grows from the root. Likewise, v. 10 is no longer concerned with the ideal king but with 'la communauté des Juifs pieux groupés autour du temple'.[28] According to Vermeylen, this is the community in which the converted heathens are to seek refuge.

In contrast to Vermeylen, *Hans Wildberger*[29] sees the root of Jesse as an image of the Messiah, and believes that it merely represents a somewhat careless link to the expressions in v. 1. The crucial aspect of the verse is its interpretation of the Messiah as a focus not only for Judah/Israel but also for the peoples. The universalistic aspect is thereby emphasized, compared with vv. 1-9's narrower horizon.

But as far as I can see this represents not only a broadening of the perspective in vv. 1-9 but also a new interpretation in relation to vv. 11-16. In vv. 11-16, the nations for whom the ensign is raised are described more precisely as the outcasts of Israel. On the other hand, in v. 10 it is the nations in general that shall seek the ensign. The only link to a concept of the nations' gathering in Jerusalem is v. 12's vague reference to the nations, גוים. It is, then, this expression which also is taken up in v. 10 in an attempt to bind the two parts of the chapter together. I must therefore see v. 10 as a reinterpretation, not only of vv. 1-9, but also of vv. 11-16, created with the object of combining the two; v. 10 is therefore later than both the first part and the second part of the chapter. The dating of v. 10 must therefore depend not so much on the dating of vv. 1-9 as on the dating of vv. 11-16. Whereas I consider it probable that vv. 1-9 date back to Isaiah himself, I believe that vv. 11-16 are later. The problem is merely whether the diaspora referred to in these verses is the result of the destruction of the Northern Kingdom or that of the Southern Kingdom. The reference to the jealousy between Ephraim and Judah in particular leads me to prefer the latter possibility.[30]

For an image analysis, it is most important to look at how the image in v. 1 is exploited in v. 10. Whereas 11,1 refers to both shoot, חטר, and branch, נצר, to both stump, גזע, and root, שרש, 11.10 uses only one of the concepts in the formulation שרש ישי. Whereas 11.1 describes the stump as Jesse's, גזע ישי, the name is linked in 11.10 to שרש. On the other hand, one is informed that שרש ישי is to stand as an ensign for the nations. Two images are thereby combined: the tree root, which is normally to be found in the ground and sends up its branches from there, and the standard on the hilltop, which rallies the scattered troops. This somewhat surprising combination leads us naturally to consider whether at the date of redaction שרש ישי may have lost so much of its image nature that the expression can be understood automatically as a reference to the expected Messiah, the new king; in other words, whether we are in the presence of a dead metaphor.

According to Hans Wildberger, שרש ישי in v. 10 is, as already mentioned, the Messiah, whereas Vermeylen believes that it is the post-Exilic community. This latter interpretation is also to be found in Hermann Barth.[31] Of the two proposals, the *Messiah interpretation* is the most feasible, since the combination with the name Jesse makes it clear that the reference is to a member of David's lineage. In his analysis of שרש, P. Joachim Becker[32] has shown that the word frequently has the meaning 'rootsucker', i.e. not the root itself but the branch produced by the root. This observation makes it even more obvious that Jesse's rootsucker would have acquired one of the meanings generally established by convention, i.e. as a name for the expected Messiah coming from the lineage of David. Analysis of Isa. 4.2 shows that the terminology was not so firmly established during the Exilic period. Isa. 11.10, therefore, may very well be an example of how the plant image, which was originally a living metaphor, died in the post-Exilic period. 'The root', שרש, in Isa. 11.10 has therefore suffered precisely the same fate as 'the branch', צמח, in Jer. 23.5 and 33.15.

But that שרש in Isa. 11.10 acts as a dead metaphor translated automatically by whoever knew the convention cannot be explained merely by the fact that in the post-Exilic period שרש became a cliché. An important factor, also valid in connexion with the use of צמח in Jer. 23.5 and 33.15, is that these metaphors are in an *isolated* position in the literary context. This helps to make the direct translation possible. It is easy for the context, which does not refer to flora, to demarcate the elements of meaning activated which prevent elements other than those directly indicated by the context from cropping up. Whereas 11.1 describes the Messiah by using נצר/חטר (shoot/branch) and the two designations for stump and root, שרש/גזע, 11.10 sums up everything in שרש ישי, Jesse's rootsucker.

Vermeylen's interpretation—that the post-Exilic community is this rootsucker around which the converted heathens are to gather— is unsupported by the text, but relies rather on Vermeylen's perception of the self-awareness of the post-Exilic community. We do not know whether the community, in its attempt to find 'written examples' of its own role in the history of salvation, interpreted ישי שרש as referring to itself. Whereas Isa. 27.2-6, with its special use of the vineyard image, describes relatively clearly the post-Exilic period's perception of itself—Jacob/ Israel—as a plant that throws out roots and flourishes, הבאים ישרש יעקב יציץ ופרח ישראל (Isa. 27.6), we can say no more in regard to Isa. 11.10 than that such a reinterpretation is possible; but neither 11.1-9 nor 11. 11-16 appears directly to set the stage for such interpretation. Read in context, the probable understanding of שרש ישי must be: the coming king is of David's lineage.

Conclusion
The analysis of Isa. 10.33–11.9, 10 has lead to a number of separate results, and, to conclude, the most important of them will be stressed.

In regard to the *tree image's informative function*, it must be emphasized that this image acts as an interpretative key to the *political situation*. With the aid of his particular version of the tree-felling myth, Isaiah points out to the audience that the correlation to be found between the world of nature and the world of the myth is also to be found in the political world. By seeing the political situation through the tree image, they will receive new understanding of the reality surrounding them. Isaiah thereby achieves the result, that what can be argued for within the tree code can similarly be argued for within the political code. If one can feel sure that the tree will sprout again, one can also feel sure that the dynasty will continue. Then, depending on situation and context, the situation indicated may be the fall of the king of Judah or the fall of the king of Assyria as a prelude to the coming of the new king.

It must also be stressed that in Isa. 10.33–11.1 we are confronted with a new version of the tree-felling myth, in that it has been supplemented by the description of the new branch, a motif we shall meet again in a number of other Isaianic texts.

But Isaiah wishes to do more than inform, and redactors preserve and reuse his message for reasons other than the purely informative. Isaiah wishes to *admonish and comfort*; he wishes to *argue with* and *stimulate* his hearers so that they themselves undertake an interpretation of the imagery; so that they permit themselves to be convinced, to adopt Isaiah's suggestion that they should see the reality as their own and draw the necessary implications from it. It is true that he uses a familiar image, but his particular twist to it forces the hearers to undertake an active interpretation. The individual must decide where the similarity lies and where the difference lies. The image also has a *performative function*.

Finally, analysis of the tree image has shown the great extent to which the image has lent itself to reuse and has been exposed to *reinterpretation*. As regards Isa. 10.33-34, such reinterpretation has not, as far as we can see, led to changes in the oracle itself. The image can be employed in precisely the same form to relate to both Judah and the king of Assyria. It is the context that helps to decide which is most probable. In the case of Isa. 11.10, on the other hand, what is concerned is a reinterpretation of Isa. 11.1-9 + 11.11-16 (but especially the image in v. 1), which has led to a production of new text, i.e. v. 10. But in regard to v. 10 we were able to establish that the original image had lost its image value, and in the context functioned as a dead metaphor.

3. *Analysis of Isa. 6.12-13*

Context

One of the central passages in the early Isaiah traditions is the so-called '*Denkschrift*'. According to Odil Hannes Steck,[1] this originally consisted of Isa. 6.1-11; 7.1-9, 10-17;[2] 8.1-8a, 11-15, 16-18. It was written by Isaiah himself in 733, and describes how Yahweh sent him as a prophet to harden the hearts of the people during the Syro-Ephraimite war.

According to Steck, the verses with which we shall deal—Isa. 6.12-13,—do not belong to the original version of Isaiah's report on his mission,[3] Isa. 6.1-11. Steck reaches this result via a form-critical analysis of the text. In part, Isaiah employs in the mission report the schema of assignment of a special task in the divine council (cf. Zech. 1.7ff.; Job 1.6-12; and especially 1 Kgs 22.19b-22). But in relation to this schema Isaiah extends it by vv. 5-7 and v. 11[4] in order to say more about the content of the special heart-hardening task assigned to him. Now, *Steck's thesis* is—and I find his reasoning convincing—that the subsequent episodes, Isa. 7.3-9; 7.10-17; and 8.1-8a, are intended to exemplify how the prophet carried out his commission, and in practice spoke to deaf ears.

If one supplements Steck's discussion of the texts by investigating the 'Denkschrift' structure, including in particular the relation between the introductory section, Isa. 6.1-11, and the concluding section, Isa. 8.11-15, 16-18, it can be seen that this is a circular composition in which the introductory themes are taken up again at the end.[5] This analysis therefore also supports, although indirectly, Steck's categorization of vv. 12-13 as a later addition, in that the concluding passage does not take up again the motifs in these two verses.

Finally, it is apparent from the chapter's use of the first and second persons that Isa. 6.12-13 must be secondary. The mission report itself, vv. 1-11, describes in the first person—and by the direct reproduction of dialogue—what Isaiah has seen, heard and said. Verses 12-13, on the other hand, are comments delivered in the third person. These must be either the prophet's own amplifying comments on what he has experienced, or an attempt by others to clarify the meaning of the prophet's mission.

It is clear from v. 10 that the report on the mission in general gave rise to comment, the last three words about the possibility of healing clarifying the heart-hardening intention—the text's central problem. These words are not organically part of the heart-hardening statement, since this falls into three statements made twice; i.e. a clear parallelism. Moreover, it should be noted that Isaiah's question and Yahweh's answer in v. 11 are both directly linked to the heart-hardening statement, but do not touch upon whether Yahweh will heal.[6]

Both commentaries in v. 10 and in vv. 12-13 operate to clarify what was the *object* of Isaiah's special assignment. Such clarification was necessary because of the historical events which occurred after the 'Denkschrift's' composition and the questions that these events raised. If, therefore, we are to come to understand vv. 12-13, it is necessary to investigate both the verses' function in the literary context in which they are placed and the situation that necessitated these commentaries on the mission report.

The question of the number of individual statements of which vv. 12-13 consist is a special problem.

Isa. 6.12-13: One, Two, or Three Oracles?
According to *Hans Wildberger*,[7] Isa. 6.12-13 reflects three phases of reinterpretation. Verse 12 stems from the period after the fall of

Samaria, and reflects the deportation[8] which then took place. Verse 13a,bα is somewhat later. It tries to warn Judah against believing itself secure now that Israel has fallen; for the last tenth (= Judah) will also be destroyed. Finally, v. 13bβ is added at an even later date in protest against the purely negative interpretation of Isaiah's message. Wildberger prudently refrains from expressing an opinion on when precisely this protest came about.

According to J. *Vermeylen*,[9] this relates—as regards vv. 12-13bα—to the Exile period. These verses express a reinterpretation of v. 11 in the light of the events surrounding the fall of Jerusalem. That the tenth referred to—Judah—had also to be destroyed is justified by the heart-hardening statement (vv. 9-10); Judah learned nothing from the events in Samaria, but shut its ears to Yahweh's warnings; therefore, Judah also had to be struck.

According to Vermeylen, v. 13bβ is a post-Exile reflection based on the concept of the holy remnant, the devout few who uphold the Law; i.e. those who returned home from Babylon in contrast to those who remained in Jerusalem. Cf. as to this the reference to the holy race, זרע הקדש, in Ezra 9.2. This reinterpetation corresponds to what is to be found in Isa. 4.3-5a.

In continuation of this, it should be briefly mentioned that Hermann Barth[10] also dates vv. 12-13bα to the Exile. This he does on the basis of the reference to deportation and the corresponding use of רחק in Jer. 27.10 and Ezek. 11.16. Moreover, he considers that the concepts about the land having to be laid waste are in fact characteristic of texts from this period. Cf. Isa. 5.14, 17; 7.21, 22b; 7.23-25. Barth also considers that Isa. 6.13bβ is a post-Exilic addition corresponding to the concepts about the salvation of the remnant familiar from other additions, i.e. Isa. 4.2; 7.22a; 11.11, 16; and in particular Isa. 28.5f.

Finally, it should be mentioned that there are still scholars who consider vv. 12-13bα to be authentic Isaiah, although not originally belonging to ch. 6.[11]

A clear tendency is evident from these references to envisage several phases when commenting in depth on Isa. 6.1-11. Whereas Wildberger envisages three phases and divides the verses into v. 12; v. 13a,bα ; v. 13bβ, both Vermeylen and Barth operate with two phases, i.e. the addition of vv. 12-13bα and v. 13bβ respectively. All three have in common that they do not consider v. 13b as an entity but as two independent statements that have only secondarily been placed in extension of one another.

But in my opinion this splitting-up of v. 13b is questionable, since it leads to the division of a cohesive image into two parts, which have been linked only secondarily. In contrast to Wildberger, Vermeylen and Barth, I believe that *v. 13b* is an *original entity*, a complete image, whose function is to give a positive corrective to vv. 12-13a's negative statement. Verse 13b cannot be divided into two parts any more than vv. 12-13a and 13b can be separated. My arguments in support of this will be set out below, and we shall then investigate vv. 12-13's meaning and function in the redactional context, i.e. as a link in Isaiah's 'Denkschrift'.

Meaning and Function

The heart-hardening commission in Isa. 6.9-10 has given rise to the dialogue between Isaiah and Yahweh in v. 11. In answer to the prophet's question, how long is this adversity to last? Yahweh answers: 'Until cities lie waste without inhabitant, and houses without men, and the land is utterly desolate'. The answer, which is in three parts like v. 10's heart-hardening statement, rounds off the mission report, and there appears to be no mistaking it. It is clear and literal language. But nevertheless there was a need for further clarification.

Verses 12-13a

The political events of 722 made an impression on Judah. The destruction of the Northern Kingdom was seen as a direct relief, and also perhaps as proof of the soundness of king Ahaz's policy. By leaning on the Assyrians, Judah avoided suffering the same fate as the Northern Kingdom. But not all resigned themselves to the fact that now there was peace and no danger. We can see from vv. 12-13a that Isaiah's circle at least had a different view of the political situation. It is true that v. 12's description of the destruction as a deportation also shows that this group had seen 722 as the fulfilment of the oracle in v. 11; it is evidently because of the Northern Kingdom's heart-hardening that Yahweh sent the Assyrians across it. But v. 13a specifies that the danger was not over by 722. Judah, the tenth part, must also be struck.[12]

What v. 13a has to say is not new compared with what Isaiah has already said—according to Isa. 8.7-8—about Yahweh's plans in

connexion with the Syro-Ephraimite war. The Assyrians will come
and inundate Judah like a flood. But the tone is sterner in Isa. 6.13a.
The image in Isa. 8.7-8 had indeed left open a certain opportunity for
hope: the waters would reach the neck—but no further. On the other
hand, in v. 13a all hope appears to have gone; destruction will be
total.

I find it reasonable therefore to *date vv. 12-13a* to the period
shortly after the fall of Samaria. It was at this time that Isaiah had
had to preach to his obdurate contemporaries that they should not
believe themselves to be safe merely because in the first round Judah
did not go the way of Israel. Judah will also be struck (cf. Isa.
28.7ff.)

The actual formulation of the oracle makes just as good sense at a
time when none of the hearers could have had any doubt that the
land laid waste (v. 12) is in fact the Northern Kingdom just
destroyed, and that the tenth (v. 13a) is the Southern Kingdom, as
yet spared. If, on the other hand, the date of its origin was the Exilic
period, as Vermeylen and Barth believe, the land in v. 12 would be
immediately understood as the Southern Kingdom just destroyed.
And if this is what the author meant, v. 13a's explicit reference to the
tenth would be superfluous. If, on the other hand, the author wished
to describe the fall of both the Northern Kingdom and the Southern
Kingdom, it is surprising that he chose to refer to the Northern
Kingdom merely as 'the land', a formulation that would automatically
cause his sixth-century contemporaries to think of their own land,
the Southern Kingdom.

To summarize, therefore, we can say that the detailing of the
consequences of heart-hardening in the form of total destruction, as
expressed in vv. 12-13a, belongs after the fall of Samaria, when the
prophet had to warn his contemporaries against the easy optimism
provoked by the fall of the Northern Kingdom. Verse 12 establishes
that Yahweh in fact had the Northern Kingdom in mind when he
pronounced judgment on the hard-of-heart, and that he was in a
position to suit the action to the word. Verse 13a makes it equally and
unambiguously clear that Judah also will not escape. The fate of the
Northern and Southern Kingdoms is compared here, and I can see no
reason to envisage, like Wildberger, two phases in this commentation.

But the text does not end with v. 13a and the judgment formulated
there; it continues into 13b, which specifies the purifying nature of
the judgment by using a tree metaphor.

The Tree Metaphor, v. 13b

Collectively, v. 13b describes what occurs when a terebinth or an oak is felled. Although the tree indeed falls, its vital force does not disappear. It can still sprout, for it is holy seed that remains in it. It is evident from the comparative particle that this description is to be seen as an image of how the destruction referred to is to take place, and what its consequences will be.

Now, as we have seen, there is a clear tendency to divide v. 13b into two independent statements and to view the words about the holy seed as a later addition. But it is questionable whether such splitting-up is necessary, let alone reasonable. We have met in another context (Isa. 10.33–11.1) an analogous combination of tree-felling and the potential for new beginnings, and argued there in support of the close association between felling and new growth.

That Isaiah saw the coming calamity as a transitional phase, and that this view was regarded as the crux of Isaiah's message, is shown not only by the use of the tree image but also by the use of a number of other images whose function is to juxtapose the negative and the positive. We have merely to think of the image of the metal to be cleaned (Isa. 1.25); the image of the washing of the daughters of Zion (Isa. 4.4); the image of the water reaching to the neck (Isa. 8.8); the image of the darkness replaced by light (Isa. 9.1; RSV 9.2); and the image of the anger that came but faded away (Isa. 12.1). The same basic idea has received its formulation in the remnant concept as we know it from Isa. 7.3, from the description of the function of Isaiah and his disciples as signs and portents (Isa. 8.18), and from the exploitation of the remnant concept in Isa. 10.20-23 and Isa. 37.31f. Or one can indicate the repeated juxtaposition of judgment statements and salvation statements; which is difficult to explain as only an expression of the redactors' theology and, like the images referred to above, must certainly have its source in Isaiah's own tension-charged message. It is therefore not unreasonable to believe that v. 13b must be an original entity, and that the image has precisely the function of prophesying the judgment as a necessary transition before the salvation, and the salvation as 'organically' linked to the judgment. It might rather be said that good arguments are needed to separate the two parts.

The tree image's form and content fit well into Isaiah's message. But why has this image been placed within the very framework of the 'Denkschrift'? A characteristic feature of the 'Denkschrift' is the mixture of threats and promises. As Odil Hannes Steck has demonstrated, the three episodes in Isaiah 7–8 are to illustrate how in practice Isaiah carried out his heart-hardening task. All three episodes employ both a negative and a positive aspect. Both Isaiah's son and the coming scion of David bear symbolic names that imply hope: שאר ישוב in Isa. 7.3 and עמנו אל in Isa. 7.14. Even though there is drastic decimation of the people (the army), a remnant will nevertheless return; even though King Ahaz will be rejected, the dynasty will continue; even though the waters of chaos overwhelm Judah, they will not reach beyond the neck. This positive aspect emerges most strongly in the Immanuel portent in Isa. 7.14, where Yahweh repeats his promise to David's dynasty through the oracle of the new prince who is to be born.

Viewed in this context, v. 13b's tree image makes good sense. This image also contains the tension between the negative and the positive. The tree is felled, but it still has the power to sprout; despite all, this is not complete obliteration. But the image is well-chosen not merely by reason of this duality: the image's meaning also fits into the context.

The Meaning of the Tree Image

The trees referred to are אלה and אלון, two types of oak-tree frequently mentioned in association with holy places and fertility cults: אלה is employed in association with holy places in Gen. 35.4; Josh. 24.26; in association with holy persons in Judg. 6.11, 19; 1 Kgs 13.14; in association with fertility cults in Ezek. 6.13; Hos. 4.13; and in association with burial places in 1 Chron. 10.12. אֵלוֹן/אַלוֹן is used in association with holy places in Gen. 12.6; Deut. 11.30; Judg. 9.6; 9.37; perhaps 1 Sam. 10.3; in association with fertility cults in Hos. 4.13; and in association with burial places in Gen. 35.8. It must therefore be assumed that concepts of the tree as holy belong to the connotations which אלה and אלון have. Cf. incidentally pp. 79ff. on the tree as the tree of life.

What happens to these trees is described by the expression בשלכת מצבת בם. שלכת is a hapax legomenon,[13] but must have been used here in reference to felling or similar forms of destruction. Apart from 2 Sam. 18.18, where it means massebe,[14] מצבת appears here only. It is translated traditionally as 'stump', but this is rather a doubtful translation. It is much more probable that it refers to the new branches that sprout forth.[15] This meaning is supported by, for example, Peshitta's rendering of מצבתה in v. 13bβ by ܢܨܒܬܗ of the root ܢܨܒ , which means 'to plant'. מצבת is then presumably a ma-nomen, derived from a root with the same meaning as ܢܨܒ , so that it means 'plant', 'branch', or more generally 'power to sprout'. The image describes how the felled trees have in themselves the power to sprout, despite all; indeed, even *holy power*.

Excursus
To a certain extent, therefore, Peshitta's translator must also have understood MT in this way. But whereas Peshitta translates vv. 12-13a very literally, in the case of v. 13b it is a matter of re-creation rather than actual translation. Peshitta renders the tree image as: 'just as with a terabinth, so with an acorn when it falls out of its acorn-cup: its branch is holy seed'.

As we have seen, מצבתה is translated in v. 13bβ by the word ܢܨܒܬܗ 'its plant', 'its branch'; but surprisingly enough מצבת בם is translated totally differently, namely by the expression ܡܢ ܚܒܝܬܗ , i.e. 'of its acorn-cup'.[16] In my opinion, Peshitta's idea that an acorn-cup from which the acorn falls is referred to results from the following: The Hebraic word אלון is translated in Peshitta by the word ܒܠܘܛܐ, in LXX by βάλανος. Ivan Engnell[17] points out that the word βάλανος can indicate both the oak-tree and its fruit. Analogously, the Syriac word ܒܠܘܛܐ has two meanings: 'oak-tree' and 'amphora'.[18] It is therefore reasonable to imagine that ܒܠܘܛܐ, like βάλανος, can indicate both the oak-tree and its amphora-shaped fruit, the acorn. This would explain why Peshitta continues by describing how something falls out of its acorn-cup. That Peshitta has been able to conceive אלון as a description of an acorn and not of an 'oak-tree' is presumably associated with the fact that MT speaks of both אלה and אלון. In Syriac, diminutives are formed by the addition of the ending -ōn; it is natural, then, for the Syriac translator to understand אלון as a diminutive of אלה.[19]

LXX has understood MT in a similar way. Now, a special point about LXX is that, in contrast to Peshitta, v. 12 is translated exceedingly freely. It is true that in LXX Yahweh allows men to be removed,[20] but on the other hand the remnant shall multiply on the earth. At the beginning, the translation of v. 13 is in accordance with the text in referring to the tenth, which is to become fodder (for animals) or spoil (for the fire)—προνομή has a double meaning, as does the Hebraic לבער—; but when we arrive at the tree image changes have again occurred. In the first place, a translation of the words זרע קדש בם מצבת is lacking. LXX renders the image: ὡς τερέβινθος καὶ ὡς βάλανος ὅταν ἐκπέσῃ ἀπὸ τῆς θήκης αὐτῆς. If we start backwards, it becomes clear that ἀπὸ τῆς θήκης αὐτῆς must be a rendering of 13bβ's last word, i.e. מצבתה, and *not* of מצבת בם. This means quite simply that the translator has seen fit, because of homoeoteleuton, to ignore the words referred to. Instead of continuing after בשלכת with בם, he has read the verse's last word מצבת.[21]

Secondly, the translator, like Peshitta's translator, saw אלון as a diminutive of אלה,[22] i.e. in the meaning 'acorn' and not 'oak-tree'. βάλανος can certainly mean both parts, but the continuation ἐκπέσῃ ἀπὸ τῆς θήκης αὐτῆς shows that it must be the acorn which falls out of its container. LXX has therefore understood מצבתה as a name for 'acorn-cup', the base from which the acorn falls.

If we now compare Peshitta's and LXX's reading of Isa. 6.12-13, it becomes clear that the versions differ, but that both translations have read the judgment to mean that it does not involve complete extermination. Peshitta stays close to MT in the rendering of vv. 12-13a, and accordingly describes the necessary judgment. Only with v. 13b is the possibility of new sprouting introduced. It must happen as in nature, where the acorn falls out of the acorn cup and sprouts again. This is a very harmonious view of Yahweh's judgment over Judah. In v. 12, LXX has referred to a positive feature at variance with MT's v. 12, but this may well be because the translator had a Hebraic text to work from which contained the positive aspect of v. 13b, and from it anticipated the positive future. However, because of homoeoteleuton, he has omitted precisely the reference in v. 13b to the holy seed. LXX therefore ends with a pure declaration of judgment. Both translations disclose in different ways that in the light of MT they have interpreted the judgment as non-total destruction, a concept that corresponds to the central point in MT's tree image: after destruction follows new life. It is not surprising that this is MT's main idea when the trees concerned are seen as holy trees.

As one might expect, Ivan Engnell also has no doubts that it is *holy trees* which are referred to in Isa. 6.13b, and that the background to Isaiah's use of the image of trees which are felled but have in them power to sprout must be found in the rites and ideas associated with the sacred kingdom. 'It is *the tree of life* itself that stands behind the mode and expression, symbolized in the cult by "the sacred pole", the *masseba*, corporalizing at the same time the "Tammuz"-figure and the king.'[23]

Although not all Engnell's ideas on, for example, the central role of Jachin and Boaz as trees of life in the royal cult in Jerusalem are equally well founded (his references to 2 Kgs 11.12ff. and 23.1ff. are in any event insufficient to support the concept that in Israel also rites known from elsewhere were to be found), I believe that his main point is correct. And it is precisely the main ideas that concern us if we are to try to reveal the connotations associated with, for example, the tree.

The trees in Isa. 6.13b connote 'the holy tree', 'the tree of life', and thereby permit association with the concepts of the king as a tree, just as we saw in Isa. 11.1. By use of the tree image, Isa. 6.13b then formulates the same hope for the future as we found expressed in the Immanuel portent in the 'Denkschrift'.

Ivan Engnell, who as we have seen believes that the whole of Isaiah 6 is authentic Isaiah, concludes his investigation with the words:

> v. 13 is by no means a late, meaningless gloss, but belongs on the contrary from the very beginning to the oracle, constituting its natural apex. We may state at the same time that the verse expresses nothing but *the consistent theme of the prophetic teaching*, its kernel: apostasy, doom—a purification, not an annihilation doom—and a remnant, linked up with the Davidic Messiah, and forming at the same time the basis of the Messianic kingdom to come.[24]

The author has therefore not chosen a fortuitous image to formulate the hope for the future. By choosing the positively connotated image of the tree capable of surviving which takes its meaning from both day-to-day experience and religious concepts, including royal ideology, the author is able to argue that the political events are not an expression of fortuitousness. The hearers can adduce from the image not only the general information that there is a cohesion in life; they can also see that the hope for the future is linked to the king and the dynasty, information further confirmed by perusing the 'Denkschrift'.

The author chooses to modify the strong and clear pronouncement of sentence in vv. 12-13a by using the tree image not only to give information about Yahweh's plans for Judah but also to comfort the anxious (performative function). The image of the tree that is felled but will sprout again is able to retain simultaneously the negative reality, which has created fear and trouble, and the hope that can overcome anxiety for the future. The image thereby has *not only* an *informative but also* a *performative function.* But who is the author of this image?

Is Isa. 6.12-13 Isaianic?

What has been said above about the tree image's importance renders it probable that one image is concerned which collates the crux of Isaiah's message in an abbreviated form. In its structure, the image resembles the tree image in Isa. 10.33–11.1, although the use of words is different. The idea of the possibility of new sprouting similarly reminds one of the reinterpretation of the vineyard parable we encounter in Isa. 27.2-6; but this is significantly later than the present passage. Also, as regards content, it accords well—as we have seen—with the 'Denkschrift'. I therefore see no reason to reject v. 13b as non-Isaianic, and I see this image as an original part of Isaiah's own commentary elaborating the mission report (Isa. 6.12-13). I therefore consider that vv. 12-13 is one coherent oracle referring back to Isaiah's own message.

The oracle does not stem from the 'Denkschrift's' date of origin, the period of the Syro-Ephraimite war, but from the period following Samaria's annihilation.

In the analysis of Isa. 11.1, I referred to Vermeylen's thesis that Isa. 11.1-5 was written in the context of young Josiah's accession to the throne in 639. I rejected this thesis and warned generally against too precise dating of the images because they can in fact be used meaningfully in different situations without permitting us to establish which situation is the original.

The same must of course apply when we attempt to date Isa. 6.12-13. We have earlier been able to show that it is a well-chosen image used in close concord with one of the main ideas in the 'Denkschrift'—the dynasty's continuation despite destruction of the land—and that it must be located in time after 722. What we must look for, then, is a situation in which there is cause for a certain amount of hope that Yahweh's final objective is not total annihilation, and in which this hope is linked to the new king.

We have perhaps such a situation in the period shortly after 722. I have in mind the time of the *accession of the new king in 715*, when king Ahaz, the rejected king to whom the Immanuel portent was given, died and handed over the throne to his son Hezekiah. Not only had the events surrounding the fall of Samaria come into their proper perspective, and the immediate euphoria—because it was neighbours who had suffered—become somewhat reduced, perhaps under the influence of Isaiah's threats about Yahweh's punishment of Judah; the accession of a new king could only help to reawaken hopes for the future. We know this from the hymns sung at the accession of kings and the names endowed on them. And perhaps there was extra reason for Yahweh-believers to be optimistic at Hezekiah's accession, for if we believe only a little of what the Deuteronomists have to tell about him he was a man who 'did what was right in the eyes of the Lord' (2 Kgs 18.3).

Hezekiah was one of the kings who purified the Yahweh cult of alien strains, dismantled sacrificial mounds, broke up the massebes and cut down the Asherahs. He must have been a man not only after Yahweh's own heart but also after the hearts of Isaiah and Isaiah's disciples. But such optimism could scarcely be maintained for very long. As early as 713 Hezekiah joined the Ashdod coalition against Assyria, thereby incurring Isaiah's wrath. (Cf. Isa. 20.)[25]

Now, as we have said, one must accept the Deuteronomists' description of Hezekiah's reign with certain reservations. Their account of it was and still is tendentious. If we look at their description of the events of around 701, there can be no doubt about their great partiality for Hezekiah. In 2 Kings, they describe him as a clear contrast to his father, Ahaz. Whereas Ahaz went out to the fortifications to inspect them when the threat of war became serious, and Yahweh had to inconvenience his prophet to go there, it is there that, in 701, according to the Deuteronomists, Hezekiah requested the prophet Isaiah to help and to intercede; similarly, the king did not go to the fortifications relying on his own forces but sought out Yahweh in the temple in Jerusalem. It is not surprising, therefore, that the Deuteronomists permitted Hezekiah to be the king who perceived that Yahweh saved Jerusalem 'for my own sake and for the sake of my servant David' (2 Kgs 19.34).

At the same time, behind these traditions and through these traditions we glimpse a very hectic period politically, when Hezekiah only just—and by large cash payments—succeeded in preventing Jerusalem from suffering the same fate as Samaria. Neither can it be concealed that in fact the king was forced to surrender large parts of the kingdom, so that Jerusalem was left like a booth in a vineyard (Isa. 1.8). The Deuteronomists make no reference to it, but the Sennacherib text of course includes it: Sennacherib, according to his own account, captured forty-six cities from Hezekiah. But not Jerusalem!

This brief outline of the historical situation in 715 and 701 is not intended to prove that vv. 12-13 *does in fact* date from 715 and represents Isaiah's interpretation of what Ahaz's death and Hezekiah's accession would mean for Judah. In the first place the precise date of Hezekiah's assumption of power is still the subject of debate,[26] and secondly the tree image is so receptive that we would be wise to

hesitate before asserting that this is its one and only meaning. What I
have tried to point out is that at the end of the eighth century also
there were situations, although shorter, which could give cause for
belief in a future for Judah despite the judgment, and confidence that
Yahweh was beside his king. It is not necessary to go right back to the
Exile to find a basis for such a prophecy.

What I have outlined here is thus a *possible* Sitz im Leben for vv.
12-13, i.e. about the time of Hezekiah's accession. My proposal has
the consequence that this oracle should most naturally be understood
as an authentic Isaiah oracle, and that in the present context its
placing belongs to Isaiah's own time. I see no reason not to assume
that Isaiah himself had an interest in declaring/justifying that this
also was a consequence of the assignment on which Yahweh had sent
him. The placing of vv. 12-13 within the 'Denkschrift' shows in any
event that this oracle, with its linking of judgment and salvation, was
considered part of the crux of Isaiah's message.

That the Sitz im Leben was the situation in about 715 rather than,
for example, the Exile period, as so many people assert,[27] is also
supported by the placing of the statement within the 'Denkschrift's'
framework, where the traditions about Hezekiah's father, king Ahaz,
play such a central part; but where also the promise of the dynasty's
continued existence is to be found. The addition of vv. 12-13 is
therefore well in keeping with Isa. 7.10-17, where the Immanuel
prophecy stands in positive contrast to the rejection of king Ahaz.
And it is at least worth considering whether the promise of the new
king in Isa. 9.1-6[28] should also be seen as such an attempt to enlarge
on the positive aspects of Isaiah's message during the Syro-
Ephraimite war. The holy seed in the tree image and the new prince
each help to emphasize that Yahweh does not forsake *the Davidic
dynasty*, although this might appear to be so for a time.

To summarize, therefore, we must conclude that Isa. 6.12-13 makes
good sense if we see it as a well-balanced, *Isaianic oracle* from the
period of *about 715*. Its function is to console the anxious, that
although punishment will also strike Judah Yahweh nevertheless
does not go back on his promise to David's dynasty. Isaiah thereby
wished to stress that the duality which characterizes Yahweh's
attitude towards the people and which the three episodes in Isa. 7-8
exemplify was already being expressed by his mission. This duality is
not an expression of history's fortuitousness but of Yahweh's wish.
The tree image is therefore in a position to argue that the same

imperatives familiar from the world of nature and which the people recognize from the world of myth and cult are also to be found in the world of politics.

Reinterpretation of Isa. 6.13b

As we have already seen, the Exile gave rise to restudy of the Isaiah traditions, with consequent reinterpetation and the production of new text. It is therefore reasonable to assume that the 'Denkschrift', and consequently the tree image in Isa. 6.13b, was also made the subject of restudy. Vermeylen and Barth date Isa. 6.12-13bα to the Exilic period and v. 13bβ to the post-Exilic period, since they believe that the thoughts these verses express accord well with the catastrophe-situation of the sixth century. But what Vermeylen and Barth consider to be the oracles' original Sitz im Leben is in my opinion a new Sitz im Leben, and what they consider to be the oracles' original meaning I see as a good definition of the reinterpretation that may have taken place during the Exile. Vermeylen and Barth are indeed correct in saying that these words must have acted as significant words of Yahweh during the Babylonian captivity. But whereas in the original eighth-century use vv. 12-13a acted as a threat, the statement of judgment in the sixth century acted as justification for Yahweh's punishment already carried out on the slow-witted people, Judah.

Neither am I in any doubt that the statement relating to the holy seed has been interpreted at a later date as referring both to Zerubbabel, 'branch of Babel' (cf. Zech. 3.8; 6.12, where there is a play using the word צמח [same word as in Isa. 4.2] on the meaning of Zerubbabel), and to those returning from Babylon, the holy seed (Ezra 9.2).

A characteristic feature of Peshitta's rendering of the tree image is the very positive and harmonious perception it expresses. We meet the same positive slant[29] in the *Targum's use of the tree image* to interpret the political situation. It is Israel's exiles גלוותא דישראל, who are to gather again and return to their country, for their plant, נצבתהון,[30] is holy seed. But the image has been changed, so that it refers to the tree that loses its leaves but is nevertheless able to preserve sufficient moisture to permit the seed to be kept alive. Again, another variation of nature's course of events for the tree.

In the same way as the Targum has clearly read Isa. 6.13b in the light of the political circumstances of its own time, so has 1QIsa, according to John Sawyer,[31] read the text as a topical saying polemically directed against the hierarchy in Jerusalem. Isa. 6.13b thereby becomes a rejection of the possibility that this 'establishment' with which the Qumran community has broken can in any way be a holy remnant; it is indeed merely a tree stump!

Sawyer's interpretation is sometimes speculative, but is well in keeping with the contemporizing reinterpretation which the commentary literature at Qumran expresses.[32] It is not therefore very unreasonable to believe that we shall also be able to find traces of this method of interpretation in the biblical writings employed at Qumran.

Conclusion

Isa. 6.12-13 presents us with another example of how, by using the tree image, Isaiah is able to *interpret the political situation of his time* so that his hearers could see the connexion between the necessary punishment and the possibilities of a future. From the choice of image, it appears that the hope for the future is linked to the royal house, David's dynasty. The object, therefore, of using the image is both to point out this connexion and to comfort and encourage those affected. Yahweh does not go back on his promises, although his punishment is inevitable. By speaking in imagery, the prophet involves the hearers in the message in such a way that, by entering into the interpretation, they can adopt as their own the image's way of seeing reality. The chosen image of oak and terebinth connotes in the culture of the time 'the holy tree', and awakens among the hearers a series of associations which support Isaiah's reasoning that destruction will not impede new life.

We have been able to see from the old translations and from the Targum that it is precisely this positive aspect which has permeated the interpretation, and it has been pointed out that the tree image was well-suited for *reuse* in the Exile period also. But then the felling of the tree, together with the preceding description of the prophet's vocation and his pronouncement of judgment, has had the same function of *justifying* Yahweh's punishment, already executed against his obdurate people.

4. *Analysis of Isa. 14.4b-20*

Genre and Dating

According to its formulation, Isa. 14.4b-20[1] is a *dirge*. The dirge is introduced by the characteristic exclamation אֵיךְ,[2] which is repeated in v. 12, and like dirges in general it is based on the contrast between past and present.[3] The themes in the text also indicate the dirge genre, but this does not mean that we are confronted with an ordinary dirge. The dead man is a feared tyrant; tears have been replaced by joy (v. 7), the dirge by the poorly concealed 'Schadenfreude': the incomparable has become like one of us, the morning star has been flung to the ground, plunged into the land of the dead (vv. 10ff.); he is not given an honourable burial, the corpse is simply cast away (v. 19). It ends with the striking words that the kin of the deceased are never again to be mentioned. He is even denied a posthumous reputation.

The text thus employs a number of recognized dirge motifs in a new and surprising way. This is not only because he was a tyrant and the sorrow over his death therefore very limited; it is also because the situation in which the dirge is used is fundamentally different from the normal dirge situation. The actual Sitz im Leben and the form-related Sitz im Leben do not tally.[4] The tyrant is not dead at the time the prophet curses him, but on the contrary in the best of health. The arrogant, self-assured king who considers himself above everything and everyone—indeed, like the gods—now experiences the derision of the prophet's declaring him dead by singing a dirge over him. The dirge, as precisely formulated by Hans Wildberger, is 'eine zum Spottlied abgewandelte *Leichenklage*'.[5]

It is clear from the heading they have given it that the redactors of Isaiah 14 also wished the dirge to be understood in this way. It is referred to as a מָשָׁל,[6] i.e. a satirical song, to be used about the king of Babylon. As we have pointed out, for the dirge to function in this way it is axiomatic that the tyrant is still alive. If he dies, the dirge must change its addressee—if of course it is still to function as a satirical song.

But who was the *original addressee*? This question is immensely difficult to answer, in the first place because the description of the tyrant is very general—*Hans Wildberger*[7] emphasizes that the author has tried to describe the typical ruler—and secondly because of the extensive use of mythical concepts and images. *J. Vermeylen* gives a survey of the suggested datings that have been presented over time,[8] from the thesis that the poem is an original Canaanite poem[9] via the various suggestions relating to kings of Assyria up to the thesis he himself advocates, i.e. that it refers to a group of some kind in post-Exilic times. But Vermeylen is forced to end by pointing out that the text gives no opportunity for a final decision on the matter. One may find this annoying, or it can make one realize that there is indeed something special about this text: it is receptive to reuse; it has both breadth and conciseness.

But the redactor of ch. 14 had no wish to allow the question of addressee to remain open; he has said in v. 4a that it refers to the king of Babylon. This makes it clear that the text was in any event in use during the Exile, and that the redactor tried to uphold one interpretation. But the text's history of utility shows that he has been unable, by using the name of Babylon, to uphold this meaning as the only possible meaning. Upon the fall of the kingdom of Babylon, the interpretation 'the king of Babylon' lost its direct meaning. The text is nevertheless reused, but now to the effect that 'the king of Babylon' is seen as a code-name for the world power.[10] The apparent closing of the text by means of a geo-political decision is cancelled by turning the name into a cipher, or, if one prefers, by understanding it figuratively.

Whereas Vermeylen in reality abandons involvement in the text's meaning before setting it in the present context, *Hermann Barth*[11] goes about it much more positively. According to Barth, the text in fact gives some basis for dating the creation of the original text (Isa. 14.4b + 6-20a). The reference in v. 8 to the felling of Lebanon's trees, the description of the tyrant's various activities in vv. 6 and v. 16f., the allusion to his death מקברך (Barth reads this as: far away from your grave= abroad), and finally the reference to חרגים, v. 19, i.e. those who have fallen in war, make it reasonable, according to Barth, to think of Sargon's death in 705 during a campaign. [12]

The difficulty about this dating is not the result itself, if it is meant thereby that the original subject of the poem was Sargon—this is in fact a reasonable and familiar suggestion[13]—but rather the way in which Barth reaches his conclusion. Barth interprets the poem as if it were a description of an historical course of events, thereby overlooking on the one hand that some of the features he accepts at face value are figurative (such as, in my opinion, v. 8), and on the other hand that the intention of the poem becomes meaningless if it

came into existence after Sargon's death; or—if not meaningless—
that it meant something else.

Barth is in fact also forced to the conclusion that the intention of
the poem is to explain Sargon's death as a consequence of his hubris.
But this misses an essential point of the poem. In the original
situation, the poem is not an expression of subsequent rationalization
but an example of how a prophet carried out the speech act that
taunts the king of Assyria. As regards Barth, therefore, I must
maintain that if it is Sargon II to whom the poem is addressed it
came into existence before 705; if, however, it is Sennacherib it is of
course later. I bring up Sennacherib's name in this connexion
because, according to Isa. 37.24, he has indeed boasted about how he
felled the great trees of Lebanon.

If, therefore, I am to try to find features in the text that might
reveal who the author had in mind when he originally formulated his
mocking dirge, I would rather look at how the Isaianic traditions
characterize the individual kings than try to adduce historical
information about their fate. Used in reference to Sennacherib, the
description of how the cedars of Lebanon rejoice at the fall of the
hewer, and how in reality he himself is merely a branch thrown
away, would be both significant and impressive. But, as we know,
there is a large gap between outlining a possible Sitz im Leben and
establishing that this is the original Sitz im Leben.

We cannot therefore finally decide whether the song goes back to
Isaiah's own time. What we can say is that its imagery reminds one of
Isaiah's use of tree images; also, the sophisticated use of well-known
genres in a new and surprising way is not foreign to Isaiah. Finally,
there is nothing in the poem itself which demands that it came into
existence only during the Exile. I therefore see no reason to conclude
that the satirical song was not created by Isaiah. But we cannot
pronounce on this with certainty; the only certain Sitz im Leben for
the poem is the present, probably secondary, location in the
collection of foreign people's oracles, under the heading: satirical
song about the king of Babylon.

The Use of Tree Images
Having determined the form and function of Isa. 14.4b-20 and
considered its dating, we must now look more closely at how tree
images function in this context. There are two references to trees,
v. 8 and v. 19; but whereas in the case of v. 19 there can be no doubt

that it is imagery (cf. the comparative particle כְּ) it is not similarly certain that v. 8 is to be read figuratively.

It may well be, as Hermann Barth believes, that this refers merely to the tyrant's ruthless exploitation of the great forests.[14] When the tyrant falls, the great trees rejoice that they escaped their fate. As referred to above,[15] we know from a number of Near-Eastern texts that the great kings fetched timber from Lebanon, and if this is what is referred to the author has simply chosen to express himself in a special style in which the trees act as speakers, but act on their own behalf. It might be called an animation of nature in a style we recognize from, for example, Isa. 55.12, where the trees clap their hands, or in Isa. 44.23, where all nature, heaven and earth, mountains and trees, is to rejoice at Yahweh's salvation. But in that event the present passage should not be understood figuratively.

If we are to decide whether or not *imagery* is concerned, it is necessary to look at the *context* in which the verse is placed. According to vv. 4b-6, the tyrant has been silenced by Yahweh, and the symbols of the ruler—staff מטה and sceptre שבט—have been broken as punishment for injustice towards his vassals. Verses 7-8 describe the reaction to this. The whole world is jubilant that rest and quiet prevail; Lebanon's trees rejoice at the tyrant's fall, since no-one will now come to fell them. That peace prevails in the whole world because the tyrant has ceased his ruthless exploitation of Lebanon's timber has a striking effect, not only because the reaction is out of proportion but primarily because the context is in general concerned with the tyrant's suppression of other peoples and his encounter with his former vassals in the land of the dead (vv. 9ff.).

It would follow, therefore, that v. 8 also concerns the relationship with the vassals, but formulated in imagery. The verse thus tells how the surviving vassals who did not end up in the land of the dead react to the tyrant's fall. The author is in a position to give his interpretation of events by using the image of the trees of Lebanon instead of plainly referring to the kings, since if the situation is observed through the tree image it becomes clear that the great king is guilty of hubris. It is indeed Lebanon's trees that he has indiscriminately felled! The author is thus able to interpret the political situation for his contemporaries and to brand the tyrant as a rebel against Yahweh himself. The context thus renders it probable that imagery is concerned and not literal language.

The Mythical Background

In the context of an analysis of Joel 1.5, *Arvid Kapelrud*[16] has discussed the ideas behind Isa. 14.8, and has shown that it refers to the fertility cult's myth of death and resurrection. According to Kapelrud, the Isa. 14.4-21 passage is a description of the divine ruler's descent into the land of the dead, and must originally have belonged to a text cycle corresponding to what we already know from the Ras Shamra texts. In the cult, the god can be symbolized by a tree (especially a cedar) and, via the king's role as the cult's representative, the tree also becomes a natural image of the king. The god's death and resurrection can therefore be presented in the cult as the felling of a tree. The point of Isa. 14.8's use of these ideas is, then, that it is the tyrant, the great hewer, הכרת, who has himself fallen/been felled, and whose fall Isa. 14.12ff. describes.

In extension of Kapelrud's analysis, I wish to point out that the 'king's fall' motif has been developed not only by means of the myth of the titan who, in punishment for his hubris, is plunged into the land of the dead (vv. 12-15)[17] but also by means of tree images. We have already seen that this is true of v. 8, but v. 19 is also involved in this context. Here, the word נצר is used for the tyrant. In Isa. 11.1, נצר is the branch sprouting from Jesse's root, i.e. an image of the new king. But whereas in Isa. 11.1 the king is to be a divinely equipped ruler of the land of peace, the tyrant in Isa. 14.19 is described as a loathed shoot which is merely cast out without even a sepulchre.[18] Whereas in the fertility-cult context the felling of the tree is a link in a sequence ending positively in the god's resurrection, the motif is used negatively here; the king remains in the land of the dead.

As will be seen from this paraphrase of the text, the author focuses alternately on the image and its interpretation, a technique which causes most scholars to reject MT's נצר and instead to correct it to נפל, a monster.[19] But this correction is in no way necessary, let alone reasonable. The text makes good sense if one is aware that the entire poem is full of ideas taken from Jerusalem king-ideology, and has its background in the fertility-cult myths. Audiences of the time were fully aware that the despised shoot was an image of a king, *in casu* the tyrant.

There was also probably no difficulty in sensing the biting irony behind such utilization of cult-myth ideas. Similar examples of the ironical use of the tree as a metaphor are to be found in Isa. 7.2, where the king and his people shake with fear as the trees of the

forest shake before the wind, and especially in Isa. 7.4, where the
opponents' fierce anger is reduced to the smoke from some
smouldering stumps of firebrands. For what indeed are these kings?
Are they Lebanon cedars or Bashan oaks? No, they are only some
smoking tree stumps. The tyrant's arrogance and the king's/people's
disbelieving cowardice is unmasked by means of images.

But let us return to the mythical background to the tree images in
v. 8 and v. 19. In my opinion, it is not enough to point out that such
mythical ideas lie behind the use of the images. The images and
motifs employed are not chosen at random; they are most carefully
matched, and assist in making Isa. 14.4b-20 a very well-constructed
poem. The connexion between the images emerges if we ask the
question: Why is the tyrant described as 'the great forest-feller'?
Kapelrud stressed that there was a cultic background to this, but was
in fact forced to abandon trying to explain of what the role as הכרת
consisted.[20]

It should, however, be possible to get somewhat further than
Kapelrud if we include the myth that appears to lie behind the
satirical song. As Stolz has shown, in Old Testament times there was
a tradition that the garden in Lebanon was in danger of being
usurped. An alien destroyer felled the divine trees, but is dispatched
to the nether world as punishment for his hubris.[21] When the author
of Isa. 14.4b-20 describes the tyrant as 'the great forest-feller' who
has used violence against the trees of Lebanon, he exploits the
hearers' preconception of Lebanon's trees as divine trees. Everyone
knows that the tyrant is guilty of sacrilege in this, and will be
punished by death. Whereas in 14.8 the tyrant's fall is described only
by the word שכבת ('you were laid low'—the idea is of course that he is
laid low in the land of the dead, cf. Ezek. 31.18; 32.28), the descent to
the land of the dead is expanded in the subsequent description of the
titan's fate (vv. 12-15). Whoever seeks to arrogate power to himself
on the mountain of the gods in the furthermost north and rises above
the clouds to become like עליון must quite logically be punished by
being sent to the negation of the world of the gods: the nether
world.

Behind Isaiah 14's use of the tree image lies the old fertility-cult
concepts of the tree as representative of the god; originally, perhaps,
the myth spoke directly of the killing of a god.[22] In Isa. 14.8, we
encounter these concepts in the utilization of the myth of the tree-
felling in Lebanon, whereby the forest-feller/tyrant is stamped as one

who unjustly seeks to come into possession of divine status. The punishment of the forest-feller is therefore justified. The images and the myths behind them thus received an *argumentative function* precisely as we saw in the analysis of Isa. 10.33ff.

Finally, it should be stressed that Isa. 14.4b-20 employs a technique we shall meet again in the context of Isa. 4.2 and Isa. 10.16-19, in that the text weaves its motifs into one another so that they mutually reinforce one another. After the introductory definition of the whole theme—Yahweh will punish the tyrant—the myth of the alien destroyer of Lebanon's holy trees who receives his well-deserved punishment is introduced in just one verse. This is immediately succeeded by a parallel myth bearing the same message: the titan who considers himself equal to God is to be banished to the nether world to the derision of everyone. Finally, we again find the punishment motif at the end of the poem in the form of the image of the severed branch. The forest-feller has now himself been reduced to a discarded shoot.

At first glance, Isa. 14.4b-20 may give a somewhat confusing impression, but as we have shown it is not a haphazard composition. The author's *prophetic intention* is simply to convince his contemporaries that pride goes before a fall (cf. Isa. 2.12-17), and that the great king who is at present threatening their existence must therefore also fall. But whereas in 10.33-34 Isaiah gives a twist to the myth, whereby the felled trees become an image of the proud, Isa. 14.8 keeps closer to the original myth, where the trees are the victims of sacrilegious encroachment from without.[23]

Excursus
Analysis of the satirical song has provided a clear impression of the way in which the author exploits known myths and images. [24] To the modern exegete, this sympathy between text and reader is a difficulty. It is all too easy to base the analysis on one's own assumptions and ideas. A way of avoiding this is to turn to parallel texts that can throw light on the preconceptions of the time.

What we shall draw on, in this connexion, is *Ezekiel 28 and 31-32*, texts which of course also played an important part in Fritz Stolz's thesis on the Lebanon myth. We shall discuss these specific Ezekiel texts because, having regard to the dating of Isa. 14.4b-20, we are in a position to establish with certainty only that the satirical song was used in the Exilic period. By drawing on other texts from this period, therefore, we can to a certain extent check the interpretation we have arrived at above in relation to the text's use of the concepts regarding Lebanon's trees and the arrogant king's descent to Sheol.

We again find in *Ezekiel 28* the motif of the arrogant great king who is punished by death. The king of Tyre has said of himself that he is a god (Ezek. 28.2); and as punishment for this hubris (יען גבה לבך) he is to be killed and thrust down into the pit (Ezek. 28.8). After the judgment follows a lament (Ezek. 28.11-19). Just as in Isa. 14.4b-20, this is based on the contrast between past and present. By using the myth of the garden of God on the mountain of God, the king is described as primitive man,[25] the chosen one walking among the sons of God in Eden. He was perfect in everything until he became arrogant. Then Yahweh intervened and cast him to the ground so that the kings could feast their eyes on his fall, על־ארץ השלכתיך לפני מלכים נתתיך לראוה בך (v. 17), and let fire consume him. Common to the tyrants in Isa. 14.4b-20 and Ezek. 28.1-10, 11-19 is their hubris. Like Adam and Eve (cf. Gen. 2-3), they try to become like God, but pride comes before a fall. As soon as man forgets the limits God has set for him God must intervene and punish him with death.

We meet in *Ezekiel 31–32* the same basic theme, but here formulated by means of a tree image. Pharaoh is a cedar of Lebanon which has been given ideal growing conditions. Its roots draw water from the depths of the world, and its top is set among the clouds.[26] God has made the cedar so beautiful that all the trees of Eden are envious of it. But just as the king of Tyre became arrogant and thought of himself as a god, so did Pharaoh the cedar become arrogant because of his/its height, יען אשר גבהת בקומה (v. 10). The tree was indeed about to grow up into heaven, i.e. to become like God. It was then that Yahweh had to surrender it for felling. Alien people are to cut it down and cast it away. It must be felled so that no tree shall ever again become arrogant and lift its crown right up into the clouds, since all trees must end among the dead in the nether world. Then shall Lebanon mourn and peoples quake because of the cedar's fate, and the trees of Eden shall share its fate. 'This is Pharaoh and all his multitude', reads the interpretation in v. 18.[27]

In ch. 32, the motif of the descent into the land of the dead is resumed in the form of another lament (Ezek. 32.18-32). Pharaoh is to find his grave among the uncircumcised, slain by the sword (!) in the nether world. He shall share the fate of other kings who ended ignominiously in the land of the dead, without a hero's grave, without armour, sword and shield.

The object of this review of Ezekiel texts has been to show how the main idea running through Isa. 14.4b-20 not only plays a central part in the book of Ezekiel but can indeed be expressed by *combining tree images* with concepts of the arrogant king's punishment in the form of *banishment to the land of the dead*. There is no complete accordance between the way in which the motifs are utilized in Isaiah 14 and in the Ezekiel texts. In Isa. 14.4b-20, it is the arrogant one who is sent to the land of the dead, described as both a hewer (v. 8) and as the tree that is felled (the severed shoot) (v. 19). In Ezekiel 31–32, Pharaoh is described only as the tree that is felled, but both the texts referred to have in common that they utilize the tree image to describe the reason for the tyrant's fall. Through the tree image, they are in a position to argue that the tyrant concerned is doomed: it is he who considers himself equal to God that must be sent to the antithesis of the divine world: the land of the dead.

Conclusion

The analysis of Isa. 14.4b-20 concludes the discussion of some important examples of the use of tree images. On each occasion we have been able to establish (a) that the tree image acts as a key to interpretation of the *political situation* (informative function),[28] (b) that imagery is employed *argumentatively*; the familiar images and the myths behind them are used not only to inform but also to influence the hearers (performative function), so that they adopt the author's way of interpreting the situation and make it their own,[29] and (c) that the use of imagery makes it possible to *reuse* the texts— but at the same time makes precise dating difficult.

The analysis of Isa. 14.4b-20 has additionally made it possible to cast a little more light upon the *mythical concepts* lying behind the use of the tree image. Up to now we have been referring relatively vaguely to the basic myth of the fertility cult in which the god/king/ tree is felled in order subsequently to arise/sprout again, and to some extent to the special tree-felling myth in which the trees in the garden of God are destroyed by an alien criminal, who is banished to the nether world as punishment.

We have seen in the analysis of, inter alia, Isa. 10.33-34 + 11.1 that Isaiah can combine tree-felling with new sprouting. This has made it possible for Isaiah to indicate a way of understanding the complex political situation commensurate with the basic structure of the cult myth on death and resurrection; but this is seen through/formulated through the image of the tree that is felled but sprouts again.

In Isa. 14.4b-20, we have encountered ideas about the forest-feller in Lebanon and the tree that is felled, and we have seen how these tree images are combinded with banishment to the nether world. But how do these motifs relate to one another? For the time being, I think it is important to emphasize that the ideas concerned are not mutually exclusive, but on the contrary supplement one another. But whereas it is possible, with no previous knowledge other than that we presumably all possess from our dealings with nature, to arrive at an understanding of what is meant by the image of the tree that is felled but sprouts again and of the tree's erectness as an expression of pride and arrogance, this does not apply to the concepts of the forest-feller in Lebanon. It is necessary here to know *the narrative behind the image* in order to grasp the author's intention: to stamp this forest-feller as a usurper, a titan, who tries to arrogate divine power to himself.

Behind this narrative lie the concepts of the tree as a holy tree. It is these concepts which give the felling of trees the nature of sacrilege. But at the same time it is these concepts which—in their close association with the myth of the god/king who dies and is resurrected—reinforce the image of the tree that is felled but sprouts again.

When these concepts of the garden of Lebanon and its holy trees are expressed in the Old Testament, Yahweh is clearly the owner of the garden. It is of course impossible, on the basis of Isaiah's theology, to identify Yahweh with the divine trees that are felled. Israel's Holy One is not a dying and resurrecting god. On the other hand, Yahweh's people or the people's enemies can die; not by accident or by reason of usurpation but as righteous punishment. And what certainly deserves punishment is the arrogance which makes man believe that he is God himself.

This gives us two possible variations: the arrogant hewer who wishes to arrogate divine status to himself but is punished for it; and the proud trees who wish to reach into heaven but are felled for it. We meet the first variation in Isa. 14.8; the other in Isa. 14.19, although only in catch-phrases. Finally, in Isa. 10.33-34 + 11.1 we have a combination of the second variation and the concepts that the tree, despite being felled, can sprout again.[30]

5. *Analysis of Isa. 37.22b-32*

Context

The two images we shall discuss in Isaiah 37 are included in the narratives referring to Isaiah's role during Sennacherib's siege of Jerusalem in 701.[1] The passage 37.22b-32 breaks the chapter's natural narrative context. Previous to v. 22b, we hear that Isaiah sends a message to Hezekiah conveying to him Yahweh's answer to his prayer about the king of Assyria, but only after v. 32, i.e. in 37.33-

35, does the reply follow, with the promise of Yahweh's protection of Jerusalem.[2]

The redactors placed vv. 22b-32 in the middle of this context because they wished to make the Isaiah traditions about the events of 701 usable for their own time, so that by means of these traditions they could arrive at an interpretation of Yahweh's will in regard to the Babylonian exile. The analysis of Isaiah 14 showed that the Exilic period's redactors utilized material from the Isaiah tradition to mock and deride the tyrant of their own time, the king of Babylon. In Isaiah 37, we are confronted with the same phenomenon; but we undeniably lack a direct indication that what is said about Yahweh's plans for the proud tyrant is to be understood as referring to the king of Babylon; in any event as referring not only to the king of Assyria, Sennacherib, with whom the context is otherwise concerned. If we look more closely at vv. 22b-32, there are a number of features that point in this direction.

Isa. 37.22b-32 as a Redactional Composition

The passage falls into three parts; vv. 22b-25, the satirical song about the great king; vv. 26-29, which interprets and amplifies the song; and vv. 30-32, which is a positive oracle about the future of Judah and Jerusalem. Whereas *Aage Bentzen*[3] considers vv. 22b-29 as a whole, and dates this 'satirical song about the world conqueror' to the later epochs of the Assyrian period, *Brevard S. Childs*[4] considers that vv. 26-29 are an addition to vv. 22b-25. Childs points out that the satirical song displays great similarities to Isa. 10.5ff., and concludes from this that it contains old material. But whether by this he means Isaianic material is not quite clear. Verses 26-29, on the other hand, are later; they are stamped by Deutero-Isaianic language and thought processes. Childs gives no examples of this, but in our context it is worthy of note that the use of grass (referred to with various glosses) as an image of the transient is well-known, particularly in Deutero-Isaiah (cf. Isa. 40.6-8; 40.24; 47.14; 51.12).[5] Similarly typical is the strong emphasis on Yahweh's 'long-term planning' of political events (cf. Isa. 45.21; 46.10; 48.3) and the importance of prophetic proof in Isa. 41.21ff. and 43.8ff.

I therefore agree with Childs in his assessment of the relationship between vv. 22b-25 and vv. 26-29, and I believe that the key to understanding the intention in inserting vv. 22b-32 is in fact to be found in the situation in which vv. 26-29 came into existence: *the Babylonian Exile.*

Whereas the narrative of Sennacherib's siege of Jerusalem in 701 proclaims Yahweh's unbounded care for Jerusalem, vv. 26-29 as well as vv. 30-32 envisage that destruction has taken place, and thus reflect a situation entirely different from that of 701. According to vv. 26-29, the great king has demonstrably made fortified cities crash into ruins, with a deadly impact upon their inhabitants. Only a remnant of Judah and Jerusalem is left (vv. 30-32).

It is fairly clear that the situation is the Exilic period, although it is noteworthy that the redactors wished to link up with the message heard in about 701, when the outcome of the political crisis was entirely different. Not only do they place their own message in the centre of the narratives about 701; they also utilize the existing oracles in vv. 22b-25 and vv. 30-32, which may very well go back to Isaiah himself, or at least to Isaiah's circle.

Taken with the concluding description of Jerusalem's salvation (Isa. 37.36-38), vv. 33-35 reflect *the Zion theology* according to which Yahweh protects and redeems Jerusalem for his own sake and for the sake of his servant David. The extraordinary rescue from Sennacherib's siege has become interpreted as Yahweh's miraculous intervention, and together with the optimism of Josiah's time the fall of the kingdom of Assyria has further assisted this theology to attain a strong position. The events of 587, on the other hand, were catastrophic for this theology. The miracle of 701 was not repeated. Reconsideration is therefore necessary if faith in Yahweh's power and wish to save is not to be lost. And Isaiah's message could be used in this reconsideration. Isaiah's idea of the remnant is an example of how the new situation can be interpreted so as to become meaningful. Destruction is unavoidable; the people must get through the crisis. But they will survive and take root again. This is therefore a redactional attempt to utilize Isaianic concepts and images to interpret events in 587.[6]

R.E. Clements considers that the events of around 587 are crucial to the reinterpretation to which Isaiah's message has been exposed. It is the need to find an explanation of external political events that leads the redactors back to the prophetic message to seek a meaning in what was happening in their own time.[7] As Carroll expressed it: dissonance gives rise to hermeneutic.

The composition and placing of Isa. 37.22b-32 must therefore originate from the period after 587, when there was a grave need for interpretation of Yahweh's attitude towards Jerusalem. The two entirely different outcomes of an alien great power's attack on Yahweh's city demanded explanation, if frustration was not to result. By going back to *Isaiah's denunciation of the great king*, now read with the king of Babylon in mind, and by combining this message with *Isaiah's concept of the remnant*, the redactors can create the necessary correlation in the events they are experiencing: Yahweh is still he who overcomes arrogant tyrants and ensures a future for his own people—although they must first go through a crisis.

The Tree Image in Isa. 37.24

As B.S. Childs, for example, has pointed out, the oracle in vv. 22b-25 reminds one of Isa. 10.5-15. Read in a narrative context, i.e. as an account of the events of 701, the oracle is directed towards the king of Assyria, Sennacherib, and as in Isa. 10.5-15 the central subject here is the great king's arrogance. Both oracles employ the technique of allowing the king to reveal himself by his boastful utterances. There is no doubt that Isa. 37.24-25, which quotes what Sennacherib is alleged to have said, is formulated as a counterpart to the Assyrian victory inscriptions, in which the kings describe their own exploits.[8] This gives the 'quotation' the stamp of authenticity. This is what the king of Assyria actually said!

Sennacherib describes his own achievements by recounting how he went up into Lebanon with his many chariots and felled its cedars and cypresses; how he dug up drinking water and even dried up the streams of Egypt, i.e. the Nile, by walking across it. The first part of the statement, v. 24, corresponds to the descriptions we have of kings from the Mesopotamian region obtaining timber for building their palaces and temples from Lebanon, among other sources. The words therefore appear to be authentic, and indeed many interpreters believe that this passage in fact refers to the ruthless exploitation to which Lebanon, for example, was exposed;[9] i.e. that v. 24 should be understood literally.

Matters are different in regard to v. 25. From an historical point of view, in any event the description of the crossing of the Nile causes difficulties. It is understandable that Sennacherib made arrangements to obtain water during his victorious campaigns;[10] but if the text and what follows allude to an actual conquest of Egypt it is unhistorical to link this to Sennacherib, since no such conquest took place until the time of his successors. The actual phrasing of his exploits is also striking, even for an Assyrian victory inscription. Otto Kaiser in fact points out that the author uses this form of words to impute to Sennacherib that he considered himself to be like a god (cf. Isa. 51.10).

I am in no doubt that the purpose of the 'Sennacherib quotation' is to reveal his hubris; but in vv. 24-25 we are not, as many have thought, confronted with literal language but *imagery*.

Viewed in this light, one must of course be careful in accepting the oracle as an indication that—historically—a conquest had taken place when it came into existence, i.e. that the oracle is later than 671 when Memphis was conquered and than 667 when Thebes was conquered. Dating should much rather take its point of reference from the fact that images and genres are used which are taken from Isaiah's message, but this does not make it possible to arrive at a dating more precise than that for which the narrative framework itself sets the scene. The satirical song directed against the great king could in fact have acted very effectively in the very context of Sennacherib's siege of Jerusalem in 701, just as could Isa. 14.4b-20.

The unmasking of Sennacherib really succeeds in vv. 24-25, where the author permits him to describe himself as him who is not only able to climb high mountains but has also felled Lebanon's cedars and cypresses, and as him who not only can obtain water for the army during his campaigns but has also dried up the Nile. In both cases, the statements are given a form that aroused a large number of connotations among the Israelite hearers. Hans Wildberger rightly points out that one gets the impression, 'daß V. 24 auf ein traditionelles Begriffsreservoir zürückgreift, wie das der Verfasser von Kap. 14 auch getan hat'.[11] Wildberger does not specify the material which is utilized in v. 24, but if the content of this verse is compared with the tree images in ch. 14 it becomes clear that it is the narrative about the garden of Lebanon. It is used here to show that the great king behaves as only Yahweh himself has a right to do. Indeed, the garden is Yahweh's, and no-one else has a right to fell its trees. Similarly, the miraculous draining of the Nile is not within the king's power; Yahweh also 'holds the patent' for this.

According to the parallel text in 2 Kgs 19.23, there is a מלון, i.e. a place to spend the night, at the top of Lebanon. This reflects the

concepts of the divine abode on the holy mountain. In Isa. 37.24, מלון
has been corrected to מרום, presumably by a transcriber who alone
understood the text as a description of Lebanon's impressive heights.
The version in the book of Kings underlines even more clearly than
the version in the book of Isaiah that Sennacherib's enterprise is
really hubris; he wishes to conquer the divine abode.

The author utilizes the myth of Lebanon's holy trees to *unmask
Sennacherib* as the blasphemer. This note is already struck in the
first stanzas of the passage in the description of the derision of
Jerusalem and the accusation of pride. Verses 26-27's interpretation
of vv. 24-25 not only makes it clear that this is Yahweh acting
through the great king, as is emphasized by Isa. 10.5ff.; what is new,
and indeed typical of the Deutero-Isaianic message, is the emphasis
that the planning of this took place long ago, but has only now been
carried out.

It is also clear from vv. 26-27 that v. 24 has been understood and
interpreted by the redactors as imagery. As in Isaiah 14, where the
context interpreted v. 8's imagery, vv. 26-27 act as clarification of
what is meant by saying that the great king has felled Lebanon's
cedars (v. 24), i.e. the conquering and destruction of cities and
people. What the author permits him to express in the self-revealing
imagery is now described in plain words, and is designated as
Yahweh's work into the bargain!

Here also, therefore, the felling of Lebanon's trees is seen as an
image[12] of political events. But whereas in, for example, Isa. 10.33-34
we have the motif: the proud trees = the leaders, the tyrants, the
trees are here, as in Isa. 14.8, positively connoted and used about the
people who are oppressed and are suffering under the great king's
usurpation.

The Tree Image in Isa. 37.31
In extension of this, I wish briefly to point out that v. 31 also takes its
imagery from the plant world. The plant concerned is not immediately
apparent, but since the image is used about Judah's remnant and the
oracle has been placed in direct extension of v. 30, which refers to
vineyards and their fruit, the reader will naturally think of a vine (cf.
Isa. 5.1-7; 27.6; Ps. 80.9ff.).

The author focuses on roots and fruit,[13] which means that Israel's
remnant, i.e. those who survive the catastrophe, will fully function
again just like a tree that has roots and bears fruit. The remnant is

not only a remnant, but something positive and fruitful.

There is little doubt that vv. 30-32 are a later addition[14] meant to clarify the positive implications for Judah of Yahweh's punishment of the arrogant great king. The oracle moves cautiously, with a slow improvement of the situation for the remnant which has survived the catastrophe, and concludes with v. 32's assurance that this is accomplished by the zeal of the Lord of Hosts. This assurance is borrowed from Isa. 9.6, and likewise the remnant concept has its basis in Isaiah's message (cf. Isa. 7.3), but we can scarcely assert that the oracle in its present form goes back to Isaiah himself.

There is much to indicate, however, that at least it was not drafted with an eye to its present position. The oracle is not directed to Sennacherib but to Hezekiah. It offers the king a sign, whose function must be to support an assertion of salvation already given; but the assertion of salvation does not appear until vv. 33-35. Furthermore, the link between the two tree images in v. 24 and v. 31 is not quite as successful as one might expect if the oracle was created for this very context, since the reader must see the plant in v. 31 as a vine, whereas v. 24 concerns cedars and cypresses. It is therefore probable that the redactors made use of an available oracle taken from the Isaiah tradition which could in their opinion provide the logical conclusion to the satirical song.

The passage's *chain of argument* is therefore as follows: vv. 22b-25, the king's self-presentation, which reveals his hubris; vv. 26-27, which on the one hand makes it clear that the king is guilty of self-conceit, and on the other hand interprets the imagery used; vv. 28-29, which announces Yahweh's just punishment of the blasphemer; and vv. 30-32, which promise a happy future for Judah and Jerusalem after the crisis. In general terms, we find the same chain of argument in Isa. 10.6-11.9.

By his choice of image, therefore, the author is in a position to deliver up the tyrant in such a way that the hearers can identify themselves with the trees and come to a new understanding of their own situation. They have been the victims of an arrogant tyrant, but the tyrant's hubris will be punished. The plant image in v. 31 is therefore used, in extension of the image in v. 24, to argue for a positive future for *the victim*. (Cf. Isa. 14.4b-20, where the interest is concentrated on *the tyrant* and his fate.) Despite the destruction of the trees, new sprouting will occur.

We have previously met, within the Isaiah traditions, examples of tree images being used to combine the negative and the positive. We saw in Isa. 10.33-34 + 11.1 a very clearly formulated *combination* of *tree-felling* and new *sprouting*, and after closer examination of the image's history of use and reuse we were able to see how suitable this had been for *reinterpretation*. We had the same experience in regard to the vineyard image in the analysis of Isa. 27.2-6's reuse of Isa. 5.1-7.

A clear parallel to Isa. 37.22b-32 is to be found in Isa. 14.4b-20, where the myth of the felling of Lebanon's trees is used just as it is in Isaiah 37 to unmask the arrogant tyrant.[15] In addition, a common feature of both texts is that they use a further tree image. In Isa. 14.19, the image of the shoot is used, in 37.31, the image of new rooting and setting of fruit; basically the same image but used exactly conversely in the two versions. In Isa. 14.19, the shoot is removed from its vital connexion with the tree; in 37.31, the symbiosis is restored, the tree puts down roots again and fulfils its function, just as Israel is to do according to Isa. 27.6. The alien great king's fate and the fate of Yahweh's people are directly opposed one to another.

Isa. 37.31's imagery therefore fits well into the patterns that gradually emerge. But in regard to this image also there is reason to look beyond the Isaiah tradition and to supplement our understanding of *the oracle's importance in the Exilic period* with a contemporary example from the book of Ezekiel, i.e. Ezekiel 17's use of the tree as an image.

Excursus
Ezekiel 17 is quite a complicated text. The introduction refers to it with the words חידה ומשל indicating that it concerns figurative language or a riddle which requires interpretation. Commentators have indeed tried to solve the text's riddles by translating the individual elements of the imagery into non-figurative language, and by examining the relationship between the figurative language (vv. 3-10 + 22-24) and the interpretation incorporated (vv. 11-21).[16] In our context, it is sufficient as regards the interpretation itself to note that the tree images (both cedar and vine) are here also to be understood in the light of the political code,[17] and that as regards the interpretation (vv. 11-21) this is a later insertion in which the redactors try to uphold one interpretation of the figurative language.

But there is reason to consider the individual elements of which the figurative language in Ezekiel 17 consists, since here we encounter a number of images and motifs with which we are familiar from the Isaiah tradition. *Ezek. 17.3-4* describes how the great eagle came to Lebanon, took the top of the cedar and carried it to a city of trade. The destruction (felling) of the cedar of Lebanon is a motif we have met on several occasions (cf. Isa. 10.33-34; 14.8; 37.24), and since the eagle is an image of the king the connexion with concepts referring to the ruthless exploitation of Lebanon appears to be clear, whether one considers, as does Bernhard Lang, that what is referred to is the king's felling of forests with a view to the export of timber,[18] or, as I do, one prefers to turn to the mythical concepts surrounding Lebanon.

The next scene in the figurative language, *Ezek. 17.5-10*, describes the planting of a vine in good and fertile soil where it can develop. But the vine is not content with the opportunities it is given; it behaves quite contrary to nature by sending its roots towards another eagle to get even more water, and as a consequence it must be punished by being pulled up by the roots so that it can be dried up and scorched by the east wind. Despite all the differences (and there are many), the sequence of action and argument corresponds to what we know about the vineyard parable in Isa. 5,1-7.

Finally, we are told in the chapter's last verses, *Ezek. 17.22-23*, that Yahweh plants a sprig from the cedar on Israel's high mountain—i.e. Zion—as a sign that Yahweh humbles the high—i.e. the proud—tree and makes high the low—i.e. the humble—tree, כי אני יהוה השפלתי עץ גבה הגבהתי עץ שפל (Ezek. 17.24). This motif also reminds one of the Isaiah tradition's concepts of the new time when the tree is to put forth new shoots (cf. Isa. 27.6; 11.1; 6.13; 37.31; and Isa. 4.2) and of the humbling of the proud, perhaps expressed most clearly in Isa. 2.12-17; but we have already encountered this in Isa. 10.33-34 and Isa. 14.4b-20.

In his analysis of Ezekiel 17, Bernhard Lang is careful to point out that there is a form of conventional image-logic behind the use of images.[19] Consequently, much of what we do not understand today was quite obvious to hearers of the time. Although in my opinion Lang has not gone far enough in his attempts to reveal the tree image's form and function,[20] I agree with him entirely in his basic approach. The use of images is not fortuitous, but follows a number of conventions known to the contemporaries which the speaker can utilize either by following them—or by breaking them and thus creating the germ of new conventions.

Conclusion

Isa. 37.22b-32 is an insertion into the account of events in 701 and, read directly, recounts Isaiah's message in the context of Sennacherib's siege of Jerusalem. Closer analysis of the text showed that this is a composition of later creation, which came into existence after Jerusalem's destruction in 587. Of this composition, the satirical song with the Lebanon motif may very well go back to Isaiah's own message in the context of 701, when the function of the song was to mock the arrogant king of Assyria. The oracle about Judah's remnant

(vv. 30-32) has also probably been taken from the Isaiah tradition, and placed secondarily in its present context.

The purpose of this composition was, in the first place, to explain to the generation of the Exile what was Yahweh's will and plan in destroying Jerusalem, i.e. to give *information about the political events*, and, secondly, to comfort those affected and disheartened (*performative function*). The means of achieving this include the tree images and the concepts associated therewith. By using the image of Lebanon's destruction, the redactors are able to argue that the destruction of 587 was a token of the king of Babylon's hubris, and must therefore lead to his fall. The great king is indeed a tool in Yahweh's hands, and he has dug his own grave by his arrogance. Moreover, the tree image can be used to comfort those affected: Jerusalem's destruction is not the end of the people's history but the introduction to a new life, since Judah's remnant will take root and bear fruit.

It is true that history did not repeat itself first time, but by making the narrative of the happy outcome of the events in 701 the framework of the message to the Exilic generation, and by reusing and reinterpreting the images from the Isaiah tradition, the redactors are able to argue strongly that the great king's days are numbered, whereas the victim still has vitality. An important point in this *reuse and reinterpretation* is, indeed, that this message is not presented as an innovation but as the words of Isaiah uttered long before what has now occurred, just as Yahweh's plans were already laid in days gone by.

6. *Analysis of Isa. 2.12-17 and 32.15-20*

Two further texts concerned with the humbling of the proud make use of the tree image. In Isa. 2.12-17 it is the cedars of Lebanon and the oaks of Bashan that are to be struck on Yahweh's day, whereas Isa. 32.19 speaks of the fall of the forest. Neither of the two texts adds anything vitally new to the observations we have already made in regard to the use of the tree image, and discussions of them can therefore be very brief.[1]

Isa. 2.12-17
The main theme of this oracle is Yahweh's day, when all that is great and arrogant is to be humbled. The oracle, whose genuineness is

undisputed, is clearly well-balanced, and from the redactional aspect a context has been added condemning idolatry.[2] In the Old Testament, Lebanon and Bashan are positively connoted regions known for their fertility. They are mentioned together in Isa. 33.9; Ezek. 27.6; Nah. 1.4 and Zech. 11.2. In Isa. 2.13 the lofty and strutting aspects of the trees are stressed; they are examples of the pride and arrogance that comes before a fall. Juxtaposed with these trees is a reference to the high mountains, the fortified cities and the beautiful ships of Tarshish, all of them things on which the people pin their faith. The mountains, which from a military aspect are safe places of refuge, and the fortified cities, with their towers and walls, lead the mind back to the political situation and the people's confidence in their own strength. They rely on themselves, and not on Yahweh—a theme well-known in the Isaiah tradition.

Viewed in this context, it is natural to interpret the trees of Lebanon and Bashan as an image of the political leaders whose greatness is interpreted as arrogance. Such an understanding of the tree image is to be found, for example, in the Targum, where 'all the trees of Lebanon' has been translated as 'all the peoples' strong and mighty kings'.[3] But more important than this late interpretation, in my opinion, is the redactional reading of the image to be found in Isa. 2.12-17's context.[4]

Closer analysis of Isa. 2.6-22 as a redactional entity shows that the redactor has consciously tried to bind the individual oracles together into one entity, for example by repeating crucial words and formulations.[5] If we look at vv. 12-17's context collectively, it can be established that the theme—arrogance which is to be humbled— indeed plays an important role here, but that a new theme seems to assert itself, i.e. the idol polemic. The redactor has wished the central oracle to be understood, using this polemic as a frame of reference.

In Isaiah's time, coalition policy was an important problem. For example, should king Ahaz join Israel and Aram to defend himself, together with them, against Assyria (cf. Isa. 7), and how should Hezekiah behave towards Assyria and Egypt (cf. Isa. 20)? And it can be seen from 2 Kgs 16.18 that Ahaz's contact with the king of Assyria resulted in Ahaz having to make certain changes in the cultic domain, changes that can only have evoked disapproval in Isaianic circles. It is not therefore surprising that the redactor of this text has seen a connexion between political coalitions with aliens and idolatry.

But it is scarcely likely that the redactor associates the tree image and idol polemics only because the destruction of the trees of Lebanon can be used as an image of the political leaders' fate, and because the political leaders became idol-worshippers as a result of their coalition policy. The trees of Lebanon and Bashan, the high and chosen trees, connote a *holy tree*, in the same way as the high mountains are often associated with holy places. I therefore consider it probable that some of the background to the redactional combination of the two motifs is to be found in the tree's function as a holy tree and the redactor's view of the tree cult as idolatry. Cf. also the connexion between trees and idolatry in Isa. 1.29-31.

To summarize, it must be said that Isa. 2.12-17 is yet another example of how central the arrogance motif is to Isaiah's message, and how the image of the high trees was employed to refer to the political leaders, who have been guilty of arrogance and therefore deserve the punishment to come. A theological interpretation of the political events is thus presented, giving the hearers/readers an opportunity to see a connexion between peoples' actions and Yahweh's actions, between the trees' erectness/pride and their fall. The tree image in this text is very little developed, and we must therefore express ourselves with great care, especially in regard to its *function* in the original situation. Consideration of how the redactor is able to *reinterpret* vv. 12-17 by surrounding this passage with other oracles and amplifying comments is of importance to an investigation of the *redactional processing* of the Isa. 2.6-22 passage.

Isa. 32.15-20
The description of the fall of the forest in 32.19 is included in the 32.15-20 passage, which acts as the positive counterpart to the judgment oracle in 32.9-14. Both Rémi Lack and Hermann Barth[6] believe that vv. 15-20 is a redactional composition created in conscious contrast to vv. 9-14 under the influence of a number of other texts from the book of Isaiah.

The fall of the forest and the humiliation of the city are thus included in a description of a cosmos, but since the ideal time can scarcely be envisaged as a time of no forests (cf. Isa. 32.15; 41.19; 55.13), the fall of the forest must be an image. The passage must be understood in the same way as Isa. 2.13, 15, where we have the description of the humiliation of trees and cities. Both texts use the root שׁפל to indicate destruction, and so provide a theological interpretation of this.

In his analysis of ch. 32, Rémi Lack[7] points out that the thematic structure of the chapter displays marked similarities with Isa. 4.2-6, but does not clarify his approach. Lack's observation is correct. The negative background to Isa. 4.2-6 is the judgment on the women in Isa. 3.16–4.1, in the same way as the negative background to 32.15-20 is in 32.9-14's demand that the complacent women should mourn the calamity. In Isa. 4.4, the judgment aspect is assimilated in the salvation statement in the form of the purification image. In Isa. 32.19, the judgment is assimilated in the same way, so that it becomes clear that the two phases belong together. The image of the forest that falls and the city that is humbled can therefore naturally be understood as an *internal purification* which conditions the time of salvation. As in Isa. 2.13, this is a polemic against those circles in Jerusalem which can be considered as arrogant, i.e. the leaders.

Chapter 32 clearly makes use of Isaianic material; thus v. 3 takes up Isa. 6.10, and vv. 1 and 2 appear to have a connexion with Isa. 11.3-5 and 4.6.[8] The redaction of the chapter must, however, be placed considerably later than Isaiah's own time. The strong emphasis that the precondition for a future time of happiness under a just king is temporary destruction would make good sense after 587, when it becomes clear that the fall of Jerusalem and the deportation of the leaders is a stage in Yahweh's plan one day to create a new time for his people. If this is the case, the composition will have come into existence on the basis of the same attitudes as those behind the redaction of Isa. 4.2-6 and its placing in the context.

To summarize, it only remains to point out that Isa. 32.19, like 2.13, uses the tree image in reference to the political circumstances in Judah.

7. Analysis of Isa. 4.2-6

Dating and Context

Isa. 4.2-6 is a *redactional composition* from *the Exilic period* whose purpose it is to balance and interpret the preceding chapters. The judgment is not Yahweh's last word but a necessary precondition for the salvation. We encounter in v. 2 an image from the plant world, the image of a new branch. In the earlier analyses of the tree image, we have seen how the tree is felled or in some other way destroyed. This motif appears to be missing here, since we are presented only with the branch, i.e. that part of the image which we know from, for example, Isa. 11.1 and Isa. 6.13. But this does not mean that the negative background for the appearance of the branch is missing. The 'negative background' is merely formed on the basis of a different code, i.e. as a condemnation of the daughters of Zion (Isa. 3.16–4.1).

It is clear that we must read these verses as a lead into Isa. 4.2 not merely from the placing itself but also from the redactor's careful readoption of the motif: the fate of Zion's daughters in Isa. 4.4.[1] By means of the image of the purification of Zion's daughters (Isa. 4.4), the connexion between the negative and positive is secured in one single image, while at the same time the punishment is defined as a purifying judgment.

In my opinion, the redactor chooses an image from the plant world to describe the happy future in Isa. 4.2 out of a wish to form a link to Isa. 2.13, where the humiliation of all that is great is described as a destruction of Lebanon's cedars, lofty and lifted up, and all Bashan's oaks. The code used in ch. 2 to describe the negative is resumed here to describe the positive. The redactor seems to wish to tell his contemporaries that there is an organic connexion between past and future, between the felling of trees and new sprouting, between the leaders' fall and the new time.

There is no doubt that the time at which the redactor undertakes his assembling of the Isaianic traditions is the Exilic period. Apart from what we can point to as a readoption of motifs, it is in fact the concentration on *Zion's fate* that binds the first four chapters together (cf. also Zion's raising up in Isa. 2.2-4). This concentration is best understood on the basis of the experience of Zion's destruction. Two aspects are upheld: Yahweh's day has struck Zion, and the people have thereby experienced the purifying process of which the prophet Isaiah had spoken, but the happy future when Zion becomes the centre of the world is still imminent. These are aspects the redactor wishes to hold fast to, since it is in their light that the people's present situation can be given meaning. The Exile and the catastrophe which Zion had to experience were Yahweh's righteous punishment. This is clear from Isaiah's many judgment oracles, which are now given importance as evidence and witness. But it must not be forgotten that the future will appear in a different light. This the prophet has also said.[2] The object of the images used in the passage, including the tree image, is therefore not only to argue that there is such a connexion in the people's history, and thereby cause them to look at the political situation in a new way, but also to *comfort* and *encourage* the Exilic generation.

Aage Bentzen refers to ch. 4 as 'a mosaic of *clichés* from different sources, bearing the mark of epigonism'.[3] He indicates here the valid point that it represents a mosaic created from available individual parts. But I cannot agree with negatively charged words such as cliché and epigonism. The text's images are not all equally successful, but the image of the new branch, the oracle of the remnant in Zion and the image of the purification of Zion's daughters really do not deserve such a designation.

What makes Bentzen and many others believe that the entire passage is something late and therefore secondary in a negative sense is presumably the way in which one image follows another. It is introduced by the image of Yahweh's branch, צמח יהוה, the description of the fruit of the land and what all this is going to mean to the survivors of Israel (v. 2). Immediately after follows an amplifying oracle about the remnant of Zion (v. 3). Verse 4 presents the image of washing away the filth of the daughters of Zion. This operates in the context to explain how the remnant will emerge. A new image (v. 5) describes the care for the remnant: Yahweh will create a cloud by day and a fire by night. It is unclear whether the image of the canopy belongs to this or is an addition whose function is to visualize the care in a new way, perhaps to connect v. 5 and v. 6. The image in v. 5 is thus an amplifying comment on the image in v. 4, while at the same time it needed amplifying itself. In any event, v. 5 has been supplemented by the image of the pavilion that is to give shelter from heat and rain (v. 6).

But how is one to interpret this complex structure? In my opinion, it is really an indication that the redactor wished to pass on available material which has a connexion with Isaiah's message, and not that subsequent prophets do not express themselves as clearly.

That scholars such as *Hans Wildberger*[4] and *J. Vermeylen*[5] date not only the redaction but also the coming into existence of the individual oracles to the post-Exilic period is of course attributable to the significance of the passage. Their analyses of what Isa. 4.2-6 meant in the post-Exilic period is indeed pertinent, and accords well with what I myself consider to be the post-Exilic period's use of this passage. But that the passage made good sense at the time it was written and could be reused in the period following thereafter does not mean that all its individual parts are similarly late. I think here that the similarity in content with Isaiah's message suggests that at least parts of v. 2 and v. 3 originate from the traditions of Isaiah's message.[6] As regards its ideas, the image of the purification process in v. 4 is also so similar to Isaiah's theology that it must have a connexion to it.

The Use of the Tree Image
Let us look more closely at Isa. 4.2 and its function in the context of *Isa. 3.16–4.6*. The fate of the daughters of Zion is described on the basis of the war code, and this is done from the women's point of view. To them, war means not only renouncing luxury but also husbands and thus children. So few men are left that the women must fight for them to avoid the disgrace of childlessness (cf. Isa. 54.4 and Gen. 30.23).

The redactor then places Isa. 4.2's description of the time to come in contrast to this situation. This redactional work clearly took place during the Exile, when there was good reason to describe *Jerusalem* by using *the image of a woman* left all alone (Isa. 3.26). The hope for the future is, then, that Jerusalem will flower once again.

The image of Jerusalem as a childless and mourning woman, perhaps a widow, is used many times in the book of Isaiah as a background to the hope of the homecoming.[7] Cf. Isa. 49.14ff.; 54.1ff.; 60.1ff.; 62.4 and 66.7ff. The image was well-adapted to interpreting the Exile situation, where Jerusalem is deserted; but the same image can also act as the bearer of dreams of the future: through Yahweh's intervention, the childless woman becomes the mother of many. This motif is also repeated in the patriarchal narratives, which played an important role particularly during the period of the Exile. The ancestresses experienced the same fate: first childlessness, then the long-expected child is born. The people's earlier history and their present history are thus perceived as reflected images of one another.

We have thus been able to establish that Isa. 3.16–4.1 + 4.2 make use of *two images* similar to one another in structure:[8] the image of the childless *woman* who (perhaps once again) becomes productive, and the image of the *tree* that is destroyed but sprouts again. Since the structure is the same, and since both images have been used to interpret the past and shape the expectations for the future, the redactor can combine them so that the negative part is taken from one image, the childless woman, and the positive part from the other, the new shoot. We cannot know whether the redactor felt that the two images are related to one another; both describe lack of vitality—new vitality. But this is decidedly possible, even though in the light of our way of thought we may find the similarity limited, perhaps far-fetched, and would prefer to emphasize that one of the images belongs to the human world and the other to the plant world.[9]

It should also be stressed that the theme in Isa. 3.16ff., the *humbling of the proud women*, is well in keeping with the theme of the tree image in Isa. 2.13, *the humbling of the proud trees*. Motifs and images are thus interwoven with one another so that together they form a strong chain of argument in which the punishment of the proud leaders must precede the re-establishment of the kingdom of the future. The negative precondition for Isa. 4.2 is thus to be found not only in Isa. 3.16ff.; it is already pronounced in the tree code in Isa. 2.13's description of Yahweh's day against the lofty trees of Lebanon and Bashan.

צמח יהוה

The term *Yahweh's branch* is understood either as a figurative expression of the fruitfulness that will eventually come or as an image of the coming king. The latter possibility is realized in the Targum, which quite simply translates the image as Yahweh's Messiah, משיחא דיהוה. But it is more important in understanding Isa. 4.2 that Jer. 23.5; 33.15; Zech. 3.8; and 6.12 use similar terms with צמח about the coming king. The objection to this interpretation of the term is primarily that צמח יהוה is parallel to, and therefore must mean the same as, פרי הארץ, and since this must be understood as referring to the land's fruit/fruitfulness (cf. Deut. 1.25) and cannot be a Messianic title, neither can צמח יהוה.[10] The parallel with the Jeremiah texts is also rejected because Jeremiah speaks of *David's* branch and not, as here, of *Yahweh's* branch.

As regards these arguments, it should first be said that the parallelism argument is not binding. Although Hebrew likes to place two parallel terms side by side, it is possible even in Hebrew to speak in terms other than pure parallelisms. As regards David's branch versus Yahweh's branch, it must be asserted that the Israelite king can with equal justification (cf. the Psalms[11]) be considered as Yahweh's or David's progeny, and so the designations can also be interchanged. It is therefore possible that the first term refers to the coming king, whereas the second term refers to the fruitfulness that will characterize the land. If this is the case, we meet the same train of thought as in Psalm 72, where the king's justice is shown not only by his righteous condemnation of his people and his overcoming of his people's enemies but also in that the land is fruitful. There is consequently a connexion between the king's justice and nature's fruitfulness.

The literal interpretation of the land's fruit does not therefore exclude a figurative interpretation of Yahweh's branch. But it is possible that here also we have a parallelism, although of such a kind that פרי הארץ, like צמח יהוה, is used figuratively. In that case, both images are used about the coming king. As an argument in support of a literal reading, reference is often made to Deut. 1.25, where the same expression is used about fruit from the plant world. But this does not of course mean that the land's fruit is to be taken literally in any context.

The arguments referred to do not exclude the possibility that צמח יהוה *can* have been used here about the coming king. But is it accordingly also the technical term for a Messiah with both priestly and royal functions? This is believed by, for example, Joyce G. Baldwin.[12] To complete her interpretation, however, she must undertake a rather heavy-handed exegesis. For example, she entirely overlooks that the washing away which she considers to be a priestly function is carried out by Yahweh himself in Isa. 4.4!

In my opinion, therefore, one must be considerably more cautious, and content oneself with reading צמח יהוה as *an image* that can be used about the king, whether the present king or the coming king. In the prophetic books, the new king can be described by several different plant terms. In Isa. 11.1, for example, both חטר and נצר are used; in Isa. 11.10, which clearly takes up again the concept from 11.1, the term שרש ישי is used; in Isa. 53.2 יונק as well as שרש is used; and as we have pointed out צמח is used both here in Isa. 4.2 and in Jer. 23.5; 33.15; Zech. 3.8 and 6.12.[13] These plant images all refer to the king as the vital force that breaks through and heralds a new time. צמח יהוה can therefore quite naturally be understood as an image taken from the king-ideology concepts, and used here about the new king under whose reign the land will bear fruit. During the Exilic period, when Isaiah 4 was redacted, the final determination of the Messianic designations had not yet taken place, but we can see that plant terms were favoured.

It is one thing to understand the image in the light of other texts' use of similar images and their rendering of these in later times, but its meaning in the specific context, i.e. as an element of Isa. 3.16–4.6, is something different. Is it reasonable in this context also to understand the branch, and perhaps the fruit, as a king-image?

The correlation back to the woman-image makes it natural to expect that 4,2 refers to those who survive the catastrophe and can perpetuate the people. Indeed, this is what the verse does, and does it very directly, with the words פליטת ישראל; similarly, these survivors are also the subject of v. 3. But the branch and the fruit are not identical with these; on the contrary, they become the pride and glory of the survivors. What the redactor succeeds in doing by including the image of the branch and the fruit is therefore to indicate that something other than the surviving people is important to the future. In Isa. 2.13, it was possible to see the destruction of the great trees as the leader's fall. Similarly, I consider it a reasonable possibility that the redactor has used the branch and the fruit as an image of the king who is to rule the people in the new future. The choice of adjectives to describe branch and fruit also supports this.

It is said of Yahweh's branch that it/he becomes צבי לצבי. צבי is used, for example, in Isa. 13.19; 23.9; 24.16; 28.1, 4, 5. In 13.19, it is Babylon that is referred to as the most glorious of kingdoms (note in the same passage the use of two other words, תפארת and גאון); in Isa. 23.9, where not only צבי but also גאון and the root כבד are used, it is similarly Tyre's proud glory and all its dignity that are described. In Isa. 24.16, it is the songs that are of glory to the Righteous One, while finally Isa. 28.1, 4, 5 concerns, on the one hand, the drunkards in Samaria who decorate themselves with faded flowers (v. 1 and v. 4) (note also the use of the words גאות and תפארת in this context) and, on the other hand, Yahweh himself (v. 5) (a typical example of reinterpretation of existing imagery). The examples referred to from the Isaiah tradition therefore support that צבי is used here also about a person and not a plant.

The same applies to the use of כבוד.[14] It is true that dead things also have their כבוד, but the word is often used about prominent persons or about Yahweh himself. Cf. e.g. as regards the latter Isa. 3.8; 4.5; 6.3 and the many examples in the Psalms; as regards the former, Isa. 8.7; 10.16; 11.10.

Equally clear is the use of גאון, which is employed to characterize פרי הארץ, primarily person-related: Isa. 2.10, 19, 21; 13.11; 13.19; 14.11; 16.6; 23.9; 24.14, although both waves and thicket can be designated by this word (but perhaps indeed to provide the nuance of proud and not only high) (cf. Job 38.11 and Zech. 11.3).

As regards תפארת, the fourth designation, the expression is used about prominent persons' splendour/pride: Isa. 3.18; 10.12; 13.19; 20.5; 28.1, 4, 5; or about the glory of Yahweh and his temple: Isa. 46.13; 60.7, 19; 62.3; 63.15; 64.10.

The choice of adjectives thus indicates that a *person* was in mind, and that he had a prominent position—such as, for example, the position a king has. But that the redactor has worked on the basis of the same contexts does not of course mean that any reader will automatically notice this and understand the image as such a king-image. צמח יהוה and פרי הארץ can also be read as a description of the land's stupendous fruitfulness[15] under the new circumstances.

Conclusion

The analysis of Isa. 4.2 and the context of the verse showed that here also the redactor has been able to use the tree image to interpret *the political situation*. The redactor utilizes the Isaianic image material very freely, and can alternate between the various images; but the choice of image is not fortuitous.

Imagery is not only used to argue in support of a continuity in the people's history, i.e. that the Exile is not a meaningless accident. The images are interwoven so that they mutually strengthen one another, and create a convincing chain of argument which can *explain* the present situation and *comfort* and *encourage* in regard to the future situation.

Finally, we must describe the use of the tree image in Isa. 4.2 as an example of redactional *reinterpretation* of image material already available. One of Isaiah's central images is utilized here to interpret the current political situation during the Exile.

8. *Analysis of Isa. 9.7-20 (RSV 9.8-21) and 10.16-19*

We have concerned ourselves above with the texts that in various ways describe the destruction of the tree as a tree-felling. In the texts now following we encounter the forest-fire theme in descriptions of the fire that consumes thorns and briers; indeed, even the forest's thickets and great trees.

Analysis of Isa. 9.7-20 (RSV 9.8-21)
Context and Dating
The image of the forest fire (Isa. 9.17; RSV 9.18) is included in the so-called 'Geschichtsparänese' (Isa. 9.7-20 + 5.26-29) in which the people are instructed about Yahweh's repeated attempts to bring them to their senses by punishing them.[1] Most scholars consider this text to be genuinely Isaianic, and since Isa. 5.26-29, which concludes the paraenesis, presumably describes a coming attack by the Assyrians, Hans Wildberger dates the entire passage to the period immediately prior to the Syro-Ephraimite war, i.e. Isaiah's first period of activity.[2] (Cf. my correction of this, pp. 211ff.)

In our context, it is noteworthy that in several places in his paraenesis Isaiah makes use of images taken from the plant world. The people's arrogance is revealed through a 'quotation'. The prevalent building material, the sycamore, has been felled (presumably by enemies); but then the people console themselves by the knowledge that they need only to plant cedars instead, as if they were kings (Isa. 9.9; RSV 9.10). In Isa. 9.13 (RSV 9.14), the image of a reed[3] whose head and tail are cut off is used to describe how Yahweh lops off the head and tail of Israel, both the top and the bottom of society are struck. For our context, however, the image in Isa. 9.17 is the most important.

The Use of the Forest-Fire Image
Whereas the use of the tree-felling image has its basis in the material conditions and in a number of culturally determined concepts, the use of the forest-fire image has its basis in the *climatic conditions* in Palestine. During the dry summer months, the great field fires and forest fires are a serious threat. Once the fire takes hold, it consumes everything. In Isa. 9.17, wickedness is compared to such a forest fire. It flares up and consumes thorns and briers; it kindles the trees of the forest so that everything goes up in smoke.

Thorns and briers, שמיר ושית, and the great forests, סבכי היער,[4] are referred to as examples not only because by giving the extremes, both small and great, the extent of the destruction can be emphasized: everything is affected, but the examples are also chosen because thorns/briers and forests can be used as metaphors, and thereby identify the persons to whom reference is made.

But let us look more closely at the image. We have already encountered סבכי היער as a parallel to Lebanon in Isa. 10.34 where, depending upon time and context, it was an image of Judah's or

Assyria's political apex. In contrast to this there is שמיר ושית. This formulation we have also met before, in Isa. 5.6. There, analysis showed that it is a distinctly Isaianic expression employed as an image of those whom society evaluated negatively. What is said in Isa. 9.17, then, is that wickedness has permeated the whole of society from top to bottom. As a forest fire ravages everything, so has wickedness done away with both those who stood lowest on the social ladder and those who stood highest. The last to be seen of the people is rising smoke. Isaiah here uses the word גאות, and thereby utilizes its ambiguity in an ironical way.[5] (Cf. Ps. 17.10, where it signifies arrogance, and the use of גאוה in Isa. 9.8 (RSV 9.9) about the people's arrogance, a theme also characteristic of Isa. 2.6-22, with the contrast between man's greatness and Yahweh's greatness (cf. גאה in Isa. 2.12 and גאון in Isa. 2.10, 19, 21)).

Not everything has been said in this clarification of the plant image's importance. As indicated, they form part of one forest-fire image in which the fire is the central metaphor. Whereas in the earlier analyses the tree was the principal element in the imagery, in this text the fire has an absolutely crucial function. As we have seen, the tree (thorns and briers + the forest's dense thicket) is not insignificant; but its significance is so firmly established by convention here that we are approaching the cliché, the dead metaphor. It is not therefore the tree that carries the text forward; it is the fire.

In v. 17, it is the wickedness of the people that is described as an all-consuming fire; but if one reads on in the context it is seen that the image of the fire continues in v. 18 (cf. the resumption of the root אכל and of אש). It is again the people who become the victims of the fire's destructive force. But a significant change has taken place, in that the fire is now employed as an image of Yahweh's wrath. The people's wickedness and Yahweh's wrath are compared by means of the fire image; a connexion between the two is created[6] by which it is indirectly argued that *Yahweh's wrath* is not fortuitous but closely bound up with the *people's wickedness*. Isaiah is thus able, by the use of images, to point out *the coherence in the people's history* which they did not themselves wish to see, and to argue that the misfortune has its foundation in the people's own sins.

The forest-fire image thus contributes to the paraenesis. The people must learn from the past, not only for them to understand that pride goes before a fall and that Yahweh knows how to punish a nation whose leaders mislead, so that it can be felt from top to bottom, but also for them to understand that their arrogance and wickedness are the true reasons for Yahweh's wrath. It is their own fault that Yahweh's anger has not lessened, and they are themselves responsible for the length of time Yahweh's hand will be raised against them. The implication is obvious, but they must themselves draw the conclusion and execute it.

To summarize, we can therefore say that in a number of respects Isaiah's use of the forest-fire image corresponds to the use of the tree-felling image. The forest-fire image is also employed to interpret the *political circumstances*, and to point out a coherence of which the people have not been aware; and like the tree images discussed earlier it is used *argumentatively*. It will be seen from the analysis of Isa. 10.16-19 that the forest-fire image also was well-suited to *re-interpretation*.

Analysis of Isa. 10.16-19

The analysis of Isa. 10.16-19 will be undertaken in three stages: A, which analyzes the oracle read in extension of Isa. 10,5-15; B, which discusses the history of use and reuse of the images employed; and C, which analyzes the oracle as a prelude to Isa. 10.20ff.

A. *Isa. 10.16-19, Read in Extension of Isa. 10.5-15*

In its actual redactional context, Isa. 10.16-19 must be read as a statement of judgment concluding the accusations in the curse upon the king of Assyria (Isa. 10.5-15). The redactors considered it insufficient to permit vv. 5-15 to end with a rhetorical question, but wished to specify what was to happen to the arrogant king of Assyria. Verses 16-19 are therefore added, in which by a series of images it is argued that *the king of Assyria's pride is about to fall*; Yahweh himself will attend to his end. The king of Assyria, who is initially cursed, is indeed doomed! (Cf. as regards the redactional processing of Isaiah 10 my analysis of Isa. 10.33ff.).

This urge to specify is a well-known phenomenon in redactional processing of the Isaiah tradition. Whereas Isaiah prefers to leave it to the hearers themselves to draw conclusions from what he says, redactors see it as their task to add what is missing. This is to be seen, for example, in connexion with the unfinished disputation speeches in Isa. 1.2-3 and 3.13-15, where the redactors have supplemented the disputation speech by what is in their opinion the missing judgment;

or in Isa. 10.9, where originally it was the hearers themselves who were to supplement the chain of cities by adding Jerusalem, but are now given in vv. 10-11 accurate information on this. The same is true of Isa. 10.27b-32, where the hearers were themselves to imagine the consequences of the army's advance; but the redactors have supplemented this by their ideas on how it will end. And one might also mention Isa. 7.8-9, where Isaiah begins a sequence but does not finish it.[7]

Imagery in Isa. 10.16-19
If Isa. 10.16-19 is read in its actual context, the verses are directed against the king of Assyria. The chain of images moves between *two images*: *the wasting sickness* which emaciates and weakens so that the sick man wastes away (Isa. 10.16, 18b), and *the forest fire* where the fire devours not only thorns and briers but also the land's forest so that scarcely anything is left (Isa. 10.17, 18a, 19).

The two images are interwoven as two parallel sequences, which in fact say the same thing. This interweaving is reinforced by the repetition of a number of crucial words: כבוד v. 16 + v. 18; אש v. 16 +v. 17; יער v. 18 + v. 19. Moreover, the statement in v. 18: מנפש ועד־בשר יכלה acts as a link between the forest image, the sickness image and the person to whom the images refer. The expression has been taken from the human world, and therefore fits directly and well into the subsequent sickness image in which the whole person is affected. Read in the forest context, it makes sense as an expression of the extent of the destruction and, based as it is in the human world, at the same time assists in pointing out that the image concerns the fate of a person, the king of Assyria, since by creating the image the two contexts meet.

The passage must be seen as *an entity*. The images form a chain; it is not only an accumulation of images but a clearly interwoven string of arguments demonstrating indirectly how the relationship between Yahweh and the king of Assyria must develop. By using both images, it is argued that the king of Assyria will suffer defeat. The imperatives that apply in the world of medicine when sickness breaks out and the imperatives that apply in the world of nature when a forest fire breaks out also apply in the political world when Yahweh turns against the king of Assyria.

The hearers can be made to accept the combination of sickness and forest fire because sickness and the destruction of trees were already to some extent linked in Israelitic awareness. We have on several occasions mentioned that the tree was seen as holy in the Near East, and entered into the fertility cult as a symbol of both the god and the king. When the tree is felled in the cult and vegetation is similarly burnt away in nature, it is the god who wastes away and dies. But just as nature is given new life, so the god rises again to new life. We do not know the extent to which such a cultic felling of trees took place on Israelite soil, but the combination of sickness, the destruction of nature, harvest, etc. which we encounter not only in Isa. 10.16-19 and Isa. 17.4-6 but also in Isa. 17.11[8] renders it probable that the Israelite saw a connexion between these things which helped to make Isa. 10.16-19 a far more coherent passage than is normally assumed.[9]

As far as I can see, this connexion follows naturally from the entire *basic idea of the fertility religion*: the close connexion between the course of nature and the course of life in the world of the gods, which is in turn associated with the human world when the king, as representative of both the god and the people, meets with this in the cult. Since the world of nature and the world of the god (symbolized in the king) are so interwoven that they can be distinguished only in theory, it is not surprising that the language and images employed can be combined. The very same is to be found in the description in Isa. 14.19 of the dead great king who is like a shoot, cast out without a sepulchre; in Isa. 53.2ff., where the shoot is described as one who is plagued by sickness and in the end dies; or quite generally in the many texts lamenting over the withered vegetation.[10]

What may also have helped to create a link between the two images is the use of the root יקד in v. 16. Hermann Barth[11] has pointed out that the words normally used in Hebrew for fever have been derived from words with meanings suggesting burning and heating. It would therefore be natural for the root יקד to have a similar double meaning, the first indicating fever-heat which is comparable with a fire. The repeated use of יקד helps to bind the oracle's individual elements together into one entity.

We have now shown a probable connexion between the images chosen, and seen how they function as an argument that well-deserved punishment will also come to the king of Assyria, whose arrogance has been clearly unmasked in vv. 5-15. Anyone who forgets that he is merely Yahweh's tool and thinks he is ruler of the world who can move the frontiers between peoples at will is guilty of hubris and will be punished for it. The king of Assyria has believed himself to be god-like and, ironically, his fall reminds one of the god's/vegetation's languishing—although to be sure without the text giving any hope of resurrection for the king! Cf. the analysis of Isa. 14.4bff. and Isa. 37.22bff. It scarcely needs further amplification that the image of the forest fire (here closely associated with the sickness image) is used in reference to political circumstances. As we have seen, the chapter's main subject is Assyria's fate and its consequences for Judah.

But what has proved difficult for scholars to determine is whether the author/redactor of Isa. 10.16-19 has seen Isa. 10.5-15, with which he links up, as a polemic against the Assyrian power that threatened Judah in the eighth-seventh century BC, or whether the redactor lived at a date later than the kingdom of Assyria, and has seen Assyria as a pseudonym for the enemies of his own time. This brings us to the question of when the text was composed and the opportunities for reinterpretation it may have occasioned.

Dating
Both J. Vermeylen and H. Wildberger consider that Isa. 10.16-19 is a late, redactionally drafted oracle. *J. Vermeylen*[12] believes that it came into existence during the post-Exilic period, and reflects internal strife among the Jews. *Hans Wildberger*[13] also supports a late dating, i.e. the (later) Persian period; whereas *Hermann Barth*, who considers that Isa. 10.16-19 is a 'nachjesajanisch-redaktionelle Arbeit',[14] is unwilling to abandon the oracle's connexion with the actual kingdom of Assyria with which Isa. 10.5-15 is concerned. Barth therefore dates the oracle to the later years of the history of the kingdom of Assyria, i.e. 620-610 BC. What is common to these suggestions is that they assume that the oracle came into existence at the date it was placed in its present context. But this does not follow naturally. Before we go into the problem, however, we should look at the date of *the composition* of ch. 10, and thus the placing of Isa. 10.16-19 in the present context.

The main subject of ch. 10 is Yahweh's relationship with Assyria and Judah respectively. The chapter is marked by a very complex perception of Yahweh's will. Both Assyria and Judah are struck by Yahweh's wrath; Assyria is Yahweh's tool for punishing Judah; but Assyria's own fall is followed by Judah's salvation. Whereas Isa. 10.16-19 speaks of a destruction which leaves as good as nothing

behind, Isa. 10.20-23 refers to a remnant that is still left after the
catastrophe. But whereas Isa. 10.16-19 concerns Assyria, Isa. 10.20-
23 concerns Israel (= Judah) and its remnant. The reader of Isaiah 10
is thereby led into parallel thought as regards the two kingdoms.
Both are clearly to undergo decimation of one form or another—to
this extent their fates follow each other; but for Judah the outcome is
different from that of the kingdom of Assyria. Isa. 10.20-21 expresses
this positive turn by utilizing the remnant idea[15] to comfort and
encourage the anxious.

Such a message bears the impress of the contradictory experiences
and the divided expectations that must have been typical of the
period between the siege of Jerusalem in 701 and Nineveh's fall in
612. It is difficult to say whether we, like Hermann Barth, can come
to an even more precise dating; here also, I wish to recommend
caution.

Following this clarification of when Isa. 10.16-19 was placed in its
present context, we can return to the question of *the date the oracle
came into existence*, i.e. by examining the images' *history of use and
reuse*.

B. *The Images' History of Use and Reuse*

Isa. 10.16-19 consists of a series of images which, according to Hans
Wildberger, are so poorly matched that Isaiah can scarcely have been
the author. What has happened is that 'ein Diaskeuast unausgeglichene
Elemente verschiedener Herkunft zu einem Gerichtsgemälde zusam-
mengefügt hat'.[16] Wildberger is correct in saying that part of vv. 16-
19 must have been borrowed from elsewhere, but that these elements
should not have been adapted to one another still presents a
problem.

Isa. 9.17-18 and Isa. 17.4-6

In examining the source of the loans for Isa. 10.16-19, two texts must
be considered: Isa. 9.17-18; RSV 9.18-19 and Isa. 17.4-6. If we look
closely at *Isa. 9.17-18*, it will be seen that in both 9.17-18 and 10.17-
18 we have the image of a forest fire,[17] and in both texts we find this
described by means of the words אכל, שית, שמיר, אש, בער and יער. Isa.
9.17-18 describes how wickedness burns and consumes thorns and
briers and the forest's dense thicket, and immediately afterwards
speaks of the wrath of the Lord of Hosts as the means by which the

land is burnt and the people become like fuel for the fire. Isa. 10.17-18 describes how the light of Israel, referred to in Isa. 10.16 as the Lord of Hosts, becomes a fire and his Holy One a flame that burns and devours briers and thorns (note the reverse sequence שיתו ושמירו) and all the glory of his forest and fruitful land.

There is little doubt that Isa. 10.17-18 is based on Isa. 9.17-18, but whereas 9.17-18 speaks of wickedness and Yahweh's wrath (cf. the wrath motif's great importance in the historical paraenesis in Isa. 9.7ff.), 10.17-18 merely says that it is Yahweh who destroys and burns. That the reason for this—the wickedness and godlessness of the people—and the wrath is omitted in the ch. 10 version may indicate that 10.16-19 is perhaps based on 9.17-18, but has been deliberately adapted to its context. In this context, the image is not to justify Yahweh's wrath against his own people but to act as a judgment on the king of Assyria, whose arrogance already is proved in the preceding text.

There is also a close connexion between *Isa. 17.4-6 and Isa. 10.16-19*. Both passages employ the image of the wasting sickness that emaciates the fat body. The image appears most clearly in the older of the texts, Isa. 17.4, which is normally considered to be Isaianic and is dated to the period shortly before Tiglath Pileser's attack in 733.[18] The oracle follows a judgment oracle against Damascus, and must be seen as a statement of judgment directed against the Northern Kingdom, here described as Jacob. The glory of Jacob, כבוד (cf. Isa. 10.16, 18) will be brought low according to 17.4, and the fat shall waste away from his body, ומשמן בשרו ירזה (cf. 10.16). The image in the two texts is the same, but the rendering of it in 10.16-19 contains a few variations connected with its having been inserted into the context.

In Isa. 17.4, the fatness of the body is referred to in the singular form משמן. (Perhaps the root שמן is a play here on the city name Samaria, שמרון; cf. Isa. 28.1ff. and Isa. 10.27.) But in Isa. 10.16, the plural form משמנים is used about the king of Assyria's fatness. The name Jacob, which in 17.4 is placed in association with כבוד and not משמן, is of course omitted and replaced by a suffix for the third person singular, which may refer back to the king of Assyria; but apart from this the word body, בשר, has also been left out. (But we can give it a nod of recognition in 10.18, where it is found in the established phrase מנפש ועד-בשר.) In my opinion, the authors' intention in these amendments was as follows.

Isa. 17.4 describes the destruction of the Northern Kingdom's fatness, which must of course be understood figuratively as referring to the land's fertile fields or some other feature of the land that can be described as 'fat', for example the leaders. The Northern Kingdom is personified by the name Jacob, but there is no doubt that it is the country which is intended. If this image is now transferred to the king-of-Assyria text, it is not similarly clear that imagery is concerned. That Yahweh wishes to send the wasting sickness into the king of Assyria's fat body can be understood quite literally: the great king's end will come in the form of sickness. If the singular form is used, and if his body is referred to, this reading appears to be the most appropriate. If a change is made to the plural form and the word for body omitted, it still refers to sickness, but it becomes easier to see that it is an image and not literal language. In both the singular and the plural, משמן can be used about fatness.[19] But the plural form makes it more appropriate, in connexion with the king of Assyria, to consider whether perhaps it relates to the fertile fields of the country,[20] or to the prominent and respected of the country,[21] those who, together with the king, are responsible for leadership in the country. The change in numbers and the omission of the word body do not have the function of making the statement an image (it could also indeed function as an image without these alterations), but act as a marker to indicate that we do in fact have an image and not literal language.

Another difference between Isa. 10.16-19 and 17.4 is the use of the term כבוד, glory. Whereas in 10.16, 18 it is included in the forest-fire image, in 17.4 it is used in the sickness image. The author of 10.16-19 must therefore have seen the forest-fire image as another way of saying the same as the sickness image.

If we look further into the context of 17.4, it will be seen that 17.5-6 consists of two other images, both taken from the harvest situation, grain harvest and olive harvest, and both with the same point as the sickness and forest-fire images. The harvesting methods are described as the careful cutting-off of the ears and the effective beating of the olive trees. In Isa. 17.4ff. sickness and harvest are combined, whereas in Isa. 10.16-19 it is sickness and forest fire. Read and understood with the fertility cult as a frame of reference, sickness/death and harvest/nature's dying (here because of forest fire) in the autumn are closely connected events. The harvest and the forest fire are also similar to one another in that they remove all that is worthy of mention. Correspondingly, wasting sickness is a sickness that emaciates the body. All that is valuable and vital—everything that is beneficent—is removed. We can thus establish that the images employed in the two chapters have the same intent, i.e. to convince that the all-destroying punishment is now at hand.

The comparison with Isa. 9.17-18 and 17.4-6 showed that Isa. 10.16-19 utilizes to a great extent *Isaianic images and formulations*; but it also showed that there has been a *conscious processing* of the material, not least by combining the forest-fire image familiar from Isa. 9.17-18 with the sickness image found in Isa. 17.4. This processing has been effected with a view to the king-of-Assyria context, by which a new understanding of the target of the oracle becomes possible. Whereas both Isa. 9.17-18 and Isa. 17.4-6 concern Yahweh's own people, Isa. 10.16-19 is so placed that, in the light of 10.5ff., it must be seen as an oracle directed against the king of Assyria.

C. *Isa. 10.16-19 Read as a Prelude to Isa. 10.20ff.*

We have so far limited the analysis of Isa. 10.16-19's context broadly to the preceding passages, and shown that the oracle has been adapted to act as a concluding statement of judgment upon the king of Assyria. But in addition the oracle acts as a link to the subsequent passages.

As already shown, by comparing the oracles now making up the Isa. 10.5–11.9 passage, the redactors wished to point out a cohesion between the fall of the kingdom of Assyria and the flowering of the kingdom of Judah. We established earlier that the tree image in Isa. 10.33-34 + 11.1 acts as the bearer of this message, and we shall now examine how the connexion between destruction and new beginning is created in Isa. 10.16-19.20ff.

It is not intended here to undertake a detailed analysis of Isa. 10.20-23, 24-27a, but rather to see how the tree image presents an opportunity for an interpretation other than that occasioned by the king-of-Assyria context. The point of reference for the remnant concept clearly developed in Isa. 10.20-23 is the tree image in Isa. 10,19. It is the formulation ושאר עץ יערו מספר יהיו that provides the basis for the further reference to שאר ישראל (v. 20); שאר ישוב (vv. 21, 22); and שאר יעקב (v. 21). Whereas the forest-fire image in Isa. 9.17-18 implies total destruction, the forest fire in Isa. 10.16-19 is described to include the sparing of some trees. Compared with 9.17-18, a change has thus taken place making a positive sequel possible.

Read in the judgment context, where the image is presumably used to refer to the leaders of the kingdom of Assyria, these trees are of no worth, but read as a background to the salvation statement to Judah, the trees suddenly acquire importance. In this context, the image indeed describes the decimation of Judah as the negative precondition for the emergence of the remnant. The *change in context* also changes the addressee, and a clear *shift in the interpretation* of the tree image takes place. We were able to establish precisely the same in regard to Isa. 10.33-34.

As regards Isa. 10.33-34, we came to the conclusion that the tree-felling image was an *original Isaiah oracle* directed against *the king of Judah*. By placing it in the king-of-Assyria context, it was given the new function of proclaiming judgment upon the king of Assyria. In extension of this, it is natural to ask whether there is any analogy in the case of Isa. 10.16-19.

We have already demonstrated the basis of this oracle in Isa. 9.17-18 and Isa. 17.4-6 respectively and its adaptation to the king-of-Assyria context. But we have expressed no opinion on whether at any time between there existed an oracle that already combined the forest-fire image and the sickness image in the same way as in Isa. 10.16-19, but had Judah and not Assyria as its addressee.

There is no possibility of giving a definitive answer to this question, but in my opinion two things support the existence of such an oracle. In analyzing the oracle, we showed the great extent to which it contains genuine Isaianic concepts and the care with which it has been drafted. These circumstances make it worth considering whether in fact it essentially goes back to Isaiah's own message, like the other two oracles, Isa. 9.17-18 and 17.4-6, i.e. whether the careful combiner of the two images was Isaiah himself.

We have also established that the oracle in v. 19 contains a basis of hope for the future, which is not particularly meaningful if the oracle was originally created with reference to the king-of-Assyria context. It would be much more comprehensible if, in line with Isa. 10.33-34, the oracle had been originally directed against Judah as an element in a message to the effect that Yahweh is about to decimate his people (perhaps, then, the oracle contained a reason for this similar to Isa. 9.17's), but that a remnant would be left. Such an oracle would accord well with Isaiah's other message, in the same way as the use of an image to express this purification judgment would accord well with Isaiah's actions in general.

But whereas in connexion with the forest-felling image Isaiah utilizes the tree's capacity to sprout again, this is not the case here. The link is the *remnant*, the remaining few. On the face of it, a more natural continuation on the basis of the tree image would be an oracle on the lines of Isa. 4.2-3 where the tree image and the remnant concept are combined, and where we also have a number of concepts and formulations that remind us of Isa. 10.20: פליטת, ביום ההוא ישראל, הנשאר בציון and קדוש (in 4.3 about the remnant; in 10.20 about Yahweh). But it is presumably relevant here that the tree image in Isa. 10.16-19 is a forest-*fire* image and not a forest-*felling* image. The forest fire connotes complete destruction; when the fire takes hold nothing is normally left. The fire is stronger than the tree. The remaining trees, therefore, as in the forest-felling image, can scarcely, qua trees, become bearers of hope for the future (cf. Isa. 9.17-18 and Isa. 1.29-31). The positive continuation must therefore be established more by 'key-words' via the remnant concept than was the case in Isa. 10.33-34 + 11.1.

We are not in a position to determine whether this is because parts of Isa. 10.20-23, like Isa. 11.1-5, also belonged to the oracle from the outset, so that the redactors' work consisted primarily in expanding this oracle by statements amplifying Yahweh's plans for punishing Judah and Assyria. But, as pointed out above, I consider that the evident parallelism in the structure of Isa. 10.5–11.9 indicates conscious redactional work in which the original Isaiah statement (Isa. 10.33–11.9) has functioned as a model for the combination of oracles in Isa. 10.16-27a. It is not therefore inconceivable that for the purpose of formulating Isa. 10.16-27a the redactors employed original Isaiah statements bearing the same message of the necessity of the purification judgment, and then, in the interest of the Assyria context, carried out the necessary minor adjustments.

According to J. Vermeylen,[22] the tangle of images, as he calls it, and the many allusions to other passages in the book of Isaiah would be against the thesis that Isa. 10.16-19 in the main goes back to an original Isaiah statement. In his opinion, both these features are typical signs of *post-Exilic* redactional work. Hans Wildberger's reasons for rejecting the thesis that Isa. 10.16-19 goes back to Isaiah are of a similar stylistic nature, although he has to admit that the author is well versed in the Isaiah tradition.[23] But as to this it must be said that they both misjudge the oracle in seeing it as a more or less fortuitous hotchpotch of different images. On the contrary, the oracle constitutes quite a sophisticated chain of images utilizing the argumentative power of imagery. Moreover, the images and concepts employed are so dependent on genuine Isaianic statements, and the changes carried out in adapting it to the context are so clearly conditioned by a wish to proclaim Yahweh's plans for the Assyrians, that there is nothing to suggest that the redactors lived after 587.

Reinterpretation
But this does not mean that Vermeylen's and Wildberger's interpretations and datings lose their importance entirely. The interpretation presented by each of them individually is certainly possible, but not as the oracle's original meaning. What they draw attention to is the *reinterpretation* that must have taken place at various times *after the Exile*, when the reader has allowed himself to be captured by the imagery and has interpreted it as spoken in his or her own time. This is also Hans Wildberger's concern when he writes that the function of Isa. 10.16-19 is *to actualize* in a certain situation Isaiah's message against the Assyrians, whereby an *'Entgeschichtlichung'* takes place, or as it also says: *'Das Geschichtsdenken* ist daran, *remythisiert* zu werden. . . .'[24] Wildberger hereby draws attention to the very characteristic feature of prophetism that we have hitherto referred to as reinterpretation. I have avoided Wildberger's terminology because it can lead to misunderstandings in the direction of a non-historical perception of prophetism.

Finally, it should be noted briefly that *the Targum* also translates the tree image in this instance so as to make it clear that the reference is to political conditions.[25] We can therefore confirm that a clear continuity appears to be present in the understanding of Isa. 10.16-19's imagery from its early use right up to the Targum's paraphrased rendering of the oracle.

Conclusion
The analysis of Isa. 10.16-19 showed that the forest-fire image, in combination with the sickness image, is used in the redactional context to give *information* about political circumstances causing the hearers/readers to look at political events through the images. It is argued via the use of images that the arrogant king of Assyria will

receive his punishment from Yahweh. The fall of the king of Assyria is unavoidable, and will be a blessing to Judah. Before this redactional use, the oracle, in a slightly different form, may have had *Judah* as its addressee, and have been used to proclaim the necessary purification judgment.

The images *argue* that imperatives prevail within the political world also, which the hearers, according to time and place, can see as a *threat* or a *consolation*.

Analyses of the images' *history of use and reuse* showed that the imagery in Isa. 9.17-18 and Isa. 17.4-6 has had a *text-producing* effect. Most scholars take the dependence on these other Isaiah statements to support the thesis that Isa. 10.16-19 does not originate from Isaiah himself. But this is scarcely binding. There is nothing against Isaiah himself having at a certain date worked on his own formulations and images. There is perhaps behind Isa. 10.16-19 a genuine Isaiah statement directed against Judah. In association with the redactional placing, it has been exposed to *reinterpretation* with corresponding minor amendments to the wording. I therefore believe, in contrast to Hermann Barth, that the oracle has a history dating from before the seventh century where the redactors place it in ch. 10, and that similarly it has a history of use and reuse after that time.

9. *Analysis of Isa. 1.29-31*

Isa. 1.29-31's Form

According to *Hans Wildberger*,[1] Isaiah 1 consists of six originally independent prophetic texts, vv. 2-3, 4-9, 10-17, 18-20, 21-26 (extended by vv. 27f.), and 29-31. The redactor has created a thematic entity from the four first, which has the form of a lawsuit, *rîb*, vv. 2-20. The last two oracles are somewhat more loosely attached. Wildberger believes that all six are genuine Isaiah texts; as regards vv. 29-31, however, this is a fragment of a longer oracle which originates from the prophet's first period of prophecy.

There is agreement among scholars that Isaiah 1 is a redactional composition consisting of a number of independent oracles.[2] In his 1962 article, 'Jesaja 1 als Zusammenfassung der Verkündigung Jesaja', *Georg Fohrer* has presented the thesis that, by ch. 1, the redactor wished to give a survey of Isaiah's message, i.e. that the juxtaposition is of a *programmatic nature*.[3] According to Fohrer, the

chapter consists of five independent Isaiah oracles brought together
so that they form a progressive train of thought. From a description
of sin (vv. 2-3), the chapter moves on to the judgment upon the sin
(vv. 4-9), to the possibility of salvation (vv. 10-17), and further to the
necessary decision: judgment or salvation (vv. 18-20), and on again
to a description of how realization of the salvation can be imagined
(vv. 21-26, extended by vv. 27f. which Fohrer refers to as a gloss).

To this is then added a fragment, vv. 29-31,[4] which Fohrer includes
in the collection itself, but he cannot explain why these verses were
added. Fohrer discusses whether there may be a link between the fire
in v. 31 and the smelting furnace in v. 25, but he quickly abandons
this question in favour of a brief demonstration that, after all,
fragments occur frequently in the traditional Isaianic collection. No
discussion of the fragment therefore follows. Both Fohrer and
Wildberger believe that vv. 29-31 is a loosely attached fragment, and
in fact forego any attempt to see a closer connexion between this and
the main part of the chapter.[5]

From its *form*, the oracle is a *statement of judgment*. Its
fragmentary nature is to be seen from the introductory כִּי, preceding
which there must have been a threat, according to Bernhard Duhm,[6]
a curse according to Karl Budde.[7] Verses 27-28, which have been
added secondarily as a reinterpretation of the clearly balanced dirge
in vv. 21-26, is not the fragment's original introduction. A new
section begins with v. 29, which is only seemingly a continuation of
the preceding text.

According to Duhm, the original threat must have turned on the
hearers' superstition, which will lead them to misfortune. Duhm
believes that this superstition is probably a consequence of alliance
with foreigners, as in Isa. 17.1-11. What the fragment otherwise
refers to is the *tree cult*, which will bring only shame and disgrace to
the cult's participants.

Budde sees the content of the text in quite a different way. In his
view, and generally speaking he is unsupported in 'recent' research,[8]
holy trees and groves are not involved, but instead the partiality for
fine trees and gardens which he believes was widespread among the
wealthy of the time. If the oracle is read in this way, its original
context can also be found, i.e. the curses in Isa. 5.8ff., where vv. 8-10
tell of the exhaustion of the land by the greedy. This corresponds
admirably to the judgment upon those who are fond of magnificent
gardens, says Budde. Budde bases the transfer of the fragment from

here, where it makes good sense, to ch. 1, where it does not fit, on all the shaking about to which the curse passages have been subjected. It is easy under such circumstances for individual elements to be damaged or shifted. As we have indicated, Budde is more or less alone in this interpretation, and he is alone in this specific suggestion as regards the meaning of *the fragment's original literary context*. But how strong is his position?

Isa. 1.29-31's Function: Judgment upon the Tree Cult?
Despite the lack of an introduction, Isa. 1.29-31 is a well-structured oracle. It is based on a series of contrasts which are juxtaposed partly by stylistic means such as paronomasia[9] and parallelism and partly by a common theme: oaks and gardens. In *v.29*, the verbs יבשו and חמדתם as well as תחפרו and בחרתם are placed antithetically, i.e. negative definitions opposed to positive definitions in a parallel construction. In the minds of the hearers, the oaks, אילים, and the gardens, הגנות prefixed by מן: מאילים—מהגנות), are positively connoted. As pointed out above (cf. the analysis of Isa. 6.12-13), אלה is employed in connexion with holy places in Gen. 35.4; Josh. 24.6; with holy persons in Judg. 6.11, 19; 1 Kgs 13.14; with fertility cult in Ezek. 6.13; Hos. 4.13; and in connexion with burial places in 1 Chron. 10.12.

In rejecting the 'cult interpretation', *Budde* mentions that אלה is used entirely without such connotations in Gen. 49.21; Isa. 6.13; 61.3; and Ezek. 31.14, which is why one should uphold the simple meaning in Isa. 1.29 also, where there is no direct reference to cultic purposes. But it should be noted in regard to this that אילה in Gen. 49.21 does not refer to a tree, as LXX translates it. As the above analysis shows, Isa. 6,13 quite obviously connotates a 'holy tree'; as a parallel to אילי הצדק, Isa. 61.3 has the term ממע יהוה, which scarcely indicates quite ordinary trees; and finally Ezek. 31.14 belongs to the great imagery about Pharaoh as the cedar of Lebanon, where the context clearly points to mythical concepts of the trees as holy trees.

Good reasons therefore exist to assume that Isaiah's hearers, when they hear the prophet speak of אילים, associate this with the holy trees. Who is the speaker is also of relevance here. Isaiah is a prophet of Yahweh, and the expectations one has about what he will say on behalf of Yahweh are not the same as the expectations one has in regard to any other person who begins to speak of trees.

The use of גנה in Isa. 65.3 and 66.17 similarly points to gardens for
cultic purposes. Budde rejects these references because the passages
are considerably later that the Isaiah text (but this does not prevent
him from himself including in his argument passages from, for
example, Nehemiah and Jeremiah) and he subsequently refers to the
paradise narrative to exemplify that a garden is considered as
something of the utmost value without having anything to do with
holy groves. The example is poorly chosen, since Genesis 2–3 to a
large extent utilizes the concepts referring to the holy place.[10]
Budde's other examples, 2 Kgs 25.4; Jer. 39.4; Neh. 3.15; 2 Kgs 21.18,
26, concern, as regards the first three, references of a 'geographical
nature' to the king's garden, which gives a basis for conclusion in
neither one direction nor the other, and, as regards the last, concerns
the use of Uzza's garden as burial place for a king, which does not
suggest a profane perception of the garden. Finally, the choice of the
verbs בחר and חמד (cf. Isa. 41.24; 65.12; 66.3f.) points in a cultic
direction. Budde does not deny this, but he believes that the use in
Isa. 1.29 is so clear that it is not affected by this.

Verse 30 also speaks of אלה and גנה. The hearers must become like
an oak which loses its leaves, like a garden which is not watered. Like
v. 29, the background to this image is the holy place with the holy
tree—the tree of life—and the holy spring. It is here that the hearers
believe they can participate in the divine life. After having been told
in v. 29 that their holy trees and gardens will give them only shame,
they must now see that they themselves are being compared to
withered trees and *waterless* gardens, i.e. a negation of what they have
set their trust in. Budde believes that such an understanding would
give a distorted image, but unfortunately he does not explain of what
the distortion would consist.

That imagery is concerned is to be seen from the comparative
particle כ. The two images, which repeat the same negative message,
are not formed syntactically in the same way, but are related partly
by use of the same two main words, אלה and גנה, which are parallel in
v. 29, and partly by means of the play on words between אלה and
אין לה.[11]

After vv. 29-30's use of the tree-and-garden motif, there follows in
v. 31 a description of what is to happen to החסן and פעלו. They are to
become tow and a spark respectively, which will make them burn
together with none to quench them. Both v. 29 and v. 30 have
pronounced judgment upon those who cultivate the holy trees. Verse

31 introduces 'the strong' and 'his work or creator'. Viewed in extension of the preceding verses, it must be expected that this also concerns cultivators of holy trees. Indeed, *Hans Wildberger*[12] also sees the text as meaning that החסן is an image of the cult participant, whereas פעלו is his idolatry. When Isaiah refers to the cult participants as the strong, this is not a term chosen fortuitously. According to Wildberger, the cult participant saw himself as a strong and vigorous oak.

Wildberger's interpretation of החסן as a designation for the great tree, which in turn is an image of the cult participant, is supported in that this word, which is used only here and in Amos 2.9, is employed in the Amos text also in association with great trees. According to this passage, the Amorites are as strong as the oaks, וחסן הוא כאלונים. That the oaks are considered to be strong is also to be seen from the actual word אילים, which according to KBL is derived from the root אול II, 'to be strong', and KBL therefore also believes that איל does not indicate a special kind of tree but merely a great and strong tree.

Bernhard Duhm[13] sees in the same way the oracle of the cult participant and his work, which Duhm, referring to, inter alia, Isa. 9.17, calls all his wrong. Frants Buhl[14] also believes that the verse must describe the fate of the idol-worshipper. The tow is the idol-worshipper himself, whereas his work, seen in extension of v. 30, must be his idol. But Buhl makes certain reservations, since the text is obscure.

In both v. 30 and v. 31, therefore, the tree has been used as an image of the idol-worshipper, provided—and here Wildberger also makes a small reservation—the two verses are to be read in extension of one another. But does this also mean that there is a connexion between what is said about the tree in v. 30 and what is said in v. 31? Or are they completely unconnected images which merely have the tree as a key-word?

I do not believe that the tree functions only as a key-word between the two verses, but perhaps I can reveal the *association* of *ideas* lying behind the combination of the image in v. 30 and the image in v. 31. In v. 30, the idol-worshippers, believing themselves to be great and strong, are branded as the direct opposite, i.e. as withered trees and gardens without water. In v. 31, the 'strong' idol-worshipper learns that he is to burn helplessly like tow. In a paraphrased form, the train of thought is as follows: 'You tree-worshippers who feel like great and strong trees; you are in fact only withered trees and gardens without water which despite all the fancied "tree power" will become prey to the fire'. Such a train of thought is possible in the light of the text's potential meanings, but is it also probable?

Yes, I believe it is, precisely because of the use of the tree images. We know that a withered tree or a dry branch can easily become prey to the fire, as does tow (cf. Judg. 16.9), and that this can be used figuratively to describe total destruction, for example as in *Ezek. 19.10-14*. According to Walther Zimmerli,[15] this describes the complete collapse of the royal house of Judah. The vine, which is used as an image of the royal house, is suddenly plucked up and cast down to the ground; the east wind dries its fruit (cf. Ezek. 17.10), its strong stem withers and the fire consumes it. It is then transplanted in the wilderness which is dry and needs moisture; cf. Ezek. 19.10 where in contrast it was described as transplanted by an abundance of water. Dry as it is, it catches fire and it is consumed by the flames.

By using this image, an interpretation is given of the fall of the royal house. According to Zimmerli, the image has been extended in certain respects by a redactor who wished to emphasize that the reason for the destruction is to be found in the vine (the royal house) itself; cf. v. 11aβb, which introduces the familiar arrogance motif, and v. 14aα, which points out that the fire is caused by self-ignition. But that a redactor's intention is to point out the Judaean royal family's responsibility for its own misfortunes need not imply that, in using imagery, he goes beyond what the hearers could accept as credible, i.e. that a vine not given water for one reason or another dries up and ends by being set on fire and destroyed. The image is not contrary to the hearers' own experience, and it can therefore argue in support of the interpretation of the political situation a redactor wishes to give.

The image in Isa. 1.30 of the withered tree and the garden without water may remind one of the introductory part of the forest-fire images in the book of Ezekiel, where drying up is described as a prerequisite for fire taking hold; cf., in addition to Ezek. 19.10-14; Ezek. 21.3 where both the fresh tree and the dry tree are to be destroyed by fire; Ezek. 17.10 (where only the drying-up is described); Ezek. 28.18 (where the fire is referred to only in connexion with the judgment upon the king of Tyre); and Ezekiel 15 (where the fire is similarly used as an image of destruction; the vine to be burnt is here an image of Jerusalem).

The connexion between drying up and fire is, as we have seen, part of the Israelite's everyday experience, and may therefore very well be the basis of the *association of ideas* reflected by vv. 30-31: drying up→ destruction by fire. The destruction by fire is not, however, described as a forest fire but by the image of the inflammable tow. Before we leave the interpretation of v. 31, one further possible reading should be mentioned, i.e. that Isaiah here focuses, as in v. 29, on the oaks as the holy trees which the hearers worship but which will bring them shame and disgrace. As the trees in v. 29 represent the idols, so is החסן in that case an image of the idol, and פעלו must be he who has fashioned the idol, i.e. the idol-worshipper.

Read in this way, it is the apparently strong idols that are unmasked by irony. These idols (possibly there is a play on words here between an implied אלים,[16] idols, and אילים, the great trees), despite all their strength, החסן, are irretrievably lost face to face with the fire.

One interpretation which reminds one of this is to be found in *H. Ehrentreu*[17] who believes that Isaiah employs the image of tow and spark about the idol and he who has made the idol in order to describe their worthlessness and their complete disappearance. Isaiah has chosen the term חסן as a name for the idol because he wishes to exploit the play on words between החסן, 'the strong', and חוסן, which refers to the uncombed flax from which tow is made. (Ehrentreu arrives at this definition of חוסן's meaning on the basis of the Mishnah that prohibits the use of חוסן as a wick in the Sabbath lamp.)[18] What Isaiah wishes to say in this play on words is then: 'Wie man aus חוסן Werg macht, so wird auch euer חסון, euer Starker, zu Werg werden'.[19]

Ehrentreu's interpretation, which was accepted by Delitzsch,[20] has since been continued by *M. Tsevat*,[21] who does not, however, accept the idea of a play on words but simply believes that חוסן and חסון are variants of the same word. The image is therefore quite simply: God himself is he who prepares the flax so that it first becomes חוסן and then נערת, but during such a process it is easy to produce a spark that burns up everything, both flax and tow, which in turn is an image of the groups placed high and low in society.

But, as *S.E. Loewenstamm*[22] shows, several weaknesses are to be found in Tsevat's interpretation. That God should be he who processes the flax, פעלו, is by no means certain, and similarly there is nothing in the context to suggest that different classes of society are

concerned. Moreover, it is unfortunate that the two which, according
to Tsevat, are to be destroyed by fire are the flax and the tow, since
the flax has just been made into tow and has therefore already ceased
to exist, '. . . and a thing that has vanished cannot burn'.[23]

According to Loewenstamm, in the image of the flax that becomes
tow (here Loewenstamm follows Ehrentreu's reading of חסון,
although he also cannot accept that it is a play on words), Isaiah
describes, as in the image of the silver that becomes dross (Isa. 1.22),
how man corrupts what is valuable. But the sinful man will become a
spark which causes a fire, so that both he himself and his sinful acts
will be irretrievably destroyed by fire.

According to Loewenstamm, the verse is an original Isaiah text
which has been placed secondarily after v. 30—perhaps because the
redactor has seen a connexion between the two verses, in that v. 30
describes the garden without water which can easily be ignited by a
spark and is then impossible to save from total destruction by fire.

Both Tsevat's and Loewenstamm's analyses show the great
difficulties that Isa. 1.31 presents. Loewenstamm also does not
succeed in coming to a clear and simple understanding of the text
and the association of ideas behind its creation. The image is
complicated by his division of v. 31a into, first, a description of how
man changes the valuable into something less valuable (figuratively,
makes flax into tow) and, secondly, a description of how this man,
now referred to as the executant of the process, becomes a spark, so
that the image represents rather a possible reinterpretation than
what may have been the original meaning of the image.

Loewenstamm is also clearly in difficulties in perceiving a link to
v. 30, but he cannot make it fit into his interpretation. He cannot do
this for two reasons. In the first place, like Tsevat, he rejects too
readily Ehrentreu's idea of the play on words between חסון and חוסן;
secondly, again like Tsevat, he interprets v. 31 as an isolated image.
If he had examined his own suggestion of a link to v. 30's garden
without water, and added to this Ehrentreu's idea of the word-play
on the strong (the idol), he would have been able to develop from this
a more coherent image. But this is obstructed by Loewenstamm's
conviction that v. 31 has been redactionally placed, and is not an
original part of vv. 29-31.

If we maintain that חסון in v. 31 is employed figuratively about the
idol, it contains the following *potential meanings*: (a) 'the strong',
connoting the great trees, and (b) the combed flax from which tow

can be made. The word-play on the uncombed flax then helps to explain how an association can be effected from חסון to נערת. Whereas the inclusion of Ezek. 19.10-14 et al. assisted in pointing out an association of ideas from the withered tree and the garden without water to the fire, Ehrentreu's demonstration of the play on words can help to explain that it was the image of the inflammable tow that Isaiah continued in v. 31, and not an actual forest-fire image in line with Isa. 9.17-18 and 10.17-18.

Ehrentreu's demonstration of possible word-play is not of course tied to his interpretation of חסון as referring to the idol, but makes just as good sense if חסון is used about the 'tree-proud' idol-worshipper. If we hold to the interpretation that it is the idol-worshipper who is the strong one, we can render the message in vv. 29-31 roughly as follows:

> 'You tree-worshippers who feel yourselves to be great and strong trees; you are in fact only withered trees and gardens without water. Despite all your imagined "tree-power" you will be the victims of the fire, since you and your strength are like flax that is processed into weak and inflammable tow, which is destroyed by a single spark.'

We can scarcely get any nearer than this in revealing *potential meanings*. It cannot be conclusively determined whether Isaiah wished to refer to the idol-worshipper or the idol as the strong one. The difference in meaning is also limited, since the point is that they are together devoured by fire, both the idol-worshipper and his idol. What we may conclude is that in its use of images the oracle motivates the hearer to try to extract from the image the information that makes best sense in his or her situation.

In regard to v. 31, *Karl Budde* has followed without further discussion his own understanding of the gardens as private gardens, and he therefore interprets the strong one as the proud garden-owner whose work includes his acts of negligence in the domain of morals. Now comes the punishment for living a life of indulgence. But as we have seen it is much more reasonable to follow the generally accepted interpretation and see the whole passage as a denunciation of the tree cult and those who participate in it. The objections Budde has advanced must be rejected; establishing this also disposes of Budde's proposal in regard to the oracle's original context. Read as a cult polemic, it has no place alongside the social indignation of the lamentations. We shall return to the question of where it may otherwise belong.

Isa. 1.29-31 as a Coherent Oracle

In extension of this interpretation of the oracle, we also wish to draw attention to a feature that may support the above attempts to see connexions and associations of ideas within the oracle, and so justify the reading of the oracle as an 'entity'; as we have seen, it lacks an introduction.

A characteristic of Isa. 1.29-31 is the use of word-play. A further example of this is the use of יבשו in v. 29. Commentators have long been surprised by the form יבש, and have preferred to correct it to תבשו. This is also true of Hans Wildberger.[24] The correction is supported not only by some manuscripts and the Targum but also by the parallel תחפרו. If a correction is made, the result is in fact a smooth and easily comprehensible text. But the question is whether the form יבשו may be the original, and whether this very form has been retained because it is able to awaken both the connotations associated with בוש, i.e. in the direction of 'shame', 'disgrace', and therefore correlates well with חפר in the parallel statement, and the connotations associated with יבש, i.e. in the direction of 'drying up', and thus accords well with v. 30's image of the withered tree and the garden without water.

The form מאילים and the entire parallel structure, which in my opinion is original, shows that the basic idea is associated with the meaning 'shame', but by employing impf. qal, third person plural of בוש Isaiah can play on the concepts which v. 30 actualizes, and which have in turn formed the background to the association with fire in v. 31.

N.H. Tur-Sinai[25] also sees no reason to correct יבשו. But he does correct מאילים to אילים, so that this word becomes the subject of the sentence. The meaning is then 'for the oaks (אילים) which you have desired shall *dry up* and (thus) ye shall be confounded for the gardens that ye have chosen'. Tur-Sinai believes that מ has been placed before אילים on the basis of the parallel in מהגנות, when one began to read יבשו as derived from בוש instead of from יבש. This means that Tur-Sinai in fact assumes a deliberate alteration to the text in the direction of the understanding 'be put to shame', whereas I assume this to be the original and a deliberate attempt to play on both possible meanings.

Such a play on the roots בוש and יבש is presumably also to be found in 2 Kgs 19.26, where the image of the withered grass is used in reference to the peoples' (שביהן—note again the use of word-play) powerlessness when they are gripped by shame: חתו ויבשו. But in Isa. 37.27 the opportunity for this play has been removed, in that the passage is rendered using the perfect form of בוש, i.e. חתו ובשו. In the book of Isaiah, the use of בוש and יבש in Isa. 19.5-9 and Isa. 42.15-17 should also be noted. Cf. also Ps. 129.5-6 and Joel 1.10-17, which quite obviously play on these two roots.

The use of יבש thus emphasizes the justification for reading and interpreting vv. 29-31 as three coherent verses.[26]

Isa. 1.29-31's Original Literary Context?
Isa. 1.29-31 is a fragment whose original literary context is still an *open question*. The analysis showed that the oracle is a statement of judgment directed against the arrogant idol-worshippers who have put their trust in the tree cult in the holy groves, and that to formulate this judgment Isaiah utilizes images which relate to trees (plants) and fire.

We are familiar with an analogous message using similar imagery in another passage from Isaiah's early preaching, i.e. the historical paraenesis in Isa. 9.7-20 (RSV 9.8-21) + 5.26-29. The people are here told about Yahweh's repeated but vain attempts to bring them to their senses—i.e. to repentance—by his judgments. The people's arrogance is revealed by means of 'the quotation', with cedars instead of sycamores (Isa. 9.9), while the punishment of the high and the low is described by the image of the reed whose head and tail are cut off. In Isa. 9.17, the image of a forest fire is used to proclaim how self-destructive is the people's arrogance. Verse 18 continues by pointing out that the fire is not only self-inflicted but is also an expression of Yahweh's wrath, and is therefore righteous punishment. It goes on to describe the horrors of war: brother devours brother, and Ephraim and Manasseh together, יחדו, fall upon Judah. But despite this his anger is not turned away; his hand is still stretched out (Isa. 9.20).

Commentators normally place Isa. 5.26-29, describing the advance of the Assyrian army, to follow this. Isa. 9.20 cannot be the end, since as Hans Wildberger phrases it: 'Der Kehrvers, der einhämmert, daß Jahwes Hand noch immer ausgestreckt bleibe, verlangt nach einer Fortsetzung'.[27] According to Wildberger, the most likely continuation is an even more strongly worded outburst of anger against the people, which may very well be Isa. 5.26-29. But according to Wildberger it is impossible to come to any conclusion about Isa. 5.25's original position.[28]

But this fourth outburst of anger could also be Isa. 1.29-31, whose content and choice of images would fit in well as an extension of the three first passages. According to Hans Wildberger, Isa. 9.17-20 probably reflects the war between the king of Judah, Amaziah, and the king of Israel, Jehoash, in which the Judaeans suffered an ignominious defeat (2 Kgs 14.8ff.). (This, strangely enough, is the very war introduced by the dialogue between Amaziah and Jehoash, in which Jehoash brands Amaziah as a thistle on Lebanon compared with the cedar on Lebanon.) As regards the rivalries also referred to in the oracle, Wildberger believes that on the basis of the Old Testament we have no possibility of adding to this.

If, then, the subsequent outburst is Isa. 1.29-31's description of the judgment upon the 'tree-proud' idol-worshippers, it becomes necessary to ask who was it precisely that Isaiah had in mind. As regards time, we find ourselves, in the light of the passage's chronology, between Amaziah's defeat by Jehoash, i.e. the beginning of the eighth century, and the events lying behind Isa. 5.26-29, which are to be dated either shortly before the Syro-Ephraimite war, according to Wildberger, or (and this I consider more likely) just after this war, as proposed by Donner et al.[29]

If we again keep to the 'great events' of which we know something from the Isaiah tradition, for example, and which we may expect to have left traces in the prophetic message, it is possible, in the light of the events of the Syro-Ephraimite war, to see Isa. 1.29-31 as an oracle about the Northern Kingdom and Aram, which together threatened Judah. The two enemy powers are here told that it will end in their total destruction by fire. That Isaiah would use such imagery in this situation is supported by the imagery in Isa. 7.4. Isaiah was sent to king Ahaz of Judah, whose heart was trembling with terror 'as the trees of the forest shake before the wind' (Isa. 7.2) under the threat of war, with the words 'Do not let your heart be faint because of these two smouldering stumps of firebrands, at the fierce anger of Rezin, Aram and the son of Remaliah' (Isa. 7.4). It can be seen from Isa. 1.29-31 that the fire will consume both of them together. Read in this way, the oracle is a statement about the immediate future. In contrast to the earlier oracles, therefore, this oracle is not kept in the perfect +

consecutive imperfect but is similar to the following oracle, Isa. 5.26-29, which also speaks of what is about to happen.[30]

That Isaiah begins by branding them as idol-worshippers relying on powerless trees does not prevent the oracle from applying to the Northern Kingdom and its coalition partners. Bernhard Duhm can take some credit for this interpretation, in that he sees from a different angle the worship of idols as a consequence of alliance with foreigners, i.e. by pointing out the similarity between Isa. 1.29-31 and Isa. 17.1-11 (which is of course directed against the Northern Kingdom).

But it is scarcely sufficient to argue on the basis of similarity of content and choice of image as regards a possible placing of Isa. 1.29-31 within Isa. 9.7ff. We know that this text is a tightly structured poem with a number of stanzas interrupted by a regular chorus. The stanzas have more or less the same number of lines, i.e. seven including the chorus.[31] The lines are mainly, although not consistently, built up of 2 x 3 words with a stressed syllable. As regards the number of lines, Isa. 1.29-31 fits well into the context, in that this oracle, supplemented by the chorus, has seven lines. But as regards the rhythm there are differences, in that the lines in vv. 29-30 consist of 2×2 and in v. 31 of 2×5. But uncertainty in regard to the metre is so great that in my opinion these differences do not damn the suggestion; cf. merely the number of omissions necessary in Isa. 5.26-29 for this section to fit into the desired schema.

The stanzas are not introduced by one and the same sentence construction, but it can be seen from 9.17's כי־בערה כעש רשעה, with which 1.29's כי יבשו מאילים would accord well, that the chorus can be naturally followed by a כי-sentence. Finally, it can be said that the use of יחדו in both 9.20 and in 1.31 may perhaps indicate a link between the two oracles. If, therefore, Isa. 5.25ab is replaced by Isa. 1.29-31, we have a much more homogeneous poem consisting of five stanzas each of seven lines, and with a regular chorus: Isa. 9.7-11; 9.12-16; 9.17-20; 1.29-31 + 5.25c; 5.26-29; the last stanza, however, of course ends without a chorus.

There is just one aspect which gives reason to assume that the original version of Isa. 1.29-31 was adapted to its present context. Like the poem's other passages, this oracle also was originally kept in the third person and not as it is now, where by using the second person there has been a degree of adaptation to ch. 1's direct addressing of Jerusalem. That the original oracle was in the third person is revealed by v. 29a, where the third person plural has in fact been maintained, in the same way as v. 31 has also been kept in the third person.

Conclusion

Finally, in summarizing the analysis of Isa. 1.29-31, it must be emphasized that we have to a large extent read this fragment, whose original context may be Isa. 9.7ff. and which is only loosely linked to the other oracles in ch. 1, as an isolated dimension. This means that we have interpreted its individual statements on the basis of one another; to illustrate the oracle, we have included material 'from outside' to only a very limited extent, mainly in the form of other tree images that describe drying up and/or forest fires.

The use of the tree image in this text is as closely associated as is at all possible with the concepts of the tree as a holy tree, since the tree is included in a polemic against the holy-tree cult itself. Tree images are employed to unmask the self-assured cult participants and to reveal to them that they will come to an abrupt end. The content of the message is thus akin to Isaiah's other threats against the arrogant whose pride is about to suffer a fall. And, should it be correct that the historical paraenesis in Isa. 9.7ff. is the original context, we are here also in the presence of tree images used in reference to political circumstances.

As with the two forest-fire images (Isa. 9.17-18 and Isa. 10.17-18), the emphasis is on the fire's all-devouring nature, but leaving no doubt that it is precisely the seemingly strong trees, i.e. the arrogant, which will be struck. Read as an isolated fragment, vv. 29-31 gave us no opportunity to establish more closely to whom the oracle was addressed, to which period in Isaiah's ministry it belongs, and whether perhaps it has been the subject of reuse and reinterpretation.[32] Only the demonstration of a possible literary context enabled us to do this.

As already mentioned, Georg Fohrer believes that Isaiah 1 is a redactional attempt to give a survey of Isaiah's message. I agree with Fohrer in this approach, but I consider it a clear weakness in the argument that such a concisely formulated and highly informative oracle as Isa. 1.29-31 in reality has no function in the chapter.[33]

Hans Wildberger[34] highlights this problem in his discussion of the history of Isaiah 1–39's creation. He also draws attention to another factor that casts doubt on Fohrer's thesis. If Isaiah 1 is intended to be a summary of Isaiah's message—and Wildberger would clearly prefer to agree with Fohrer here—why are there missing such important points as the warnings against the coalition policy, the exhortation to trust in Yahweh and the 'Messianic hope? As regards the latter, Wildberger arrives at a partial solution, supported by P.R. Ackroyd,[35] by introducing *Isa. 2.2-4* as a redactional addition to ch. 1, whose very purpose it was to ensure that the positive aspect of Isaiah's message was also included in the introductory summary.

But we are left with the problem of Isa. 1.29-31's lack of function and the absence of the two central themes: the coalition policy and trust in Yahweh. The analysis of Isa. 1.29-31, including particularly the suggestion that the oracle's original function was to act as a link in the historical paraenesis, gives reason to believe that the two problems should be seen—and resolved—together. It does indeed look as if the 'superfluous' oracle and the 'missing oracles' had something to do with one another. But such a conclusion calls for further investigation into what are the main themes in *Isaiah's theology* and their connexion with *Isaiah's imagery.*

10. *The Main Themes in Isaiah's Theology*

Like the other prophetic books, Isaiah 1–39 is primarily a collection of prophetic *statements*. Narratives about Isaiah's activities are present to a limited extent (Isa. 6–8; 20; 36–39); but on only two occasions, in two political-crisis situations, do we learn that Isaiah performs his office by means other than words. The first situation is the Syro-Ephraimite war, where three persons with symbolic names appear: the two sons of Isaiah (Isa. 7.3; 8.1, 3) and Immanuel (Isa. 7.14). These three incarnate Yahweh's promise to Judah, and by their very existence argue that Judah must seek its support in Yahweh, and neither fear nor rely on others. The other situation is the period of the Ashdod revolt, when by going about naked for three years the prophet himself became the visible warning against reliance on support from Ethiopia and Egypt (Isa. 20). But during both these crises the political leadership chose to safeguard Judah by *coalitions with other nations*, and on both occasions Isaiah employed—although in vain—the strongest possible form of expression, *the sign-act*,[1] to warn his contemporaries against this.

The use of sign-acts gives reason to expect that we are face to face with one of the central themes of Isaiah's message, and the many other examples of warnings against reliance on foreigners support this assumption. The reason for Isaiah's strong reaction is not only Realpolitik, although according to Herbert Donner Isaiah had a good sense of this side of the matter, but is primarily of a theological nature.[2]

In his analysis of Isaiah's view of the relationship between Yahweh, Judah and the other nations, *Friedrich Huber* has examined the functions of these foreign nations in relation to Judah. During the Syro-Ephraimite war, they appear on the one hand as 'eigenmächtige Bedroher Judas', such as Aram and Ephraim, and on the other hand as 'vermeintlicher Helfer', such as Assyria. But in both cases Isaiah requires Judah to rely on Yahweh, since the foreigners are no more a real danger than they are a real support. Judah's only possible coalition partner is Yahweh, and for this reason Isaiah tries to convince the people that they must choose Yahweh, hold fast to him and rely on him if they wish to continue to exist[3] (cf. Isa. 7.9).

Isaiah has also to adopt a position towards the coalition policy later in the people's history. In association with the Ashdod revolt, he stresses that it is in Zion that they must seek refuge, and not among the Philistines (Isa. 14.28-32).[4] The people are indeed doomed[5] if they seek help other than in Yahweh himself (Isa. 30.1ff.). For if they seek refuge among the Egyptians the protection of Pharaoh will come to their shame, and shelter in the shadow of Egypt will bring only disgrace; 'since this is a people that cannot profit them, that brings neither help nor profit, but shame and disgrace' (Isa. 30.5).

The other nations are unable to carry through what they plan; only Yahweh can do this. Therefore, it is not they who decide Judah's fate; it is decided by the state of the relationship between Judah and Yahweh.[6] For if they do not *return* and *rest* on Yahweh, as he has said to them, destruction will befall them (Isa. 30.15-17).[7] Isaiah's warnings against coalitions with foreigners thus have their positive counterpart in the call to rely on Yahweh instead.

That Yahweh is in control of events is also to be seen from Isaiah's assessment of Assyria's role. Huber shows in his analysis that Assyria acts not only as a putative helper of Judah, as was the case during the Syro-Ephraimite war, but also as a self-appointed threat. But this is a threat Yahweh wishes to set aside, if only the people will rely on him.[8] Assyria has to a certain extent acted as Yahweh's tool for punishing Judah,[9] but the events of 701 reveal the king of Assyria's arrogance, and Isaiah must now turn against him and threaten him with Yahweh's punishment. The function of these threats is, then, to reassure Judah and to encourage trust in Yahweh, the same purpose as the message during the Syro-Ephraimite war.[10]

The main thrust of Isaiah's polemic against the coalition policy is, as we have seen, that Judah's fate depends on its relationship with Yahweh, and not on the foreign nations' threat or their help. But how does this theme relate to the other themes in Isaiah's message? And how does it relate to the tree images we have discussed above?

Isaiah's Theology

In his review of twentieth-century research into Isaiah 1–39, *Rudolf Kilian*[11] points out that, although the methodological approaches change, the same themes are discussed over and over again, i.e.: Messiah, the remnant, Zion, Assyria, repentance, heart-hardening. Kilian arranges his review of the main results of research on this basis; but it soon becomes clear that one basic question lies behind these apparently very different subjects: How to combine the judgment message and the salvation message in Isaiah 1–39?[12]

Kilian's account shows that in general terms scholars can be divided into two groups. The most recent representative of the first group is Hans Wildberger, but the group relies very largely on opinions advanced by Gerhard von Rad. A characteristic of the views of this group is that Isaiah's original message contained both judgment statements and salvation statements. But these statements are not unintegrated with one another. By use of his remnant concept, Isaiah has been able to link the two forms of statement in such a way that the inevitability of the judgment is maintained, while at the same time salvation for a selected group can be proclaimed. If the judgment is perceived as such a purification judgment, it is similarly possible to accept the 'Messianic passages' as genuine expressions of Isaiah's hope for the future. This hope originates from, for example, the Zion theology that Isaiah took over from the Zion psalms. It may be asserted that the alternating views of Assyria as the tool of Yahweh's anger against Judah and as itself the subject of Yahweh's anger accord well with the statement referring to the ambivalence of Isaiah's message. Yahweh first punishes his people with the aid of Assyria; then he removes their main enemy and permits the punishment to cease. For the very reason that there is hope for a remnant, Isaiah can be defined by this group as a prophet of repentance, and for the very same reason—but now underlined—

that only a remnant will be saved Isaiah can see his task as unavailing: he spoke to deaf ears.[13]

Opposed to this group of scholars is another to which Kilian himself belongs. In their opinion, there is no such tension in Isaiah's message. The themes referred to—both positive and negative—indeed exist, but only the negative themes go back to the prophet himself, who was and remains a prophet of judgment. He did not visualize that a Messiah would come, or that a holy remnant would survive; Zion was no guarantee of Yahweh's salvation, and Isaiah's attitude towards Assyria was quite simple: Assyria was a tool to strike Judah. Since Isaiah visualized judgment and destruction alone, he did not of course try to exhort his contemporaries to repent, but from the outset saw his task as that of accomplishing the heart-hardening assignment, which occurred by the very pronouncement of the judgment.[14]

Kilian and the scholars whom he cites in support, including Georg Fohrer, arrive at this result because they deprive Isaiah of all positive statements and date them to later periods, in particular the period after 587. If the texts are graded in this way, a clear image emerges of Isaiah as a prophet who believed that his only task was to pronounce judgment and destruction, the later redaction originating from a group that radically reinterpreted Isaiah's message.[15]

If we compare Kilian's presentation of the two main directions in Isaiah research, it becomes evident that analysis of the use of tree images in Isaiah 1–39 led to results which accord far better with Hans Wildberger's view of Isaiah's message than with Rudolf Kilian's. Like Wildberger, I come to the conclusion that an important aspect of Isaiah's message is that Yahweh plans both judgment and salvation, and it was shown in the individual analyses that the tree images formed part of this message. By using tree images, Isaiah was able not only to express both judgment and salvation but also to point out continuity in the apparently random series of historical events that he and his contemporaries were witnessing.

The arrogance motif was given a central position to form a link in justification of the judgment as righteous punishment. It is the proud tree or the blasphemous tree-feller that is about to fall; it is the political leaders who consider themselves strong and therefore in no need of Yahweh's support that are struck. The absence of trust in Yahweh is thus the implicit subject whenever the prophet polemizes against arrogance, whether manifested in coalitions with foreigners or in the idol-worship associated therewith. An important theme in the tree images—judgment upon those who put their trust elsewhere than in Yahweh—thus accords with what we encounter in other contexts in Isaiah's polemic against the coalition policy—and without the use of tree images. This theme plays such an important part in Isaiah's message because it is closely associated with the core of his theology: his view of God.[16]

In this survey of research, Rudolf Kilian discusses the subjects that have played an essential part in the debate surrounding Isaiah 1-39, and comes to the conclusion that Isaiah was a judgment prophet. In his commentary, Wildberger of course considers the same subjects, although his conclusion is different. Whereas Kilian stops after establishing the content of Isaiah's message, and thus his prophetic function, Wildberger goes on to arrive at an understanding of the motivation of Isaiah's message. Kilian is correct in saying that research has concentrated on the themes referred to, but Wildberger's summary of Isaiah's theology[17] shows that Isaiah's view of God lies behind these themes. Wildberger therefore begins by explaining the relationship between Yahweh and the foreign gods, since it was the God of Israel, the holy God, by whom Isaiah felt himself to be called; he is the lord of history, the king, who is the vital point of reference of Isaiah's message.[18] Isaiah's prophetic assignment and the relationship between Israel and Yahweh must be seen in this light.

And this brings us back to the theme we took as our point of reference: *the polemic against the coalition policy.* By choosing to seek support elsewhere than from Yahweh, the political leaders reveal their own blasphemous arrogance. Isaiah's polemical attacks are thus accusations of blasphemy; but at the same time, by their threats of judgment, the attacks act as indirect calls to rely on Yahweh instead.

Walter Dietrich especially has drawn attention to the fact that Isaiah speaks in political-crisis situations. Dietrich points out in his book 'Jesaja und die Politik' that about two-thirds of Isaiah's message is concerned with political situations. [19] That such a predominant part of a prophet's message concentrates on this subject is of course reflected in his theology. Dietrich's analyses of this lead to the same results as our analyses of the tree images, i.e. that for Isaiah there is a necessary connexion between political events and Yahweh as he who gives meaning to history. Axiomatic to Isaiah's message is his confidence that the many individual events are an expression of Yahweh's will.[20]

The image analyses have been able to show not only that, in general, the themes referred to by Kilian can be expressed by means of tree images (cf. the concepts of the coming king, the remnant, Assyria's fate), but also that the actual use of imagery accords well with the repentance—or rather the decision—theme, and should probably also be seen in the context of the heart-hardening theme.[21] But, as we have seen, what they have mainly been able to show is that for Isaiah there is a connexion between the individual events.

Tree images have shown themselves to be well-adapted for expressing this theology in a concise and assertive message that can be reused century after century. This should not be taken to mean that Isaiah was looking for a suitable and durable image with which to illustrate his otherwise fully rounded theology. It is far more probable that the tree image gripped him and gave him an opportunity, by experimenting with it (and several others), to arrive at an understanding of Yahweh's intention in the events which were happening to his people.[22] It is true that language is a tool which can be used to give shape to existing ideas, but it is not merely such a tool; it can also provoke new thought, point out new opportunities and create new correlations.

The many potential meanings of the tree image have made it well-suited for interpreting such a complex historical period as that in which Isaiah lived. The many threats against Judah made the question of the people's survival crucial; a factor that had of course to repeat itself after 587. Isaiah's answer, which the redactors repeated (for example during the Exilic period), was that Yahweh had planned both judgment and salvation. He can argue in support of this by the use of images able to juxtapose what is apparently self-contradictory. But analysis of the tree images showed us not only how Isaiah could juxtapose both negative and positive points but also how Isaiah could argue that the negative, the judgment, was an expression of Yahweh's righteousness when arrogance had to be cut down.

We have shown by this that the polemic against the coalition policy is not just one of several themes in Isaiah's theology but a main theme. If Judah chooses to enter into a coalition with other nations, this is not what we would understand as a 'Realpolitik' choice. If they choose foreign support, this represents rejection of Yahweh himself, and that must have its consequences (cf., for example, Isa. 8.5ff.). Coalition policy and idol-worship are therefore two sides of the same coin.

The polemic against the tree cult played a crucial part in the analysis of *Isa. 1.29-31*. It is said directly here that their oaks and gardens would bring shame and disgrace to the people. This form of words refers not only to the emotion that grips the disappointed but also to the impotence. The root בוש is frequently used in the Psalms, where the speaker asks Yahweh to put his enemies to shame, i.e. to deprive them of their power[23] (cf. Pss. 6.11; 31.18; 35.4, 26; 40.15; 70.3; 71.13, 24; 83.18; 86.17; 97.7; 109.28; 119.78), or formulates his plea for help as a request not to be put to shame (cf. Pss. 25.2f., 20; 31.2, 18; 71.1). In Ps. 97.7, in one of the enthronement psalms in which Yahweh is praised as king, it is all worshippers of images and those who praise worthless gods who are put to shame, יבשו. In Isa. 1.29, it is those who worship the holy trees who will be put to shame, יבשו, and in Isa. 20.5 it is those who put their trust in the coalition with Ethiopia and Egypt who will be dismayed and confounded, וחתו יבשו. According to Isa. 20.5, they had considered Egypt their pride, תפארתם, but this indeed shows that they had confused Yahweh with the foreigners, since Israel's pride is Yahweh; any other pride set in place of Yahweh is an expression of arrogance (cf. Isa. 28.1, 4, 5; Isa. 10.12).

We advanced in the analyses of Isa. 1.29-31 the suggestion that the oracle's *original context* was the historical paraenesis (Isa. 9.7ff.), and that the situation to which the oracle referred was the Syro-Ephraimite war. If I am correct in this suggested dating, the situation is that the two aggressors wish to force Judah to participate in a joint coalition against Assyria. We know from Isa. 7.4-6 that Isaiah exhorted Ahaz not to abandon his neutral stand,[24] and we know from 2 Kgs 16.7 that Ahaz did not enter into a coalition with the small states but, in contrast, sent for the king of Assyria and concluded a treaty with him.

Viewed in this context, Isa. 1.29-31's judgment upon the Northern Kingdom and Aram as 'tree-proud' but worthless idol-worshippers who must be annihilated by fire also becomes addressed to Judah. Just as the unmasking of the Northern Kingdom and Aram in Isa. 7.1-9 as 'two smouldering stumps of firebrands' occurred to convince Ahaz that it was Yahweh on whom he should lean, so the unmasking of them in Isa. 1.29-31 contains an indirect summons to Judah not to put its trust in such idol-worshippers. And so Isaiah's crucial point was the same as that expressed in the Yahweh oracle: 'If you will not believe, surely you shall not be established' (Isa. 7.9).

The question of the function of this oracle in ch. 1 was raised in the context of the analysis of Isa. 1.29-31. If we compare the interpretation of Isa. 1.29-31, read in the original literary context, with Isaiah's theology in general, it becomes clear that Isa. 1.29-31 represents a main theme: the rejection of any policy that sets human power in place of Yahweh. The polemic against the coalition policy and the call to trust in Yahweh were the two themes Hans Wildberger missed in ch. 1's summary of Isaiah's message. But Wildberger overlooks that these themes, which are very closely connected, are in fact represented by the chapter's last oracle.

PART C. CONCLUSION

It is not the purpose of this conclusion to repeat in detail the results to which the analyses of the tree image have led. They may be referred to in the exegetic sections, where they are to be found in their proper context. I wish, however, to assemble the most important insights into three specific theses, and to support these theses by the understanding we have gained:

a. *The tree metaphors in Isaiah 1-39 have the informative function of acting as theological interpretations of the political situation.*

As referred to in the methodological section, a major part of recent discussion of the parable has been concerned with whether the function of imagery is to describe a tangible matter, i.e. to give information, or whether imagery must be defined as performative, i.e. that the function of imagery is to involve the hearers in the world of the image, and thereby to create participation. But it was also shown in my initial description of Old Testament imagery that I could not accept such an alternative, and I asserted *both* an informative *and* a performative function.

It also became clear that, because of imagery's receptiveness to interpretation, I must reject the suggestion that its informative and performative possibilities have been frozen in advance; on the contrary, images have a history. The basis on which the image is understood must therefore always be given careful consideration. Every reading of an image is historically conditioned.

If, therefore, we are to comment in general on the information of which the tree image is a bearer in Proto-Isaiah, we must express ourselves in relatively general terms. We can only point out the focus of the tree metaphor; we cannot stake out its boundaries. The 'translation' we attempt should be seen only as a paraphrase, with all the limitations this implies; above all, the limitation that we can never exhaust the metaphor.[1] That being said, we shall try to summarize the information which can be passed on by/derived from the tree image.

To begin with, it must be placed on record that the use of trees as images was not invented by Isaiah. On the contrary, we are in the presence of a *traditional* form of imagery. This means that the tree is associated with very many connotations familiar to both the author and the hearer. To the hearers, it is not surprising that circumstances in the human world are interpreted by means of images from the plant world. Indeed, their expectations in regard to what the prophet wishes to say in using the image are fairly specific. These are the expectations we have expounded in Chapter 3, section 2, where we considered the tree's role in Near-Eastern culture; this included the tree as building material, as the bearer of fruit and as the tree of life. It was made clear here that the tree had positive connotations. (The exception to this is of course the established term, 'thorn and thistle', which always has negative connotations.)

Where the tree is used as an image, one of the *preconceptions* is that the tree is something of value. The hearers are interested to learn what was to happen to the tree. Will it grow and bear fruit? Or will it be felled, consumed in a forest fire, dry up from lack of water? What is surprising is not the tree as an image but the statements or the narrative about the tree that the prophet conveys. The tree can be used typically, but also a-typically; new connotations can be created and utilized; a well-known myth can be given a special twist, and an expected meaning can turn out to be a false trail. The more traditional the image, the more surprising is the effect of a-typical use and the easier it is for the author to exploit the hearers' preconceptions and prejudices.

The main content of the *information* to be derived from the images employed is as follows: As the God of Israel, Yahweh is the master of the political events, both when they denote misfortune and when they denote success for his people; similarly, Yahweh can use foreign nations to accord with his plans. History is not therefore fortuitous; it has its own coherence. It has been possible in various ways to express this message by use of the vineyard image, the forest-felling image and the forest-fire image, or combinations of them. But a characteristic is that it was possible to use the tree images to *argue* that this coherence is *righteous*. It is the unnatural vineyard that must be destroyed (cf. Isa. 5.1-7); it is the proud trees that are felled (cf. the analysis of Isa. 10.33-11.9, 10; Isa. 2.12-17 and Isa. 32.15-20); it is the arrogant forest-feller who is himself struck (cf. the analysis of Isa. 14.4b-20 and Isa. 37.22b-32), or the proud tree-worshipper who is consumed in an unquenchable fire (cf. Isa. 1.29-31). The use of the thorn-and-thistle motif also emphasizes this interest in *justifying* Yahweh's acts (cf. e.g., Isa. 24.4; Isa. 9.17 and Isa. 10.17).

But tree images can inform not only about misfortune. The possibility of new life is part of Yahweh's plan. The felled tree can sprout again (cf. Isa. 10.33-11.9, 10; Isa. 37.22b-32; Isa. 6.12-13; Isa. 4.2). The forest-felling image can thus juxtapose two apparent contrasts: destruction of life—resurrection of life,[2] a combination found again in connexion with the vineyard parable in Isa. 27.2-6 and in the redactional composition of Isa. 10.16-19, 20-23.

The Tree Image

As we have seen, the tree is not a new image in the Old Testament context. It was therefore important to unearth the concepts behind the use of the image in Isaiah 1-39. The analyses showed that some of the tree-felling images played on a more coherent complex of ideas—the myth to which *Fritz Stolz* has drawn attention. This tells in the main of an encroachment into the garden of God by a knave who tries to win divine power but is banished to the nether world in punishment for this.

Both *Isa. 14.4b-20* and *Isa. 37.22b-32* are clearly in keeping with this. It is the tyrant and his blasphemous act that occupy the central position, and the 'king of Babel' and Sennacherib must both pay the penalty for this hubris. But if we look at the other tree-felling images we see that some changes have occurred, associated with the fact that the tree-feller is no longer an alien but the owner of the forest: Yahweh.

It is thus Yahweh himself who fells the trees or otherwise brings about their fall in *Isa. 10.33-34; Isa. 6.13; Isa. 2.13 and Isa. 32.19.* As owner of the trees, Yahweh has the right to do what he pleases with them; but in all the cases referred to the tree-felling is seen as a just punishment because of the trees' hubris. Isa. 6.13 does not say this directly, but since this verse is a continuation of the heart-hardening statement and its consequences this must also relate to Yahweh's punishment of the stubborn.

Whereas in the original myth and in the two versions of it in Isaiah

14 and Isaiah 37 it was the tree-feller who suffered well-deserved punishment, in the other examples it is the trees which suffer punishment. This creates a new way of looking at the high, upright trees. The uprightness is interpreted as pride, and the positively connoted trees now become negatively connotated. This forms a basis for the use of the tree image we encounter in Isa. 32.19, where the forest is an image of the negative. If the trees thought themselves to be as safe and protected as God's own garden, they must now think otherwise. Yahweh can also turn against his own, provided of course they have turned away from him in pride. The precondition for protection is indeed, as expressed in Isa. 7.9, that they hold fast to him.

If we try to describe the pride within the tree code, we must say that it consists in the trees' attempt to grow up into heaven. Translated into non-figurative language: the arrogant try to disregard the limits set for man. Pride is the basic sin of wishing to be like God, who, as 'the One', has no need of a god to lean on. Thematized in the form of the myth, we are familiar with this view of man's arrogance from Genesis 3's narrative of how man tried to become like God by eating of *the tree in the garden of God*. In the Isaiah context, arrogance is unmasked, for example by the fact that the people seek support from foreign alliance-partners, thereby giving these partners the position to which Yahweh alone is entitled. In so doing they substitute human power, including their own, for God's power.

That tree-felling can be employed as an image of Yahweh's relationship with the people themselves means yet another change in terms of the original myth. Whereas the original myth leaves the blasphemous in the nether world, the special version of the myth we have found in Isaiah's message operates with the possibility of a new beginning; a new branch can sprout. The felling is not necessarily the last one hears of the tree; Yahweh's punishment of the people is not necessarily a final rejection. They are not left in the kingdom of the dead, as was the tyrant who profaned the garden of God, but after the felling/'death' they can obtain new life. Isaiah gives the original myth this twist because of his trust and hope that, in spite of the necessity of punishing the people, Yahweh still stands by his promises to be their God, and thus their protector.

By using the *tree-felling myth* combined with the concept of *the new branch*, Isaiah is able to transfer to history the context familiar from nature and to everyone, so that apparently unconnected events become linked. Imagery becomes a means of bringing order to the chaotic, so creating a cosmos, and Isaiah is able to point out a series of contexts that the people have not previously understood. Imagery gives new information.

The historical events referred to must be determined from text to text, taking into consideration the context (in the very broadest sense of the word) in which the image is read. But in very general terms it may be said that the tree images play on what in our terminology we would call a political code.[3] The tree can thus be employed as an image of the people themselves, of their leaders and of their king, and similarly it can be used of foreign nations and their king.

By assembling *the basic theological ideas* that Isaiah was able to express by using the tree image in formulating his message, we gain a good impression of the remarkable flexibility and adaptability of the image. We discover in doing so that in general terms all the important ideas in Isaiah can indeed be expressed by means of the tree image. This is true of the polemic against the proud (cf. e.g. Isa. 2.13); the polemic against idol-worshippers/political leaders (cf. e.g. Isa. 1.29-31); the polemic against the king of Assyria (cf. e.g. Isa. 14.8, 19); the necessary punishment of the people (cf. e.g. Isa. 5.1-7); the remnant concept (cf. e.g. Isa. 6.13); and the hope of a new ruler (cf. e.g. Isa. 11.1). And where Isaiah gave up the redactors carried on.

Tree images were therefore especially serviceable in very many *different situations*; similarly, they could be used as bearers of *different messages*. That Isaiah employs tree images does not mean that his message became stereotyped. He has certain basic viewpoints which cannot be shaken, such as his view of the proud and of the alliance policy, but in regard to the fate of the people Isaiah clearly fluctuated between more confidence or less confidence that there was a future. Whereas the forest-felling myth had already been utilized by Isaiah himself to express the concept of the link between judgment and salvation, it seems that the forest-fire image and the vineyard image were used by Isaiah to underline the punishment's inevitability. Only the redactors' reinterpretation rendered a positive sequel possible after the destruction.

One of the aspects which must be included in extension of this is that the images describe *sequences of events*. The image is not static; nor should the history of Israel and the relationship to Yahweh be considered as static. The function of the image is not to describe the people's situation as deadlocked, but to indicate some continuity which the people have failed to understand.

As regards the tree image, it is also important to note the extreme subtlety with which Isaiah balances between the use of *the tree cult's imagery* and the adoption of its ideology. Just as Hosea, Isaiah's contemporary in the Northern Kingdom, can extensively utilize the language and images from the sexual cult against which he polemicizes, so can Isaiah utilize the language and the images from the tree cult which he himself must reject. The boundary between use of religious language and acceptance of the fundamental ideas and cultic acts associated with these ideas can often be difficult to establish. Thus, as regards Hosea's use of the marriage image, one often has the impression that it is not so much the perception of the relation with God in the light of sexuality that is polemicized against but the people's choice of the wrong partner: Baal. But in the case of Isaiah he clearly avoids using the tree image in such a way that Yahweh himself can be regarded as a tree.

Hosea is alone in using the image of a tree in reference to Yahweh when, in Hos. 14.9; RSV 14.8, he permits Yahweh to compare himself to an evergreen cypress and to remind Ephraim that it receives its fruit from Yahweh, and therefore has no need of idols. Whereas in general the Old Testament displays no reticence in describing Yahweh by images from the world of nature, the Canaanite tree cult has had the result that any attempt to identify Yahweh with the holy tree has been as good as entirely avoided. This reticence is in line with the repeated rejection of the concept that Yahweh is a god who dies and is resurrected. Yahweh is, on the contrary, the living God whose life cannot be identified with the annual cycle of the flora, since this would imply Yahweh's death. This reservation towards the fertility cult has not, however, prevented extensive use of its imagery; but as regards the tree image this has meant that it is used only about people in Isaiah, with the consequence that Yahweh must be either the tree's protector or its destroyer. Thus, in Isaiah it is the people who may experience something like cultic death and resurrection—not Yahweh.[4]

b.   *The performative function of the tree metaphor in Isaiah 1– 39 is to involve the hearers in such a way that they adopt the metaphor's interpretation of reality as their own.*

Imagery not only contains information; it can also *influence the hearers* so that something happens to them. When they go along with the interpretation and adopt it as their own perception of reality it causes a *change in their attitude*. The despondent can be given new courage and the anxious comforted through the image of the new branch. Similarly, the tree-felling image can be perceived as a threat to the proud, a judgment upon those who rely on their own strength.

Only when image and hearer/reader meet does the actual meaning come into existence. We emphasized earlier that three important components are involved in the creation of meaning: the author, the text and the hearer/reader. That the author of the text is involved should be self-evident, but this needs perhaps to be stressed at a time when language is allotted increasing independence in relation to the user of language. Analysis of Isaiah's use of imagery shows that we are in the presence of an extremely competent user of language who can exploit its many possibilities; but it also shows that the author is not the master of his text in the sense that he can freeze its meaning.

Isaiah is often referred to as a judgment prophet, which is in itself correct if this merely describes a major part of his message. But this description should not be taken to mean that the prophet mediates information about a coming judgment exclusively. In fact, Isaiah chooses to express himself about a coming judgment *and* salvation in imagery not because his ideas on how this judgment will occur are too imprecise to be expressed in non-figurative language, but because he wishes to make something happen by means of his message. He wishes to create a change in attitude among his hearers. A textbook example of this 'transference of judgment' is the vineyard parable in Isa. 5.1-7.

The means for creating this effect are numerous. We mentioned earlier Isaiah's predilection for making the hearers draw their own conclusions from what has been said by rhetorical questions and incomplete statements and descriptions. But a number of other features of Isaiah's message must also be emphasized: his use of various forms of word-play intended to stimulate the hearers' imagination and their capacity to see similarities between otherwise dissociated phenomena (cf. e.g. the analysis of Isa. 1.29-31); the use of antithesis, particularly in connexion with paronomasia (cf. e.g. the analysis of Isa. 5.1-7), in which the reader is forced to compare two contradictions and thus test the degree of dissimilarity; and the a-typical use of familiar genres and concepts (cf. the different variants of the tree-felling myth), that help to awaken and involve the hearer in what is said.

But above all it is the *imagery* and its performative function that must be stressed here, recognizing that the means referred to above are also used together with imagery. Since imagery requires interpretation, the hearer is stimulated and activated: the uncertainty about the image's correct application leaves the mind in sufficient doubt to be activated.[5] That imagery requires interpretation means, as we have said, that the hearer must himself complete it. It therefore captures the hearer, since, as Voltaire expressed it: 'Malheur à l'auteur qui veut toujours instruire! Le secret d'ennuyer est celui de tout dire.'[6] Imagery is indeed a language that does not say everything.

But important though it is to emphasize the uncertainty into which the hearer is plunged, it is equally necessary to show how the hearer's interpretation is guided by the author's choice of images, the context in which the author employs the image and the entire culture-determined situation to which the hearer belongs and on which he bases his understanding. This latter aspect is important where one is concerned with the Old Testament prophetic texts, which as repeatedly stressed are traditional literature that has been the subject of constant reuse and the reinterpretation associated therewith.

In the texts analysed, we have repeatedly discovered that the images are used for the purpose of argument, especially to *argue* that the many seemingly fortuitous events are meaningful, i.e. are part of a whole (cf. e.g. the analyses of Isa. 5.1-7 and 27.2-6; Isa. 10.33–11.9, 10; Isa. 14.4b-20; Isa. 37.22b-32; Isa. 32.15-20; Isa. 4.2-6; Isa. 9.7-20, Isa. 10.16-19). But the purpose of the argument is not only to create one form or another of what we, with our way of distinguishing between things, would call an 'intellectual effect' among the hearers; the images must also, according to their content, time and place, *judge, threaten*, and *warn* (cf. Isa. 5.1-7; 27.2-5; 10.33-34; 6.12-13a; 10.16-19; 1.29-31), or *comfort* and *encourage* (cf. Isa. 27.2-6; 11.1-9, 10; 6.13b; 37.22b-32; 32.15-20; 4.2-6; 10.16-19, 20-23). If this succeeds, something happens when the prophet speaks; the threats and warnings cause the people to stop and think, and the promises and the consolation give the people new hope and new trust in Yahweh.

That Isaiah exploits the performative function of the language to such a great extent is because of the intention of his message. Isaiah is convinced that a great catastrophe awaits his people (cf. Isa. 6.11ff.); but alongside his proclamation of the judgment's catastrophic consequences is the confidence that a future is still possible. It is true that the trees will fall; but the power to sprout remains (Isa. 6.13; 11.1); the judgment shall pass over the people like a purification (Isa. 1.25), since despite all there is a remnant that will return (Isa. 7.3).

Who is to form this remnant is *not* decided in advance; it depends upon whether or not they hold fast to Yahweh. King Ahaz had an opportunity, but he lost it when he refused to accept Yahweh's sign and chose to rely on powers other than Yahweh. The remnant is not of a dimension that can be staked out in advance. If that were so, Isaiah's repeated attempts to make the hearers enter actively into interpretation of the message and draw the implications of the message would be incomprehensible. No, the remnant must be fought for and fought over, and the prophet's weapon is first and foremost language.[7]

In his book, 'Die Intention der Verkündigung Jesajas',[8] *Hans Werner Hoffmann* reacts against the one-sided definition of Isaiah as a judgment prophet. He tries instead to show that Isaiah was a repentance preacher until the Assyrians abandoned the siege of Jerusalem in 701 and the people revealed their obduracy. Only then did he become a judgment prophet; this can be seen from Isa. 22.1-14 and 29.9-10, which according to Hoffmann are the prophet's last (transmitted) words.[9]

If in this connexion we ignore Hoffmann's not very convincing thesis that Isaiah radically changed his role after 701, his specific analyses—which it should be noted are not analyses of imagery—support what we have said above about Isaiah's prophetic intention.[10] But Hoffmann's definition is not without its difficulties. One of the weakest points in his argument is his interpretation of the *heart-hardening statement* (Isa. 6.9-11),[11] which he does not succeed in harmonizing with the definition of the prophet as a *repentance preacher*.

But if these two interpretations do not harmonize it is not only Hoffmann who is faced with a problem. I have myself pleaded above that Isaiah uses imagery to appeal to 'the remnant'; but this approach may also encounter difficulties when confronted with Isaiah 6's

description of Isaiah's commission during the Syro-Ephraimite war.
Isaiah's use of imagery gives an impression of a prophet who puts all
his effort into making the hearers open their eyes, their ears and their
hearts to the message with which Yahweh has commissioned him.
Isaiah 6 insists that Isaiah was sent to tell his contemporaries: 'Hear
and hear, but do not understand; see and see, but do not perceive'.
(Isa. 6.9). Is it in any way possible to maintain both these points of
view?

Yes, the two approaches are in fact closely linked. Detailed analysis
of Isaiah's 'Denkschrift'[12] shows that the three episodes in Isa. 7.3-9,
7.10-17 and 8.1-8a must be seen as exemplifications of the special
heart-hardening commission. Central to these three episodes are the
symbol-names. The three children with the symbolic names act as
signs and, as in the *Exodus traditions* so in the 'Denkschrift', it is the
divine sign that occasions the quite unnatural reaction. That
Pharaoh refuses to believe in the signs Moses makes is just as
unreasonable and unnatural as Isaiah's contemporaries' refusal to
take Isaiah's message to their hearts. For the very reason that Isaiah's
message was such that under normal circumstances it would not only
make the hearers open both eyes and ears but also open their hearts
to it, the only reasonable explanation for the people's hardening their
hearts against it is that this heart-hardening is motivated by Yahweh.
Our emphasis that Isaiah's message is a very convincing and
powerful message makes it indeed meaningful to see the rejection as
just as extraordinary as Yahweh's heart-hardening of his own
people.

The special task with which Isaiah was commissioned and which
he performed in the context of the Syro-Ephraimite war does not
therefore preclude the understanding of the intention of Isaiah's
message to which analysis of the imagery led. We might rather say
that if Isaiah had not exploited *the performative function of language*
to such a degree the reference to *heart-hardening* would become
meaningless.

    c.   *The use of metaphors has made continuous reinterpretation of
        the original message possible, including opportunities for the
        production of new text.*

The fact that imagery is suitable for reuse is closely associated with
its receptiveness to reinterpretation. If the image changes its context,

its meaning will also change; but just as changes can occur in the information the image bears, so can changes take place in regard to the performative function. For example, the justification aspect may attain a far more prominent role with reuse (cf. the analysis of Isa. 5.1-7). But as regards these specific changes in the informative and performative functions respectively reference should be made to the individual text analyses. Our aim here is to give a survey of the *various forms of reuse* we have encountered in association with the tree image.[13]

The first form to be noted is the repetition of Isaianic statements that has *not* involved *changes* in the form of the statement and does *not* require actual *reinterpretation*. I have in mind here the reuse, mainly by Isaiah himself but perhaps also by his disciples, of major images. But this reuse cannot be identified, and cannot therefore be subjected to analysis.

The next form of reuse to consider is also difficult to identify, in that one must assume a reuse which has involved reinterpretation *without* having involved *changes in the text*. The external situation itself was able to emphasize special aspects of the image. In this connexion, one may refer to the reuse of Isa. 11.1-9, which may very well have occurred in association with the eight-year-old Josiah's accession to the throne following the murder of his father. Under these circumstances, the image of the shoot may certainly be perceived as emphasizing the tender age of the new king, whereas this aspect would play no part under other circumstances. Furthermore, it should be noted that the form of reuse here employed accords with the reuse which became the only form possible after the text's final redaction and the establishment of the canon.

While this form of reuse has not resulted in changes to the text, there are examples where images have been placed in a *new literary context*, and thereby made the subject of reinterpretation. A very large part of this *redactional adaptation* of Isaiah's message indeed consisted in juxtaposing various oracles, thereby setting the scene for a definitive interpretation of them. A typical example of this is the composition of Isa. 10.5–11.9.

Even clearer than the redactional juxtapositions are the directly *redactionally created additions* whose function is to define the manner of interpreting a certain image. Cf. e.g. the framework surrounding Isa. 2.12-17, which consists in part of redactional additions and in part of redactionally placed oracles that can be traced back to Isaiah himself; or the introduction to Isa. 14.4bff., which is intended to emphasize who the tyrant is. This includes the Targum's direct translation of the tree images, which is an attempt to safeguard the texts against reinterpretation.

Finally, the *production of text* should be noted to which imagery can give rise, not only in the form of the redactional additions already mentioned but also in the form of new versions of the original statements, including corrections to the text itself.

One example of this is Isa. 10.16-19. But it is disputable here whether the use of the plural form במשמניו in Isa. 10.16 should be seen as an example of correction of a text in order to indicate a specific interpretation of the image or whether Isa. 10.16-19 is a new production of text on the basis of Isa. 9.17 and Isa. 17.4. The most obvious example is, of course, the vineyard parable in Isa. 27.2-6; but in addition the different variants of the forest-felling myth we have met while discussing text analyses should also be mentioned. The many different aspects of the tree image have made it possible to produce new text here, where new aspects of the image are utilized.[14]

The possibilities of reuse thus outlined are of vital significance in understanding the *genesis of prophetic literature*. A characteristic of the OT's understanding of the prophetic word as the actual word of Yahweh is thus the tension between the word's historical constraints and its claim, as the living word of God, to be always topical.

What we have said up to this point about imagery shows how suitable it is for passing on such words of Yahweh. In the specific situation, the image can be the bearer of information that is to be seen as an actual communication of Yahweh's intention; but this does not exhaust the meaning of the image. In a new situation, it can convey new information. It is not therefore surprising that a large part of the preserved and transmitted message is indeed structured in imagery.

In the context of this emphasis on imagery's great value in reuse, I wish to refer briefly to the extensive use of images in *apocalyptic literature*,[15] conveyed in the form of dreams and visions, for example. In many cases this involves a revival of traditional motifs and images,[16] now associated with the final and authoritative interpretation. The reinterpretation carried out in various ways by redactors of the prophetic books, by which they tried to ensure that the images were seen in a certain way, is matched in a number of apocalyptic texts of

angelus interpres,[17] which as representative of the celestial world
gives the final and true interpretation of the old words and images.[18]
Imagery requires interpretation, which is reflected, for example, in
all redactional activities; but the authoritative interpretation of
apocalyptic literature means *in principle* the end of that part of the
text's history of use and reuse expressed by the continuous attempts
at reinterpretation. The final time and thus the final interpretation of
what is God's will for Israel *has* now arrived. (The whole of the New
Testament's reinterpretation of the Old Testament is clear evidence
that events turned out differently in practice.)

Having thus concerned ourselves with the possibilities of imagery's
reuse, we shall now consider the possibilities the exegete has of
tracing and analysing the *different phases* of reuse. It should first of
all be noted here that reuse which has left no traces in the
transmitted texts cannot of course be demonstrated. We can only try
to outline the effect that a known event such as the destruction of
Jerusalem in 587 must have had on the understanding of, for
example, the image of forest-felling in Isa. 10.33-34. That we are in a
position to say anything at all about this is due in part to our
knowledge of the events of 587 and literary conclusions derived from
other sources, and in part to our knowledge of the method of
reinterpretation otherwise occasioned by images such as these.

As concerns the methods of reinterpretation reflected in the
redactional changes in the text itself or in its context, caution should
generally be exercised in regard to precise dating, since these
changes, additions, readjustments, etc. rarely signal clearly datable
changes in the external situation, but most often reflect a shift from a
more negative to a more positive view of the future—or vice versa.
We must therefore, as is also evident from the exegetical sections,
focus our attention mainly on the great events in the people's history
of which we know, and which were of such crucial importance to the
entire political situation that we must also expect them to have an
impact on texts of the same period.

This means that we must concentrate our attention on events such
as the Syro-Ephraimite war, Samaria's destruction, the Ashdod
revolt, Sennacherib's siege of Jerusalem, the fall of the kingdom of
Assyria and the corresponding ascent of Judah under Josiah,
Jerusalem's destruction, with the subsequent deportation, the Exile
in Babylon, and finally the people's return to Jerusalem and the
subsequent attempts to rebuild the country. This does not in

principle preclude some changes having taken place under the influence of events other than those referred to above. This is possible, but on the basis of the source material available we can come to no conclusion.

This is in fact also how we have proceeded in the individual analyses, where we have tried to understand the specific statements in the light of *the events* that appear otherwise to have *made their mark on the traditions*. The oldest examples of the use of tree images within Isaiah 1–39 originate from the period *before the Syro-Ephraimite war*. It is at that time that Isaiah tries, by using his vineyard parable, to make the people accept that Yahweh must condemn their unnatural behaviour (Isa. 5.1-7), just as, presumably in connexion with the *Syro-Ephraimite war*, he urges the people in Isa. 9.7-20 to learn from Yahweh's punitive intervention into history, and in Isa. 1.29-31 unmasks the people's current enemies, Ephraim and Aram, as arrogant idol-worshippers who will themselves be consumed by fire. *Shortly after 722*, Isaiah warns those Judaeans who in facile optimism believe themselves to be saved. Yahweh's plans apply not only to the Northern Kingdom; his judgment upon the hard-of-heart shall also strike Judah (Isa. 6.12-13a), a message that should make it possible to reinterpret the vineyard parable which sees a *partial* fulfilment of Isa. 5.7 in the Northern Kingdom's destruction, but understands that Judah must suffer the same fate. It is possibly in this period that the original version of Isa. 10.16-19 as a judgment oracle against Judah came into existence.

Hezekiah's accession to the throne in *715* awakened a number of expectations for the future, and this *may* be the background to the oracle of the tree that is felled but sprouts again (Isa. 10.33–11.9), in the same way as the accession of the new king may have occasioned Isa. 6.13b's consolation of the anxious and afflicted: the tree's capacity to sprout is holy. This concept is also to be found in Isa. 4.2's image of the branch of Yahweh and the fruit of the land, and in Isa. 37.31-32's description of the remnant as a tree that takes root again and bears fruit. But in regard to these two images we were extremely cautious in our dating.

But the expectations awakened are soon frustrated, since Hezekiah, like his predecessor Ahaz, chooses to enter into political coalitions. This led to a sharp reaction on the part of Isaiah. Isa. 2.12-17's polemic against the proud (cf. also the image in Isa. 32.19) *may* originate from this period, but it can also be understood in the light of similar political events under King Ahaz.

Sennacherib's siege of Jerusalem in *701* evokes Isaiah's condemnation of the blasphemous prince who believes himself to be like God, but will in punishment for this be sent to the kingdom of the dead (Isa. 14.4b-20), a theme to be found again in Isa. 37.22b-32. The redaction of Isa. 10.5ff., with its placing of the oracles in Isa. 10,16-19 and Isa. 10.33–11.9, has its basis in this event, which reveals that the king of Assyria is not only an implement of punishment in Yahweh's hand. It is impossible for us to establish how close this redactional work is to the events of 701, but the fall of Nineveh of course sets a lower limit to this phase of redaction.

Whereas *the period of decline of the kingdom of Assyria* and its final fall again actualized Isaiah's words about Yahweh's wish to care for his people after their punishment, *the destruction of Jerusalem* and *the Babylonian Exile* at first gave rise to reflection in regard to the necessity and justification of the judgment. And here Isaiah's tree images were well-suited to maintain the cohesion in the political events and so justify Yahweh's acts. But this cohesion applied not only to the connexion with the people's offences and Yahweh's punishment; some of the tree images could also highlight the new possibility of life when the tree would begin to sprout again after the destruction, and thus comfort and encourage the Exilic generation. Cf. as regards the Exilic period's reflections the reuse of Isa. 5.1-7; 10.33–11.9; 6.12-13; 14.4b-20; 37.22b-32; 2.12-17; 32.19; 4.2-3.

Upon *termination of the Exile* and *the return to Judah*, a number of new problems arose, including the strong tension between various groups within the community. The situation not only gave rise to a reuse of Isaianic statements (cf. Isa. 32.15-20; 4.2-6; 10.16-19) but also to a new production of text based on them (cf. Isa. 27.2-6 and Isa. 11.10). A characteristic of this period's reuse and reinterpretation is the confidence that a new age will dawn: 'In days to come Jacob shall take root, Israel shall blossom and put forth shoots, and fill the world with fruit' (Isa. 27.6).

The chain of events I have been able to outline here shows the complexity of Isaiah's message. In contrast to Rudolf Kilian and W. Werner,[19] for example, I therefore believe I can prove that the salvation prophecy also belongs to Isaiah's message. But by concerning myself with imagery I have also been able to show, for example, how the positive message received its central position in the Exilic and post-Exilic period which many scholars afford it; my point is simply that this is not because the positive message came into existence at that time, but that it was reused.

The value of the work on the use of the tree image as a metaphor in Isaiah 1–39 is therefore to demonstrate the *reuse of the images*. The image analyses should thereby represent an important corrective to the ever stronger trend towards dating the prophetic texts to the Exilic period. No-one can be in any doubt that the Exilic period was extremely productive, but this production, as shown by the—certainly limited—textual material, has been to a great extent *interpretive reproduction*. My analyses are therefore a *corrective* to J. Vermeylen's repeated *late datings* of the Isaianic texts, but should also be seen, although more indirectly, as a plea against Hermann Barth's attempt to provide more precise datings for the Isaianic oracles. I therefore find an analysis such as that undertaken by R.E. Clements[20] on the reuse of the Isaianic judgment oracles in connexion with the fall of Jerusalem more convincing than Hermann Barth's attempt to explain *in detail* the reinterpretation of Isaiah's message probably brought about by the fall of the kingdom of Assyria.

My endorsement of *R.E. Clements's* approach to the study of Isaianic prophecies should also be supplemented by an endorsement of the ideas forming the basis of *R.P. Carroll's* work. But what I miss in both cases is more fundamental consideration and analysis of the language of the prophetic message employed. I therefore consider that analysis of the special nature of imagery is an absolute necessity if one wishes to study the continual reuse of the prophetic message.

Finally, I wish to point out that work on the Isaianic imagery, its reuse and the reinterpretation to which it has been subjected has most certainly raised the question: What do we in fact understand as the meaning of the image? As frequently asserted, it is impossible to speak of *the* image without defining the period in its history of use and reuse with which one is concerned; similarly, it is not possible to speak of *the* meaning without adding for whom the image has this or that meaning. To a great extent, therefore, the exegetes work consists in laying bare *imagery's possible meanings* and pointing out the elements in the context—both literary and cultural-historical—that can influence the hearer's perception of the image. This consequence must follow from imagery's polyvalence, and the fact that its meaning does not come into existence until the actual encounter between image and hearer.

The study of Isaianic imagery is a literary task, but it is hoped this treatise has shown that such work can be undertaken only if one is prepared to adopt both *literary* and *historical* approaches to the texts, taking into account imagery's function and the implications of using this form of language.

We have now come to the end of the road, and in conclusion I wish only to summarize the *main result* of the treatise by emphasizing that the tree images in Isaiah 1–39 act as theological interpretations of the political situation, that their function is to involve the hearers in the message in such a way that they adopt as their own the images' interpretation of reality, and that the images have given an opportunity for reinterpretation and the production of new text. An important part of this reuse of the tree image is founded on Isaiah's own confidence that the judgment is not Yahweh's last word. In the image of the tree that is felled but sprouts again Isaiah and the redactors of the Isaiah tradition have found the key to the understanding of the political situation best described by the quotation from Job : THERE IS HOPE FOR A TREE.

NOTES

Notes to Introduction

1. Luis Alonso Schökel, 'Stilistische Analyse' (1960).
2. Luis Alonso Schökel, 'Stilistische Analyse' (1960), pp. 161 and 164.
3. Luis Alonso Schökel, 'Literary Study' (1975), p. 14. Cf. also J. Cheryl Exum, 'Broken Pots' (1981), pp. 331ff.

Notes to Chapter 1

Proto-Isaiah as Traditional Literature and Religious Utility Literature

1. Johannes Lindblom, *Servant Songs* (1951), p. 10.
2. Johannes Lindblom, *Servant Songs* (1951), p. 102.
3. Rolf Rendtorff, *Einführung* (1983), pp. 132f.
4. J.H. Eaton, 'Origin' (1959), p. 138. Eaton is not alone in this view of the genesis of the book of Isaiah. Cf. Hans Wildberger, *Jesaja 28–39* (1982), p. 1545, and, in the scholarly of discussion of the genesis of the book of Isaiah, Wildberger's very clear and instructive survey (pp. 1529-47).
5. Rolf Rendtorff, *Einführung* (1983), p. 138.
6. Eduard Nielsen, 'Literature' (1971), pp. 25f.
7. R.E. Clements, *Fall of Jerusalem* (1980), p. 433.
8. As regards the content-related reasons, I must in this connexion indicate the complexity of the preserved part of the message. The tension between judgment and salvation which is so characteristic of Isaiah's message has made a large contribution to its utility. I therefore agree with Rolf Rendtorff (who in his interpretation of Isaiah cites in support/relies on his American colleague Brevard S. Childs) when he stresses the inextricable connexion between judgment and salvation in both Proto-Isaiah and the book of Isaiah as a whole. Cf. Rolf Rendtorff, *Einführung* (1983), pp. 211f. and Brevard S. Childs, *Introduction* (1979), pp. 336-38, where Childs indicates the theological and hermeneutic consequences of the analysis of the book of Isaiah.
9. Joachim Jeremias, *Gleichnisse* (1970), p. 113.
10. Eduard Nielsen, *Shechem* (1955), p. 151.
11. Cf. e.g. R.P. Carroll's, H. Barth's and J. Vermeylen's work dating from the end of the 1970s. See also Douglas Jones, 'Traditio' (1955), which, although with other concepts, expresses the views that later manifested themselves in regard to reinterpretation.
12. R.P. Carroll, *Prophecy Failed* (1979), and the articles: 'Dissonance' (1977); 'Isa. 1-11' (1978); 'Second Isaiah' (1978) and 'Prophetic Tradition' (1980).

13. R.P. Carroll, *Prophecy Failed* (1979), p. 110. See also p. 215 and
R.P. Carroll, 'Prophetic Tradition' (1980), where views are advanced with
rather more prudence, and a sense that other factors also play a part.
   14. Cf. e.g. Annemarie Ohler, who, in her irritation that all images in the
OT are not as clear as Isaiah's war image in Isa. 9.4, writes: 'Bilder werden
nur selten zur Veranschaulichung eingesetzt, sie dienen im Gegenteil öfter
der Verunklärung' (Annemarie Ohler, *Gattungen* [1972], p. 74).
   15. Cf. as regards this Rolf Rendtorff's warning against 'making a fetish
of' ipsissima verba, so that we regard these words only as genuine
expressions of the prophetic message. Such an historical approach to the
texts is—and remains—a modern phenomenon (Rolf Rendtorff, *Einführung*
[1983], p. 200). See also Hans Wildberger's emphasis of the intention of Isa.
1–39: 'Aber Jesaja I ist weder eine Dogmatik noch eine Sammlung religiöser
Dokumente, der man lediglich historisches Interesse bewahrte, sondern eine
solche von Glaubenszeugnissen für die jeweilige Gegenwart' (Hans Wildberger,
Jesaja 28–39 [1982], p. 1683).
   16. In his study of the book of Isaiah, B.S. Childs draws attention to how
the Deutero-Isaianic message, which was originally spoken in a specific
historical situation, has had removed in the final redaction what might
remind of this context (with the exception of the reference to Kyros) and has
been set in the canonical context, where the words—read together with
Proto-Isaiah's message—from being a special message to the Exilic generation
become a general message about God's plan for history as a whole (Brevard
S. Childs, *Introduction* [1979], pp. 325ff.).
   17. Cf. David Robertson, *Literary Critic* (1977). See also William A.
Beardslee, *Literary Criticism* (1970), pp. 5-7, which expresses a more precise
view of the relation between an historical and a literary approach to the
texts.
   18. Cf. Rolf Rendtorff, *Einführung* (1983), pp. 137f.
   19. R.E. Clements, *Fall of Jerusalem* (1980).
   20. Cf. as regards such 'contextless' use of biblical texts Jan Lindhardt's
article on biblical interpretation in the Middle Ages and the Renaissance (Jan
Lindhardt, *Bibeludlaegning* (Biblical Interpretation) [1979], pp. 203ff.).

Notes to Chapter 2

The Use of Imagery in the Old Testament

   1. Adolf Jülicher, *Gleichnisreden*, I–II (1910). The first edition appeared
in 1886 (Vol. I) and 1899 (Vol. II) respectively.
   2. Cf. as regards literature on the subject Luis Alonso Schökel, *Kunstwerk*
(1971), pp. 312-18. The oldest work in this bibliography is Albert Werfer,

Poesie (1875), which, however, must be considered as primarily a collection of material.

3. The most recent research review is Warren S. Kissinger, *Parables* (1979). In addition, reference should be made to Hans Weder, *Gleichnisse* (1978), pp. 11-57. A more extensive review of both Weder's and Klauck's (see below) books is to be found in Charles E. Carlston, 'Review' (1981). Cf. also Bertil Wiberg, *Lignelser* (Parables) (1954); Eta Linnemann, *Gleichnisse* (1975; 1st edn, 1961); Sigfred Pedersen, 'Metodeproblemer' (Problems of Method) (1965); Dan Otto Via, *Parables* (1967); Norman Perrin, *Parables* (1967); James M. Robinson, 'Parables' (1968); Norman Perrin, *Interpretation* (1971); John Dominic Crossan, 'Bibliography' (1974); Elisabet Engdahl, 'Språkhändelser' (1974); Turid Karlsen Seim, 'Lignelsesforskningen' (Parable Research) (1977); Hans-Josef Klauck, *Allegorie* (1978); Gerhard Sellin, 'Allegorie' (1978); Wolfgang Harnisch, 'Metapher' (1979); J. Lambrecht, 'Paraboles' (1980), which each give a individual impression of the development of parable research. Finally, cf. G.B. Caird, *Imagery* (1980), which provides a general discussion of language and imagery in the Bible.

Notes to Chapter 2§1

Main Viewpoints in Old Testament Research

1. Johannes Lindblom, 'Bildspråk' (1949).

2. Johannes Lindblom, *Servant Songs* (1951). Cf. the promise in Bildspråk (1949), p. 223 of a specific analysis of the Ebed-Yahweh songs and the description in the same passage (p. 208), of the 1949 article as a little, fragmentary, preliminary study.

3. Cf. Johannes Lindblom, 'Bildspråk' (1949), p. 209.

4. Johannes Lindblom, 'Bildspråk' (1949), p. 209, where in note 3 Lindblom refers to Adolf Jülicher, *Gleichnisreden* (1910), Vol. I, pp. 52f. Cf. also Jülicher's own formulation in Vol. I, p. 55: 'Mithin ist die *Metapher uneigentliche* Rede; es wird etwas gesagt, aber etwas andres gemeint . . . '

5. According to Jülicher, John 10 is just such a metaphorical description. Cf. Johannes Lindblom, 'Bildspråk' (1949), p. 211.

6. Ivan Engnell, 'Bildspråk' (1962).

7. Aug. Wünsche, *Bildersprache* (1906).

8. Johannes Hempel, 'Jahwegleichnisse' (1924). Cf. as regards Hempel's attempt to include psychological considerations in the interpretation of imagery Klaus Seybold, 'Bildmotive' (1974), who, in connexion with Zechariah's visions, refers to the possibility of involving interpretation of dreams, but refrains from this because methodological certainty within this field is not yet sufficient. Klaus Seybold, 'Bildmotive' (1974), p. 97.

9. Johannes Hempel, *Gott/Mensch* (1926).

There is Hope for a Tree

10. Harold Fisch, 'Analogy of Nature' (1955). See in particular p. 162.

11. Rudolf Mayer, 'Bildersprache' (1950), p. 55. Note also that Mayer refers in Note 1 to both Wünsche and Hempel.

12. Rudolf Mayer, 'Sünde' (1964).

13. Cf. Luis Alonso Schökel, 'Stilistische Analyse' (1960); 'Is. 27, 2-5' (1960); *Kunstwerk* (1971); 'Literary Study' (1975).

14. Cf. Luis Alonso Schökel, *Kunstwerk* (1971), pp. 318ff.; in particular as regards water as a metaphor pp. 326ff. See also 'Stilistische Analyse' (1960), pp. 159-61.

15. Eva Hessler, 'Deuterojesaja' (1965).

16. Christine Downing, 'Exodus' (1968), pp. 35 and 38.

17. G. Johannes Botterweck, 'Löwenbilder' (1972).

18. G. Johannes Botterweck, 'Löwenbilder' (1972), p. 119. Johannes Hempel, in a 1939 article, has dealt with analogous ideas, in that he examines the anthropomorphism in the OT. Cf. Johannes Hempel, 'Anthropomorphismus' (1939).

19. Erling Hammershaimb, 'Pseudepigrafer' (1975).

20. Anders Jørgen Bjørndalen, 'Allegorier' (Allegories) (1966).

21. Anders Jørgen Bjørndalen, 'Allegorier' (1966), pp. 149f.

22. Cf. e.g. the very copious note 14, p. 147, on New Testament parable research, the meticulous review of, inter alia, Bultmann's view of allegories, pp. 150ff., and note 66 on the transition from use of myths to use of imagery, pp. 156f.

23. Anders Jørgen Bjørndalen, *Allegorische Rede* (1986).

24. The 'allegory' concept is defined as 'Texte, die eine Reihe oder, mehr bildhaft gesagt, eine Kette von in gewisser Weise aufeinander bezogenen Metaphern bieten' (Anders Jørgen Bjørndalen, *Allegorische Rede* [1986], p. 1).

25. Cf. Anders Jørgen Bjørndalen, *Allegorische Rede* (1986), pp. 1-5.

26. Cf. Anders Jørgen Bjørndalen, *Allegorische Rede* (1986), pp. 7ff. See also my discussion of this problem, pp. 62ff.

27. Anders Jørgen Bjørndalen, *Allegorische Rede* (1986), pp. 27ff.

28. Anders Jørgen Bjørndalen, *Allegorische Rede* (1986), pp. 34-39. Cf., as regards an understanding of metaphor, the formulation: 'Dies ist disjunktive (disjunct) Anwendung der Bedeutung: der Sprachverwender kennt in der Bedeutung gleichzeitig noch andere Bedeutungselemente, die nicht auf dasjenige, worüber er spricht, bezogen werden können' (pp. 37f.). A brief account of Reichling's theory is also to be found in Anders Jørgen Bjørndalen, 'Allegorier' (1966), p. 162.

29. Anders Jørgen Bjørndalen, *Allegorische Rede* (1986), pp. 46ff.

30. Anders Jørgen Bjørndalen, *Allegorische Rede* (1986), pp. 54, p. 352.

31. Anders Jørgen Bjørndalen, *Allegorische Rede* (1986), pp. 135ff.

32. Leonard L. Thompson, *Literature* (1978), pp. 251-56.

33. Leonard L. Thompson, *Literature* (1978), p. 251. Cf. also on the use of the משל concept the following excursus on משל.

34. Hans-Peter Müller, *Vergleich* (1984).

35. Hans-Peter Müller, *Vergleich* (1984), p. 18.

36. Claus Westermann, *Vergleiche und Gleichnisse* (1984).

37. Claus Westermann, *Vergleiche und Gleichnisse* (1984), pp. 104f.

38. Claus Westermann, *Vergleiche und Gleichnisse* (1984), pp. 121ff. and 134f.

Excursus משל, māshāl

The Old Testament has no specific concepts for imagery forms such as parable and allegory; but both these forms (and more) can be described as משל. Cf. Anders Jørgen Bjørndalen, 'Allegorier' (1966), p. 146 and *Allegorische Rede* (1986), pp. 8ff. According to Otto Eissfeldt, *Maschal* (1913), the root משל originally indicated similarity, and could be used about both proverbs and parables. The basic meaning has been forgotten over the years, and therefore משל could also be used about proverbs that contained no comparative or figurative elements, about the satirical poem, and about various other forms of speech. Cf. also Eissfeldt's diagram p. 43 concerning משל's possible meanings.

In Isa. 1–39, משל is used only in relation to a certain speech-form in Isa. 14.4a, where it refers to the subsequent satirical song (see discussion of this on pp. 159ff.), and in Isa. 28.14, where it describes the scoffers in Jerusalem. We are not therefore confronted with a terminology characteristic of the texts we are to analyse. The purpose for which the Israelite used imagery will therefore come to light from analysis of the specific examples of imagery rather than from analysis of the משל concept.

In conclusion, it should be mentioned briefly that not all scholars are in agreement with Eissfeldt's definition of משל's meaning. Allen Howard Godbey, '*Mašal*' (1922-23) advances the thesis that משל often signifies a ritual act of a magical nature whereby destruction of the enemy can be invoked, i.e. a form of sympathetic magic that relies on similarity between the ritual act and what it occasions. A.S. Herbert ('*Māšāl*' [1954]) believes that משל always indicates a parable. If it has a linguistic form (which is not always the case, since a person can also be a משל), it is formulated briefly and tersely. In the OT, the concept usually has the same meaning, and there is consequently no reason to differentiate between 'satirical song', 'popular proverb', 'instruction', 'oracle' and 'apocalyptic statement', as did Eissfeldt.

Cf. also as regards this: D. Buzy, *Paraboles* (1912), pp. 52ff.; *TWNT* V, pp. 744ff.; Maxime Hermaniuk, *Parabole* (1947), pp. 62ff.; Jean Pirot, '*Māšāl*' (1950); Bertil Wiberg, *Lignelser* (Parables) (1954), pp. 22ff.; A.R. Johnson משל(1955); Madeleine Boucher, *Parable* (1977), pp. 87-88 and

Timothy Polk, 'Māšāl' (1983), who gives the following broad definition: 'I want to suggest that the speech-acts designated *mĕšālîm* are aptly suited for religious discourse (and Scripture) by virtue of a heightened performative and reader-involving quality' (p. 564).

39. Cf. e.g. Eduard König, *Einleitung* (1893); E. Sellin, *Einleitung* (1910); Otto Eissfeldt, *Einleitung* (1934); Robert H. Pfeiffer, *Introduction* (1952; 1st edn, 1941); Artur Weiser, *Einleitung* (1957); G.W. Anderson, *Introduction* (1959); R.K. Harrison, *Introduction* (1969); Otto Kaiser, *Einleitung* (1969); Georg Fohrer, *Das AT*, I (1969); *Das AT*, II-III (1970).

40. In addition, as concerns König and Sellin, König has discussed imagery meticulously in his hermeneutic, Eduard König, *Hermeneutik* (1916), pp. 96ff., while Sellin, in his definition of what Old Testament introduction is, has pointed out that it is no more than Israelitic literary history (E. Sellin, *Einleitung* [1910], p. 1).

41. Aage Bentzen, *Introduction*, I (1948). See in particular pp. 9-19 and 102ff.

42. Aage Bentzen, *Introduction*, I (1948), p. 13.

43. Cf. e.g. Aage Bentzen, *Introduction*, I (1948), pp. 177-81 and Otto Kaiser, *Einleitung* (1969), p. 124.

44. Cf. e.g. Georg Fohrer, *Das AT*, II-III (1970), pp. 23-24 and 28. Otto Eissfeldt, *Einleitung* (1934), pp. 82ff.

45. Hermann Gunkel, 'Jes. 33' (1924), pp. 182f.

46. Brevard S. Childs, *Introduction* (1979).

47. Werner H. Schmidt, *Einführung* (1979), pp. 177f. may perhaps be interpreted, with some goodwill, as an initiative in this direction. Schmidt here refers quite briefly to the prophets' audacious use of imagery, and then continues, in brevier, with a brief and quite general discussion of the shift in meaning that can occur when an individual statement is moved from its original Sitz im Leben to a new context.

48. Rolf Rendtorff, *Einführung* (1983), p. 223. See also p. 220.

Notes to Chapter 2§2

General Principles of New Testament Parable Research

1. Adolf Jülicher, *Gleichnisreden*, Vol. I (1886); Vol. II (1899). See especially Vol. I pp. 58ff. and 70. My references to Jülicher apply not to this first edition but to the second edition of 1910, in which Vol. I is revised. Cf. also as regards the history of research note 3 p. 243 in this treatise.

2. Cf. Adolf Jülicher, *Gleichnisreden*, I (1910), p. 145 and Hans Weder, *Gleichnisse* (1978), pp. 14-15.

3. Adolf Jülicher, *Gleichnisreden*, I (1910), pp. 146-48. Cf. my discussion of the heart-hardening concept pp. 231f.

4. Cf. Sigfred Pedersen, 'Metodeproblemer' (Methodological Problems) (1965), p. 151ff. See also Bertil Wiberg, *Lignelser* (1954), pp. 22ff. as regards the criticism of Jülicher's use of Latin and Greek rhetoric instead of Semitic material.

5. C.H. Dodd, *Parables* (1961).

6. Cf. C.H. Dodd, *Parables* (1961), p. 22 and the formulation p. 144: 'the *eschaton*, the divinely ordained climax of history, is here'.

7. Joachim Jeremias, *Gleichnisse* (1970; 1st edn, 1947); quoted here from the 1970 edition.

8. Joachim Jeremias, *Gleichnisse* (1970), p. 113. See also this treatise p. 18. Moreover, Joachim Jeremias's method of reconstructing the original parables has recently been strongly criticized by a representative of Literary Criticism's view. John W. Sider believes that the laws of change which Jeremias claims to be able to demonstrate have nothing to do with laws but are individual observations from different parables (John W. Sider, 'The Jeremias Tradition' [1983]).

9. C.H. Dodd, *Parables* (1961), p. 16.

10. C.H. Dodd, *Parables* (1961), p. 21.

11. Joachim Jeremias, *Gleichnisse* (1970), p. 227

12. Cf. William A. Beardslee, *Literary Criticism* (1970), where Beardslee introduces 'Literary Criticism'. See especially pp. 12f.

13. Cf. Elisabeth Engdahl, 'Språkhändelser' (1974), which gives a brief and clear introduction to Robert W. Funk, Dan Otto Via and Norman Perrin, rounded off with some critical comments. See also Hans Weder, *Gleichnisse* (1978), pp. 31ff. and 45ff.

14. Robert W. Funk, *Language* (1966).

15. Robert W. Funk, *Language* (1966), p. 162.

16. Robert W. Funk, *Language* (1966), pp. 136ff. and 140ff.

17. Robert W. Funk, *Language* (1966), p. 143. But note Funk's special interpretation of the argumentative as 'a "revelation" which calls for response' (p. 145).

18. Robert W. Funk, *Language* (1966), p. 140.

19. Dan Otto Via, *Parables* (1967).

20. Dan Otto Via, *Parables* (1967), pp. 2 and 17.

21. Dan Otto Via, *Parables* (1967), pp. 24-25. See also pp. 73ff.

22. Dan Otto Via, *Parables* (1967), p. 79.

23. Dan Otto Via, *Parables* (1967), p. 86.

24. Dan Otto Via, *Parables* (1967), p. IX.

25. Dan Otto Via, *Parables* (1967), p. 52.

26. Dan Otto Via, *Parables* (1967), p. 54.

27. John Dominic Crossan, 'Experience' (1973).

28. John Dominic Crossan, 'Experience' (1973), p. 346. See also pp. 339f.

29. John Dominic Crossan, 'Experience' (1973), p. 349.

30. John Dominic Crossan, *Parables* (1973).

31. John Dominic Crossan, *Parables* (1973), p. 14.

32. John Dominic Crossan, *Parables* (1973), p. 13.

33. Cf. Elisabet Engdahl, 'Språkhändelser' (1974), pp. 95 and 107.

34. John Dominic Crossan, *Articulate* (1976).

35. John Dominic Crossan, *Articulate* (1976), p. 115.

36. Cf. e.g. Norman Perrin, 'Parables' (1967), pp. 344f. and Norman Perrin, 'Interpretation' (1971), pp. 145ff.

37. Norman Perrin, 'Scholarship' (1967), pp. 467f.

38. Norman Perrin, 'Parables' (1967), p. 343; 'Scholarship' (1967), pp. 467f.; 'Interpretation' (1971), p. 143.

39. Norman Perrin, 'Interpretation' (1971), p. 148. See also Norman Perrin, 'Historical Criticism' (1972), p. 375.

40. Norman Perrin, 'Symbol' (1975).

41. Norman Perrin, 'Symbol' (1975), p. 366.

42. I end my survey of Perrin's 1975 article not because there has since been no research into parables (cf. note 3, p. 243 on the subject of research) but because I believe that in these surveys I have covered the main points.

43. Hans Wildberger, *Jesaja 28–39* (1982), pp. 1694f.

44. The standard method is to list the images according to the fields they are drawn from. This in itself is an excellent way of obtaining a comprehensive survey of the material and an impression of the author or circle behind the texts. But it is not sufficient to perform this preliminary work if one wishes to understand the use of the images.

Notes to Chapter 2§3

Description of the Function of Imagery in the Old Testament

1. A brief survey of the position of research in about 1975 is to be found in H.G. Koch, 'Metaphor' (1975), in which the traditional understanding of the metaphor (from Aristotle to Vico) is compared with more recent trends in religious philosophy and theology, including, very briefly, New Testament parable research. In addition, reference should be made to an analysis of the New Testament parables just published in which profound philosophical reasons are given for the assertion that the synoptic parables can be defined as metaphors in regard to functional structure and cognitive function. This analysis substantiates in many respects the results arrived at in this treatise in regard to the form and function of Old Testament imagery. See Mogens Stiller Kjärgaard, *Metaphor* (1986).

2. The example chosen differs in one respect from the images discussed in the textual analyses. The tree images in Isa. 1–39 are always used about

human relations; the image of the waters of Shiloah, on the other hand, is used about Yahweh. If the Israelite wished to speak of his Creator, it was very important that the language should not imply an identification of God with that which is created. Under the ban on images, this would be blasphemy. The language must therefore have such a form that it avoids blasphemy without ending up in tautology lacking in informative value. Imagery is able to maintain the balance between these extremes. The tension in the image between the two different statements ensures that the Creator is not identified with the created, and at the same time prevents the radical distancing of the Creator from the created, which would mean that Yahweh remained the unknown, the one about whom, according to Wittgenstein, one must be silent. Cf. Kirsten Nielsen, 'For et trae' (For a tree) (1983), p. 434.

As regards imagery's function, however, there is no difference between images used about transcendent matters and images used about non-transcendent matters; what we derive from Isa. 8.6-8 is therefore also relevant to images not used about Yahweh.

3. Cf. ThHAT on םאנ.

4. Cf. on the interpretation of Ps. 46 Benedikt Otzen, Hans Gottlieb, Knud Jeppesen, *Myths* (1980), pp. 73ff., 119ff.

5. Max Black, 'Metaphor' (1954-55), p. 285. See also Black's discussion of the metaphor in his 'More' (1979), pp. 19-43, which is a supplement to the first article. But this changes nothing in regard to the points where I find it necessary to criticize Black.

6. Max Black, 'Metaphor' (1954-55), p. 285. Cf. also K.E. Løgstrup's very concise formulation of the metaphor's way of acting: 'The difference is insisted on so that the similarity can surprise.' K.E. Løgstrup, *Vidde* (Width) [1976], p. 79).

7. Cf. this treatise p. 40. See also G.B. Caird, *Imagery* (1980), p. 153.

8. Robert W. Funk, *Language* (1966), pp. 134f. points out that there is a tendency for the parable's meaning to become established in the course of tradition.

9. Cf. Paul Tillich's emphasis of the difference between a sign and a symbol. Signs can be invented and deliberately changed; symbols, on the other hand, are born and die (Paul Tillich, *Culture* [1964] p. 58).

10. This latter is the opinion of K.E. Løgstrup, *Vidde* (1976), p. 76.

11. On this, cf. what scholars such as John Dominic Crossan and Robert W. Funk have stressed in regard to the hearers' importance to the interpretation of imagery.

12. Cf. Anders Jørgen Bjørndalen's way of differentiating between the metaphorical statement and the non-metaphorical statement. Anders Jørgen Bjørndalen, 'Allegorier' (Allegories) (1966), p. 162 and *Allegorische Rede* (1986), pp. 27ff.

13. Paul Ricoeur, 'Metaphorical Process' (1979), p. 146.

14. Jan Lindhardt *Luther* (1983), pp. 126f.

15. Cf. Ian G. Barbour, *Myths* (1974), p. 13. See also Paul Ricoeur, 'Hermeneutics' (1975), p. 77, where Ricoeur stresses the same in the words: 'When a poet speaks of a "blue angelus" . . . he places two terms in tension . . . of which only the whole constitutes the metaphor. In this sense we must not speak of words used metaphorically, but of metaphorical *statements*. *Metaphor proceeds from the tension between all the terms in a metaphorical statement.*'

16. It is worth-while in this context to remember that the understanding of what the river context covers is culturally determined. For example, in the Old Testament the snake is perceived as cunning and in our culture the wolf is perceived as ferocious, whatever zoologists may think of these animals. Cf. Max Black, 'Metaphor' (1954–55), pp. 287f.

17. Cf. Earl R. MacCormac, *Metaphor* 1976, p. 74.

18. Cf. e.g. the account of the attempt of the verification theory and the function theory to resolve the problems surrounding the relation between language and reality in Mogens Stiller Kjärgaard, 'Sproget' (Language) (1981). It is concluded here that both attempts fail.

19. Cf. Paul Ricoeur's reference to the metaphor's referential function as 'split reference'. Paul Ricoeur, 'Metaphorical Process' (1979), p. 151.

20. Cf. J.L. Austin, *Things* (1977), pp. 1-11 and 150. A brief and concise account of Austin's main views is to be found in Justus Hartnack, 'Analytisk filosofi' (Analytical Philosophy) (1980), pp. 174–80. Hartnack tries here to establish the difference between constatives and performatives, since in his opinion the term performative loses its meaning if every statement is also a performative. According to Hartnack, the difference is that constatives presuppose an already existing fact, whereas the performative first creates this. Austin has not claimed such a difference, and Hartnack gives no specific examples of pure constatives. It is indeed also difficult for me to conceive that any of the statements with which we are concerned in this treatise could be included in this.

21. John R. Searle, *Speech Acts* (1979), pp. 17f.

22. Austin himself is not content with such a broad, blanket description, but distinguishes between three types of performative usage: a) locution, which signifies the actual act of using the language in speech; b) illocution, which signifies the way in which or the force with which the language is used, for example warning or persuasive, and c) perlocution, which signifies the effect the speech act has, for example that the person addressed really permits himself to be warned or persuaded. This distinction can be useful if one wishes to define the intention and the effect respectively of a prophetic message. Cf. the analysis of Isa. 5.1-7 and the entire discussion of the heart-hardening. I bring in Austin in this connexion only to illustrate that even the

scholar who coined the description 'performative' must abandon the categorical distinction between performative statements and non-performative statements and recognize that all speech is also performative. For Austin's way of using the term performative cf. J.L. Austin, *Things* (1977), pp. 98ff.

23. Elisabet Engdahl, 'Språkhändelser' (1974), p. 107.

24. Robert W. Funk, *Language* (1966), p. 143.

25. R.P. Carroll, *Prophecy Failed* (1979). As regards the formulation of the thesis, cf. p. 110.

26. Cf. R.P. Carroll, *Prophecy Failed* (1979), pp. 69-75. Carroll seems very uncertain as regards the performative aspect's significance in the prophetic message. The main argument is the somewhat questionable one that the hearers actually rejected the prophets, which shows that their message did not have the performative effect the theory should assume! Cf. also p. 58, where Carroll himself points out that his thesis is dependent upon the fact that the prophets really prophesied future events.

27. It should be noted here that the possibilities of falsification of a figurative statement are not nearly as great as of a non-figurative statement, since the lack of fulfilment is easily explained as a consequence of the failure to understand the meaning of the statement. Cf. R.P. Carroll, *Prophecy Failed* (1979), p. 106, where Carroll opens up the possibility that hermeneutic endeavours may be an *alternative* to dissonance.

28. Cf. Atle Kittang & Asbjørn Aarseth: Strukturer (Structures) (1976), p. 72 and Paul Ricoeur 'Hermeneutics' (1975), pp. 75ff.

29. Ivan Engnell, 'Bildspråk' (1962), col. 283.

30. Cf. e.g. John Dominic Crossan, *Articulate* (1976), p. 115, where he emphasizes that he no longer considers parables and allegories to be antitheses. On the other hand, Gerhard Sellin ('Allegorie' [1978], p. 289) does so.

31. John R. Searle, *Speech Acts* (1979).

32. John R. Searle, *Speech Acts* (1979), p. 78.

33. K.E. Løgstrup, *Vidde* (1976), pp. 78-79.

34. K.E. Løgstrup, *Vidde* (1976), p. 81. Cf. also Svend Bjerg's criticism of this in Svend Bjerg, *Grundfortaelling* (Basic Narrative) (1981), pp. 160-63.

Excursus

Further to the discussion of Old Testament imagery, it is natural to refer briefly to a possible connexion between imagery and another form of language that also cannot be translated into the language generally preferred. I am thinking here of jokes.

Charles Brenner has pointed out that jokes can function only if it is assumed that the primary process is activated (Charles Brenner: *Psychoanalysis* [1973], pp. 154ff.). If a joke is translated into secondary-process language, the amusing aspect quite simply disappears. In continuation of this, it is natural to think of imagery, which also cannot be translated without losing its effect. It is merely a matter of different effects. The joke paves the way for laughter or a smile as releasing factors; but for what does imagery pave the way?

It probably quite simply sets the scene for interpretation and acceptance of what is said, so that one falls in with it and acts according to it. It is common to the strategy of the joke and imagery that they construct a tension (uncertainty about outcome/interpretation) which is thereupon released by—in the case of the joke—understanding the point and the subsequent laughter, and—in the case of the image—by interpretation, acceptance and the subsequent appropriate behaviour.

It may perhaps be surprising initially to compare imagery with a joke, but both the joke and the image subsist in reality on the fact that two different areas are combined in an unexpected way, whereby new insights can be created.

It is this to which Erling Jacobsen draws attention when he points out that creative thought indeed arises from a clash of two trains of thought, and says, with a reference to A. Koestler, that '... a short circuit between trains of thought or matrixes (is) the unavoidably essential condition for all creative mental activity in humour, science and art' (Erling Jacobsen, *Grundprocesser* [Basic Processes]. [1971], p. 146).

Notes to Chapter 3

The Tree as a Central Metaphor in Proto-Isaiah

1. The Choice of the Tree Image

1. In addition to the tree images that I analyse in Chapter 4, there are a number of images with a certain relationship to the tree, including harvest images. These are included to only a limited extent.

2. On this see Kirsten Nielsen, *Prosecutor* (1978), where I analyse the prophetic judgments and Yahweh's dual role.

3. Gilbert Durand, *L'Imaginaire* (1960), p. 370.

2. The Cultural Background to the Use of the Tree Image

1. Cf. Dalman, *AuS* VII (1942), pp. 32-45; Friedrich Lundgreen, *Pflanzenwelt*, (1908), pp. 57ff.

2. 'Cypress' is the traditional rendering of ברושים. According to KBL, this refers to a kind of juniper berry, Juniperus Phoenicea, which, however, is scarcely distinguishable from the cypress. See also KBL as regards the

traditional designation of 'cedar'. This may refer to another conifer with a very long trunk.

3. Cf. ANET, p. 307 and AOT, p. 365.

4. Cf. also Assurnasirpal II's account of a similar expedition to Carchemish and Lebanon (ANET, p. 275), and Asarhaddon's account (ANET, p. 291).

5. See also II D VI, 21 as regards the quality of trees from Lebanon.

6. Cf. ANET, pp. 252, 254; see also ANET, pp. 27b, 240b, 243. The Old Testament also refers to 'cedars' in connexion with shipbuilding (cf. Ezek. 27.5).

7. M.B. Rowton, 'Woodlands' (1967).

8. See also the use of the images in Song 5.15. In 1 Kgs 5.13 (RSV 4.33) there is a reference to the cedars of Lebanon as the peak of the vegetable kingdom, and to hyssop as the lowest.

9. Cf. Vilhelm Møller-Christensen & K.E. Jordt Jørgensen, *Växtvärld* (1957), p. 86; Dalman, *AuS* IV (1935), pp. 162f.

10. Cf. Vilhelm Møller-Christensen & K.E. Jordt Jørgensen *Växtvärld* (1957), pp. 88f.; Yosef Kahaner, 'Metaphors' (1973-74), p. 16.

11. Yosef Kahaner, 'Metaphors' (1973-74), p. 17.

12. On the care of olive trees, cf. Dalman, *AuS* IV (1935), pp. 171ff, and on the care of vines cf. Dalman, *AuS* IV (1935), pp. 307ff. and Vilhelm Møller-Christensen & K.E. Jordt Jørgensen, *Växtvärld* (1957), pp. 120ff.

13. Dalman, *AuS* IV (1935), p. 173.

14. Cf. Edmond Jacob, 'Esaïe 27,2-5' (1970), p. 329.

15. On wine production generally, cf. Dalman, *AuS* IV (1935), pp. 356ff.

16. Cf. also the special rules for the Nazirites, Num. 6.2ff., and the Rechabites, Jer. 35.6-7, 14 and e.g. the polemic in Isa. 28.7ff. against the inebriated priests and prophets.

17. Cf. also Johannes Pedersen, *Israel III–IV* (1960), p. 354; Flemming Friis Hvidberg, *Graad* (Weeping) (1938), p. 128.

18. Cf. Vilhelm Møller-Christensen & K.E. Jordt Jørgensen, *Växtvärld* (1957), pp. 29ff., and Dalman, *AuS* IV (1935), pp. 327f. and 315f.

19. Karl Jaroš, *Elohist* (1974), p. 231. For literature on the subject see p. 214 note 1.

20. Karl Jaroš, *Elohist* (1974), pp. 235ff.

21. Hos. 4.12-13; Jer. 2.20; 3.6; 3.13; Ezek. 6.13; Isa. 57.5. Cf. also Deut. 12.2, where the Israelites are told to destroy the holy groves; Deut. 16.21 which bans the planting of Asherahs/trees beside Yahweh's altar, and the reference to the Israelites' high places for sacrifices, 1 Kgs 14.23; 2 Kgs 16.4; 17.10.

22. Friedrich Lundgreen, *Pflanzenwelt* (1908), p. 24. Oaks and terebinths are thus frequently referred to in connexion with holy places. Cf. Gen. 12.6; 13.18; 35.4, 8; Josh. 24.26; Judg. 6.11, 19; 1 Kgs 13.14; 1 Chron. 10.12.

23. Cf. E.O. James, *Tree of Life* (1966), p. 37; Friedrich Lundgreen, *Pflanzenwelt* (1908), pp. 33-43.

24. Cf. Friedrich Lundgreen, *Pflanzenwelt* (1908), pp. 74-79.

25. In his article on the image motifs in Zechariah's visions, Klaus Seybold shows how the traditions about Solomon's temple influenced the wording of the visions (Klaus Seybold, 'Bildmotive' [1974], pp. 97ff.). See also Klaus Seybold, *Visionen* (1974), where a more detailed study is to be found. Isaiah's use of the tree as an image is not however included.—For Wildberger's definition of Isaiah as a Jerusalem prophet see his *Isaiah 28-39* (1982), pp. 1596ff.

26. See Flemming Hvidberg, 'Gen. I-III' (1960), p. 286, where Hvidberg stresses that Gen. 2-3 in fact refers to things that belong to a Canaanite Bāmā: the tree of life, the water of life, the guards at the entrance to the holy place and first of all the holy pillar, the snake.

27. Cf. Ivan Engnell, *Kingship* (1943) and 'Planted' (1953), pp. 92ff.; Geo Widengren, *Tree of Life* (1951); E.O. James, *Tree of Life* (1966) and Friedrich Lundgreen, *Pflanzenwelt* (1908), pp. 136-40.

28. Ivan Engnell in *SBU* (1962), I, cols. 1518ff. (Livets träd). See also Hans Wildberger's excursus on the Canaanite fertility cult in Hans Wildberger, *Jesaja 13-27* (1978), pp. 652-55 and the excursus pp. 657-58 on the gardens of Adonis.

29. Ivan Engnell in *SBU* (1962), I, col. 1521 (Livets träd).

30. Ivan Engnell, *Kingship* (1943), pp. 26ff., 82ff.

31. Geo Widengren, *Tree of Life* (1951). As regards Engnell's promise, see Ivan Engnell, *Kingship* (1943), pp. 174f.

32. Geo Widengren, *Tree of Life* (1951), p. 42. The connexion between god/king and the tree of life has since been discussed by, for example, Ivan Engnell, '"Knowledge"' (1955); Ilse Seibert, *Hirt* (1969), see especially pp. 35ff.; Bernhard Lang, *Aufstand* (1978), pp. 65ff.; Karl Jaroš, *Elohist* (1974), pp. 213ff.; Karl Jaroš, 'Gen. 2-3' (1980).

33. Cf. Ivan Engnell, *Kingship* (1943), pp. 26ff. and Mowinckel's criticism of this in Sigmund Mowinckel, *Han som kommer* (He who shall come) (1951), p. 303 note 173.

34. Ivan Engnell in *SBU* (1962), I, col. 1333 (Konung, kungadöme).

35. Fritz Stolz, 'Bäume' (1972).

36. Fritz Stolz, 'Bäume' (1972), p. 148. On the interpretation of Ps. 29 and its background in Canaanite religion cf. also Hans-Joachim Kraus, *Psalmen 1-63* (1972), p. 235.

37. Cf. Stolz's very cautious treatment of the dependence problem (Fritz Stolz, 'Bäume' [1972], pp. 153ff.).

38. Cf. Luis Alonso Schökel's emphasis that water as an image is polyvalent and therefore particularly employable (*Kunstwerk* [1971], p. 329).

39. Cf. Hans Wildberger, *Jesaja 1-12* (1972), p. 221. See also Luis Alonso Schökel's analysis of fire as an image in Isa. 5.24-25 and 9.7-20 (*Kunstwerk* [1971], pp. 358-60).

40. Cf. Bernhard Lang, *Aufstand* (1978), p. 110 and Lang's references to Dalman, *AuS* I,2 (1928), p. 320 and *AuS* IV (1935), p. 293.

41. Cf. Bernhard Lang, *Aufstand* (1978), pp. 111ff.

42. In the review, we have held to the general ideas in the Palestinian region, and can therefore only agree with Othmar Keel that 'Der primäre Verstehenshorizont der konventionellen Bilder sind das Alte Testament und Palästina' (Othmar Keel, *Metaphorik des Hohen Liedes* [1984], p. 16). Only where this does not suffice should one assume an influence from elsewhere.

Notes to Chapter 4

Analysis of Tree Images in Isaiah 1–39

1. *Analysis of Isa. 5.1-7 and Isa. 27.2-6*

1. J. Vermeylen, *Isaïe* (1977-78), pp. 159-68 and Anders Jørgen Bjørndalen, *Allegorische Rede* (1986), whose copious notes on the analysis of Isa. 5.1-7, together with the extensive bibliography, are very helpful.

2. Cf. Hans Wildberger, *Jesaja 1-12* (1972), p. 166. See also Anders Jørgen Bjørndalen, 'Echtheit' (1982), pp. 93-98.

3. Cf. Hans Wildberger, *Jesaja 28-39*. 1982, p. 1557.

4. Luis Alonso Schökel, *Kunstwerk* (1971), p. 296, whose rendering of the use of עשׂה is not however wholly correct; it rather covers a loose paraphrase of the text.

5. Cf. Karl Budde, *Jesaja 1-5* (1932), p. 52; Anders Jørgen Bjørndalen, *Allegorische Rede* (1986), p. 247.

6. John T. Willis, 'Isaiah 5:1-7' (1977).

7. John T. Willis, 'Isaiah 5:1-7' (1977), p. 359.

8. I am thus in agreement with O. Loretz that the text consists of different genres; but on the other hand I do not agree that this must be because the text consists of different fragments which have only secondarily been joined together to form an entity: the prophetic song of protest. Cf. O. Loretz, 'Weinberglied' (1975), pp. 573-76. But the employment of different forms of language need not necessarily mean that what is concerned is later amplifications relative to an original text. I must likewise reject Paul Haupt's attempt at 'cleaning the text' of additions on the basis of prosodial considerations. The very alternation between different genres makes it unreasonable to expect a completely homogeneous prosody (Paul Haupt, 'Isaiah's Parable' [1903]). See also Peter Höffken, 'Jesaja 5,1-7 (1979), where the possible history of development is analysed, emphasizing the allegorizing element as a new interpretation of available material. Cf. in addition my criticism in note 40 of Gerald T. Sheppard.

9. The term דוֹדִי is vocalized by some as דּוֹדַי, i.e. the plural of דּוֹד.

10. Hans Wildberger, *Jesaja 1-12* (1972), p. 167. Ahlström's treatment of the question is to be found in G.W. Ahlström, *Psalm 89* (1959), pp. 163-73; as regards Ahlström's interpretation of Isa. 5.1, see pp. 163f., where Ahlström mentions quite briefly that Isaiah utilizes words and motifs from the דוד cult's liturgies. But the text itself is scarcely such a liturgy. See also Hans-Peter Müller, 'Funktion des Mythischen' (1971), pp. 268-71, who interprets the song in the light of mythical concepts about Yahweh as Israel's beloved.

11. Anders Jørgen Bjørndalen, *Allegorische Rede* (1986), pp. 257-66.

12. H. Junker, 'Is. 5,1-7' (1959).

13. Cf. also Isa. 3.14; 27.2; Jer. 2.21; 5.10; Ps. 80.9ff., which in various ways use the vineyard (vines) as an image.

14. Cf. John T. Willis, 'Isaiah 5:1-7' (1977), p. 362.

15. I am not therefore in agreement with Willy Schottroff, who believes that it is surprising to the hearers *that* it is spoken in imagery. Cf. Willy Schottroff, 'Jes. 5,1-7' (1970), p. 69. It is remarkable that Schottroff of all people, who defines Isa. 5.1-7 as a fable and stresses how familiar such fables were in the Near East, can believe that it surprised the hearers *that* imagery is concerned.

16. Anders Jørgen Bjørndalen, *Allegorische Rede* (1986), pp. 286ff.

17. Cf. Julien Harvey, *Le plaidoyer* (1967), p. 92. Cf. also Kirsten Nielsen, *Prosecutor* (1978), p. 40, where I point out that *rîb*'s basic structure is of such a general nature that it is not possible to associate it with only one specific situation in life, such as the great lord's accusation against the faithless vassal. See also Michael de Roche, '*Rîb*' (1983) and his attempt at terminological justification in this connexion.

18. Cf. my analysis of this in Kirsten Nielsen, *Prosecutor* (1978), pp. 34-38.

19. Cf. Aage Bentzen, 'Jes 5,1-7' (1927) and H. Junker's contribution, 'Is 5,1-7' (1959), where Junker joins Bentzen, and in the light of Jn 3.29 interprets the friend as the bridegroom's friend.

20. Hans Wildberger, *Jesaja 1-12* (1972), pp. 167f.

21. Cf. Hans Wildberger, *Jesaja 1-12* (1972), p. 169; John T. Willis, 'Isaiah 5:1-7' (1977), pp. 345f.

22. According to Karl Budde, one has to imagine a pause after v. 4. The hearers must now reply; but they are still at a loss for a reply to the owner of the vineyard. According to Budde, this is because of their embarrassment; they feel that something unpleasant is about to happen. While Budde thus allows the hearers to anticipate a development of the matter by their eloquent silence, Bentzen believes that the reason for the lack of reply is the hearers' approval of the development and their anticipatory pleasure about what is to happen to the faithless woman. I am in no doubt that Bentzen's psychological sense and his understanding of the text's structure and

technique is greater than Budde's. Cf. Karl Budde, 'Jesaja 1-5' (1932), p. 56.

23. Cf. Gillis Gerleman, *Ruth. Hohelied* (1965), pp. 126f.

24. As regards this perception of בתה cf. P.-R. Berger: 'Jes. 5,6' (1970), and as regards the description of the wilderness Johannes Pedersen, *Israel I-II* (1920), pp. 355ff.

25. Cf. e.g. Bernhard Duhm, *Jesaia* (1922), p. 56, who believes that it is precisely here that Isaiah throws off the mask of a popular bard and surprises his hearers with his talk of punishment. '"Den Wolken gebiete ich"—es ist kein Mensch, der das spricht, es ist Jahwe!' The same view can also be found in Jochen Vollmer's study of Isa. 5,1-7 in *Geschichtliche Rückblicke* (1971), p. 153.

26. Aage Bentzen, 'Jes 5,1-7' (1927), pp. 209f.

27. Cf. e.g. John T. Willis, 'Isaiah 5:1-7' (1977), pp. 353-58, where Willis reviews the scholars who see Isa. 5.1-7 as an allegory and a parable respectively.

28. The term is used by Hans Werner Hoffmann, 'Form' (1970). Cf. also my discussion of the form-critical method in Kirsten Nielsen, *Prosecutor* (1978), pp. 3f.

29. Gale A. Yee, 'Juridical Parable' (1981), p. 30.

30. It is on this aspect that Adrian Graffy focuses when he defines Isa. 5.1-7 as belonging to the 'self-condemnation parables' genre, a genre that includes the Nathan parable, 2 Sam. 12.1-7a; the parable in 2 Sam. 14.1-20 about the woman of Tekoa; the parable of the escaped captive in 1 Kgs 20.35-42; and the parable of the cast-off woman who marries again in Jer. 3.1-5. See Adrian Graffy, 'Isaiah 5,1-7' (1979), pp. 408 and 404ff. Analogously, Gale A. Yee, 'Juridical Parable' (1981) strongly emphasizes the juridical aspect.

31. Text correction with BHSa. See also the analysis of Isa. 27.4 on p. 118.

32. Cf. Hans Wildberger: *Jesaja 13-27* (1978), p. 1009. Wildberger suggests on p. 1011 that it may refer to an image of external enemies who, if that is the case, are converted to Yahweh.

33. I thus entirely disagree with William McKane, 'Isaiah VII 14-25' (1967), pp. 216f. who believes that vv. 23-25 is a continuation of the positive statement in vv. 21-22, and thus expresses a return to the Israelitic life-style (as smallholders/stock breeders) in contrast to the Canaanite culture with its many vineyards. There is nothing positive in the book of Isaiah about the wilderness's thorns and briers, and nothing negative about the vineyard; merely that it bears genuine grapes.

34. Cf. Aage Bentzen, *Jesaja* (1944), p. 266, who believes that it is a confusion of two expressions, קוץ ודרדר (Gen. 3.13; Hos. 10.8) and שמיר ושית.

35. Cf. Targum, which in all other places sees שמיר ושית as an image, whereas Isa. 7.23, 24, 25 takes it literally.

36. Cf. *TWAT* (1973), col. 731.

37. Cf. KBL, where בער is translated as 'destroyed by fire' both here in Isa. 5,5, and in Isa. 3,14; 6,13. Cf. also Jochen Vollmer, *Geschichtliche Rückblicke* (1971), p. 151, who quite characteristically, in his discussion of לבער's meaning, views the two possibilities, 'burned down' and 'devoured' as alternatives, and does not consider whether the duality might involve special possibilities of reinterpretation.

38. See Gerald T. Sheppard, 'Redaction' (1985), who, although he considers Isa. 5.1-7 as redactionally formulated, stresses the redactional exploitation of existing images in the Isaianic tradition.

39. As regards the dating of Deut. 32, cf. Kirsten Nielsen: *Anklager* (1977), p. 111.—In extension of the examples given of the use of the rain image, Job 29.22f. should also be mentioned. Job's words dropped, נטף , upon his hearers, and they waited for him as one waits for rain. The root נטף is used in the hiphil about the prophecy that flows (Ezek. 21.2, 7; Amos 7.16; Mic. 2.6, 11), which could also indicate a certain tradition of using rain as an image of the prophetic word. In any event, this possibility should be carefully considered before one accepts the traditional interpretation, that the root is used because of the froth that runs from the mouth of the ecstatic prophet. Cf. Zimmerli's indication of this in his *Ezechiel 1–24* (1969), p. 464.

40. Gale A. Yee, 'Juridical Parable' (1981). In a 1982 article, Gerald T. Sheppard described as a step in the right direction Yee's definition of Isa. 5.1-7 as a juridical parable. But Sheppard believes that he can supplement and support her analysis. According to Sheppard, Isa. 3.13-15 would originally have been part of the parable, which would then have had the following structure: Isa. 5.1-2; 3.13-14; 3.15; 5.7; 5.3-4; 5.5-6. A quick run-through of the text thereby emerging should be sufficient to show that Sheppard is on the wrong track. If 3.13-15 is introduced as suggested, the interpretation of the imagery is given before the call to judgment, so that the whole basic idea disappears. Moreover, I find it difficult to bring the two accusations (according to ch. 3, the leaders have devoured the vineyard; according to ch. 5, the house of Israel/men of Judah have behaved like a vineyard that bears wild grapes) into harmony. See Gerald T. Sheppard, 'Juridical Parable' (1982), pp. 45-47. See also Gerald T. Sheppard, 'Redaction' (1985), where the main idea is taken further; v. 7, however, is placed as the end of the text. But here also Sheppard permits the interpretation, by way of 3.13-14, to follow directly after v. 2.

41. Cf. Yee's excellent introduction of Deut. 32.1-29, which is indeed referred to as a song, שירה, Deut. 31.19, 21-22, 30; 32.44, but is formed as a *rîb*.

42. Employed in the book of Hosea only in 2.17, where Israel is given the vineyards in the wilderness by Yahweh.

43. Cf. Hans-Joachim Kraus, *Psalmen 64-150* (1972), pp. 555-57.

44. Cf. Hans Walter Wolff, *Micha* (1982), pp. 21 and 25f.

45. Cf. also Hans Walter Wolff, *Micha* (1982), pp. 67f.

46. Cf. *TWAT* cols. 783-85, where it is stressed that Israel is used primarily as a religious concept.

47. The authenticity of Isa. 10.20, 22 is, however, questionable.

48. J. Vermeylen, *Isaïe* (1977-78), pp. 159-68.

49. Cf. my discussion of *rîb* in Kirsten Nielsen, *Prosecutor* (1978), pp. 43ff.

50. Cf. Kirsten Nielsen, *Prosecutor* (1978), pp. 62ff.

51. Cf. Kirsten Nielsen, 'Opgør' (Revolt) (1976), p. 230, and 'Gudsbillede' (God's Image) (1978), p. 105.

52. Edmond Jacob, 'Esaïe 27,2-5' (1970), p. 325. This text is often considered to have been so poorly handed down over the centuries that it needs a great deal of correction to make it comprehensible. But in my opinion this is not necessary. Cf. Edmond Jacob, 'Esaïe 27,2-5' (1970), pp. 325f.

53. Hans Wildberger, *Jesaja 28-39* (1982), pp. 1014f.

54. Cf. also in support of the demarcation of Isa. 27,2-6 J. Vermeylen, *Isaïe* (1977-78), p. 376 and Otto Kaiser, *Jesaja 13-39.* (1973), pp. 179f, who considers v. 6 to be an apodosis to the song, a view also to be found in Bernhard Duhm, *Jesaia* (1922), pp. 190f. According to Duhm, v. 6 originates from a poem other than 27.2-5.

55. As regards Isa. 5.1-7, the anger motif is most clearly expressed in the context, where Yahweh's anger is in part formulated directly in the chorus to the historical paraenesis (cf. Isa. 5.25) and in part lies behind the many lamentations following directly after 5.7.

56. Edmond Jacob, 'Esaïe 27,2-5' (1970), p. 328 points out that חֹזֶק is used in the light of the concepts of asylum in the holy place. The last chance of the doomed is to hold fast to the horns of the altar.

57. Cf. P. Joachim Becker, 'Wurzelspross' (1976), pp. 30f.

58. J. Vermeylen, *Isaïe* (1977-78), pp. 375ff.

59. Hans Wildberger, *Jesaja 13-27* (1978), p. 1009 here leans on Edmond Jacob, 'Esaïe 27,2-5' (1970). See also Benedikt Otzen, 'Isaiah XXIV–XXVII' (1974), pp. 203f., who likewise dates the text to the post-Exilic period, in that he distinguishes between oracles that concern the world's catastrophe and the city's destruction, and oracles introduced later (including 27.2-6) that concern Zion.

60. The examples here referred to are in my opinion most convincing in Luis Alonso Schökel, 'Is 27,2-5' (1960), pp. 771f.

61. Luis Alonso Schökel, 'Is 27,2-5' (1960), p. 772.

62. Cf. Edmond Jacob, 'Esaïe 27,2-5' p. 327, who describes שמיר ושית as a stereotypical Isaianic term vaguely used about an enemy.

63. Cf. both J. Vermeylen, *Isaïe* (1977-78), p. 376 and Edmond Jacob, 'Esaïe 27,2-5' (1970), p. 328.

64. This outline could of course be supplemented by study of the use of the vineyard as an image in the New Testament. Cf. e.g. the parable of the wicked husbandmen, Mk 12.1-11; Mt. 21.33-44; Lk. 20.9-18 and Joachim Jeremias's treatment of the link with Isa. 5.1-7 in Joachim Jeremias, *Gleichnisse* (1947 [1970]), pp. 67ff.

Notes to Chapter 4§2

Analysis of Isa. 10.33-11.9, 10

1. Cf. Hans Wildberger, *Jesaja 1-12* (1972), p. 433. But Wildberger himself sees vv. 33-34 as an authentic Isaianic oracle turned against the circles in Jerusalem that wished to enter into a coalition with Ashdod. Only with the redactional placing was there a reinterpretation of the oracle, so that it was seen as a judgment on the Assyrians.

2. J. Vermeylen, *Isaïe* (1977-78), pp. 265-68.

3. Read in the redactional context, vv. 27b-32 must be seen as the king of Assyria's march against Jerusalem. I therefore see no reason to refrain from 'identifying' the army, as does Friedrich Huber. According to Huber, the description represents neither the historical circumstances of the Syro-Ephraimite war nor the events of 701 (712 is not a possibility), and he can therefore omit including the passage in his analysis of the foreign people's role in Isaiah. This criterion is of course acceptable if one wishes to use the texts as a historical source but not if—as here (and perhaps also to a certain extent in Huber's case)—one wishes to investigate the texts' use of historical events. See Friedrich Huber, *Die anderen Völker* (1976), p. 32.

4. J. Vermeylen, *Isaïe* (1977-78), p. 268.

5. J. Vermeylen, *Isaïe* (1977-78), pp. 271ff.

6. Hermann Barth, *Josiazeit* (1977), pp. 54-76.

7. Cf. also G. Vermes, 'Lebanon' (1958), who has analysed the rendering of Lebanon in the Targum and shown the great extent to which Lebanon is there also regarded as a metaphor. See also E. Lipiński, 'Lebanon' (1973) and *TWAT*, IV, cols. 461-71.

8. Cf. Fritz Stolz, 'Bäume' (1972) and my opinion of his views, pp. 82ff.

9. Sigmund Mowinckel, 'Paradiselvene' (Rivers of Paradise) (1938).

10. Walther Zimmerli, *Ezechiel 25-48* (1969), pp. 685, 757ff.

11. Fritz Stolz, 'Bäume' (1972), pp. 147ff.

12. It is not sufficient merely to interpret the reference to Lebanon as a superlative expression of what is best and most precious, as does Gillis Gerleman, *Ruth. Hohelied* (1965), p. 161. Cf. also as regards the connexion between Gen. 2-3 and the Song of Solomon Phyllis Trible, *Rhetoric* (1978), pp. 72ff, and 152f., where Trible quotes Song 4.12 and 4.16, but does not really cover the text. Note also that Lebanon is referred to no fewer than

seven times in such a short text as the Song of Solomon: Song. 3.9; 4.8[2]; 4.11; 4.15; 5.15; 7.5 (RSV 7.4).

13. Cf. *ThHAT* cols, 753-61: רום, article by H -P. Stähli.

14. Cf. *TWAT* cols. 394-97: גבה, article by H.-P. Stähli, and Hentsche's article in *TWAT*, Vol. I, cols. 890-95.

15. Cf. Hermann Barth, *Josiazeit* (1977), pp. 75f.

16. Johann Gottfried von Herder, *Poesie* (1825), pp. 406f. Cf. also Hans Wildberger, *Jesaja 1-12*, p. 425, who points out that Otto Kaiser also goes along with this connexion. See also Hermann Barth, *Josiazeit* (1977), p. 57, where Barth meticulously lists the literature on the question and also himself accepts the idea of a close connexion between Isa. 10.33-34 and 11.1ff. (but 10.33a + 11.1-5).

17. Cf. Geo Widengren: *Tree of Life* (1951), p. 50, where Widengren points out that חטר means sceptre in Phoenician, and exploits this in support of his thesis. As regards the thesis itself cf. pp. 20ff. and 37ff.

18. Cf. the use of the same image in Isa. 53.2, a text also strongly marked by concepts of royal ideology. But this is not the same terminology, apart from the use of the gloss שרש. Cf. also Ivan Engnell, 'Ebed Jahve' (1945), p. 56 and Geo Widengren, *Tree of Life* (1951), p. 53.

19. Cf. Hans Wildberger, *Jesaja 1-12* (1972), p. 443, where Wildberger refers to the use of שרש in Isa. 5,24 and 14.29f. To this may be added Isa. 11.10; 37.31 and 53.2.

20. Hermann Barth, *Josiazeit* (1977), p. 63. See also his inclusion of metrical considerations to support the thesis, p. 75, note 340.

21. Cf. e.g. P. Joachim Becker, 'Wurzelspross' (1976), where Ginsberg's attempt to understand שרש as a word for 'stem' is completely rejected.

22. In his discussion of the passage, Benedikt Otzen reviews briefly the ideas of Scandinavian research as regards the tree-and-plant image's background in royal ideology. Lebanon and the trees felled are images of Jerusalem and its nobles, especially the king and the royal house (cf. ארז in the singular in Zech. 11.2). As regards the plural form in v. 2 (the glorious trees), it states that this can perhaps be explained in that it was referring to the entire dynasty (Benedikt Otzen, *Deuterosacharja* [1964], pp. 163-64). Whereas Otzen appears to find the explanation of the image's complexity in its interpretation (the king and his entire lineage), I try to show here that we are dealing with a complex tradition with *implications* for the interpretation.

23. Cf. as regards Isaiah's view of the foreign people as coalition partners Friedrich Huber, *Die anderen Völker* (1976). As regards Isaiah's condemnation of this in Isa. 31.1-3, cf. Huber pp. 122-30, where it is stressed that Judah's policy of friendliness towards the Egyptians in the period 705-701 is, according to Isaiah, an expression of Judah's confusion of God and man, and the outcome will therefore also be unfortunate for Judah.

24. Herman Barth, *Josiazeit* (1977). As regards Barth's general thesis, cf. pp. 4f.; as regards Isa. 10,27bff., cf. p. 76.

25. J. Vermeylen, *Isaïe* (1977-78), pp. 274 and 282.

26. Cf. Hans Wildberger, *Jesaja 1-12* (1972), p. 435, who also refers to a reinterpretation of Isa. 10.33-34 determined by the redactional context.

27. Cf. as regards this Hans Wildberger's investigation of the use of שרשׁ in connexion with Isa. 14.29, where, after a survey of a number of examples of the combination of 'root' and 'fruit', he concludes: 'Es hat den Israeliten offensichtlich Eindruck gemacht, daß auch ein Baumstrunk oder ein Wurzelstock noch Schosse treiben kann (6,13; 11,1; 37,31; Hi. 14,7f). Solange die Wurzel 'lebt', ist Hoffnung da (Hans Wildberger, *Jesaja 13-27* [1978], p. 582). In my opinion, it is these very connotations that prevail in the use of the tree as an image—even if forestry experts will observe that cedars do not usually sprout again.

28. J. Vermeylen, *Isaïe* (1977-78), p. 277.

29. Hans Wildberger, *Jesaja 1-12* (1972), pp. 458f.

30. Cf. Hans Wildberger: *Jesaja 1-12* (1972), pp. 466f. as regards the dating to the post-Exile period, and Seth Erlandson's attempt at dating the text in the eighth century (Seth Erlandson, 'Jesaja 11:10-16' [1971], p. 43).

31. Hermann Barth, *Josiazeit* (1977), p. 59.

32. P. Joachim Becker, 'Wurzelspross' (1976).

Notes to Chapter 4§3

Analysis of Isa. 6.12-13

1. Odil Hannes Steck, 'Jesaja 6' (1972). See also Odil Hannes Steck, 'Jesaja 7,3-9' (1973) and 'Jesaja 7,10-17 und 8,1-4' (1973). On the state of research up to 1959 cf. Ernst Jenni, 'Berufung' (1959).

2. But except for a few words. Moreover, the whole 'Denkschrift' was originally kept in the first person singular, according to Odil Hannes Steck, 'Jesaja 6' (1972), p. 199 n. 28.

3. Cf. Steck's rejection that an account of a call in the style of e.g. Exod. 3; Judg. 6.11-17 or Jer. 1.4-10; Ezek. 1-3 was concerned (Odil Hannes Steck, 'Jesaja 6' [1972], pp. 189ff.).

4. Odil Hannes Steck, 'Jesaja 6' (1972), p. 193.

5. Cf. Kirsten Nielsen, 'Isa. 6:1-8:18*' (1986), where I discuss the 'Denkschrift' as a dramatic composition.

6. It is worth noting that the addition keeps within the precise sickness image, as used in v. 10.

7. Hans Wildberger, *Jesaja 1-12* (1972), pp. 241, 257f.

8. The root רחק is also used in Jer. 27.10; Ezek. 11.16, where it clearly refers to an exile. Cf. Hans Wildberger, *Jesaja 1-12* (1972), p. 257.

9. J. Vermeylen, *Isaïe* (1977-78), pp. 195-97.

10. Hermann Barth, *Josiazeit* (1977), pp. 195f.

11. Cf. Hans Wildberger, *Jesaja 1-12* (1972), p. 241. Note also Ivan Engnell, *The Call* (1949), pp. 52-53, who thinks that *all* ch. 6 dates back to Isaiah. See also J.A. Emerton, 'Translation' (1982), who, by including the versions, gives a thorough review and evaluation of the attempts made by scholarship to come to an understanding of v. 13's meaning. Emerton also considers that the last sentence is a secondary addition.

12. Cf. the possible reinterpretation of Isa. 5.7 at this point in time; it takes place in the light of the same question: Will the same happen to Judah as happened to Israel?—see pp. 108ff.

13. Cf. as regards the text-critical problems of the verse Hans Wildberger, *Jesaja 1-12* (1972), pp. 233f.

14. Cf. Walter Baumgartner, *Lexicon* (1974).

15. Cf. Walter Baumgartner, *Lexicon* (1974). See also N.H. Tur-Sinai, 'Isaiah i-xii' (1961), p. 169 and Hans Wildberger, *Jesaja 1-12.* (1972), p. 234.

16. Cf. *Thesaurus* II, col. 3684.

17. Ivan Engnell, *The Call* (1949), p. 50 n. 1.

18. *Thesaurus* I, cols. 531f.

19. See Theodor Nöldeke, *Syrische Grammatik* (1898), §131.

20. Unless, like Ivan Engnell, one goes as far as understanding the verb μακρύνω as positive, i.e. in the meaning 'become indulgent'. But I think this translation is not acceptable. In the light of the following reference to the remnant, the best sense is obtained by retaining the verb's normal meaning. Cf. Ivan Engnell, *The Call* (1949), p. 14.

21. Cf. Ivan Engnell: *The Call* (1949), pp. 14-15. J. Vermeylen believes the same as Engnell, and stresses that this does not mean that LXX was without knowledge of the words about the seed. The positive rendering of v. 12 shows that LXX knew these words, but left them out by accident. Cf. J. Vermeylen, *Isaïe* (1977-78), p. 196 n. 2. Wildberger also explains the missing words in LXX as an accident, a 'aberratio oculi' (cf. Hans Wildberger, *Jesaja 1-12* [1972], p. 234), and thereby follows a tradition going back to a 1923 article by K. Budde. On the basis of LXX, therefore, one cannot argue that v. 13b is secondary.

22. In Greek, the diminutive is formed by the suffix -ιον. Cf. Friedrich Blass, *Grammatik* (1961), §111, 3.

23. As regards the cultic background to Isa. 6.13, cf. Ivan Engnell, *The Call* (1949), pp. 49f. Note also Engnell's own reservation (p. 50 n. 3) in regard to the rites still practised in Isaiah's time.

24. Cf. Ivan Engnell, *The Call* (1949), pp. 50f.

25. As regards the political transactions surrounding the Ashdod coalition cf. Hans Wildberger, *Jesaja 13-27* (1978), pp. 751ff. and Siegfried Hermann, *Geschichte* (1973), pp. 315ff.

26. Cf. Benedikt Otzen, *Israeliterne* (The Israelites) (1977), p. 271ff.

27. Cf. also, in addition to Vermeylen and Barth, Wolfgang Metzger, 'Jesaja 6,13' (1981), p. 284, who assigns to Jeremiah's scribe Baruch a new and surprising role as 'proof-reader' etc. of Isa. 6.13.

28. Cf. Karl Marti, 'Jes 6,1–9,6' (1920), pp. 114f.

29. Cf. also how Isa. 6.9-10's heart-hardening statement has become subdued in later renderings. Craig A. Evans stresses that this trend begins in Ch. 6 itself with the addition of v. 13, and can be found again in 1QIsa^a 6.9-10, in LXX, partly in the Targum and partly in Peshitta. On the other hand, the Vulgate retains the acerbity in the statement, which Evans sees as an expression of the Christian interpretation of the heart-hardening (Craig A. Evans, 'Isaiah 6,9-10' [1982]).

30. The root נצב also means 'a plant' in Aramaic. Cf. Syriac ܢܨܒ.

31. John Sawyer, 'Isaiah 6,13' (1964).

32. Cf. *Dødehavsteksterne* (The Dead Sea Scrolls) (1959), p. 2, where Eduard Nielsen describes the interpretation of the book of Habakkuk as 'actualizing *re-interpretation*'.

Notes to Chapter 4§4

Analysis of Isa. 14.4b-20

1. Hans Wilderberger deals with v. 4b-21 as an entity, but points out that v. 21 should probably be considered as an addition. In my opinion, this assumption is supported by the shift from apostrophe, 2nd pers., to comment, 3rd pers., and I therefore find it most natural to consider only vv. 4b-20 as an entity. Cf. Hans Wildberger, *Jesaja 13–27* (1978), pp. 539-41.

2. Cf. Hedwig Jahnow, *Leichenlied* (1923), p. 249.

3. Cf. Hedwig Jahnow, *Leichenlied* (1923), p. 243.

4. On this differentiation between form-related and actual Sitz im Leben cf. Kirsten Nielsen, *Prosecutor* (1978), pp. 3f.

5. Hans Wildberger, *Jesaja 13–27* (1978), p. 537.

6. Cf. excursus, pp. 245f.

7. Hans Wildberger, *Jesaja 13–27* (1978), p. 562.

8. J. Vermeylen, *Isaïe* (1977-78), pp. 292ff. See likewise Hans Wildberger, *Jesaja 13–27* (1978), p. 543.

9. Cf. in support of this thesis e.g. Fritz Stolz, *Strukturen* (1970), pp. 163-64.

10. Cf. e.g. the use of Babylon as a code name in Rev. 14-18.

11. Hermann Barth, *Josiazeit* (1977), pp. 119-41.

12. See also Barth's discussion of the connexion between vv. 18-20a and

the remaining part of the poem (Hermann Barth, *Josiazeit* [1977], p. 137).

13. Cf. J. Vermeylen, *Isaïe* (1977-78), p. 293, who is strongly tempted to subscribe to this interpretation, but rejects it as he does not believe that Isaiah would have expressed himself in this way. As regards this, it must be said that Vermeylen probably overlooks the great extent to which this text uses traditional material.

14. Cf. e.g. Aage Bentzen's interpretation of Isa. 14.8 in Aage Bentzen, *Jesaja* (1944), p. 113, where he speaks of 'ruthless exploitation in order to ornament the metropolis' magnificent temples', and R.E. Clements, *Isaiah 1-39* (1980), pp. 141f.

15. Cf. section on wood as building material, pp. 75ff.

16. Arvid S. Kapelrud, *Joel* (1948), pp. 26ff. Kapelrud's presentation is unfortunately not quite clear. It is difficult to see whether in fact he is content to indicate a certain general background in the fertility cult or whether he really identifies the forest-feller with Karit, the fertility god Baal's representative in the cult, so that the king of whom Isa. 14.8 speaks is described as the dying god. Cf. also Eduard Nielsen's analysis of the cultic background to the book of Habakkuk, Eduard Nielsen, 'Habaqquq' (1952), where he emphasizes (p. 61) that the cedars of Lebanon signify things other than building material, and shows by including the imagery in the fable of Jotham that the cedar signifies the righteous, legitimate leader, which in turn supports the use of the tree image in Ps. 1.3 and elsewhere (cf. pp. 67ff.).

17. Cf. Hans Wildberger, *Jesaja 13-27* (1978), pp. 550ff.

18. Cf. as regards the terminology Ezek. 19.12, where the vine is plucked up and cast down to the ground (likewise hophal of שלך), and where the tree image is also used in reference to political circumstances.

19. Cf. as regards this Hans Wildberger, *Jesaja 13-27* (1978), p. 536, and Hermann Barth, *Josiazeit* (1977), p. 123.

20. Arvid S. Kapelrud, *Joel* (1948), p. 29.

21. Cf. Fritz Stolz, 'Bäume' (1972), p. 153.

22. Cf. Fritz Stolz, 'Bäume' (1972), pp. 150ff. The OT does not refer directly to god-killing as in the Epic of Gilgamesh; but is this perhaps expressed in the imagery?

23. Cf. Hans Wildberger, *Jesaja 13-27* (1978), pp. 546f., where Wildberger refers to Stolz's thesis about the garden of God in Lebanon, and shows how Isa. 14.8 (see also Isa. 37.24bff.) is closer to the original myth than Isa. 2.13; 10.33f. and Ezek. 31.

24. Cf. also the concepts about the mountain of God in the North, for example. See Aarre Lauha, *Zaphon* (1943), pp. 38ff.

25. Cf. Walther Zimmerli, *Ezechiel 25-48* (1969), p. 688.

26. Emendation with LXX, BHSc in Ezek. 31.3 and 31.10, and BHSa in 31.14.

27. Cf. Walther Zimmerli, *Ezechiel 25-48* (1969), pp. 751ff.

28. Also as regards Isa. 14.8 the political interpretation can be found again in the Targum, where the cypresses and the cedars of Lebanon are rendered as the rulers and the prosperous.

29. The hearers of Isa. 14.8 are of course both the tyrant who is to be humbled by the satirical song and Israel which is to be comforted and encouraged by the words about the fall of the despot.

30. Cf. also the analyses of Isa. 2.13; 4.2 and 32.19, where the combination appears as a result of redactional processing.

Notes to Chapter 4§5

Analysis of Isa. 37.22b-32

1. On the literary problems surrounding Isaiah narratives, apart from the commentary literature, cf. Brevard S. Childs, *Isaiah* (1967) and R.E. Clements, *Deliverance* (1980).

2. Cf. Hans Wildberger, *Jesaja 28–39* (1982), pp. 1420-21.

3. Aage Bentzen, *Jesaja* (1944), p. 303. See also Otto Kaiser, *Jesaja 13–39* (1973), pp. 298, 314, who merely defines the passage as secondary.

4. Brevard S. Childs, *Isaiah* (1967), p. 103. Note that Childs bases himself on the book of Kings version, and therefore gives the verses on the basis of 2 Kgs 19.21ff.

5. Whereas Deutero-Isaiah uses grass negatively, it is used positively in Trito-Isaiah, which describes how bones 'shall flourish like grass' at the sight of Jerusalem's salvation (Isa. 66.14).

6. As regards this interpretation cf. R.E. Clements, 'Fall of Jerusalem' (1980) and P.R. Ackroyd, 'Babylonian Exile' (1974).

7. R.E. Clements, *Fall of Jerusalem* (1980), p. 432.

8. Cf. Frants Buhl, *Jesaja* (1912), p. 469. Buhl refers to a victory inscription in which Sennacherib describes how, in his chariot, he drove over the high wooded mountains and over the mountain torrents. See *Keilschriftliche Bibliothek* (1890), pp. 87, 99.

9. Thus e.g. Frants Buhl, *Jesaja* (1912), p. 469; Aage Bentzen, *Jesaja* (1944), p. 304; Otto Kaiser, *Jesaja 13–39* (1973), p. 314. But Kaiser also mentions that there may be some connexion with the concepts about breaking into the garden of God, as is found in Ezek. 28.13. R.E. Clements, *Isaiah 1–39* (1980), p. 286 describes v. 24's reference to the forest as an image of Assyria, and refers to an analogous use of the image in Isa. 10.18f., but unfortunately he does not amplify his approach.

10. Cf. e.g. Asarhaddon's description of his expedition to Egypt (AOT, p. 358 and ANET, p. 292).

11. Hans Wildberger, *Jesaja 28–39* (1982), p. 1432.

12. Cf. also the Targum, which here also translates the image of the felling

of the trees of Lebanon in such a way that the hearers do not take this at face value but see that acts of war are concerned, just as in vv. 26f.

13. As regards this meaning of שרש and פרי, cf. Joachim P. Becker, 'Wurzelspross' (1976), pp. 24-26, where Becker rejects Ginsberg's view.

14. Cf. Hans Wildberger, *Jesaja 28-39* (1982), pp. 1421 and 1434f., where Wildberger shows how poorly these verses fit into the context of the Sennacherib situation, but otherwise gives no opinion on the origin of the oracle.

15. Cf. K.E. Løgstrup, *Vidde* (1976), p. 87 about the ironical unmasking by means of metaphors.

16. Cf. Walther Zimmerli, *Ezechiel 1-24* (1969), pp. 377-90.

17. Cf. also, in addition to Walther Zimmerli, Bernhard Lang, *Aufstand* (1978), pp. 28-88, where Lang analyses Ezek. 17 as a contribution to the political debate down to 587.

18. Cf. Bernhard Lang, *Aufstand* (1978), pp. 38-41.

19. Bernhard Lang, *Aufstand* (1978), p. 33.

20. As concerns an actual definition of what imagery is, or rather how imagery functions, Lang has not gone much beyond a cautious criticism of Jülicher's allegory concept and his use of this on Ezek. 17; cf. Bernhard Lang, *Aufstand* (1978), pp. 46-49. I also miss discussion of the myths behind the tree image. On the other hand, his attempt to bring in iconographic material is especially promising (cf. Lang, pp. 41-46).

Notes to Chapter 4§6

Analysis of Isa. 2.12-17 and 32.15-20

1. Cf. the more detailed analysis of the passage's redactional history in Kirsten Nielsen, *For et træ* (1985), pp. 257-71, where, among others, the following scholars' views of Isa. 2.12-17 are discussed: J. Vermeylen, *Isaïe* (1977-78); Hermann Barth, *Josiazeit* (1977); Hans Wildberger, *Jesaja 1-12* (1972); Joseph Blenkinsopp, 'Jes. 2,6-22' (1981); Hubert Junker, 'Is 2' (1962); R. Davidson, 'Is. II 6ff.' (1966).

2. Hans Wildberger, *Jesaja 1-12* (1972), p. 96.

3. J.F. Stenning in *Targum of Isaiah* (1949), pp. XIII and 11. Also כל אלוני הבשן (all Bashan's oaks) is paraphrased in the form of a political interpretation: כל שורני מדינתא translated by Stenning as: 'all the princes (or *tyrants*) of the provinces', pp. 10-11. Bertil Wiklander arrives at precisely the same interpretation as the Targum on the basis of his textual-linguistic and rhetorical method; but I find it difficult to see how the analysis of Isa. 2.13 can justify his very general statement that the cedars of Lebanon appear to be a stock metaphor for 'foreign and powerful foreign nations'. It is also striking that in reality he does not argue that the trees are used metaphorically,

although according to him this possibility is only one of several (Bertil Wiklander, *Literature* [1983], pp. 112-14).

4. Cf. J. Vermeylen, *Isaïe* (1977-78), pp. 135-42, who considers vv. 6-8, 11+18 to be an expounding of vv. 12-17, a first 'relecture' that originates from the Exilic period, whereas vv. 9-10+19-22 are post-Exile reinterpretations. Hermann Barth also envisages an Isaianic core (vv. 10+12-17 and vv. 7-8a, 9a—fragmentary), to which additions have been made, in part during the Exilic period and in part later (Hermann Barth, *Josiazeit* [1977], pp. 222f.).

5. Cf. Kirsten Nielsen, *For et træ* (1985), pp. 257f.

6. Cf. Rémi Lack, *Symbolique* (1973), p. 243 and Hermann Barth, *Josiazeit* (1977), p. 212.

7. Rémi Lack, *Symbolique* (1973), p. 73.

8. Cf. Hans-Wilhelm Hertzberg, 'Nachgeschichte' (1936), pp. 78f.

Notes to Chapter 4§7

Analysis of Isa. 4.2-6

1. A very meticulous study of the lines of connexion in Isa. 3.16-4.6 is to be found in Bertil Wiklander, *Literature* (1983), pp. 96, 124-34. According to him, however, not only 3.16-4.6 constitutes an entity but the whole of Isa. 2-4 (cf. pp. 98, 134-36, 141-42, 152-53). Cf. also Hans-Wilhelm Hertzberg, 'Nachgeschichte' (1936), pp. 75f.

2. Cf. Douglas Jones, 'Traditio' (1955), pp. 237ff.

3. Aage Bentzen, *Introduction* II (1949), p. 108.

4. Hans Wildberger, *Jesaja 1-12* (1972), pp. 153f. Wildberger considers the whole passage to be secondary, v. 2 being first extended by vv. 3-5a and later by vv. 5b-6.

5. J. Vermeylen, *Isaïe* (1977-78), pp. 152ff.; see especially p. 157. According to Vermeylen, 4.2-3, 4-5a, 5b-6 originate from various post-Exilic periods. Verses 4-5a clarify vv. 2-3, whereas vv. 5b-6 are a later commentary. Whereas vv. 2-3 refer to the whole community as Israel's remnant—the strong polarization has not yet begun—the following verses distinguish between the just and the sinners.

6. Cf. as regards this the connexion between Isa. 4.2-3 and Isa. 37.31-32; both texts use the words פרי, פלימה, [ה]נשאר[ה], ציון and ירושלם in a description of the new times when there will again be growth. Whereas the growth in Isa. 37.31 is an image of the remnant, this is not the case in Isa. 4,2, where the remnant is something different. Cf. in addition to the use of the words צבי, גאון, תפארת and הנשאר Isa. 28.1-4, 5's use of צבי, גאות, תפארת and שאר in the polemic against Samaria.

7. Cf. Douglas Jones, 'Traditio' (1955), p. 243, where Jones refers to the use of this image in Lamentations, where it is clearly Jerusalem's destruction in 587 that is concerned.

8. Cf. the analysis of Isa. 14.4b-20, where we saw the same technique utilized.

9. In his linguistic-rhetorical analysis of Isa. 3.16–4.6, Bertil Wiklander arrives at the result that the passage is structured on the basis of the 'family' metaphor. The family is used as a metaphor of the covenant between Yahweh and the people. Wiklander also believes that both images in Isa. 4.2—the branch of Yahweh/the fruit of the land—are used about the coming king, Yahweh's offspring, who stems from the new marriage between Yahweh and Judah. Cf. especially pp. 125, 130. Also worthy of note is the great extent to which Wiklander utilizes the metaphors, with their two semantic fields, when he wishes to argue in support of the connexion in Isa. 2–4. Wiklander uses the terminology 'principal subject' and 'subsidiary subject' about the two contexts compared in the metaphor. Cf. Bertil Wiklander, *Literature* (1983), pp. 124ff., and for his analysis of Isa. 2.8b-22. pp. 112ff.

10. Cf. Hans Wilderberger, *Jesaja 1–12* (1972), p. 154.

11. Cf. as regards the Old Testament perception of the king's relationship to Yahweh, e.g. Ps. 2.6-7; 89.20ff. and 2 Sam. 7.14.

12. Joyce G. Baldwin, '*Ṣemaḥ*' (1964).

13. On the use of חטר and נצר also cf. pp. 132f. and 163.

14. Cf. *ThHAT* I, cols. 798ff.

15. Cf. *SBU* Vol. II, the article 'Telning', cols. 1186f., where Ivan Engnell lists the terms used about the branch. But Engnell does not believe that צמח יהוה in Isa. 4.2 is a Messianic term; what the expression alludes to is the stupendous fruitfulness in the Messianic time. See also Karl Budde, 'Jesaja 1–5' (1932), p. 48, where Budde refers to other passages in the OT where the new time of salvation is described as stupendously fruitful: Isa. 1.19; Amos 9.13f.; Hos. 2.23; Isa. 30.23ff.; 61.7; Jer. 31.12f.; Ezek. 34.29; Mal. 3.11f.; Zech. 9.16f.; 14.7f. and Joel 4.18 (RSV 3.18).

Notes to Chapter 4§8

Analysis of Isa. 9.7-20 and 10.16-19

1. See Hans Wildberger, *Jesaja 1–12* (1972), p. 209, where Wildberger notes a parallel with Amos 4.6ff.

2. Hans Wildberger, *Jesaja 1–12* (1972), pp. 211-12. But see also J. Vermeylen, *Isaïe* (1977-78), pp. 185f., who envisages that the Isaianic text has been the subject of reinterpretation in two periods, in the first case turned against the Northern Kingdom shortly after 722, and in the second case in the light of a theology inspired by the Deuteronomists during the Exilic period, where the emphasis was on Yahweh's righteousness.

3. As regards the concepts about the destruction of reeds cf. Isa. 42.3.

4. According to Hans Wildberger (*Jesaja 1–12* [1972], p. 171), it is not possible to give a precise botanical definition of thorn and brier. As will be made clear below, this is not crucial since it is imagery that is concerned. On the forest's thicket cf. Dalman, *AuS* I,1 (1928), pp. 73-89, 254-61.

5. Cf. Hans Wildberger, *Jesaja 1–12* (1972), p. 221.

6. Cf. Luis Alonso Schökel, *Kunstwerk* (1971), p. 359, where in his analysis of fire as an image in Isa. 5.24-25 and 9.7-20 he shows how the image unites different elements.

7. Cf. also the clarifications we encounter in the form of key-word additions such as Isa. 7.8b, the duplicated 'king of Assyria' in Isa. 7.17 and 7.20, and perhaps Isa. 7.16's אשר sentence.

8. Cf. Hans Wildberger, *Jesaja 13–27* (1978), pp. 657ff. concerning the cultic concepts behind Isa. 17.10-11 and Flemming Friis Hvidberg, *Graad* (1938), pp. 94-96.

9. Cf. Hermann Barth, *Josiazeit* (1977), pp. 32f., who also believes that this is a coherent entity. I therefore disagree with Hertzberg, who considers vv. *17*-19 to be an independent oracle, an original threat against Israel, which because of linguistic similarities with v. 16 was placed later in continuation of the king of the Assyria polemic and thereby became the subject of *misinterpretation*. Where Hertzberg is correct is that the Assyrian context signifies *reinterpretation* of an original oracle; but this is vv. *16*-19, not vv. 17-19 (Hans-Wilhelm Hertzberg, 'Nachgeschichte' [1936], pp. 73f.).

10. See e.g. within the book of Isaiah Isa. 15.1-9; 16.7-12; 24.7-12; 32.9-14 and Flemming Friis Hvidberg, *Graad* (1938), pp. 119ff.

11. Hermann Barth, *Josiazeit* (1977), pp. 28-29.

12. J. Vermeylen, *Isaïe* (1977-78), pp. 259-60.

13. Hans Wildberger, *Jesaja 1–12* (1972), p. 408.

14. Hermann Barth, *Josiazeit* (1977), p. 34.

15. Cf. R.P. Carroll, 'Isa 1–11' (1978), pp. 301f., where Carroll shows how the remnant idea from Isa. 7.3 is reused and reinterpreted in Isa. 10.21. See also John Day, 'Is VII 3' (1981). According to Day, שאר ישוב (Isa. 7.3) must originally have indicated the enemy's remnant. If this is so, it is evidently a reinterpretation of the concept when it is used in Isa. 10.20f. about Jacob's remnant as a positive dimension.

16. Hans Wildberger, *Jesaja 1–12* (1972), p. 407.

17. On the forest-fire motif cf. Luis Alonso Schökel, *Kunstwerk* (1971), pp. 358-59, on the use of fire as an image.

18. Cf. Hans Wildberger, *Jesaja 13–27* (1978), pp. 646f.

19. Cf. use of the plural about the rich and strong. That dictionairies translate the same passages in the OT with the plural form by either 'corpulent, imposing persons' or 'fertile tracts of land' only proves that, in their specific context, the relatively few examples we have in the OT have this meaning.

20. Thus Hans Wildberger, *Jesaja 1–12* (1972), p. 405. See also Gen. 27.28, 39 and Dan. 11.24.

21. Cf. KBL, where the plural of מִשְׁמַן in Isa. 10.16 and Ps. 78.31 is understood as referring to persons, 'fette, stattliche Leute', and where there is a reference to an analogous use in Arabic.

22. Cf. J. Vermeylen, *Isaïe* (1977-78), p. 259 including note 3.

23. Hans Wildberger, *Jesaja 1–12* (1972), pp. 407f.

24. Hans Wildberger, *Jesaja 1–12* (1972), pp. 410-11.

25. Note also that the Targum associates the connexion directly with Isa. 10.5-15 by beginning the misfortune oracle with a reference to the king of Assyria's arrogance.

Notes to Chapter 4§9

Analysis of Isa. 1.29-31

1. Hans Wildberger, *Jesaja 1–12* (1972), pp. 8 and 69ff. See also p. 74, where Wildberger suggests the possibility that the passages vv. 21-28 and vv. 29-31 may have been written by a pupil of Isaiah. But according to Wildberger this cannot be finally decided.

2. Cf. Susan Niditch, 'Composition' (1980), pp. 509f. See especially note 1.

3. Georg Fohrer, 'Jesaja 1' (1962). See especially p. 268 and note 32, where Fohrer points out that his thesis is akin to the views of Weiser and Kuhl.

4. Georg Fohrer, 'Jesaja 1' (1962), pp. 265 n. 26 and 254.

5. That vv. 29-31 is a fragment is also stressed by Frants Buhl, *Jesaja* (1912), p. 29 and Bernhard Duhm, *Jesaia* (1922), p. 35. Aage Bentzen, *Jesaja* (1944), p. 13, on the other hand, believes that it is not a fragment but merely a new oracle with no true connexion with the preceding text. One of the most recent students of Isa. 1 is Susan Niditch: 'Composition' (1980), where Niditch defines Isa. 1.2-3, 21-31 as a prophetic description of a lawsuit from the Exilic period and Isa. 1.4-20 as an Isaianic sermon. Despite her interest in the larger contexts, Niditch does not succeed in explaining the object of joining together precisely these traditional elements, let alone placing them first in the book of Isaiah. Neither does it seem convincing to date the whole of Isa. 1.2-3, 21-31 to the Exilic/post-Exilic period.

6. Bernhard Duhm, *Jesaia* (1922), p. 35.

7. Karl Budde, 'Jesaja 1-5' (1931), pp. 36f.

8. Budde's article dates from 1931, but save for Fohrer's commentary (cf. Hans Wildberger, *Jesaja 1–12* [1972], pp. 70f.) is it alone in rejecting the 'cultic interpretation', and for this reason Budde's arguments should be investigated.

9. On the use of antithesis and paronomasia cf. Luis Alonso Schökel, *Kunstwerk* (1971), pp. 28-34, 289-94, 301.

10. Cf. Flemming Friis Hvidberg, 'Gen. I-III' (1960).

11. Cf. Luis Alonso Schökel, *Kunstwerk* (1971), p. 32. Alonso Schökel also points out that the sound l is used three times in v. 30a, which also helps to create continuity in the verse.

12. Hans Wildberger, *Jesaja 1-12* (1972), p. 72.

13. Bernhard Duhm, *Jesaia* (1922), pp. 35f.

14. Frants Buhl, *Jesaja* (1912), p. 30. The same interpretation is already to be found in Franz Delitzsch, *Jesaia* (1879), p. 33. See also Aage Bentzen, *Jesaja* (1944), p. 14, which is largely in agreement with this interpretation, but does not dare to express a definite opinion on whether 'his work' is the godless act in a general sense or the idol.

15. Walther Zimmerli, *Ezechiel 1-24* (1969), pp. 429-31. Cf. also the exhaustive discussion of the image in Bernhard Lang, *Aufstand* (1978), pp. 109-14. In contrast to Zimmerli, Lang does not treat v. 11aβb and v. 14aα as additions.

16. In Isa. 57.5, אילים is written in a similar context without the letter yod: אלים as parallel to כל־עץ רענן. Note also that Isa. 1.29 in VQa (= 1QIsa) is rendered as אלים, and that in LXX this is rendered as: ἐπὶ τοῖς εἰδώλοις. Cf. Hans Wildberger, *Jesaja 1-12* (1972), p. 69, whose account and use of P. Wernberg-Møller, 'Isaiah-Scroll' (1958), p. 254 unfortunately relies on a misunderstanding (where Wildberger writes אילים, Wernberg-Møller writes אלים).

17. H. Ehrentreu, 'Talmud' (1910 [1911]), pp. 6-8.

18. Cf. also Gustaf Dalman, *AuS* V (1937), p. 28 and *AuS* VII (1942), p. 232 on the use of flax as a wick in an oil lamp, as well as Isa. 42.3; 43.17.

19. H. Ehrentreu, 'Talmud' (1910 [1911]), p. 7.

20. Cf. H. Ehrentreu, 'Talmud' (1910 [1911]), p. 8 n. 2 and Franz Delitzsch, *Jesaia* (1879), p. 33.

21. M. Tsevat, 'Isaiah I 31' (1969).

22. Samuel E. Loewenstamm, 'Isaiah I 31' (1972).

23. Samuel E. Loewenstamm, 'Isaiah I 31' (1972), p. 247.

24. Hans Wildberger, *Jesaja 1-12* (1972), p. 69.

25. Cf. N.H. Tur-Sinai, 'Isaiah i-xii' (1961), p. 157.

26. In v. 30, the root נבל is used to indicate that the tree wilts and loses its leaves. Since the whole passage is concerned with idolatry, it is natural to assume that there is here a play on the phonetic similarity between נבלת and נבלה, i.e. 'folly', 'godlessness' (cf. Isa. 9.16; RSV 9.17), that possibly belongs to the oracle's original context, as well as Isa. 32.6. From the aspect of the history of language, it is in this connexion immaterial whether the same root is used or two different roots. The point is the phonetic similarity that activates both words' connotations.

27. Hans Wildberger, *Jesaja 1–12* (1972), p. 208.

28. Hans Wildberger, *Jesaja 1–12* (1972), pp. 208 and 222f.

29. Hans Wildberger contests this dating, saying that the prophet could scarcely describe the Assyrians after 732 by such a vague formulation as 'the people from a far country'. But in reply it can be said that what Isaiah wished to express here scarcely has anything to do with the degree of familiarity with the enemy. After all, viewed from the Palestinian region, the region to which the Assyrians belong is far away (cf. Isa. 39.3; 43.6; 60.4). To refer to this as far away acts to emphasize Yahweh's power. Cf. Hans Wildberger, *Jesaja 1–12* (1972), p. 211.

30. Cf. Hans Wildberger, *Jesaja 1–12* (1972), p. 223.

31. Cf. Hans Wildberger, *Jesaja 1–12* (1972), p. 210.

32. As regards reuse cf. J. Vermeylen, *Isaïe* (1977-78), pp. 105-11 and 747. A question not covered in the analysis is whether Isa. 1.29-31 has also occasioned a production of new text. A number of scholars have pointed out that there is a relatively high degree of agreement between Isa. 1 and Isa. 65–66, which indicates a deliberate attempt from the redactional side to cause the book of Isaiah to appear to be an entity. On this question cf. Leon J. Liebreich, 'Compilation' (1955-57), pp. 276 and 127, and Rémi Lack, *Symbolique* (1973), pp. 139ff.

33. Weiser and Kuhl, to whom Fohrer refers, also can find no function in these verses, and therefore pass over them lightly. See also Georg Fohrer, 'Jesaja 1' (1962), p. 268 n. 32.

34. Hans Wildberger, *Jesaja 28–39* (1982), pp. 1554f.

35. Peter R. Ackroyd, 'Is 2,1' (1963).

Notes to Chapter 4§10

The Main Themes in Isaiah's Theology

1. Cf. Kirsten Nielsen, 'Is. 6:1-8:18*' (1986), where I analyse, inter alia, the connexion between sign-act and heart-hardening.

2. Herbert Donner attributes great political insight to Isaiah, but emphasizes that the political and theological motifs form such an indissoluble entity in Isaiah that he can justify his rejection of the coalition policy by the fact that Judah, as Yahweh's property, has no need for any coalition partner (Herbert Donner, *Israel* [1964], pp. 170-71).

3. Friedrich Huber, *Die anderen Völker* (1976). See especially the summary on p. 26. Cf. also Hans Werner Hoffmann, *Intention* (1974), pp. 76-77.

4. Despite the difficulties as regards dating, the passage is a clear example of Isaiah's referral to Yahweh and rejection of other coalition partners (Hans Wildberger, *Jesaja 13–27* [1978], pp. 575ff.). As regards the political

situation cf. *ANET* p. 287 and Siegfried Hermann, *Geschichte* (1973), pp. 315f.

5. In Isa. 30.1ff., the woe of the dirge is pronounced on those who, according to Isa. 28.14ff., believe that they have safeguarded themselves by making a covenant with 'death'.

6. Cf. Huber's conclusion (pp. 68 and 182) in Friedrich Huber, *Die anderen Völker* (1976).

7. On the use of שובה and בטחה in Isa. 30.15 cf. Friedrich Huber, *Die anderen Völker* (1976), pp. 140-47, where Huber argues that בטחה describes unconcern rather than trust in Yahweh, whereas שובה describes repentance. But the difference between unconcern and trust in Yahweh proves to be of limited extent, since according to Huber the unconcern can indeed be based on trust in Yahweh. Cf. also Huber's analysis of בטח (pp. 148-60), which shows that the actual root בטח is used about having trust in Yahweh.

8. Friedrich Huber, *Die anderen Völker* (1976), pp. 35ff.

9. Cf. Friedrich Huber, *Die anderen Völker* (1976), p. 59, where 711 is given as terminus ante quem non for Isaiah's anti-Assyrian message. I agree with Huber in this interpretation of Isaiah's view of Assyria, and find no reason to assume that, as suggested by Walter Dietrich, *Politik* (1976), p. 114, there would have been two changes in Isaiah's attitude, from message of salvation to message of judgment, in about 713 and 705 respectively.

10. Cf. Friedrich Huber, *Die anderen Völker* (1976), pp. 64-67.

11. Rudolf Kilian, *Jesaja 1-39* (1983).

12. Rudolf Kilian, *Jesaja 1-39* (1983), pp. 27ff.

13. As regards this group's views cf. the individual passages from Kilian and his summary of Isaiah's message: Rudolf Kilian, *Jesaja 1-39*. (1983), pp. 131-33.

14. As regards this group's views cf. the individual passages from Kilian and his summary of Isaiah's message: Rudolf Kilian, *Jesaja 1-39* (1983), pp. 133-40.

15. A clear example of this is the treatment by Kilian's pupil Wolfgang Werner (whom Kilian also heavily relies upon in his survey) of the Messiah, holy remnant and nations themes, in which Werner rejects, for example, that Isa. 11.1-9 can be a continuation of the Isaianic message, since this is an unqualified message of salvation, although he has himself pointed out the evident thematic connexion with the judgment oracle in 10.33-34 and the experience from every-day life lying behind the concept that a *felled* tree can sprout again. Werner does not appear to consider that this connexion might be something original and not an expression of reinterpretation, which makes it surprising that the Isaianic message of judgment should be so radically reinterpreted, and that it has been supplemented by the message of salvation. Cf. Wolfgang Werner, *Eschatologische Texte* (1982), pp. 198 and 49-50.

16. Cf. Kirsten Nielsen, 'Is. 6:1-8:18*' (1986), where in fact I reach the conclusion that the 'drama' (Isa. 6.1-8.18) continually circles around what Yahweh's intentions are towards his people, when Yahweh, figuratively speaking, is both he who conceals his face and he who lives in the midst of his people on the mountain of Zion. Cf. also Werner H. Schmidt, 'Die Einheit' (1977), p. 272, where Schmidt concludes that true continuity between misfortune and salvation for Isaiah is to be found in Yahweh himself.

17. Hans Wildberger, *Jesaja 28-39* (1982), pp. 1634-67.

18. Hans Wildberger, *Jesaja 28-39* (1982), pp. 1634-40.

19. Walter Dietrich, *Politik* (1976). See e.g. p. 9 including n. 6, pp. 9-10.

20. Walter Dietrich, *Politik* (1976), pp. 303-304.

21. Cf. Kirsten Nielsen, 'Is. 6:1-8:18*' (1986).

22. By saying that the tree image grips the prophet, I mean something on the lines of what E. Hammershaimb describes when he says, in reference to Amos' visions, that they are neither a pure stylistic form nor true hallucinations, but have their origin in exterior phenomena that appear to the prophet as a means by which Yahweh makes known his will. E. Hammershaimb, *Amos* (1946), p. 106. Now, we of course know nothing from the book of Isaiah about whether Isaiah on a specific occasion witnessed a felled tree that sprouted again, for example, and at that very time arrived at his understanding of what Yahweh intended. What I wish to indicate by the comparison with Amos is merely, therefore, the way in which a prophet is able to see in familiar and everyday circumstances an image of Yahweh's will for his people.

23. Cf. *ThHAT*, cols. 269-72.

24. Cf. Benedikt Otzen, *Israeliterne* (1977), pp. 266f.

Notes to Conclusion

1. Cf. Paul Ricoeur, 'Hermeneutics' (1975), p. 80.

2. Cf. as a supplement to this Gilbert Durand, who emphasizes that the duality in the tree image makes the tree one of the fundamental symbols in a long series of cultures, in that the tree symbolizes totality. Durand further points out that the tree connotes progression: 'Aussi n'est-il pas étonnant de constater que l'image de l'arbre est toujours inductrice d'un certain messianisme, de ce que nous pourrions appeler le 'complexe de Jessé'. Tout progressisme est arborescent' (Gilbert Durand, *L'Imaginaire* [1960], p. 370).

3. Cf. also Benedikt Otzen, *Deuterosacharja* (1964), p. 163 and Eduard Nielsen, 'Habaqquq' (1952), p. 61, who both interpret specific examples of tree images in the light of a political code.

4. Cf. the discussion of the concepts of death and resurrection in Knud Jeppesen, *Myths* (1980), where Knud Jeppesen points out the differences that

appear to exist between the Northern Kingdom and the Southern Kingdom on this point: 'Whereas, everything considered, there were circles in the Northern Kingdom that celebrated Yahweh's death and resurrection, this was not the case in Jerusalem' (p. 103).

5. Cf. C.H. Dodd's definition of the parable quoted above, p. 36.

6. Voltaire, *Sur la nature de l'homme. Sept Discours* (1737), 6.172.

7. Cf. Kirsten Nielsen, 'RIB-Pattern' (1979), pp. 320-24, where I analyse Isaiah's use of the lawsuit image and advance the thesis that Isaiah and others used the tree image as an argument for the necessity of deciding in favour of Yahweh.

8. Hans Werner Hoffmann, *Intention* (1974).

9. Hans Werner Hoffmann, *Intention* (1974), pp. 58-59.

10. That Hoffmann's analyses support my analyses of imagery in regard to the intention of Isaiah's message does not mean that I therefore agree with all that Hoffmann writes about Isaiah's message. My main objection concerns, of course, his total rejection that Isaiah preached salvation (cf. Hans Werner Hoffmann, *Intention* [1974], pp. 38f. n. 129) and the consequent lack of feeling for the tension in Isaiah's message. This is associated with the fact that Hoffmann has no sense of the central role of the images in Isaiah's message, but has eyes only for the very directly formulated calls to repent; formulations that I, on the other hand, have not subjected to special analysis, since I consider that their intentions are obvious. Confidence in this is of course supported by the fact that, despite these differences, we reach results similar to one another.

11. Cf. Siegfried Wagner's review of this in *ThLZ* 101 (1976), cols. 255-57.

12. Cf. Kirsten Nielsen, 'Is. 6:1-8:18*' (1986), where the relation between heart-hardening and prophecy in Isa. 6.1-8.18* is analysed more closely. Cf. also Kirsten Nielsen, 'Forkyndelsesintention' (Prophetic Intention) (1982).

13. I wish to point out in this connexion that the different forms of reuse merge into one another, so that it can be difficult to be sure about whether a certain phenomenon or example should be classified in one group or another.

14. One obvious example of this is also Isa. 28.5-6, where the image of the wreath and the crown in Isa. 28.1-4 is adopted, but is used positively about Yahweh himself.

15. Cf. R.P. Carroll, *Prophecy Failed* (1979), p. 205, who perceives the connexion between prophetism and apocalyptic literature on the basis of his theory that disappointed expectations lead to hermeneutic activity, i.e. to reinterpretation.

16. Cf. Josef Schreiner, *Apokalyptik* (1969), pp. 90-98.

17. Cf. Josef Schreiner, *Apokalyptik* (1969), pp. 86-90. Schreiner points out in conclusion (p. 90) the connexion between the use of polysemantic images and symbols and the neccessity of an *angelus interpres*.

18. Cf. e.g. Dan. 9, where Gabriel gives the true interpretation of the 70 years during which, according to the book of Jeremiah, Jerusalem is to lie in ruins; or the role of *angelus interpres* in Zech. 1.9 et al. On the Zechariah passages cf. Lars Gösta Rignell, *Nachtgesichte* (1950), pp. 34ff.

19. Rudolf Kilian, *Jesaja 1–39* (1983), and Wolfgang Werner, *Eschatologische Texte* (1982).

20. R.E. Clements, 'Fall of Jerusalem' (1980).

BIBLIOGRAPHY

The Bibliography covers only the literature to which reference is made in the text. The abbreviated form employed in the notes is given first, followed by the full title.

Ackroyd, Peter R., 'Is. 2,1' (1963) = 'A Note on Isaiah 2,1', *ZAW* 75 (1963), pp. 320-21.
—'Babylonian Exile' (1974). = 'An Interpretation of the Babylonian Exile: A Study of 2 Kings 20, Isaiah 38-39', *SJT* 27 (1974), pp. 329-52.
Ahlström, G.M., *Psalm 89* (1959). = *Psalm 89. Eine Liturgie aus dem Ritual des leidenden Königs* (Lund, 1959).
Alonso-Schökel, Luis: 'Is 27,2-5' (1960). = 'La canción de la viña Is. 27,2-5', *Estudios Eclesiásticos* 34 (1960), pp. 767-74.
—'Stilistische Analyse' (1960). = 'Die stilistische Analyse bei den Propheten', *VTSuppl* 7 (1960), pp. 154-64.
—'Hermeneutics' (1963). = 'Hermeneutics in the Light of Language and Literature', *CBQ* 25 (1963), pp. 371-86.
—*Kunstwerk* (1971). = *Das Alte Testament als literarisches Kunstwerk* (Köln, 1971).
—'Literary Study' (1975). = 'Hermeneutical Problems of a Literary Study of the Bible', *VTSuppl* 28 (1975), pp. 1-15.
Anderson, G.W., *Introduction* (1959). = *A Critical Introduction to the Old Testament* (London, 1959).
Austin, J.L., *Things* (1977). = *How to Do Things with Words*, ed. J.O. Urmson and Marina Sbisà (2nd edn, Cambridge, 1977; 1st edn, 1962).
Baldwin, Joyce G., '*Şemaḥ*' (1964). = '*Şemaḥ* as a Technical Term in the Prophets', *VT* 14 (1964), pp. 93-97.
Barbour, Ian G., *Myths* (1974). = *Myths, Models and Paradigms. A Comparative Study in Science and Religion* (New York, 1974).
Barth, Hermann, *Josiazeit* (1977). = *Die Jesaja-Worte in der Josiazeit. Israel und Assur als Thema einer produktiven Neuinterpretation der Jesajaüberlieferung* (Neukirchen-Vluyn, 1977).
Baumgartner, Walter, *Lexikon* (1967). = *Hebräisches und aramäisches Lexikon zum Alten Testament* (3rd edn, Leiden, 1967).
—*Lexikon* (1974). = *Hebräisches und aramäisches Lexikon zum Alten Testament* (3rd edn, Leiden, 1974).
Beardslee, William A., *Literary Criticism* (1970). = *Literary Criticism of the New Testament* (Philadelphia, 1970).
Becker, P. Joachim, 'Wurzelspross' (1976). = 'Wurzel und Wurzelspross. Ein Beitrag zur hebräischen Lexikographie', *BZ* 20 (1976), pp. 22-44.
Bentzen, Aage, 'Jes 5.1-7' (1927). = 'Zur Erläuterung von Jesaja 5.1-7', *AfO* 4 (1927), pp. 209-210.
—*Jesaja* (1944). = *Jesaja*, I: *Jes. 1-39* (København, 1944).
—*Introduction*, I (1948). = *Introduction to the Old Testament*, Vol. I: *The Canon of the Old Testament. The Text of the Old Testament. The Forms of the Old Testament Literature* (København, 1948).

—*Introduction* II (1949). = *Introduction to the Old Testament*, Vol. II: *The Books of the Old Testament* (København, 1949).

Berger, P.-R., 'Jes 5.6' (1970). = 'Ein unerklärtes Wort in dem Weinberglied Jesajas (Jes 5.6)', *ZAW* 82 (1970), pp. 116-17.

Bjerg, Svend, *Grundfortaelling* (1981). = *Den kristne grundfortaelling. Studier over fortaelling og teologi* (Århus, 1981).

Bjørndalen, Anders Jørgen, 'Allegorier' (1966). = 'Metodiske bemerkninger til spørsmålet etter allegorier i Det gamle Testamente', *TTKi* 37 (1966), pp. 145-66.

—'Echtheit' (1982). = 'Zur Frage der Echtheit von Jesaja 1.2-3; 1.4-7 und 5.1-7', *NTT* 83 (1982), pp. 89-100.

—*Allegorische Rede* (1986). = *Untersuchungen zur allegorischen Rede der Propheten Amos und Jesaja* (Berlin, 1986).

Black, Max, 'Metaphor' (1954-55). = 'Metaphor', *Proceedings of the Aristotelian Society*, n.s. 55 (1954-55), pp. 273-94.

—'More' (1979). = 'More about Metaphor', in: *Metaphor and Thought*, ed. Andrew Ortony (Cambridge, 1979), pp. 19-43.

Blass, Friedrich, *Grammatik* (1961). = *Grammatik des neutestamentlichen Griechisch*, ed. Albert Debrunner (11th edn, Göttingen, 1961).

Blenkinsopp, Joseph, 'Jes 2,6-22' (1981). = 'Fragments of Ancient Exegesis in an Isaian Poem. (Jes 2,6-22)', *ZAW* 93 (1981), pp. 51-62.

Botterweck, G. Johannes, 'Löwenbilder' (1972). = 'Gott und Mensch in den alttestamentlichen Löwenbildern', *Wort, Lied und Gottesspruch. Festschrift für Joseph Ziegler*, ed. Josef Schreiner (Echter Verlag, 1972), pp. 117-28.

Boucher, Madeleine, *Parable* (1977). = *The Mysterious Parable. A Literary Study* (Washington, 1977).

Brenner, Charles, *Psychoanalysis* (1973). = *An Elementary Textbook of Psychoanalysis* (rev. and expanded edn, New York, 1973; 1st edn. 1955).

Budde, Karl, 'Jesaja 1-5' (1931). = 'Zu Jesaja 1-5', *ZAW* 49 (1931), pp. 16-39 + 182-211.

—'Jesaja 1-5' (1932). = 'Zu Jesaja 1-5', *ZAW* 50 (1932), pp. 38-72.

Buhl, Frants, *Jesaja* (1912). = *Jesaja* (rev. edn, København, 1912).

Buzy, D., *Paraboles* (1912). = *Introduction aux paraboles évangéliques* (Paris, 1912).

Caird, G.B., *Imagery* (1980). = *The Language and Imagery of the Bible* (London, 1980).

Carlston, Charles E., 'Review' (1981). = 'Parable and Allegory Revisited: An Interpretive Review', *CBQ* 43 (1981), pp. 228-42.

Carroll, R.P., 'Dissonance' (1977). = 'Ancient Israelite Prophecy and Dissonance Theory', *Numen* 24 (1977), pp. 135-51.

—'Isa. 1-11' (1978). = 'Inner Tradition Shifts in Meaning in Isaiah 1-11', *ExpT* 89 (1978), pp. 301-304.

—'Second Isaiah' (1978). = 'Second Isaiah and the Failure of Prophecy', *StTh* 32 (1978), pp. 119-31.

—*Prophecy Failed* (1979). = *When Prophecy Failed. Reactions and responses to failure in the Old Testament prophetic traditions* (London, 1979).

—'Prophetic Tradition' (1980). = 'Prophecy and Dissonance. A Theoretical Approach to the Prophetic Tradition', *ZAW* 92 (1980), pp. 108-19.

Childs, Brevard S., *Isaiah* (1967). = *Isaiah and the Assyrian Crisis* (London, 1967).

—*Introduction* (1979). = *Introduction to the Old Testament as Scripture* (London, 1979).

Clements, R.E., *Deliverance* (1980). = *Isaiah and the Deliverance of Jerusalem. A Study of the Interpretation of Prophecy in the Old Testament* (Sheffield, 1980).

—'Fall of Jerusalem' (1980). = 'The Prophecies of Isaiah and the Fall of Jerusalem in 587 B.C.', *VT* 30 (1980), pp. 421-36.

—*Isaiah 1-39* (1980). = *Isaiah 1-39* (New Century Bible Commentary; London, 1980).

Crossan, John Dominic, 'Experience' (1973). = 'Parable as Religious and Poetic Experience', *JR* 53 (1973), pp. 330-58.

—*Parables* (1973). = *In Parables. The Challenge of the Historical Jesus* (New York, 1973).

—'Bibliography' (1974), A basic Bibliography for Parables Research. *Semeia* 1 (1974), pp. 236-74.

—*Articulate* (1976). = *Raid on the Articulate. Comic Eschatology in Jesus and Borges* (New York, 1976).

Dalman, Gustaf, *AuS* I, 1 (1928). = *Arbeit und Sitte in Palästina* Vol. I, 1 (Gütersloh, 1928).

—*AuS* I, 2 (1928). = *Arbeit und Sitte in Palästina*, Vol. I, 2. (Gütersloh, 1928).

—*AuS* IV (1935). = *Arbeit und Sitte in Palästina*, Vol. IV (Gütersloh, 1935).

—*AuS* V (1937). = *Arbeit und Sitte in Palästina*, Vol. V (Gütersloh, 1937).

—*AuS* VII (1942). = *Arbeit und Sitte in Palästina*, Vol. VII (Gütersloh, 1942).

Davidson, R., 'Is II 6ff.' (1966). = 'The Interpretation of Isaiah II 6ff.', *VT* 16 (1966), pp. 1-7.

Day, John, 'Is VII 3' (1981). = 'Shear-Jashub (Isaiah VII 3) and "the Remnant of Wrath" (Psalm LXXVI 11)', *VT* 31 (1981), pp. 76-78.

Delitzsch, Franz, *Jesaia* (1879). = *Biblischer Commentar über den Propheten Jesaia* (Leipzig, 1879).

Dietrich, Walter, *Politik* (1976). = *Jesaja und die Politik* (München, 1976).

Dodd, C.H., *Parables* (1961). = *The Parables of the Kingdom* (first published 1935; rev. edn, London: Fontana, 1961).

Donner, Herbert, *Israel* (1964). = *Israel unter den Völkern. Die Stellung der klassischen Propheten des 8. Jahrhunderts v.Chr. zur Aussenpolitik der Könige von Israel und Juda* (Leiden, 1964).

Downing, Christine, 'Exodus' (1968). = 'How Can We Hope and not Dream? Exodus as Metaphor: A Study of the Biblical Imagination', *JR* 48 (1968), pp. 35-53.

Duhm, Bernhard, *Jesaia* (1922). = *Das Buch Jesaia* (Göttinger Handkommentar zum Alten Testament), Part III. *Die prophetischen Bücher*, Vol. I (4th, rev. edn; Göttingen, 1922).

Durand, Gilbert, *L'Imaginaire* (1960). = *Les Structures anthropologiques de l'imaginaire. Introduction à l'archétypologie générale* (Grenoble, 1960).

Dødehavsteksterne (1959). = *Dødehavsteksterne. Skrifter fra den jødiske menighed i Qumran i oversaettelse og med noter ved Eduard Nielsen og Benedikt Otzen* (København, 1959).

Eaton, J.H., 'Origin' (1959). = 'The Origin of the Book of Isaiah', *VT* 9 (1959), pp. 138-57.

Ehrentreu, H., 'Talmud' (1910). = 'Sprachliches und Sachliches aus dem Talmud', *Jahrbuch der Jüdisch-Literarischen Gesellschaft* 8 (1910 [1911]), pp. 1-34.

Eissfeldt, Otto, *Maschal* (1913). = *Der Maschal im Alten Testament. Eine wortgeschichtliche Untersuchung nebst einer literargeschichtlichen Untersuchung der* משל *genannten Gattungen 'Volkssprichwort' und 'Spottlied'* (Giessen, 1913).

—*Einleitung* (1934). = *Einleitung in das Alte Testament unter Einschluss der*

282   There is Hope for a Tree

Apokryphen und Pseudepigraphen. Entstehungsgeschichte des Alten Testaments (Tübingen, 1934).

Emerton, J.A. 'Translation' (1982). = 'The Translation and Interpretation of Isaiah vi.13', *Interpreting the Hebrew Bible. Essays in honour of E.I.J. Rosenthal*, ed. J.A. Emerton and Stefan C. Reif (Cambridge, 1982), pp. 85-118.

Engdahl, Elisabet, 'Språkhändelser' (1974). = Jesu liknelser som språkhändelser', *SEÅ* 39 (1974), pp. 90-108.

Engnell, Ivan, *Kingship* (1943). = *Studies in Divine Kingship in the Ancient Near East* (Uppsala, 1943).

—'Ebed Jahve' (1945). = 'Till frågan om Ebed Jahve-sångerna och den lidande Messias hos "Deuterojesaja"', *SEÅ* 10 (1945), pp. 31-65.

—*The Call* (1949). = *The Call of Isaiah. An Exegetical and Comparative Study* (Uppsala, 1949).

—'Planted' (1953). = '"Planted by the Streams of Water". Some Remarks on the Problem of the Interpretation of the Psalms as Illustrated by a Detail in Ps. I', *Studia Orientalia Ioanni Pedersen Dicata* (København, 1953), pp. 85-96.

—'Knowledge' (1955). = '"Knowledge" and "Life" in the Creation Story', *VTSuppl* 3 (1955), pp. 103-19.

—'Bildspråk' (1962). = 'Bildspråk', *SBU*. Andra Upplagan, Vol. I, A-L (Stockholm, 1962), cols. 283-312.

Erlandson, Seth, 'Jesaja 11:10-16' (1971). = 'Jesaja 11:10-16 och dess historiska bakgrund', *SEÅ* 36 (1971), pp. 24-44.

Evans, Craig A., 'Isaiah 6,9-10' (1982). = 'The Text of Isaiah 6,9-10', *ZAW* 94 (1982), pp. 415-18.

Exum, J. Cheryl, 'Broken Pots' (1981). = 'Of Broken Pots, Fluttering Birds and Visions in the Night: Extended Simile and Poetic Technique in Isaiah', *CBQ* 43 (1981), pp. 331-52.

Fisch, Harold, 'Analogy of Nature' (1955). = 'The Analogy of Nature, a Note on the Structure of Old Testament Imagery', *ThSt* 6 (1955), pp. 161-73.

Fohrer, Georg, 'Jesaja 1' (1962). = 'Jesaja 1 als Zusammenfassung der Verkündigung Jesajas', *ZAW* 74 (1962), pp. 251-68.

—*Das AT*, I (1969). = *Das Alte Testament. Einführung in Bibelkunde und Literatur des Alten Testaments und in Geschichte und Religion Israels*, Part I (Gütersloh, 1969).

—*Das AT*, II-III (1970). = *Das Alte Testament. Einführung in Bibelkunde und Literatur des Alten Testaments und in Geschichte und Religion Israels* Parts II and III (Gütersloh, 1970).

Funk, Robert W., *Language* (1966). = *Language, Hermeneutic, and Word of God. The Problem of Language in the New Testament and Contemporary Theology* (New York, 1966).

Gerleman, Gillis, *Ruth • Hohelied* (1965). = *Ruth • Das Hohelied*, BK 18 (1965).

Godbey, Allen Howard, *'Mašal'* (1922-23). = 'The Hebrew *Mašal*', *AJSL* 39 (1922-23), pp. 89-108.

Gottlieb, Hans, 'Myths' (1980). = Benedikt Otzen, Hans Gottlieb, Knud Jeppesen: *Myths in the Old Testament* (London, 1980), pp. 62-93.

Graffy, Adrian, 'Isaiah 5.1-7' (1979). = 'The Literary Genre of Isaiah 5.1-7', *Bibl* 60 (1979), pp. 400-409.

Gunkel, Hermann, 'Jes 33' (1924). = 'Jesaia 33, eine prophetische Liturgie', *ZAW* 42 (1924), pp. 177-208.

Hammershaimb, Erling, 'Pseudepigrafer' (1975). = 'Om lignelser og billedtaler i de gammeltestamentlige Pseudepigrafer', *SEÅ* 40 (1975), pp. 36-65.

Harnisch, Wolfgang, 'Analogie' (1974). = 'Die Sprachkraft der Analogie. Zur These vom "argumentativen Charakter" der Gleichnisse Jesu', *StTh* 28 (1974), pp. 1-20.

—'Metapher' (1979). = 'Die Metapher als heuristisches Prinzip. Neuerscheinungen zur Hermeneutik der Gleichnisreden Jesu', *VuF. Neues Testament* 1 (1979), pp. 53-89.

Harrison, R.K., *Introduction* (1969). = *Introduction to the Old Testament with a comprehensive review of Old Testament studies and a special supplement on the Apocrypha* (USA 1969).

Hartnack, Justus, 'Analytisk filosofi' (1980). = 'Analytisk filosofi', *Filosofien efter Hegel*, med bidrag af Jørgen K. Bukdahl et al. (København, 1980), pp. 155-82.

Harvey, Julien, *Le plaidoyer* (1967). = *Le plaidoyer prophétique contre Israël après la rupture de l'alliance. Etude d'une formule littéraire de l'Ancien Testament* (Bruges, Paris, 1967).

Haupt, Paul, 'Isaiah's Parable' (1903). = 'Isaiah's Parable of the Vineyard', *AJSL* 19 (1903), pp. 193-202.

Hempel, Johannes, 'Jahwegleichnisse' (1924). = 'Jahwegleichnisse der israelitischen Propheten', *ZAW* 1 (1924), pp. 74-104.

—*Gott/Mensch* (1926). = *Gott und Mensch im Alten Testament. Studie zur Geschichte der Frömmigkeit* (Stuttgart, 1926).

—'Anthropomorphismus' (1939). = 'Die Grenzen des Anthropomorphismus Jahwes im Alten Testament', *ZAW* 57 (1939), pp. 75-85.

Herbert, A.S., '*Māšāl*' (1954). = 'The "Parable" (*Māšāl*) in the Old Testament', *SJTh* 7 (1954), pp. 180-96.

von Herder, Johann Gottfried, *Poesie* (1825). = *Vom Geist der Ebräischen Poesie. Dritte rechtmässige, sorgfältig durchgesehene und mit mehreren Zusätzen vermehrte Ausgabe von Dr. Karl Wilhelm Justi* (Leipzig, 1825).

Hermaniuk, Maxime, *Parabole* (1947). = *La Parabole Evangélique. Enquête exégétique et critique* (Bruges, Paris, 1947).

Herrmann, Siegfried, *Geschichte* (1973). = *Geschichte Israels in alttestamentlicher Zeit* (München, 1973).

Hertzberg, Hans-Wilhelm, 'Nachgeschichte' (1936). = 'Die Nachgeschichte alttestamentlicher Texte innerhalb des Alten Testaments', in: *Beiträge zur Traditionsgeschichte und Theologie des Alten Testaments* (Göttingen, 1962), pp. 69-80. Cf. BZAW 66 (1936), pp. 110-21.

Hessler, Eva, 'Deuterojesaja' (1965). = 'Die Struktur der Bilder bei Deuterojesaja', *EvTh* 25 (1965), pp. 349-69.

Höffken, Peter, 'Jesaja 5,1-7' (1979). = 'Probleme in Jesaja 5,1-7', *ZThK* (1979), pp. 392-410.

Hoffmann, Hans Werner, 'Form' (1970). = 'Form—Funktion—Intention', *ZAW* 82 (1970), pp. 341-46.

—*Intention* (1974). = *Die Intention der Verkündigung Jesajas* (Berlin, 1974).

Huber, Friedrich, *Die anderen Völker* (1976). = *Jahwe, Juda und die anderen Völker beim Propheten Jesaja* (Berlin, 1976).

Hvidberg, Flemming Friis, *Graad* (1938). = *Graad og Latter i Det gamle Testamente. En Studie i kanaanaeisk-israelitisk Religion* (København, 1938).

—'Gen. I–III' (1960). = 'The Canaanitic Background of Gen. I–III', *VT* 10 (1960), pp. 285-94.

Jacob, Edmond, 'Esaïe 27,2-5' (1970). = 'Du premier au deuxième chant de la vigne du prophète Esaïe. Réflexions sur Esaïe 27,2-5', *Wort—Gebot—Glaube. Walter Eichrodt zum 80. Geburtstag*, ed. H.J. Stoebe (Zürich, 1970), pp. 325-30.

Jacobsen, Erling, *Grundprocesser* (1971). = *De psykiske grundprocesser* (2nd edn, København, 1971).

Jahnow, Hedwig, *Leichenlied* (1923). = *Das hebräische Leichenlied im Rahmen der Völkerdichtung* (Giessen, 1923)

James, E.O., *Tree of Life* (1966). = *The Tree of Life. An Archaeological Study* (Leiden, 1966).

Jaroš, Karl, *Elohist* (1974). = *Die Stellung des Elohisten zur kanaanäischen Religion* (Göttingen, 1974).

—'Gen. 2-3' (1980). = 'Die Motive der heiligen Bäume und der Schlange in Gen. 2-3', *ZAW* 92 (1980), pp. 204-15.

Jenni, Ernst, 'Berufung' (1959). = 'Jesajas Berufung in der neueren Forschung', *ThZ* 15 (1959), pp. 321-39.

Jeppesen, Knud, *Myths* (1980). = Benedikt Otzen, Hans Gottlieb, Knud Jeppesen: *Myths in the Old Testament* (London, 1980), pp. 94-123.

Jeremias, Joachim, *Gleichnisse* (1947). = *Die Gleichnisse Jesu* (Zürich, 1947; cf. 8th rev. edn, Göttingen, 1970).

Johnson, A.R., משל (1955). = 'משל', *VTSuppl* 3 (1955), pp. 162-69.

Jones, Douglas, 'Traditio' (1955). = 'The Traditio of the Oracles of Isaiah of Jerusalem', *ZAW* 67 (1955), pp. 226-46.

Junker, H., 'Is. 5,1-7' (1959). = 'Die literarische Art von Is. 5,1-7', *Bibl* 40 (1959). pp. 259-66.

—'Is. 2' (1962). = 'Sancta Civitas, Jerusalem Nova. Eine formkritische und überlieferungsgeschichtliche Studie zu Is. 2', *Ekklesia. Festschrift für Bischof Dr. Matthias Wehr* (Trier, 1962), pp. 17-33.

Jülicher, Adolf, *Gleichnisreden I (1910)*. = *Die Gleichnisreden Jesu Erster Teil, Die Gleichnisreden im Allgemeinen* (2nd edn, repr. Tübingen, 1910; 1st edn, 1886).

Kahaner, Yosef, 'Metaphors' (1973-74). = 'The Metaphors of the Vine and the Olive Tree', *Dor leDor* 2 (1973-74), pp. 15-20.

Kaiser, Otto, *Einleitung* (1969). = *Einleitung in das Alte Testament. Eine Einführung in ihre Ergebnisse und Probleme* (Gütersloh, 1969).

—*Jesaja 1-12* (1970). = *Der Prophet Jesaja. Kapitel 1-12*, ed. and trans. Otto Kaiser (ATD, 17; 3rd edn, Göttingen, 1970).

—*Jesaja 13-39* (1973). = *Der Prophet Jesaja. Kapitel 13-39*, ed. and trans. Otto Kaiser (ATD, 18; Göttingen, 1973).

Kapelrud, Arvid S., *Joel* (1948). = *Joel Studies* (Uppsala, 1948).

Keel, Othmar, *Metaphorik des Hohen Liedes* (1984). = *Deine Blicke sind Tauben: Zur Metaphorik des Hohen Liedes* (Stuttgart, 1984).

Keilinschriftliche Bibliothek (1890). = *Keilinschriftliche Bibliothek. Sammlung von assyrischen und babylonischen Texten in Umschrift und Übersetzung*, ed. Eberhard Schrader, Vol. II (Berlin, 1890).

Kilian, Rudolf, *Jesaja 1-39* (1983). = *Jesaja 1-39* (Erträge der Forschung, 200; Darmstadt, 1983).

Kissinger, Warren S., *Parables* (1979). = *The Parables of Jesus. A History of Interpretation and Bibliography* (London, 1979).

Kittang, Atle & Aarseth, Asbjørn, *Strukturer* (1976). = *Lyriske strukturer. Innføring i diktanalyse* (3rd edn, Oslo, 1976).

Kjärgaard, Mogens Stiller, 'Sproget' (1981). = 'To teorier om forholdet mellem sproget og virkeligheden' (Studier i filosofi; Odense, 1981), pp. 260-84.

—*Metaphor* (1986). = *Metaphor and Parable. A Systematic Analysis of the Specific Structure and Cognitive Function of the Synoptic Similes and Parables qua Metaphors* (Acta Theologica Danica, 20; Leiden, 1986).

Klauck, Hans-Josef, *Allegorie* (1978). = *Allegorie und Allegorese in synoptischen Gleichnistexten* (Münster, 1978).

Koch, H.G. 'Metapher' (1975). = 'Theologie und Metapher. Zur Wiederentdeckung eines sprachlichen Urphänomens', *Herder Korrespondenz* 29 (1975), pp. 85-88.

Kraus, Hans-Joachim, *Psalmen 1-63* (1972). = *Psalmen*, Vol. I: *Psalmen 1-63* (4th edn, BK 15/1 [1972])

König, Eduard, *Einleitung* (1893). = *Einleitung in das Alte Testament mit Einschluss der Apokryphen und der Pseudepigraphen Alten Testaments* (Bonn, 1893).

—*Hermeneutik* (1916). = *Hermeneutik des Alten Testaments mit spezieller Berücksichtigung der modernen Probleme* (Bonn, 1916).

Lack, Rémi, *Symbolique* (1973). = *La Symbolique du Livre d'Isaïe. Essai sur l'image littéraire comme élément de structuration* (Rome, 1973).

Lambrecht, J., 'Paraboles' (1980). = 'Les paraboles dans les Synoptiques', *NRTh* 102 (1980), pp. 672-91.

Lang, Bernhard, *Aufstand* (1978). = *Kein Aufstand in Jerusalem. Die Politik des Propheten Ezechiel* (Stuttgart, 1978).

Lauha, Aarre, *Zaphon* (1943). = *Zaphon. Der Norden und die Nordvölker im Alten Testament* (Helsinki, 1943).

Liebreich, Leon J., 'Compilation' (1955-57). = 'The Compilation of the Book of Isaiah', *JQR* 46 (1955-56), pp. 259-77 + 47 (1956-57), pp. 114-38.

Lindblom, Johannes, *Bildspråk* (1949). = *Profetiskt bildspråk* (Acta Academiae Aboensis, Humaniora 18; 1949), pp. 208-23.

—*Servant Songs* (1951). = *The Servant Songs in Deutero-Isaiah. A New Attempt to Solve an Old Problem* (Lund, 1951).

Lindhardt, Jan, 'Bibeludlaegning' (1979). = 'Middelalderens og (Renaessancens) Bibeludlaegning', *Fønix* 3 (1979), pp. 200-13.

—*Luther* (1983). *Martin Luther. Erkendelse og formidling i renaessancen* (København, 1983).

Linnemann, Eta, *Gleichnisse* (1975). = *Gleichnisse Jesu. Einführung und Auslegung* (6th rev. edn, Göttingen, 1975; 1st edn, 1961).

Lipiński, E., 'Lebanon' (1973). = 'Garden of Abundance, Image of Lebanon', *ZAW* 85 (1973), pp. 358-59.

Loewenstamm, Samuel E., 'Isaiah I 31' (1972). = 'Isaiah I 31', *VT* 22 (1972), pp. 246-48.

Loretz, O., 'Weinberglied' (1975). = 'Weinberglied und prophetische Deutung im Protest-Song Jes 5,1-7', *UF* 7 (1975), pp. 573-76.

Lundgreen, Friedrich, *Pflanzenwelt* (1908). = *Die Benutzung der Pflanzenwelt in der alttestamentlichen Religion* (Giessen, 1908).

Løgstrup, K.E., *Vidde* (1976). = *Vidde og praegnans. Sprogfilosofiske betragtninger. Metafysik I* (København, 1976).

MacCormac, Earl R., *Metaphor* (1976). = *Metaphor and Myth in Science and Religion* (Durham, 1976).

McKane, William, 'Isaiah VII 14-25' (1967). = 'The Interpretation of Isaiah VII 14-25', *VT* 17 (1967), pp. 208-19.

Marti, Karl, 'Jes 6,1-9,6' (1920). = Der jesajanische Kern in Jes 6,1-9,6. *Beiträge zur alttestamentlichen Wissenschaft. Karl Budde zum siebzigsten Geburtstag . . . von Karl Marti* (Giessen, 1920), pp. 113-21.

Mayer, Rudolf, 'Zur Bildersprache' (1950). = 'Bildersprache der alttestamentlichen Propheten', *MThZ* 1/2 (1950), pp. 55-65.

—'Sünde' (1964). = 'Sünde und Gericht in der Bildersprache der vorexilischen Prophetie', *BZ* n.s. 8 (1964), pp. 22-44.

Metzger, Wolfgang, 'Jesaja 6,13' (1981). = 'Der Horizont der Gnade in der Berufungsvision Jesajas. Kritische Bedenken zum masoretischen Text von Jesaja 6,13', *ZAW* 93 (1981), pp. 281-84.

Møller-Christensen, Vilhelm & K.E. Jordt Jørgensen, *Växtvärld* (1957). = *Bibelns växtvärld* (Stockholm, 1957).

Mowinckel, Sigmund, 'Paradiselvene' (1938). = 'De fire Paradiselvene' *NTT* 39 (1938), pp. 47-67.

—*Han som kommer* (1951). = *Han som kommer. Messiasforventningen i Det gamle Testament og på Jesu tid* (København, 1951). Cf. *He that Cometh* (Nashville and New York, 1956).

Müller, Hans Peter, 'Funktion des Mythischen' (1971). = 'Zur Funktion des Mythischen in der Prophetie des Jesaja', *Kairos* n.s. 13 (1971), pp. 266-81.

—*Vergleich* (1984). = *Vergleich und Metapher im Hohenlied* (Göttingen, 1984).

Niditch, Susan, 'Composition' (1980). = 'The Composition of Isaiah 1', *Bibl* 61 (1980), pp. 509-29.

Nielsen, Eduard, 'Habaqquq' (1952). = 'The Righteous and the Wicked in Habaqquq', *StTh* 6 (1952), pp. 54-78.

—*Shechem* (1955). = *Shechem. A Traditio-Historical Investigation* (København, 1955).

—'Literature' (1971). = 'Literature and Structure', *Religion och Bibel* 30 (1971), pp. 23-28.

Nielsen, Kirsten, 'Opgør' (1976). = 'Profeternes opgør med kulten', *DTT* 39 (1976), pp. 217-30.

—*Prosecutor* (1978). = *Yahweh as Prosecutor and Judge. An Investigation of the Prophetic Lawsuit (Rîb-Pattern)* (Sheffield, 1978).

—'Gudsbillede' (1978). = 'Det gammeltestamentlige gudsbillede belyst ud fra de profetiske retstaler', *DTT* 41 (1978), pp. 90-106.

—'RIB-Pattern' (1979). = 'Das Bild des Gerichts (RIB-Pattern) in Jes. I-XII. Eine Analyse der Beziehungen zwischen Bildsprache und dem Anliegen der Verkündigung', *VT* 29 (1979), pp. 309-24.

—'Forkyndelsesintention' (1982). = 'Om billedsprog og forkyndelsesintention i Jes 1-12', *DTT* 45 (1982), pp. 81-95.

—'For et træ' (1983). = '"For et træ er der håb" (Job 14,7). Om billedsprog og fremtidshåb i det gamle og det nye testamente', *Praesteforeningens Blad* 25 + 26 (1983), pp. 429-36 + 445-53.

—*For et træ* (1985). = *For et træ er der håb. Om træet som metafor i Jes 1-39* (København, 1985).

—'Is 6:1-8:18*' (1986). = 'Is 6:1-8:18* as Dramatic Writing. The "Drama" of Proclamation and Hardening during the Syro-Ephraimite War', *StTh* 40 (1986), pp. 1-16.

Nöldeke, Theodor, *Syrische Grammatik* (1898). = *Kurzgefasste syrische Grammatik* (2nd edn, Leipzig, 1898).

Ohler, Annemarie, *Gattungen* (1972). = *Gattungen im AT. Ein biblisches Arbeitsbuch* (Düsseldorf, 1972).

Otzen, Benedikt, *Deuterosacharja* (1964). = *Studien über Deuterosacharja* (København, 1964).

—*Myths* (1980). = Benedikt Otzen, Hans Gottlieb, Knud Jeppesen: *Myths in the Old Testament* (London, 1980), pp. 1-61.

—'Isaiah XXIV-XXVII' (1974). = 'Traditions and Structures of Isaiah XXIV-XXVII' *VT* 24 (1974), pp. 196-206.

—*Israeliterne* (1977). = *Israeliterne i Palaestina. Det gamle Israels historie, religion og litteratur* (København, 1977).

Pedersen, Johannes, *Israel I–II* (1920). = *Israel I–II. Sjaeleliv og Samfundsliv* (København, 1920).

—*Israel III–IV* (1960). = *Israel III–IV. Hellighed og Guddommelighed* (2nd edn, København, 1960; 1st edn, 1934). Cf. *Israel, Its Life and Culture*, I–II (1926); III–IV (1940).

Pedersen, Sigfred, 'Metodeproblemer' (1965). = 'Den nytestamentlige lignelsesforsknings metodeproblemer', *DTT* 28 (1965), pp. 146-84.

—'Lignelse' (1972). = 'Lignelse eller allegori. Eksegetisk-homiletiske overvejelser', *SvenskTKv* 48 (1972), pp. 63-68.

Perrin, Norman, 'Parables' (1967). = 'The Parables of Jesus as Parables, as Metaphors, and as Aesthetic Objects: a Review Article', *JR* 47 (1967), pp. 340-46.

—*Rediscovering* (1967). = *Rediscovering the Teaching of Jesus* (London, 1967).

—'Scholarship' (1967). = 'Biblical Scholarship in a New Vein', *Interp* 21 (1967), pp. 465-69.

—'Interpretation' (1971). = 'The Modern Interpretation of the Parables of Jesus and the Problem of Hermeneutics', *Interp* 25 (1971), pp. 131-48.

—'Historical Criticism' (1972). = 'Historical Criticism, Literary Criticism, and Hermeneutics: The Interpretation of the Parables of Jesus and the Gospel of Mark Today', *JR* 52 (1972), pp. 361-75.

—'Biblical Symbol' (1975). = 'The Interpretation of a Biblical Symbol', *JR* 55 (1975), pp. 348-70.

Pfeiffer, Robert H., *Introduction* (1952). = *Introduction to the Old Testament* (London, 1952; 1st edn, 1941).

Pirot, Jean, 'Mâšâl' (1950). = 'Le "Mâšâl" dans l'Ancien Testament', *RSR* 37 (1950), pp. 565-80.

Polk, Timothy, 'Mašal' (1983). = 'Paradigms, Parables, and Mĕšālîm: On Reading the Mašal in Scripture', *CBQ* 45 (1983), pp. 564-83.

Rendtorff, Rolf, *Einführung* (1983). = *Das Alte Testament. Eine Einführung* (Neukirchen-Vluyn, 1983).

Ricoeur, Paul, 'Hermeneutics' (1975). = 'Biblical Hermeneutics', *Semeia* 4 (1975), pp. 27-148.

—'Metaphorical Process' (1979). = 'The Metaphorical Process as Cognition, Imagination, and Feeling', *On Metaphor*, ed. Sheldon Sacks (Chicago, 1979), pp. 141-57.

Rignell, Lars Gösta, *Nachtgesichte* (1950). = *Die Nachtgesichte des Sacharja. Eine exegetische Studie* (Lund, 1950).

Robertson, David, *Literary Critic* (1977). = *The Old Testament and the Literary Critic* (Philadelphia, 1977).

Robinson, James M., 'Parables (1968). = 'Jesus' Parables as God Happening', *Jesus and the Historian*, ed. F. Thomas Trotter (Philadelphia, 1968), pp. 134-50.

de Roche, Michael, 'Rîb' (1983). = 'Yahweh's Rîb against Israel: A reassessment of the so-called "Prophetic Lawsuit" in the Preexilic Prophets', *JBL* 102 (1983), pp. 563-74.

Rowton, M.B., 'Woodlands' (1967). = 'The Woodlands of Ancient Western Asia', *JNESt* 26 (1967), pp. 261-77.

Sawyer, John, 'Isaiah 6,13' (1964). = 'The Qumran Reading of Isaiah 6,13', *ASTI* 3 (1964), pp. 111-13.

Schmidt, Werner H., 'Die Einheit' (1977). = 'Die Einheit der Verkündigung Jesajas. Versuch einer Zusammenschau', *EvTh* 37 (1977), pp. 260-72.

—*Einführung* (1979). = *Einführung in das Alte Testament* (Berlin, 1979).

Schottroff, Willy, 'Jes 5,1-7' (1970). = 'Das Weinberglied Jesajas (Jes 5,1-7). Ein Beitrag zur Geschichte der Parabel', *ZAW* 82 (1970), pp. 68-91.

Schreiner, Josef, *Apokalyptik (1969)* = *Alttestamentlich-jüdische Apokalyptik. Eine Einführung* (München, 1969).

Searle, John R., *Speech Acts* (1979). = *Expression and Meaning. Studies in the Theory of Speech Acts* (Cambridge, 1979).

Seibert, Ilse, *Hirt* (1969). = *Hirt—Herde—König. Zur Herausbildung des Königtums in Mesopotamien* (Berlin, 1969).

Seim, Turid Karlsen, 'Lignelsesforskningen' (1977). = 'Nye veier i lignelsesforskningen', *NTT* 4 (1977), pp. 239-58.

Sellin, E., *Einleitung* (1910). = *Einleitung in das Alte Testament* (Leipzig, 1910).

Sellin, Gerhard, 'Allegorie' (1978). = 'Allegorie und "Gleichnis". Zur Formenlehre der synoptischen Gleichnisse', *ZThK* 75 (1978), pp. 281-335.

Seybold, Klaus, 'Bildmotive' (1974). = 'Die Bildmotive in den Visionen des Propheten Sacharja', *VTSuppl* 26 (1974), pp. 92-110.

—*Visionen* (1974). = *Bilder zum Tempelbau. Die Visionen des Propheten Sacharja* (Stuttgart, 1974).

Sheppard, Gerald T., 'Juridical Parable' (1982). = 'More on Isaiah 5.1-7 as a Juridical Parable', *CBQ* 44 (1982), pp. 30-41.

—'Redaction' (1985). = 'The Anti-Assyrian Redaction and the Canonical Context of Isaiah 1-39', *JBL* 104 (1985), pp. 193-216.

Sider, John W., 'The Jeremias Tradition' (1983). = 'Rediscovering the Parables: The Logic of the Jeremias Tradition', *JBL* 102 (1983), pp. 61-83.

Steck, Odil Hannes, 'Jesaja 6' (1972). = 'Bemerkungen zu Jesaja 6', *BZ* 16 (1972), pp. 188-206.

—'Jesaja 7,3-9' (1973). = 'Rettung und Verstockung. Exegetische Bemerkungen zu Jesaja 7,3-9', *EvTh* 33 (1973), pp. 77-90.

—'Jesaja 7,10-17 und 8,1-4' (1973). = 'Beiträge zum Verständnis von Jesaja 7,10-17 und 8,1-4', *ThZ* 29 (1973), pp. 161-78.

Stenning, J.F. (see Targum of Isaiah).

Stolz, Fritz, *Strukturen* (1970). = *Strukturen und Figuren im Kult von Jerusalem. Studien zur altorientalischen, vor- und frühisraelitischen Religion* (Berlin, 1970).

—'Bäume' (1972). = 'Die Bäume des Gottesgartens auf dem Libanon', *ZAW* 84 (1972), pp. 141-56.

Targum of Isaiah (1949). = *The Targum of Isaiah*, ed. and trans. J.F. Stenning (Oxford, 1949).

Thesaurus I, II. = *Thesaurus Syriacus*, ed. R. Payne Smith, Vol. I (1879); Vol. II (1901).

Thompson, Leonard, L., *Literature* (1978). = *Introducing Biblical Literature: A More Fantastic Country* (Englewood Cliffs, 1978).

Tillich, Paul, *Culture* (1964). = *Theology of Culture* (Galaxy; New York, 1964; 1st edn, Oxford, 1959).

Trible, Phyllis, *Rhetoric* (1978). = *God and the Rhetoric of Sexuality* (Philadelphia, 1978).

Tsevat, M., 'Isaiah I 31' (1969). = 'Isaiah I 31', *VT* 19 (1969), pp. 261-63.

Tur-Sinai, N.H., 'Isaiah i-xii' (1961). = 'A Contribution to the Understanding of Isaiah i-xii', *Scripta Hierosolymitana* 8 (1961), pp. 154-88.

Vermes, G., 'Lebanon' (1958). = 'The Symbolical Interpretation of *Lebanon* in the

Targums: The Origin and Development of an Exegetical Tradition', *JThSt* 9 (1958), pp. 1-12.

Vermeylen, J., *Isaïe* (1977-78). = *Du Prophète Isaïe à l'Apocalyptique. Isaïe, I-XXXV, miroir d'un demi-millénaire d'expérience religieuse en Israël*, I-II (Paris, 1977-78).

Via, Dan Otto, *Parables* (1967). = *The Parables. Their Literary and Existential Dimension* (Philadelphia, 1967).

Vollmer, Jochen, *Geschichtliche Rückblicke* (1971). = *Geschichtliche Rückblicke und Motive in der Prophetie des Amos, Hosea und Jesaja* (Berlin, 1971).

Voltaire, *Sur la nature de l'homme. Sept Discours* (1737).

Wagner, Siegfried, 'Hoffmann' (1976). = 'Review of Hans Werner Hoffmann: *Die Intention der Verkündigung Jesajas*, Berlin, 1974', in: *ThLZ* 101 (1976), cols. 255-57.

Weder, Hans, *Gleichnisse* (1978). = *Die Gleichnisse Jesu als Metaphern. Traditions- und redaktionsgeschichtliche Analysen und Interpretationen* (Göttingen, 1978).

Weiser, Artur, *Einleitung* (1957). = *Einleitung in das Alte Testament* (6th edn, Göttingen, 1957).

Werfer, Albert, *Poesie* (1875). = *Die Poesie der Bibel* (Tübingen, 1875).

Wernberg-Møller, P., 'Isaiah-Scroll' (1958). = 'Studies in the Defective Spellings in the Isaiah-Scroll of St. Mark's Monastery', *JSSt* 3 (1958), pp. 244-64.

Werner, Wolfgang, *Eschatologische Texte* (1982). = *Eschatologische Texte in Jesaja 1-39. Messias, Heiliger Rest, Völker* (Würzburg, 1982).

Westermann, Claus, *Vergleiche und Gleichnisse* (1984). = *Vergleiche und Gleichnisse im Alten und Neuen Testament* (Stuttgart, 1984).

Wiberg, Bertil, *Lignelser* (1954). = *Jesu lignelser. En gennemgang af lignelsesforskningen 1900-1950* (København, 1954).

Widengren, Geo, *Tree of Life* (1951). = *The King and the Tree of Life in Ancient Near Eastern Religion* (Uppsala, 1951).

—*Värld* (1953). = *Religionens Värld. Religionsfenomenologiska studier och översikter* (rev. edn, Stockholm, 1953).

Wiklander, Bertil, *Literature* (1983). = *Prophecy as Literature. A Text-Linguistic and Rhetorical Approach to Isaiah 2-4* (Uppsala, 1983).

Wildberger, Hans, *Jesaja 1-12* (1972). = *Jesaja*, I: *Jesaja 1-12*, BK 10/1 (1972).

—*Jesaja 13-27* (1978). = *Jesaja*, II: *Jesaja 13-27*, BK 10/2 (1978).

—*Jesaja 28-39* (1982). = *Jesaja*, III: *Jesaja 28-39*, BK 10/3 (1982).

Willis, John T., 'Isaiah 5:1-7' (1977). = 'The Genre of Isaiah 5:1-7', *JBL* 96 (1977), pp. 337-62.

Wolff, Hans Walter, *Micha* (1982). = *Micha*, BK 14/4 (1982).

Wünsche, Aug., *Bildersprache* (1906). = *Die Bildersprache des Alten Testaments. Ein Beitrag zur aesthetischen Würdigung des poetischen Schrifttums im Alten Testament* (Leipzig, 1906).

Yee, Gale A., 'Juridical Parable' (1981). = 'A Form-Critical Study of Isaiah 5:1-7 as a Song and a Juridical Parable', *CBQ* 43 (1981), pp. 30-40.

Zimmerli, Walther, *Ezechiel 1-24* (1969). = *Ezechiel*, I: *Ezechiel 1-24*, BK 13/1 (1969).

—*Ezechiel 25-48* (1969) = *Ezechiel*, II: *Ezechiel 25-48*, BK 13/2 (1969).

INDEX

INDEX OF BIBLICAL REFERENCES

INDEX OF AUTHORS

JOURNAL FOR THE STUDY OF THE OLD TESTAMENT

Supplement Series

1988

sten, 1943-

pe for a tree